Problems of Protection

Problems of Protection
The UNHCR, Refugees,
and Human Rights

Edited by
Niklaus Steiner, Mark Gibney,
and **Gil Loescher**

ROUTLEDGE
NEW YORK AND LONDON

Published in 2003 by
Routledge
29 West 35th Street
New York, NY 10001
www.routledge-ny.com

Published in Great Britain by
Routledge
11 New Fetter Lane
London EC4P 4EE
www.routledge.co.uk

Routledge is an imprint of the Taylor & Francis Group.
Printed in the United States of America on acid-free paper.

10 9 8 7 6 5 4 3 2 1

Library of Congress Cataloging-in-Publication Data

Problems of protection : the UNHCR, refugees, and human rights / edited by Niklaus
Steiner, Mark Gibney, and Gil Loescher.
  p. cm.
 Includes bibliographical references and index.
  ISBN 0-415-94573-9—ISBN 0-415-94574-7 (pbk.)
  1. Office of the United Nations High Commissioner for Refugees. 2.
 Refugees—Government policy. I. Steiner, Niklaus. II. Loescher, Gil. III. Gibney, Mark.
HV640.3 .P76 2003
352.87—dc21

                      2002036929

Contents

Foreword

Chances are that, because you are holding this book, you know of the importance and complexity of refugee protection. Nearly 15 million people are currently defined as "refugees" by the United Nations High Commissioner for Refugees (UNHCR) and another 5 million are "of concern" to the world's oldest and largest refugee protection agency. An additional 20 million people have fled their homes but because they have not crossed an international frontier, they are termed "Internally Displaced People" (IDPs). Together, these 40 million uprooted people constitute about 1 of every 150 persons on earth.

On some fronts the worldwide refugee situation is getting worse, while on others there are signs of hope. Because of the recent turmoil in Afghanistan, hundreds of thousands of Afghans have fled the country or have become IDPs, although repatriation efforts are now underway. Civil war has also recently uprooted over one quarter of a million people in Colombia and Liberia, and one fears what the current escalation of tensions in the Middle East may bring. And massive protracted refugee situations involving Somalis, Iranians, Iraqis, Burmese, and Bhutanese remain unresolved over a decade after they began. On the other hand, nearly 1 million Eritreans have been able to return home now that a peace with Ethiopia seems to be in place. Also, the 20 million people currently "of concern" to UNHCR is 2 million lower than last year, although UNHCR notes that this drop reflects conflicting trends: while significant numbers of people continue to be uprooted, an even larger number of people, especially IDPs, are able to return home. The number of asylum seekers worldwide has also dropped slightly to under 1 million, which may be the result of reduced conflict or it may be the result of discouraging policies in the countries of asylum.

While it remains difficult to establish and interpret statistics of people forced to flee, it is clear that the issue is a chronic one. When there is a calming of tension in one region that allows people to return home, conflict flares elsewhere and drives people away. In the early 1990s, the cessation of civil wars in Central America, Cambodia, and Mozambique were contrasted by the rise of violence in the Balkans. Today, the fall of the Taliban in Afghanistan may usher in an era of return, but violence in West Africa continues to trigger waves of displacement there. Tragically, refugee scholars, policymakers, and advocates continue to have much work to do.

As the title of this book indicates, our focus is on UNHCR and its role in protecting refugees. UNHCR has recently marked its fiftieth anniversary, but we are not interested in issuing a glossy retrospective. Instead, we want to offer a critical assessment, issuing praise where deserved and criticism where needed. With a staff of 5,000 and a $1 billion budget, UNHCR is the world's largest organization mandated to protect refugees and is therefore an obvious target for such an assessment in light of the continuing plight of refugees worldwide. Few scholars are better equipped to make such an assessment than Gil Loescher, who examines the important role UNHCR plays in world politics, but one that has been limited by both internal and external forces. He concludes that, perhaps now more than ever, UNHCR needs to reassert its primary role as the protector of refugees and of the asylum principle.

In evaluating the complexity of refugee protection at the beginning of the twenty-first century, we deliberately cast our net wider than just this single institution. Elizabeth Ferris, for example, offers an evaluation of the growing role that non-governmental organizations (NGOs) are playing in refugee protection vis-à-vis other NGOs, UNHCR, and governments. Niklaus Steiner analyzes asylum debates and stresses the often counterintuitive roles that national interests, international norms, and morality play in these debates. Emily Copeland focuses on gender as a basis of persecution and examines the efforts to formally and informally expand the refugee definition to include gender.

As these three pieces suggest, refugee protection involves complex ethical and legal dimensions, and three more chapters view the issue directly through these lenses. Focusing on ethics, Bonny Ibhawoh explores the evolving debate between universalism and cultural relativism in the context of the refugee definition and of broader notions of human rights. With an eye more on legal matters, Brian Gorlick argues that there is an emerging convergence between international human rights law, criminal and humanitarian law, and that this development can be used to complement gaps in international refugee law. Finally, Erik Roxström and Mark Gibney offer a criticism of UNHCR's Temporary Protection policy for what they argue are both ethical and legal shortcomings.

By casting our net widely, we are also able to draw upon established scholars as well as bring into the discussion new voices working in the field, and we hear from the perspective of anthropology, history, international relations, law, and political science. Furthermore, the book offers analysis of regions that are often not given due attention in much of the refugee literature. Beth Whitaker redresses this deficit with her focus on Tanzania's handling of Rwandan refugees in the wake of the 1994 genocide. This inattentiveness is especially evident with regard to Palestinian refugees, and Randa Farah argues that precisely because they are not under the mandate of UNHCR, Palestinians need to be included in discussions of refugee protection.

The book also spans the whole process of protecting refugees. Arthur Helton focuses on the early stages of this process in his criticism of the reactive nature of the efforts to protect refugees, while Patricia Weiss Fagen analyzes the factors that enable refugees to return home and be reintegrated once conflict has subsided.

We are especially pleased to include two chapters that reflect upon the realities of refugee protection in this post-September eleventh world. Monica Juma and Peter Kagwanja argue that refugee protection, already compromised in East Africa, has been made even more precarious because of ramifications of the war on terrorism. Joanne van Selm examines what lasting impact the fear spawned by the 9/11 attacks may have on asylum policies in the U.S. and Europe.

The common thread that ties together all these chapters are the provocative arguments that are sure to engage readers into thinking about refugee protection and UNHCR's role in this endeavor. These arguments are the outcome of an ongoing dialogue that began with a conference in spring 2000 organized by the University Center for International Studies (UCIS) at the University of North Carolina at Chapel Hill. I would like to thank UCIS director James Peacock and the wonderful staff for all the support they offered this project. I especially thank Narvis Green, Emily Neely, and Tessa Dean for their help in organizing the conference, and Carrie Matthews for her assistance in editing this manuscript.

True to its mission of bridging intellectual communities, UCIS brought to this conference a rich and diverse array of scholars and policy makers. In addition to the contributors in this book, the conference benefited from the active and thoughtful presentations and reflections of Dennis McNamara and Eduardo Arboleda of UNHCR, Bill Frelick of the U.S. Committee for Refugees, Alex Cunliffe of the University of Plymouth, Peter Takirambudde of Human Rights Watch, and David Rieff, board member of Medicins Sans Frontiers. My co-editors Mark Gibney and Gil Loescher were invaluable in bringing such an illustrious group together and in framing this project, and I take this opportunity to thank them both.

Finally, none of this would have been possible without the generous financial support from the Andrew W. Mellon Foundation and the U.S. Department of Education's Office of Postsecondary Education and the encouragement of Harriet Zuckerman and Amy Wilson, respectively. This project and its fruition owes them deep appreciation.

Niklaus Steiner
Chapel Hill, North Carolina
Autumn 2002

1
Introduction: Refugee Protection and UNHCR

1

UNHCR at Fifty

Refugee Protection and World Politics

GIL LOESCHER

There is probably no more appropriate time than now to re-examine the role of the United Nations High Commissioner for Refugees (UNHCR) regarding the protection of refugees. Fifty years ago, on January 1, 1951, UNHCR began operations out of three rooms at the Palais des Nations in Geneva, Switzerland. On July 28 of that year, the 1951 Convention Relating to the Status of Refugees was adopted. This, like the UNHCR mandate, defined a refugee as someone who has fled his or her home country owing to a "well-founded fear of persecution." Over the next five decades, the global refugee problem grew enormously from about 2 million in 1951 to over 12 million at the beginning of the twenty-first century.[1] At the same time, the numbers of "persons of concern to UNHCR," namely asylum seekers, returned refugees, internally displaced persons, and others of concern, when added to the global refugee total, numbered almost 23 million.[2] To respond to the ever-expanding refugee crisis, the international community channeled substantial assistance to refugees through UNHCR, and consequently the agency became the centerpiece of the international refugee regime.

The evolution of UNHCR has not taken place within a political vacuum.[3] During the past half century, the growth and direction of the agency has been framed by the crucial events of international politics. Not only is it important to situate UNHCR within the context of world politics but it is also important to appreciate how, in turn, the actions of past High Commissioners and the diffusion of international refugee norms have helped shape the course of recent world history. Indeed, the history of UNHCR demonstrates that international organizations matter in international relations.

Scholars and practitioners of international relations have been slow to recognize either the rationality or significance of UNHCR in world politics. Among UN agencies, UNHCR is unique. It is both an individual, represented in the High Commissioner, and a bureaucracy with its own distinct culture and value system. The High Commissioner has little or no political authority but is vested with considerable moral authority and legitimacy dating back not just to its own founding in 1951 but to 1921 when Fridtjof Nansen was appointed as the first High Commissioner for Refugees by the League of Nations.

UNHCR is an organization with its own identity, comprising over 5,000 individuals of different nationalities who share similar values. One cannot fully
understand UNHCR without a knowledge of its organizational culture. Fifty
years after its founding, the agency still embodies a unique international commitment to refugees. There exists no other UN agency where values and principled ideas are so central to the mandate and raison d'être of the institution
or where some committed staff members are willing to place their lives in danger to defend the proposition that persecuted individuals need protection. As
UNHCR itself claims, if the Office did not exist, hundreds of thousands, if not
millions, of refugees would be left unassisted and unprotected.

However essential the agency is, it is important not to take the rhetoric and
self-presentation of UNHCR at face value. While UNHCR has had many successes over the past fifty years, it has also had many failures. A number of internal and external constraints inhibit the organization from achieving its full
impact. The Office has an organizational culture that makes innovation and
institutional change difficult,[4] and the Office remains largely unaccountable
for violation of its mandate.

UNHCR also has endemic political problems. UNHCR was created by UN
member states to be both a strictly non-political agency and an advocate for
refugees. However, from its beginning, it was clear that the agency's role would
be an intensely political one. The existence of refugees indicates political up-
heaval in their homelands. UNHCR's primary mandate is to protect refugees
from repression. This often requires the Office to directly challenge governments and places the agency in a conflictive relationship with states that produce refugees. However, UNHCR is not just an advocacy organization; it also
exists to facilitate state policies towards refugees. States did not establish
UNHCR from purely altruistic motives, but also from a desire to promote regional and international stability and to serve the interests of governments.
Governments created the Office to help them resolve problems related to
refugees who were perceived to create domestic instability, to generate inter-
state tensions, and to threaten international security. UNHCR is also an inter-
governmental organization and part of the UN system and therefore cannot
always act in a strictly neutral fashion. This was certainly the case in Bosnia
and Kosovo as well as in other places. Thus, UNHCR often walks a tightrope,
maintaining a perilous balance between the protection of refugees and the
sovereign prerogatives and interests of states.

One cannot fully understand UNHCR without placing it within the context
of world politics. In the international political system today, states remain the
predominant actors. But this does not mean that international organizations
like UNHCR are completely without power or influence. Successive High
Commissioners quickly realized that in order to have any impact on the world
political arena they had to use the power of their expertise, ideas, strategies,
and legitimacy to alter the information and value contexts in which states

made policy. The Office has tried to project refugee norms into a world politics dominated by states driven by concerns of national interest and security. Successful High Commissioners have convinced states to define their national interests in ways compatible with refugee needs.

UNHCR not only promotes the implementation of refugee norms; it also monitors compliance with international standards. For most of its history, the Office has acted as a "teacher" of refugee norms.[5] The majority of UNHCR's tactics have mainly involved persuasion and socialization in order to hold states accountable to their previously stated policies or principles. Past High Commissioners have frequently reminded Western states in particular that as liberal democracies and open societies they are obliged to adhere to human rights norms in their asylum and refugee admissions policies. In the past, because UNHCR possessed specialized knowledge and expertise about refugee law, states often deferred to the Office on asylum matters. This was particularly the case before the 1980s when UNHCR had a monopoly on information about refugee law and refugee movements. During the early decades of its existence, the Office enjoyed maximum legitimacy as it simultaneously tried to define the refugee issue for states, to convince governments that refugee problems were soluble, to prescribe solutions, and to monitor their implementation. In recent decades, as a result of states developing their own immigration and refugee machinery and as a result of increasing restrictionism on the parts of states, UNHCR has lost its monopoly on information and expertise. Consequently, its authority and legitimacy in the realm of asylum has declined.

UNHCR not only acted as a transmitter of refugee norms but also socialized new states to accept the promotion of refugee norms domestically as part of becoming a member of the international community. This socialization occurred first in the 1960s and 1970s in the newly independent or developing countries of Asia, Africa, and Latin America, and later in the 1990s in the republics of the former Soviet Union. The political leaders of most newly independent governments in Africa, Asia, and the Commonwealth of Independent States cared deeply about their international image and sought international legitimacy through cooperation with UNHCR. Thus, UNHCR became one of the "gatekeepers" in determining which governments were worthy of membership in international society.

In addition to exercising moral leverage to gain influence with states, UNHCR has repeatedly tried to link the refugee issue to states' material interests. Material assistance programs provided UNHCR with significant leverage. States have occasionally been willing to adapt their behavior to UNHCR pressures for purely instrumental reasons. Thus, through a mixture of persuasion and socialization, UNHCR communicated the importance of refugee norms and convinced many new states that the benefits of signing the refugee legal instruments and joining UNHCR Executive Committee (either as a member or an observer) outweighed the costs of remaining outside the international refugee regime.

UNHCR has not just been an agent in world politics but also a principal actor. This has been particularly true in situations where there has been a coincidence of humanitarian and political factors. However, this view of UNHCR as an actor and not just an agent has largely not been recognized by international relations scholars. Most international relations literature on refugees adopts a Statist perspective, which is still the dominant paradigm in international relations. This perspective claims that UNHCR, like all international organizations, is just a mechanism through which states act; it is not an autonomous actor but just a structure to do states' bidding.

One can find considerable support for this argument. UNHCR is totally dependent on donors and states for funding operations and on host governments for permission to initiate operations on their soil. Fifty years ago governments established a voluntary funding system for UNHCR, thereby avoiding increasing states' financial obligations to the UN and leaving to UNHCR the problems of raising the means to carry out its programs. Lacking a system of mandatory assessed contributions from governments, the High Commissioner has to directly seek contributions from possible donor countries. Not surprisingly, 98 percent of the agency's funding comes from a handful of industrialized states. The US, Japan, and the EU account for 94 percent of all government contributions to UNHCR.[6] Donations are frequently driven by politics and donors' interests in particular refugee crises. Some 80 percent of funding is earmarked for particular operations or programs.[7] Most importantly, UNHCR's ability to operate independently depends on the role that host governments choose to play. As an international organization, UNHCR depends on sovereign host governments to ensure access to, and order, in its operational environment. Frequently, host states have interfered with and obstructed both the agency's entry to countries of origin and its activities there, thus compromising the Office's autonomy and legitimacy. Thus, it is a commonly held view that UNHCR has only partial control over circumstances key to its performance, is in no position to challenge the policies of its funders and host governments, and merely acts as an instrument of states.

But this may be too simplistic a view. While UNHCR is constrained by states, the notion that it is a passive mechanism with no independent agenda of its own is not borne out by the empirical evidence of the past five decades. For example, it seems clear that the autonomy and authority of UNHCR has grown over the years and the Office has become a purposive actor in its own right with independent interests and capabilities. This was especially the case in the formative phase of the organization but it is also the case that UNHCR has not solely been an instrument of state interests in the more recent period. Rather it is more correct to say that UNHCR policy and practice have been driven both by state interests and by the Office acting independently or evolving in ways not expected nor necessarily sanctioned by states.

There are many examples during the past fifty years illustrating the Office's relative independence of states. I will briefly mention two. The first comes from the early Cold War period and the second from the more recent post–Cold War period.

The Cold War Period

When the UNHCR opened its doors in January 1951, there was a remarkable symmetry in world politics. In the conflict between communism and capitalist democracy, each camp's view of good and evil was unquestionably identifiable. From its founding, UNHCR was enmeshed in the international politics of the East–West conflict and refugees were perceived as elements of power in the bipolar rivalry.

In some respects, Cold War politics made life easy for UNHCR and for Western governments. In a Manichean political world, there was a clarity and simplicity in deciding refugee status. Recognizing persecution and identifying its perpetrators caused no headaches and the grant of asylum was generally used to reaffirm the failures of communism and the benevolence of the West. UNHCR proved valuable to the West as an agency able to handle flows out of Eastern Europe for resettlement in the "Free World," particularly after the 1956 Hungarian Uprising. International refugee policy not only saved many individuals who were subject to repression in communist dictatorships, but it also clearly served the geopolitical interests of the United States and its allies.

During the 1950s, Europe was the principal area of refugee concern as the Cold War intensified and new refugee flows moved from East to West. While the Eurocentric orientation of UNHCR reflected the international political environment, it also reflected the foreign policy priorities of the United States and the other major Western governments.[8] At the height of the Cold War, American leaders considered refugee policy too important to permit the United Nations to control it. To this end, the United States sought to limit severely the functional scope and independence of UNHCR and instead created two other U.S.-led organizations that were parallel to and outside the purview of the United Nations. These were the International Committee of European Migration, now the International Organization for Migration, and the U.S. Escapee Program. The United States was also instrumental in establishing specially created UN agencies in the Middle East for the Palestinians[9] and the Korean Peninsula for the Koreans displaced in the Korean War.[10] These were refugee populations that were located in strategic conflict areas where U.S. geopolitical interests were significant. The United States funded all of these organizations much more generously than it did UNHCR, and until late 1955 these organizations provided the United States with a pretext for completely withholding financial support from the UN based refugee regime.

The denial of American financial and diplomatic support directly affected UNHCR's ability to define an independent role and to implement its goals and programs. Even five years after its founding, and despite large refugee flows around the world, governments deliberately kept UNHCR small and confined to providing legal protection for displaced persons who had not been resettled by the International Refugee Organization (IRO). Until the mid-1950s, the UNHCR was a sideshow, largely irrelevant to regional and international high politics and limited to finances barely adequate to keep it going.

Despite the opposition of Western governments, UNHCR began to exercise power autonomously in ways unintended by states at its creation. The first High Commissioner, Gerrit van Heuven Goedhart, initially enlarged the scope of his office by obtaining the capacity to independently raise funds and by assuming material assistance responsibilities. A grant from the Ford Foundation enabled UNHCR to take the lead role in responding to a refugee crisis in West Berlin in early 1953, thereby demonstrating its usefulness to the major powers and raising the Office's international profile. These early successes legitimized the need for UNHCR material assistance to refugees and directly led to the establishment of a UNHCR program for permanent solutions and emergency assistance. This paved the way for the UN to designate UNHCR as the "lead agency" directing the international emergency operation for Hungarian refugees in 1956 despite initial American opposition.

The Hungarian operation also demonstrated the important diplomatic role that the High Commissioner could play in events at the center of world politics. In the midst of the first major Cold War refugee crisis, UNHCR played an essential mediating role between East and West involving the repatriation of nearly 10 percent of the Hungarian refugees. This operation was extremely controversial and was initially opposed by Western governments who considered repatriation to socialist countries unthinkable.

Thus, largely on its own initiatives, UNHCR grew from a strictly nonoperational agency with no authority to appeal for funds to an institution with a long-range program emphasizing not only protection but, increasingly, material assistance. This remarkable transition not only demonstrated the tension between state interests and the drive for relative autonomy on the part of an international organization but it also underlined the capacity of UNHCR to have an independent influence on events at the center of world politics.

During the 1950s, UNHCR took initial steps to lay the groundwork for an expansion of its activities to the developing world. This new approach was the "good offices" formula, which involved the UN General Assembly granting UNHCR the authority to raise funds or to initiate assistance programs for operations outside Europe.

The first major expansion of UNHCR into the developing world occurred as a result of refugees from the Algerian War of Independence fleeing to neighboring Tunisia and Morocco.[11] The second High Commissioner, Auguste Lindt, felt assistance to the Algerian refugees presented an opportunity for UNHCR to use the new international support and goodwill it had earned in its response to the Hungarian refugee emergency to confirm its position as the leading international refugee agency. Lindt feared UNHCR would be accused of discriminatory treatment if it neglected the Algerians, and he did not want to be perceived as the "High Commissioner for European refugees only."[12] He felt that the UNHCR mandate, as defined in its founding statute, was world-wide and that his office had a responsibility for dealing, in the High Commissioner's own words, "with completely different people and not only refugees from communism."[13] He was concerned that to refuse assistance to Tunisia and Morocco would estrange the organization from a growing bloc of developing nations and would weaken the more favorable attitude that the Soviet bloc had recently adopted towards the agency.

The decision to aid Algerian refugees was politically difficult, however, and UNHCR had to overcome strong government opposition. The French government denied the authority of UNHCR to give assistance in this case, fearing its involvement would internationalize the crisis. Only through persistent and courageous diplomacy on the part of the High Commissioner was French resistance to UNHCR involvement overcome. Indeed, it was one of Lindt's most noteworthy diplomatic accomplishments.

Thus, even in the early Cold War period, UNHCR initiated and capitalized on international political developments to expand its scope both operationally and geographically. In the view of many developing states, UNHCR's action on behalf of Algerians signified a turning point in the Office's geographical reach and function. The Algerian operation was a bridgehead leading to a period of both global and institutional growth for UNHCR.

UNHCR and Its Focus on Repatriation

A second, more recent, example of UNHCR acting not solely as a consequence of state pressures but also by its own initiatives involves UNHCR's repatriation policies from the late 1980s on. Before the late 1980s, UNHCR's Western donors actively discouraged repatriation, as most of the world's refugees originated from communist countries.[14] When repatriation did occur, to a large extent, refugees themselves decided when to return and under what conditions. The precondition for the involvement of UNHCR in repatriations included such factors as "fundamental change of circumstances in the country of origin, voluntary nature of the decision to return, and return in safety and dignity." With the ending of the Cold War, repatriation was increasingly perceived as the only effective solution to refugee problems.[15] As the superpowers withdrew from long-standing regional conflicts in the late 1980s and early 1990s, the numbers of refugees returning home increased dramatically.

State pressure to promote repatriation was accompanied by new thinking about repatriation within UNHCR. To respond to the new international political environment, repatriation became a central part of UNHCR's new global strategy.[16] In UNHCR's eyes it was far better for most refugees to return home at the earliest opportunity to benefit from UNHCR's repatriation programs than to remain in refugee camps that could offer them no future. The Office developed terminology and concepts like "safe return," which stipulated that conditions in the home country did not have to improve substantially but only enough to allow refugees to return home in safety. This shift in terminology made it much more likely that UNHCR would promote repatriations under less strict conditions than voluntary repatriation. For UNHCR this was a dramatic shift from its traditional position that repatriation had to be a strictly voluntary decision on the part of refugees. Rather, it would now be the UNHCR who would make the assessment as to whether conditions were safe enough for refugees to return. Moreover, there was a growing view that refugee safety did not necessarily always outweigh the security interests of states or broader peace building and conflict resolution goals. Thus, by the early 1990s, repatriation came to be perceived as part of the Office's emphasis on preventive protection and encouraging the responsibility of countries of origin toward their own citizens. Unfortunately, repatriation did not always serve refugees' interests. The return of refugees from Bangladesh to Burma and from Tanzania and former Zaire to Rwanda and Burundi[17] are only two illustrations of situations in which UNHCR cooperated with host governments to compel refugees to return home before conditions had become safe for their return. These repatriations constituted part of a larger international trend towards declining refugee protection standards worldwide.

Because UNHCR focused almost entirely on repatriation during the past decade, it also virtually ignored other possible solutions, often to the detriment of refugees. With less donor funding for operations other than repatriation and emergency relief, a range of traditional solutions—local integration projects, educational programs, income-generating projects, and the promotion of refugee participation—disappeared from the Office's possible options for long-staying refugee populations. Instead, believing that return provided the only humane solution to refugee problems, UNHCR essentially ran long-term programs in an emergency mode that were damaging to the long-term welfare of refugees stuck in protracted camp situations.

Thus, from uncertain beginnings in January 1951, UNHCR has demonstrated quite an extraordinary capacity for perpetuation and growth. A large, complex international organization such as UNHCR did not spring up overnight nor was it designed and built in one piece. The Office evolved gradually in a complex historical process in which state interests have been extremely significant. At the same time, the history of UNHCR demonstrates that it is not simply a passive mechanism of states. Rather, its growth and evolution is a result of the Office having initiated and capitalized on international political developments and having expanded its scope and authority both operationally and geographically.

However, this expansion has not come about without cost. In recent years, UNHCR has come under increasing pressure in regard to both its functions and identity. New developments in UNHCR policy directions also raise questions about the adequacy of the agency's mandate given recent changes in international relations. There is, for example, a widespread concern as to whether UNHCR's expansion into humanitarian and other kinds of assistance has distorted its identity as a refugee agency and has come at the expense of the protection of refugees. Indeed, many persons within UNHCR, governments, and the non-governmental community fear for the survival of the Office's primary mandate, namely the international protection of refugees.

UNHCR and the Erosion of Refugee Protection

Deepening and strengthening the concept of the worldwide protection of refugees is one of the most urgent tasks facing the international community in the twenty-first century. Current trends do not paint a particularly positive picture for refugee protection in the years ahead. States are either increasingly unwilling or increasingly unable to offer protection to those who are forcibly displaced, whether within their countries or across borders. Refugees are perceived as destabilizing to national, regional and international security and as triggers for regional instability. Everywhere pernicious laws now exist to turn away refugees and restrict their rights. This situation is a significant departure from state practice in the Cold War when—largely for political purposes—attitudes towards refugees were far more tolerant and welcoming. The present reality is that the Cold War interest in taking refugees from the Communist world has passed with the collapse of European Communism and has now been replaced by a growing state interest in keeping refugees out, or in sending them back home. This is a worldwide trend.

While we have many examples of states regressing in their commitment towards the protection of refugees over the past fifty years, this chapter emphasizes the role of UNHCR in the decline of the international protection of refugees. UNHCR's refugee protection responsibility makes it distinct among international organizations. Of all the international organizations created during the past century to deal with refugees, it is the only one specifically charged with protection responsibilities. For UNHCR, refugee protection traditionally means "life-saving interventions, fair treatment upon reception, compliance with essential humanitarian standards and non-return to a place of prospective persecution (*non-refoulement*)."[18] As Arthur Helton explains: "When we speak of 'protection,' we mean *legal* protection. The concept must be associated with entitlements under law and, for effective redress of grievances, mechanisms to vindicate claims in respect of those entitlements."[19] Traditionally, refugee protection is reserved for those forced migrants who have left their countries of origin and crossed state boundaries. At this point, forced migrants are transformed into an object of international concern under the international refugee legal instruments. Having lost or been deprived of protection under law in his or her country of origin, the forced migrant is in need of another source of protection. Thus, refugee protection is often closely associated with the concept of asylum in a host country.

In recent years, UNHCR's work has been transformed by its efforts to respond to the proliferation of conflicts in the post–Cold War era. Consequently, by the early 1990s, an increasing proportion of UNHCR's operations shifted to work within countries of origin, in zones of active conflict, and often in close association with UN mandated peacekeeping forces. Parlaying growing international concern about the security implications of refugee movements into increased government donations and an expanded interpretation of its mandate, UNHCR was well positioned in the early post–Cold War period to become the international community's humanitarian "fireman," intervening in internal conflicts in northern Iraq, the Balkans and other global hot spots.

During the past decade, the agency has assumed a number of different responsibilities not directly related to its traditional refugee protection role. Its main focus is to provide humanitarian aid and to try to monitor human rights violations in countries of origin in the hopes of stemming refugee flows before they begin. The transformation of UNHCR into a more general humanitarian emergency agency has put the agency at the mercy of a much broader set of political and strategic calculations, thus compromising its capacity to provide protection to refugees. Because UNHCR needs to raise more and more voluntary funds for its operations, obtain access to increasingly volatile internal conflicts, win the confidence of not only governments but also of opposition factions, paramilitaries and warlords, and promote compromise and often unsatisfactory solutions, the agency is not well placed to stand up for protection principles regarding refugees. To fully promote protection would threaten funding, access to internal wars, and the ability to be operational.[20] Thus, during the 1990s, in several internal conflicts involving massive displacement, the pressure to subordinate human rights and refugee protection concerns to strategic, political, or even economic considerations were at times extreme.

Pressures on UNHCR to engage in roles in countries of origin that are well beyond its direct responsibilities have inevitably taxed its human and financial resources. For example, at the height of the war in Bosnia-Herzegovina, the Office committed one-quarter of its staff worldwide and one-third of its global budget to the humanitarian relief operation there. Moreover, the agency's experience in the Balkans underlined the danger of balancing refugee protection concerns with the need to remain operational in internal conflicts.[21] In Bosnia, the Office became increasingly dependent on the funding, logistical assistance, and authority of parties to the conflict in which they operated. UNHCR's involvement with Bosnian and Kosovar refugees also entrapped the agency in the political and strategic priorities of the UN and NATO forces and severely compromised the Office's independence and autonomy. In other parts of the world, particularly in failed states in Central and West Africa, Asia and the Caucasus, where the agency has been caught up in conflicts, both state and non-state actors have violated UNHCR's immunity and brutalized refugees and international and local humanitarian aid personnel alike. In some situations, UNHCR involvement reinforced the political structures that threatened human rights and generated refugees.

In addition to the effects of the external operational environment on UNHCR's capacity to provide protection to refugees, in recent years there have been fundamental internal changes within UNHCR itself, affecting its culture, self-identity and orientation. For several decades after 1951, the protection of refugees reflected the core values and practices of the Office and gave UNHCR special meaning, identity, and coherence. As its operational activities gained precedence over protection from the mid 1980s on, UNHCR's culture of legal protection declined. Organizational changes that took place within the agency in the late 1980s and solidified in the 1990s, sidelined the Division of International Protection (DIP) in favor of the more pragmatic and operational regional bureaus.[22]

During recent years, UNHCR has not mainly been concerned with preserving asylum or protecting refugees. UNHCR's objectives are increasingly pragmatic—to do the best in difficult circumstances and to implement the least bad options—and not chiefly to uphold universal principles. Rather, its chief focus has been humanitarian action.[23] UNHCR is identified primarily with assistance—the delivery of food, shelter and medicine—to refugees and war-affected populations. Successes and failures of humanitarian action are judged primarily in terms of technical standards of aid delivery and in fulfilling the material needs of refugees and threatened populations. It is with UNHCR as it is with most other aid organizations today: success is measured quantitatively—how much relief can be delivered how quickly. The central importance of human rights protection of displaced and threatened populations is frequently neglected. This is a qualitative aspect of the agency's work and less easily measured and less easily sold to donor nations as worthy of funding. While UNHCR and other humanitarian organizations are able to deliver large quantities of humanitarian supplies under extremely difficult conditions, they are much less successful in protecting civilians from human rights abuses, expulsions, and ethnic cleansing.

The Need to Raise the Protection Profile of UNHCR

So what might be done to halt this decline in the protection of refugees? A key issue for the new High Commissioner is to raise the protection profile of the agency. It is true that relief operations provide for the physical security of refugees and give UNHCR staff a presence with which to monitor human rights violations and other developments in the field. It is also claimed that material assistance gives UNHCR some leverage over host states but this is extremely limited since host governments or dissident warlords ultimately exercise control over the agency's operational environment. Thus, while protection and assistance are closely linked, material assistance operations must not dominate the agency's policies to such an extent that traditional protection of refugees and asylum seekers is undermined. Moreover, both material assistance and human rights reporting can often be better accomplished by other organizations, including local and international non-governmental organizations (NGOs), whose mandates expressly incorporate such activities.

While the new High Commissioner has signaled that he would like to make the protection of refugees his "core concern," protection issues do not figure consistently as a real priority in UNHCR's management culture. Currently the role of the Department of International Protection on operational issues is marginal and the director of protection has no independent authority to act, even on the most pressing protection crises. UNHCR staff now see job experience in operations, not in protection, as the way to advance their careers and ensure regular promotions. The sidelining of protection within the Office over the past decade and a half has not only damaged the traditional protection ethos of the organization but also severely limits the staff expertise needed to pursue a vigorous protection policy. Recent personnel have little or no knowledge or memory of institutional history and lack appropriate experience or awareness to learn from UNHCR's pre-1990s policies or programs. This is unfortunate because UNHCR staff face difficult political and moral dilemmas, often without the benefit of knowledge about either the underlying nature of refugee disasters or about the success or failure of past UNHCR interventions in similar situations.

The most significant single step that the High Commissioner could take to redress this imbalance between protection and operations would be to restore a close link between the Department of International Protection and field operations with an oversight capacity and authority for the director of protection. At the same time, operations managers should be held as accountable for shortcomings and failures in protection activities as they are for assistance. Without adequate authority given to the Department of International Protection and the necessary priority given to protection issues, the UNHCR will be unable to ensure consistency in its approach to the worldwide protection of refugees.

The Department of International Protection not only needs to be given greater authority but it also needs the essential human resources to upgrade the role of protection. This is particularly the case in field operations where refugee problems may be neglected or responses delayed because of inadequate staffing and limited human resources. Adequate resources are also required for the comprehensive protection training of UNHCR staff at all levels, and particularly at the management level. Although progress has been achieved in recent years to improve professional development, the Office needs to ensure that all staff receive regular training of all kinds. Recent humanitarian emergencies in Kosovo and elsewhere have revealed a serious shortage of senior staff capable of assuming leadership roles on short notice. A future priority should be that heads of missions be trained on how to handle emergencies and how to ensure protection for refugees in such situations.

Finally, at times the Office lacks a well-focused self-identity and is confused about the role it plays in the international system. At times, UNHCR acts as if it were independent—almost like the International Committee of the Red Cross—with little connection to the other parts of the UN system. At other times, it works alongside UN peacekeeping and peace enforcement troops and other UN agencies as part of a broad UN-led effort. The Office's overall mission combines international protection and seeking durable solutions with an expanded mandate centered on "persons of concern to UNHCR." However, the limits to UNHCR's practical work are not clear. Increasingly the organization has taken on more general humanitarian and development assistance tasks and expanded the roster of its clients to include many different kinds of forced migrants. Not only is it questionable whether UNHCR has the necessary resources or expertise to take on such a broad range of activities, but the ambitious though ambiguous nature of its expanded mandate and programs also leads to confusion and loss of autonomy, particularly when there have been so few clear policy statements about its overall responsibilities.

A key to making its institutional structure stronger and more unified is to identify a particular niche for the Office in humanitarian affairs. One of UNHCR's strengths is its clear original mandate. Only UNHCR has the legitimacy from its charter to protect refugees and to promote solutions to refugee problems. Because of this, the Office is indispensable and deserves the fullest support of governments. But UNHCR loses authority and autonomy when it steps outside of its mandate to take on tasks that other agencies or governments do better. Work in countries of origin either during conflicts or in post-conflict situations is extremely important and essential if progress is to be made towards resolving the global refugee problem, but organizations other than UNHCR are better able to manage these activities.[24] The Office should act as a catalyst for provoking other UN and non-governmental agencies to undertake programs for which UNHCR now claims responsibility. The agency should re-focus its attention on refugee protection. The advantage of reaffirming and clarifying its original protection mission would be to convey to personnel what is important and to provide them with a sense of overall purpose.

A distinctive niche would also provide the external public with a strong message about UNHCR commitment and focus and would build up trust and confidence in the authority of the organization.

The Need to Reverse the Erosion of Refugee Protection

UNHCR also has an important role to play in convincing states that it is in their own national interests to find satisfactory solutions to refugee problems. The task ahead is formidable, particularly at a time when political leaders are reluctant to take positions that they feel might expose them to electoral risks. Being the international "watchdog" on asylum and balancing the protection needs of refugees with the legitimate concerns of states requires courage and a willingness to confront governments when necessary. As the guardian of international refugee norms, UNHCR has a role to play in reminding liberal democracies of their own identities as promoters of international human rights. Refugee and human rights norms enjoy a special status among Western states because they help define the identities of liberal states. They are also important to non-Western states because adherence to these norms constitute a crucial sign to others of their membership in the international community of law-abiding states. Most states are not proud of practices and policies that contradict international refugee norms. The most powerful, liberal democratic states are particularly sensitive to the criticism they have received for not providing the leadership role on these humanitarian principles. Political leaders are floundering in their search for effective responses to refugee movements·and are looking for intellectual and political leadership and guidance on this policy issue. While individual governments may feel uncomfortable being criticized, UNHCR will gain greater respect in the long term for speaking up for refugee protection principles than for remaining silent.

UNHCR and other refugee rights advocates have a unique opportunity to insert human rights ideas into the contemporary policy debate about refugees. UNHCR needs to help states transform their perceptions of their national interests and alter their calculations of the costs and benefits of their refugee, asylum and migration policies. States need to be encouraged to adopt a principled approach to managing asylum and migration issues. With globalization, it will be increasingly difficult to maintain open borders for the free movement of capital and goods and services while building new walls to keep out the world's dispossessed and pursuing a "zero immigration" policy. Placing unduly harsh restrictions on the movements of people will simply lead to greater isolation and deprivation and pose yet new threats to regional and international security. It is also the case that if states remain indifferent to the plight of the world's refugees, the social and political fiber of their own societies will suffer. The way states deal with refugees speaks volumes about their human rights health and their tolerance for ethnic and racial minorities.

UNHCR should aggressively promote and monitor the obligations states have taken on through international refugee and human rights instruments.

An independent monitoring mechanism or ombudsman should be established to provide oversight of state activities in refugee protection and should report regularly to UNHCR's Executive Committee of state members. The Office should also strengthen its cooperation with the UN human rights regime. A key to strengthening UN capacity to monitor human rights in the future is enhancing its capacity to undertake a protection role in the field. But as it now stands, the UN Human Rights Office is severely handicapped by lack of resources with an annual official budget of only $22 million or 2 percent of the total UN budget.[25] Until that time when the UN human rights regime is properly resourced and fully developed, NGOs will have to assume a larger share of responsibility for ensuring the protection of forcibly displaced people. There are a number of practical ways in which NGOs could play a protection role in the field either on their own or in collaboration with the UN human rights and refugee regimes. In addition to monitoring human rights developments, fact-finding and advocacy, these include relocating refugee camps away from borders to minimize the danger of cross-border raids, ensuring that camps are laid out in ways to promote the security of women refugees, screening out combatants from noncombatants in refugee camps and settlements, and taking active measures to protect refugee children from recruitment as soldiers.

In recent years, UNHCR has taken a number of important initiatives to collaborate more closely with human rights and humanitarian relief agencies in support of the international refugee protection system.[26] In 1996, UNHCR and NGOs undertook an extensive series of global consultations and meetings called "Partnership in Action (PARINAC)" which outlined an action program for more effective collaboration in the fields of refugee protection and assistance worldwide. In 1999, the Division of International Protection launched the "Reach-out Process" with senior NGO officials with the objective of identifying the roles that NGOs can play in protecting refugees and establishing a training program for NGO staff working in the field on refugee protection. In 2001, UNHCR convened the "Global Consultations on Refugee Protection" process with governments in an attempt to seek common understanding on the future of international protection and to revitalize the international refugee instruments on the occasion of the fiftieth anniversary of the 1951 UN Refugee Convention.[27] UNHCR needs to build on these initiatives to establish partnerships with NGOs while at the same time becoming more assertive in exercising its protection mandate.

UNHCR is not a static organization but has constantly changed and evolved over the past fifty years. Dramatic and bold steps should now be taken to revitalize UNHCR's primary role as the protector of refugees and the guardian of asylum worldwide. Action on the protection front could not be more timely. In his initial year as the new High Commissioner, Ruud Lubbers is confronted with a funding crisis that will force UNHCR to reevaluate its recent priorities and return to its essential mission. He has a unique opportunity to rethink the fundamentals of the Office and to project them into a new century. His principal challenge, therefore, will be not only to examine ways in which to halt and reverse the erosion of the protection of refugees by states in the future, but also to critically assess the role of UNHCR itself in the protection of refugees and asylum seekers.

2

What Is Refugee Protection?
A Question Revisited

ARTHUR C. HELTON

A series of humanitarian crises over the past decade, coupled with the growing phenomenon of international migration, have produced unprecedented challenges to refugee protection around the world. Beginning in the mountains of northern Iraq in 1991, and continuing in Bosnia and later Kosovo in 1999, and later in Afghanistan, audacious attempts to deal with needy people before or after they flee across an international border have created complexities that exceeded the capacities of the international humanitarian system. Approximately 25 million people are displaced within countries by reason of conflict, and over 180 million people now reside outside of their home countries, including 12 million refugees (not counting 5 million Palestinian exiles) who have fled their countries with a well-founded fear of persecution upon return.

Humanitarian catastrophes have been unrelenting in such places as Afghanistan, the Balkans, and many countries in Africa. The adequacy of the UN refugee treaty regime, now over fifty years old, is in question, especially by governments wishing to block the arrival of a growing group of unwanted asylum seekers. The Office of the United Nations High Commissioner for Refugees (UNHCR), the principal international institution responsible for refugees, has been increasingly criticized for failing to protect refugees from forced return by unwelcoming governments, and is now shrinking under budgetary pressure. In other words, a new crisis in refugee protection has emerged at the outset of the new century.

It is rare for an author to be able to publicly review his own work on dynamic issues like the meaning of refugee protection and the work of UNHCR. That is what drew me to contribute this article, really an essay in three components. The first element is a legally-oriented article, published initially in 1990 in the *International Journal of Refugee Law*.[1] The second component is an opinion piece published in the same journal in 1994 on the new protection responsibilities of UNHCR.[2] The permission of Oxford University Press to reprint these articles is gratefully acknowledged. The third element is my current reflection on the first two works in light of the ensuing events and trends of the past decade. I conclude with suggestions, drawn from my recent book,

The Price of Indifference: Refugees and Humanitarian Action in the New Century (Oxford 2002), for giving a new proactive dimension to refugee protection.

What Is Refugee Protection?
A Question Posed at the Outset of a Decade of Refugees[3]

The terms "refugee" and "protection" are often invoked in discussions of the needs of individuals for shelter and asylum. Their use, however, is frequently imprecise and definitions can be somewhat elusive. This brief essay will seek to define these terms for the purposes of assessing the state of international refugee protection.

When we speak of "protection," we mean *legal* protection. The concept must be associated with entitlements under law and, for effective redress of grievances, mechanisms to vindicate claims in respect of those entitlements. An inquiry, then, into whether a population has "protection" is an examination of the fashion in which the pertinent authorities comply with the entitlements of individuals under international law, and the manner in which these legal precepts are implemented and respected.

At the outset, the term "refugee" has a specific legal connotation. The 1951 United Nations Convention[4] (and 1967 Protocol[5] that expanded the temporal and geographic coverage of the Convention) defines "refugee" as a person who is outside of the country of nationality (or place of last habitual residence for a stateless person), who has a well-founded fear of persecution on account of race, religion, nationality, membership of a particular social group, or political opinion.[6] If an individual cannot meet the requisites of this definition, then he or she is not entitled to protection under the Convention or Protocol.

Traditionally, therefore, refugee protection is reserved for those who have left their countries of origin. The decision to leave and cross a national border transforms an individual into an object of concern under international refugee law, wherever the circumstances are such that he or she has lost, or been deprived of, protection under law in his or her country of origin, and is in need of another source of protection.

Individuals who do not cross a national boundary thus find themselves without recourse to the international refugee legal regime, notwithstanding internal displacement or a fear of persecution by the authorities. Frequently, at the request of the Secretary-General and General Assembly of the United Nations, UNHCR has extended its mandate to internally displaced persons under a "good offices" jurisdiction.[7] Another approach has been to establish a special authority to assist displaced persons, such as the United Nations Border Relief Operation (UNBRO) along the Thai-Cambodian border.[8] These displaced individuals, more numerous than those who cross borders, can have similar needs for protection, but are beyond the protective umbrella of the international refugee legal regime.

Also, those individuals who flee across a border from the generalized threats posed by war or civil disturbance are outside the ambit of international refugee law. Such persons are considered not to have a sufficiently individualized fear of persecution. Member states of the Organization of African Unity have subscribed to a broadened refugee definition, which includes war and civil disorder.[9] Governmental and expert discussions in Latin America[10] and Asia[11] have also recognized the positive utility of adopting such a broadened definition.

Humanitarian law provides a source of protection for civilian noncombatants under the terms of the 1949 Geneva Conventions relating to war. The implementation of those conventions is largely the responsibility of the International Committee of the Red Cross, which must depend in situations of internal armed conflict, frequently a cause of population displacement, upon the cooperation and tolerance of both the government and insurgent forces. Protection and assistance activities in situations not covered as the ones described above by international humanitarian law are even less certain. This has led some commentators to call for a new declaration relating to situations of internal strife, drawing upon established human rights law precepts and humanitarian law traditions.[12]

The continuing need for protection for internally displaced persons, as well as those who flee generalized violence in their home countries, must be studied and assessed. These issues affect large populations, particularly in Central America, Asia, and Africa, and include questions of both doctrinal coverage and implementation.

There are also ambiguities in the refugee definition. Meaning is offered under guidelines issued by UNHCR, the international organization established by the General Assembly to be responsible for supervising the implementation of the Convention and Protocol.[13] "Persecution," for example, is ordinarily considered to include a threat to an individual's life or freedom.[14] A deprivation of liberty must be significant, that is, for a lengthy period and/or in onerous conditions.[15] Under certain circumstances, discrimination or deprivation with respect to other basic rights can constitute persecution.[16] For example, the inability to earn a living, to receive education or to have a normal family life can constitute persecution, if imposed for one of the stated reasons, even if the deprivation does not rise to the level of "a threat to life or freedom." However, more than harassment is required to constitute persecution.

Additionally, persecution must generally come from a government source.[17] Under certain circumstances, forces that a government either cannot or will not control can become "agents" of persecution for purposes of refugee protection; they may include death squads or even insurgent forces not susceptible to government control.[18]

For an individual to be entitled to refugee protection, the persecution in question must be on account of race, religion, nationality, membership of a particular social group, or political opinion.[19] Two basic concepts are involved—group membership and belief. Mere membership of a particular race, religion, nationality, or social group, is generally not sufficient to warrant refugee protection. The individual must show a nexus between himself or herself and the possibility of persecution. In certain circumstances, however, where a group has been singled out by a persecutor for abuse, mere membership may be sufficient for the purposes of protection.[20]

With respect to belief, that is, religion or political opinion, it is not absolutely necessary that the individual previously have acted on the belief in question. However, the belief must be one that the authorities in the home country will not tolerate, and it must be held with sufficient strength that it is likely to be expressed in the future, even if it has not been expressed in the past. Under certain circumstances, refugee protection is warranted where the authorities impute a political opinion to an individual, even if the person does not possess the actual belief.[21]

The term "asylum" is not defined in international law, but for present purposes it can be taken to mean the act of providing territorial "protection" to refugees. Under international refugee law, there is no categorical right for a refugee to receive asylum. The concept of "protection," again not defined, can be taken to mean the act of respecting and upholding fundamental human rights, such as the core rights declared in the Covenants on Civil and Political Rights,[22] and on Economic, Social, and Cultural Rights.[23]

Apart from the question of coverage with respect to international refugee law, there is an issue of compliance, which can be assessed in the varied circumstances in which refugees find themselves. Upon flight, a refugee becomes subject to the jurisdiction of the authorities in a country of reception. Treatment must correspond with obligations to respect fundamental human rights, including the right not to be returned to a territory where the individual may be subjected to serious persecution, that is, *non-refoulement*.[24] This prohibition includes nonrejection at the border or shore, and in certain circumstances, it may even limit the exercise of a government's power on an extraterritorial basis, for example, the United States–Haiti high seas interdiction program (intercepting and returning boat people to Haiti).[25]

Other governmental measures hostile to refugee protection include limiting access to asylum procedures, for example, by the imposition of carrier fines and visa restrictions, as well as the "principle of first asylum," which seeks to identify a particular state as responsible for examining an asylum request, and which is used particularly in certain European countries.[26] One problem is that states typically cannot agree on which country should be responsible for the examination, and asylum seekers have been shuttled from border to border and airport to airport, creating "refugees in orbit," who frequently wind up in detention and may be returned to their country of origin. The restrictive harmonization of asylum procedures being discussed in Europe in relation to common economic and political arrangements may exacerbate those protection problems.[27]

Detention policies, as well as restrictions on movement and permission to work, have also been used by governments to discourage arrivals and to divert asylum seekers elsewhere. Policies followed in the United States, Hong Kong, and Germany provide recent examples of such "deterrent measures."[28]

A critical element of refugee protection is fair and nondiscriminatory status determination in a country of reception. While the particular procedures used may vary according to the national system in question, to meet international standards decision-making should be individualized and separated from ideology and foreign policy considerations, as well as from immigration enforcement priorities. Improperly restrictive criteria should not be used. The adjudication system established by the Comprehensive Plan of Action (CPA), agreed to at the 1989 Indochinese Refugee Conference,[29] and practiced under the CPA, is a recent example of an overly restrictive application of criteria.[30] The situation in North America is also pertinent.[31]

A critical aspect of refugee protection is the treatment of refugees held in camps following flight from persecution; they have lost the protection of their homelands and yet are often not accorded the protection by host governments that would usually be given nationals of those countries. Though there is no set of international law standards expressly governing the treatment of persons in refugee camps, certain United Nations agreements, as well as basic principles of law and human rights, are applicable.

Host governments are sometimes reluctant to assert their authority to police territory within refugee camps. Often countries which bear the brunt of first asylum are themselves economically and socially strained, and their governments are reluctant to recognize a duty to protect those interned.[32] The 1951 Convention has nevertheless codified the principle that a state is under a duty to protect refugees residing within its borders, declaring that, "except where this Convention contains more favorable provisions, a Contracting State shall accord to refugees the same treatment as is accorded to aliens generally."[33] Such a duty is a well-established principle of international law, and countries not signatories to the 1951 Convention remain obliged to protect refugees on their soil.[34]

Regardless of whether persons seeking asylum are recognized by the host government as "refugees" or are classified as unauthorized "aliens," a state is obligated to provide legal protection and to respect fundamental individual rights. The standard of treatment to which all noncitizens are entitled is the same as that which applies to a state's treatment of its own nationals, and should not fall below that level.[35] Whether a non-national's entry into a state was lawful affects only that individual's claim to benefits beyond the right to protection to which all persons within a state's borders are entitled.[36]

Non-refoulement also imposes an obligation to protect refugees residing within a state's borders. The principle that no refugee should be returned to any country where his or her life or freedom is endangered is perhaps the basis of all refugee protection.[37] The failure to provide tolerable conditions effectively promotes return and thus undermines the principle of *non-refoulement*.[38] This view has been taken by UNHCR, which has stressed that all individuals given refuge be allowed to enjoy basic humanitarian standards of treatment.[39] In order for this principle to be given full effect, refugees should be granted at least temporary asylum under humane living conditions.

International concern over human rights issues, and the right to humane treatment in all situations, has led to the adoption of a number of treaties and protocols. These instruments speak in broad terms of minimum standards of treatment for all persons; they therefore extend to refugees seeking asylum, who do not forfeit their fundamental rights when they leave their home countries. Concern with fundamental rights informs the Charter of the United Nations,[40] and is clearly expressed by the Universal Declaration of Human Rights, adopted by the General Assembly on 10 December 1948.[41] Although the Declaration does not contain a specific provision regarding treatment of non-nationals, it can be inferred that they are covered.

The Declaration ". . . is couched in universal terms which either state affirmatively that 'everyone' shall be entitled to such and such a right, or provide negatively from the viewpoint of States, that 'no one' shall be subjected to a particular deprivation."[42] It follows that, except for those provisions that explicitly grant benefits to nationals, the declaration extends its protection to refugees.[43]

In 1985, the General Assembly also adopted the Declaration On the Human Rights of Individuals Who Are Not Nationals of the Country in Which They Live.[44] It provides that aliens shall enjoy the right to security of person, and that no alien shall be subject to arbitrary arrest or detention, or be subjected to cruel, inhumane, or degrading treatment.[45]

Although the United Nations has not adopted a declaration to deal specifically with the treatment of refugees who are women or children, several instruments extend protection. UNHCR has noted that the majority of the world's refugee population comprises women and children, and has recognized that woman and girls who are refugees are particularly vulnerable to "physical violence, sexual abuse, and discrimination."[46] Accordingly, UNHCR has recommended that states establish programs to ensure the physical safety and equality of treatment.[47] In 1974, the General Assembly drafted the Declaration on the Protection of Women and Children in Emergency and Armed Conflict, which proclaims that women and children belonging to civilian populations who, "[find] themselves in circumstances of emergency and armed conflict . . . or who live in occupied territories, shall not be deprived of shelter, food, medical aid or other inalienable rights, in accordance with the provisions of the Universal Declarations of Human Rights, the International Covenant on Civil and Political Rights, the International Covenant on Economic, Social and Cultural Rights, the Declaration of the Rights of the Child or other instruments of international law."[48]

Although the declaration seeks specifically to address the danger to women and children in civilian populations in the midst of war, families who have been forced to flee owing to persecution resulting from armed struggle need protection for the same reasons. Furthermore, refugee populations are frequently encamped in border areas on the edge of war torn territories and subjected to military fire.[49] Thus, refugee women and children are within the group for which the General Assembly meant to encourage protection.

The United Nations view that refugee children should be protected by the countries in which they are interned can also be inferred from the Declaration of the Rights of the Child. This declaration recognizes that children shall enjoy special protection and that "[t]he child shall in all circumstances be among the first to receive protection and relief."[50] The protection requirement is made more explicit by the United Nations Convention on the Rights of the Child, adopted by the General Assembly in 1989.[51]

Countries not under treaty obligations to uphold the United Nations instruments are still bound in so far as these instruments reflect customary international law. For example, arbitrary prolonged detention has been prohibited by both the Universal Declaration of Human Rights,[52] and by the International Covenant on Civil and Political Rights.[53] Prolonged arbitrary detention is also prohibited by the Standard Minimum Rules for the Treatment of Prisoners.[54] The International Court of Justice has cited the Charter of the United Nations, as well as the Universal Declaration of Human Rights, in support of holding that it is a violation of international law to deprive persons of their freedom of movement and to confine them in conditions of hardship.[55] The proliferation of instruments condemning arbitrary and prolonged detention under inhumane conditions, widely adopted by the international community, and recognized by the International Court of Justice, indicates that it is prohibited under customary international law. Refugees are no less protected than are all other persons under international human rights law.

UNHCR and Protection in the 90s: The Institutional Dimension of Protection[56]

The office of the United Nations High Commissioner for Refugees is viewed increasingly as the humanitarian arm of the United Nations. The agency's work is being transformed in the post–Cold War era by its efforts to respond to the proliferation of conflicts and causes of displacement that have produced in 1994 nearly 20 million refugees and another 24 million internally displaced persons. From the mountains of northern Iraq to the besieged city of Sarajevo, UNHCR has been required to respond in new ways to new responsibilities. Whether it be meeting "winterization" needs, providing humanitarian assistance in the midst of conflict, or undertaking liaison relationships with UN peacekeeping forces, UNHCR's programs have had to address an increasing variety of circumstances. This includes concerted efforts to promote voluntary repatriation in the midst of situations of fragile peace.

Conceptual developments have not kept pace with social and political realities. Thus, the work of the Division of International Protection, that section within UNHCR that is primarily responsible for ensuring the discharge of protection responsibilities, must be fundamentally redirected to provide a conceptual foundation for new program approaches. This would not be an academic exercise; it is a crucial need. A philosophical basis and set of principles to inform UNHCR's work in this new era must be developed. Recent experience, both good and bad, should be drawn upon. Conceptual coherence would assist the work of UNHCR and provide an important source of guidance to the wider international community.

UNHCR's protection responsibility, which is entrusted to it by the international community, makes it distinct among international organizations. The protection concept is considered traditionally to include maintaining physical security and providing redress under law. For refugees, protection traditionally means lifesaving interventions, fair treatment upon reception, compliance with essential humanitarian standards and non-return to a place of prospective persecution (*non-refoulement*). Taken together, these are elements of the concept of asylum. But protection is a broad humanitarian principle; in a fundamental sense, protection means to secure the enjoyment of basic human rights and to meet primary humanitarian needs. Granting asylum is a very effective way to protect a refugee in flight, but other protection measures can be just as effective, including to protect those who have yet to flee across a national border.

Among UNHCR's most difficult current challenges is the need to identify protection strategies for its evolving work in so-called "countries of origin," including clarity with respect to exactly who should be protected. Increasingly, staff are deployed in situations of civil conflict or severe repression. Protection officers witness and document severe human rights violations. They sometimes act on the information they receive and intervene with authorities in an effort to prevent, ameliorate, or redress violations. Their work is a blend of human rights monitoring, negotiation, and activism, oftentimes in situations of considerable insecurity.

The implications are profound for UNHCR's protection work. Specifically consideration must be given to expanding the UNHCR mandate, particularly to encompass systematically the provision of protection and assistance to internally displaced persons. Regional protection strategies must be developed. A deeper understanding must be given to conventional protection concepts. Additionally, UNHCR's institutional protection capacities must be enhanced. Each of these points is discussed below.

Mandate

If UNHCR is to be significantly involved in countries of origin, it will be necessary to resolve underlying tensions in its protection responsibilities. Under what circumstances does promotion of the right of people to remain in their places of origin serve to expose them in an unjustified fashion to risk of serious harm? How can the exercise of the right of people to seek asylum abroad be assisted or facilitated without UNHCR becoming complicit in realizing the "ethnic cleansing" objectives of certain conflicts? Authoritative principles must be promulgated and founded upon tenets of law, ethics, and morality.

Protection strategies must be articulated. Can more precise objectives be identified for the human rights reporting engaged in by protection officers? Formal arrangements may be needed with the various components of the UN system, including those offices responsible for human rights and peacekeeping activities. What about instances where such reporting activities may be incompatible with high diplomatic and political responsibilities? Genuine partnerships with independent human rights groups are required to further protection objectives.

The new emphasis on preventive diplomacy and early humanitarian action necessarily results in policy makers focusing upon the situation of internally displaced persons. The vast magnitude of the population in need of assistance and protection, along with a new emphasis on work in countries of origin and prevention of the causes of refugee flight, underscore the need for a new conceptual framework. Prevention as a rationale for UNHCR's involvement with the internally displaced was recently explicitly recognized by the Executive Committee along with the conventional requisites of an exercise of the "good offices" jurisdiction. These include a request by the Secretary-General or the General Assembly, consent of the government in question, and oftentimes involvement with refugee repatriation. Of course, criteria could be identified by the international community for situations when a request to UNHCR would be appropriate, and when governments should consent to its involvement on behalf of the internally displaced or when such consent would not be required.

As an elemental term, "displaced persons" must be clearly defined, and the process and methods of determining whether groups of individuals meet the definition must be established in order to fix the nature of the responsibility of the international community and the claims affected individuals may make upon it. Although governments are likely to react cautiously, new circumstances demand new thinking. A new treaty instrument may well evolve and a corresponding institutional framework will be required. The role of UNHCR will undoubtedly be the subject of continuous inquiry.

Regional Strategies

Universal protection arrangements necessarily evolve in an incremental fashion. As a basic strategy, UNHCR should work to promote protective national practices, seek to embody such practices in regional schemes, and ultimately secure universal application. Such an approach presently could be pursued, for example, with concepts of protection for internally displaced persons (or those at risk of such displacement) or a broadened refugee definition. The newly independent states of the former Soviet Union could provide a crucible for the creation of regional instruments on forced migrants and internally displaced persons. The Conference on Security and Cooperation (now Organization for Security and Cooperation) in Europe might be an appropriate forum for development of regional standards on these issues. Temporary Protection policies in Western Europe will necessitate the consideration of standards on solutions for the beneficiaries in terms of permissible limits on the duration of such an insecure status, the circumstances under which repatriation should be promoted, and the relationship to the conventional refugee regime.

Other regional strategies could include codifying a broadened refugee definition that includes war and civil strife along the lines of the 1969 Organization of African Unity (OAU) refugee treaty. Initially, such an effort should be undertaken in Latin America where a broadened refugee concept has been accepted in non-binding declarations, including the 1984 Cartagena Declaration. Relationships should be strengthened with regional inter-governmental bodies such as the OAU and the Organization of American States in order to make them more effective. Given the need for comprehensive approaches, appropriate links should be forged with the International Organization for Migration, and other entities involved in the area of humanitarian migration.

Deepening the Concept of Protection

State compliance with tenets of conventional refugee protection must be thoroughly monitored and zealously promoted. The basic human rights of refugees must be scrupulously respected, including asylum and non-return to places of persecution, freedom from arbitrary detention, and provision of basic civil, social, and economic rights. This includes assessing the human rights dimension of development, and clarifying the content of protection itself as a humanitarian concept. Much in the conventional refugee regime is worth not only saving, but, indeed, fortifying. But the dilemma faced by states is real. How can asylum be preserved in large scale influxes that are predominantly economic in character? Protection leadership will be crucial. It is a principal function of the Division of International Protection to represent a countervailing force to negative international trends.

Institutional Issues

Protection sensibilities must be better integrated in the program work of UNHCR. A comprehensive planning process and the involvement of the Division of International Protection in formulating responses to emergencies are crucial. Consideration should be given to organizing a roster of prominent jurists and legal scholars who could be drawn upon for advice and research in appropriate circumstances. Such a resource would enhance UNHCR's capacity to reflect and conceptualize, and would be part of a larger exercise by UNHCR to strengthen ties to the academic and applied research communities.

New functions will require continuing education of UNHCR staff. New training programs should be established for protection officers on human rights and humanitarian law and institutions. In this regard, there should be collaboration with other UN agencies and sections, including the Department of Peacekeeping Operations, the Department of Humanitarian Affairs, and the Center for Human Rights. Specialized agencies such as the United Nations Relief and Works Administration, and non-governmental organizations such as the International Committee of the Red Cross, and others, should also be involved. Conflict resolution, negotiation, and conciliation techniques should be covered in such training programs in order to assist protection officers in discharging their new responsibilities. Protection must be professionalized and fully integrated into the ongoing work of the office.

In sum, UNHCR's metamorphosis into the humanitarian branch of the UN must be supported by clear and workable principles derived from law and international politics. In a fundamental sense, this will require reinventing both refugee protection and the Division of International Protection. Law and experience must be synthesized in an ongoing process to achieve ordered principles for action. This will be UNHCR's principal protection challenge for the 90s.

A Look Backward and Forward in 2002

The essays above still resonate at the end of a decade that has been extraordinary in terms of refugee crises and responses. Innovations in international efforts to deal more effectively with internal displacement through the promulgation of guidelines and agency coordination, and the prospect for greater accountability through an international criminal court, may add to the policy tools that decision makers can use to mitigate humanitarian emergencies. But the efforts to achieve more proactive policy have given rise to new complexities. This becomes clear in a brief review of the events of the past decade.

The decade of the 1990s[57] began with 500,000 Kurdish asylum seekers being turned away from the Turkish border in 1991. They were accommodated in an enclave in northern Iraq, courtesy of U.S.-led military forces, establishing a precedent for attempts later in the decade to secure in-country protection for the displaced. The United Nations at the time discovered that its institutional architecture was not adequate to deal with new complex emergencies which involved both military as well as humanitarian components, and the Department of Humanitarian Affairs (DHA) was established in the UN Secretariat. The international bureaucracy continued to wrestle with humanitarian emergencies, and DHA has now become the UN Office for the Coordination of Humanitarian Affairs, the centerpiece of an international system that so often still seems desperately inadequate.

In 1993, the crisis in Somalia featured a massive famine relief operation, and ultimately the killing of eighteen U.S. soldiers who were initially deployed as peace enforcers. The prompt withdrawal of U.S. forces was followed shortly by the retreat of other troop contingents. The evolution of peace operations in Somalia led the military to coin the term "nation building," virtually an epithet now, at least among some U.S. military leaders. Nevertheless, that is exactly the mission in post-Taliban Afghanistan. A pre-emptive strike against Iraq may lead to another ambitious recovery operation.

A 1994 emergency involving Haitian boat people was followed by an influx of Cuban rafters, presenting new asylum crises to the United States. A high-tech humanitarian response resulted, involving the projection of U.S. force in the form of Coast Guard and Navy vessels which were used to intercept and return thousands of boat people. An effort was then made to examine their individual claims for refugee protection before they could set foot on U.S. soil. Had they made it to land, they would have been entitled under our law to apply for asylum. But the numbers overwhelmed official capacities, and the prospect of a migration refugee emergency ultimately led to the deployment of U.S. troops in Haiti in 1994.

Perhaps the singular humanitarian tragedy of the past decade was the 1994 genocide in Rwanda. Approximately 800,000 Tutsis and moderate Hutus were killed by Hutu extremists, prompting massive displacement and the establishment of ominous border camps in Eastern Zaire (now the Democratic Republic of Congo), posing serious security threats to Rwanda. The ensuing failure to bring to justice those displaced persons who were guilty of genocide, and curtail the emerging threat, prompted attacks by the Rwandan army to break up the camps and the forced return of refugees. Even in Tanzania, a relatively benign refugee-hosting state, soldiers marched Rwandan refugees back home at gunpoint in December 1996. The failure to achieve a justice framework in the midst of this refugee crisis contributed to a further descent into conflict, and an ongoing inter-state war in Central Africa that will hopefully end in the foreseeable future.

While there were many crucial events relating to refugee policy over the past decade, it was in the former Yugoslavia that the twists and turns of refugee policy were perhaps most pronounced. As the Socialist Federal Republic of Yugoslavia disintegrated, conflict raged throughout most of the decade. In 1991, fighting in Croatia resulted in population displacement and "ethnic cleansing." Conflict spread in 1992 to Bosnia and Herzegovina, where it lasted until 1995. Bosnia remains even today very much a work in progress as a state. The reality on the ground is that there are three separate ethnically divided "statelets." The crisis in Kosovo prompted a 1999 NATO bombing campaign that resulted in the displacement of 800,000 Kosovars. When the victorious ethnic Albanians rushed back behind NATO ground forces, about 200,000

Serbs, Roma, and others were then forced from their homes in retaliation. In early 2001, ethnic tensions erupted into conflict in Macedonia, prompting 40,000 persons to flee their homes.[58] The situation in the region remains unresolved and tense.

In relation to the former Yugoslavia, the decade was characterized by efforts to contain human displacement through the presence of humanitarian workers and provision of material relief to needy people. This was coupled with restrictive admissions policies in Western Europe, which granted only temporary protection to those from the Balkan region who could make it there. But this was hardly a successful human protection policy: witness the UN-declared safe enclaves for Muslims being overrun by Serb forces in 1995. Approximately 200,000 persons died in the course of the conflicts, and the effort now is to manage the separation of ethnic groups in the Balkans.

The decade ended with an extraordinary effort in East Timor in 1999 to build a new state out of the devastation wrought by Indonesian militia members who had quit that tiny disputed land after a pro-independence referendum. The weaknesses and gaps in the capacities of the international community to undertake ambitious endeavors such as policing, civil administration, establishing the rule of law, and economic revival, have become painfully obvious. This is so even after East Timor gained its nominal independence in May 2002 under the continued tutelage of a UN mission.

The experience of the last decade reveals once more the deeply reactive character of the world's humanitarian system to protect and assist refugees. Perversities in aid giving and gaps in protection have demoralized humanitarians. Assistance sometimes prolongs conflict. Because they have yet to cross an international border, internal exiles do not have systematic recourse to international refugee protection. Military intervention is selective and is likely to remain an exceptional response to humanitarian emergencies. For the most part, the relatively capable states in Europe and North America seek to contain human displacement elsewhere, particularly in Africa.

There is clearly a need for more proactive refugee policy. This would mean enhancing international cooperation, including in the resettlement of refugees. In addition, preventive approaches are needed to mitigate humanitarian catastrophes. But these words are easy to say, and the real question is whether such new directions can be achieved. Indeed, what would a proactive refugee policy look like?

Take West Africa, in which a refugee crisis has recently produced predictable images of pathos and loss. In 2001, upwards of 140,000 refugees were pushed by fighting from Sierra Leone and Liberia into the Parrot's Beak area of southwest Guinea, where they were joined by dislocated Guineans as conflict spread. Though most of these refugees have since been relocated out of the extremely dangerous and desolate Parrot's Beak area, the fundamental issues have not been resolved. Another generation of exiles is caught between homes and risks being wasted in the course of this emergency. Wrenching refugee images from this region may produce at least a temporary infusion of humanitarian aid as well as a spate of solemn hand-wringing by the United Nations Security Council. But a more comprehensive international initiative is needed to address the underlying causes of this humanitarian catastrophe.

As Ruud Lubbers, the High Commissioner for Refugees, discovered during a visit to West Africa early in his tenure in 2001, the point of entry for international action is the refugee crisis. Lubbers should be commended for calling the international community's attention to this festering human disaster. But a humanitarian response, while necessary, will not be sufficient. What is needed is an operational political framework much closer to the setting and the problem. While the UN system has made modest internal adjustments to promote peace building, these bureaucratic efforts have so far been inadequate. A genuine measure of international cooperation and a forward-looking preventive orientation are needed.

Specifically, a broad international plan of action should be prepared under the auspices of the United Nations, the African Union, and the Economic Community of West African States (ECOWAS). The plan should include as stakeholders the three most affected countries, Guinea, Liberia, and Sierra Leone. In addition, traditional donor states, mainly from the European Union and North America, as well as key international organizations involved in development assistance and economic reform, notably the United Nations Development Program and the international financial institutions, should also be included. Non-governmental organizations should be involved as well since many have had long-standing programs in the region, and such groups are likely to implement any international plan.

One important component of any such plan would deal with justice for the grisly atrocities and abuses perpetrated during the conflict. A justice element would be critical to helping manage revenge and sustaining a peace process. Security could be provided by ECOWAS peacekeeping troops with logistical assistance, if necessary, from militaries outside of Africa.

A serious international strategy would have to deal broadly with the economic, social, and political dimensions of the crisis. Coming up with a specific package of policy options designed to supplant the destructive impacts of conflict, including diamonds and wartime economies, will require a strategy deeply rooted in the situation of these countries. An effective plan would identify the bundles of "sticks and carrots" necessary to diminish the power and influence of those responsible for promoting conflict in the region, most notably President Charles Taylor of Liberia.

This would be an ambitious approach, especially considering that even the modest and reactive safety net for refugees that has evolved over the past fifty years is now itself coming under great pressure. In 2001, UNHCR's budget was cut by $130 million (14 percent) and 939 posts were eliminated. The agency's budget crisis results from unreliable and diminished funding. Its future as the principal international protector of refugees has been called into question by lack of donor support.

While UNHCR staff are understandably upset, others, notably refugees, will really feel the pain. Most internal exiles will be required to subsist without international support. Efforts to strengthen refugee self-sufficiency and promote their integration in situations of prolonged exile are likely to erode under budget pressure. This poses a question to the relatively small group of traditional donors: How committed is the international community to refugees and displaced persons? The answer to this question, now decidedly uncertain, will dictate the state of the protection of the world's refugees over the next decades.

Conclusion

The current debate over refugee protection contains both back-to-the-basics and onward-to-the-future elements. The tension between these two directions is reflected well in recent "Global Consultations on Refugee Protection" process with governments. Reality, of course, will inevitably impinge upon these discussions and further define the concepts and tools of refugee protection. But clearly we need new strategies to make international protection smarter. In this regard, a successful effort to learn lessons from the recent past and infuse policy with a more proactive character will be needed in order to make protection more effective and enduring.

2
The Ethics of
Refugee Protection

3

The Legal and Ethical Obligations of UNHCR

The Case of Temporary Protection in Western Europe

ERIK ROXSTRÖM AND MARK GIBNEY

Like all other UN agencies, the Office of the United Nations High Commissioner for Refugees (UNHCR) must be governed by high ethical standards. In this chapter we begin to define what these standards should be. To do this we examine the role played by UNHCR in developing and promoting the concept of temporary protection (TP) in Western Europe as a response to the humanitarian crisis involving Bosnian refugees. This focal point means that we will be primarily concerned with UNHCR's interaction with Western European states, bearing in mind that this has profound implications on UNHCR's work elsewhere.

The tragic and brutal war in the former Yugoslavia placed UNHCR in what undoubtedly seemed like an impossible situation. On the one hand were the protection needs of tens of thousands Bosnian refugees, while at the same time UNHCR was faced with the political realities of deep anti-immigrant sentiment in each of the European countries. Certainly UNHCR quite understandably felt a need to respond in a "pragmatic" and "realistic" way. One of its "solutions" was to promote TP, a policy premised on the idea that European states would respond more generously to the refugees from the former Yugoslavia at their doorsteps if they could be assured that refugees would eventually return.[1]

As we will argue here, UNHCR's TP policy failed in a number of ways—legally, ethically, and politically. Empirically, it is by no means clear how pragmatic UNHCR's "pragmatic" solution actually was. Which is to say that there is no good evidence that Western European states provided protection to a greater number of refugees than they otherwise would have without UNHCR's input. Nor is there any evidence that this policy created any other sustainable gains in terms of refugee protection writ large.

Beyond this, UNHCR's initiative represented a failure of principle. In promoting TP as it did, UNHCR departed from its obligations concerning the treatment and protection of individuals. Moreover, UNHCR's modus operandi in this particular matter manifests some deeper problems concerning the accountability and legitimacy of international organizations, most notably the manner in which democratic principles have come to be sacrificed in the name of political pragmatism.

We begin with an overview of the legal and ethical framework that should guide the conduct of UNHCR, and then place refugee protection in Western Europe within a broader human rights context. Finally, we assess the main arguments that were used to justify UNHCR's TP scheme in light of the context in which this notion was introduced.

As a final point to this introduction, let it be said that because of the interface between the North and the South, refugee protection serves as the most obvious and visible indicator of the North's purported commitment to human rights, and any shortcomings and failures in this realm will reverberate far beyond the issue of refugee protection alone. For this reason, TP sent a rather disturbing message that Northern states generally, and Western European states in particular, have no qualms compromising principle when it is perceived to be in their collective self-interest to do so. Beyond that, however, that UNHCR apparently has few qualms in assisting this effort.

The Legal and Ethical Framework

Principles

The specific authority of the Office of the High Commissioner for Refugees comes from two separate sources: (1) under the powers of the United Nations General Assembly (GA)—as specified in UNHCR's Statute (Statute) and subsequent GA resolutions,[2] and (2) under the Convention Relating to the Status of Refugees (1951 Convention)[3] and its Protocol (1967 Protocol).[4]

Paragraph 1 of the Statute states that the function of UNHCR is to provide international protection to refugees (as defined by paragraph 6 of the Statute) and to seek permanent solutions for the problem of refugees. According to paragraph 2, the work of UNHCR "[s]hall be of an entirely non-political character; it shall be humanitarian and social and shall relate, as a rule, to groups and categories of refugees." What international protection entails is further developed in paragraph 8(a) of the Statute, which states that UNHCR

> shall provide for the protection of refugees by: (a) Promoting the conclusion and ratification of international conventions for the protection of refugees, supervising their application and proposing amendments thereto: (b) Promoting through special agreements with governments the execution of any measures calculated to improve the situation of refugees and to reduce the number requiring protection; (c) Assisting governmental and private efforts to promote voluntary repatriation or assimilation within new national communities; (d) Promoting the admission of refugees, not excluding those in the most destitute categories, to the territories of States.

In accordance with article 35 of the 1951 Convention, States Parties have conferred a supervisory responsibility on the High Commissioner.

> The Contracting States undertake to cooperate with the Office of the United Nations High Commissioner for Refugees, or any other agency of the United Nations that may succeed it, in the exercise of its functions, and shall in particular facilitate its duty of supervising the application of the provisions of this Convention.[5]

The Statute and the 1951 Convention implicitly make clear that the ultimate end of UNHCR is (1) to promote and protect the human rights of refugees and (2) to prevent refugee situations from occurring—an objective that is inseparable from the larger goal of the UN to promote the respect for human rights writ large. The connection between human rights and refugee protection, and its implication for UNHCR's mandate, is quite unambiguous. For one, refugees are persons who have a well-founded fear that they will be victims of human rights abuse.[6] Most importantly, however, human rights belong to everyone by virtue of their humanity.[7] Refugees do not forfeit their human rights based on their refugee status. Rather, the purpose of refugee protection is to enable refugees to enjoy them—to the largest extent possible. Of course, this does not mean that UNHCR's immediate responsibility is to promote the implementation of key human rights instruments. Its function is limited to a particular context and it is important that UNHCR does not become (or try to become) an all-embracing human rights body.[8] It does mean, however, that in the exercise of its functions, UNHCR must make sure that its actions and policies are consonant with human rights values.[9]

All human rights treaties—including the 1951 Convention—have the same ethical foundation, characterized by an overriding concern with individual dignity and autonomy. Hence, human rights are not in harmony with a strict consequential or utilitarian ethics. Because of this, UNHCR should not trade the rights of some refugees for the perceived benefits to many. Certainly one of the strongest principles in international human rights law is the principle of non-discrimination. Thus, UNHCR cannot promote a policy whereby states select refugees on the basis of some kind of nativist "affinity" in terms of race, ethnicity, culture, language, and so forth. And this is true even if such a policy would greatly increase the number of refugees that a particular country might be willing to accept.

Still, it might be claimed that paragraph 2 of the Statute, which stipulates that "UNHCR should, as a rule, deal with groups and categories of refugees," conflicts with the individualistic paradigm mentioned above. However, this provision cannot be read in isolation. It must be read in light of the 1951 Convention and other human rights instruments affording individual rights to refugees. Consequently, the phrase "groups and categories of refugees" must be understood as "groups and categories of refugees" consisting of individuals endowed with human rights.

As seen above, paragraph 8a of the Statute states that the High Commissioner may propose amendments to international conventions for the protection of refugees. The purpose of this is to highlight shortcomings in international refugee protection. UNHCR's authority in this respect is not without limits. UNHCR is not a norm creating body, meaning that it does not have the right to redefine the core values and ideals that it should work towards. These norms already exist: in the 1951 Convention and in other key international human rights instruments. In other words, its proposals must be in line with fundamental human rights values. Further, since the function of UNHCR is to promote the rights of refugees, the amendments it proposes must be aimed at strengthening—not weakening—individual rights already afforded to refugees.

While it is beyond dispute that the authority of UNHCR is derived from, and its discretion limited by, international human rights and refugee law, the specific content of this law may well be disputed. International rules on treaty interpretation attach considerable weight to the object and purpose of a treaty. And in this regard it is important to underscore the fact that the 1951 Convention is an instrument that seeks to protect the rights of individual refugees. Furthermore, the entire purpose of assigning an international body to supervise its implementation is to realize this objective. In this way, the 1951 Convention actually anticipates that governments may occasionally seek to avoid their responsibilities toward refugees. UNHCR is an integral means of preventing this from taking place whenever possible. In other words its purpose is to balance politics with law.[10] For these reasons, UNHCR should identify with those individuals whose rights it is legally bound to promote and protect, rather than with supposed political interests of governments.[11]

According to paragraph 9 of the Statute, UNHCR "shall engage in such additional activities as the General Assembly may determine, and is required to follow policy directions given to her or him by the General Assembly or the Economic and Social Council (ECOSOC)." In addition, UNHCR may, at the Office's request, receive advice on its *statutory* functions from the Executive Committee of the High Commission's Programme (EXCOM).[12] The EXCOM also advises UNHCR on the appropriateness of humanitarian assistance programs, makes decisions on funding, and scrutinizes all the financial and administrative aspects of such programs.

It is often submitted that a tension may arise between the functions assigned to UNHCR by the GA or ECOSOC and the supervisory role assigned to the Office by State Parties to the 1951 Convention. For example, in accordance to its Statute and subsequent policy directives and authorizations by these bodies, UNHCR has assumed a role as a key provider of humanitarian relief. Recently, this role has been significantly expanded both in extent and scope, covering not only refugees as defined by the 1951 Convention, but also other categories of displaced persons. Because a few states control funding for UNHCR's relief efforts, some claim that the Office cannot efficiently scrutinize state's behavior under the 1951 Convention.

Of importance in this context is that the 1951 Convention is a treaty that establishes an independent regime among the States Parties, of which UNHCR is presently an integral part. When acting as a supervisory organ under the 1951 Convention, UNHCR assumes a role similar to that of other treaty monitoring bodies. The GA, ECOSOC, and EXCOM do not supervise UNHCR in the exercise of this function.[13] Since these forums are not legislative bodies, in any ordinary sense of the term, they do not have the authority to dictate that UNHCR undertake activities that would compromise the Office's functions under the 1951 Convention. Whatever policy directives these bodies provide to UNHCR, it must be presumed that they do not interfere with UNHCR's role under the 1951 Convention. If necessary to avoid conflicts of interest, UNHCR should remind them not to assign to it tasks that might undermine its functions under the 1951 Convention. Notably, however, UNHCR has quite willingly assumed responsibilities that clearly could have been expected to create various conflicts of interest with respect to its core functions.[14]

Absent a formal amendment of the 1951 Convention itself, UNHCR has no reason to believe that the law, or its role under it, has undergone any significant change. Indeed, citizens of States Parties have a right to expect that UNHCR will act in accordance with the directives that they have given to this office.[15] Democratic states have particular procedures for assuming or changing their international obligations, the purpose of which is to ensure democratic control over them. For that reason the treaty-making powers of states— the power to bind the state internationally—is generally in the hands of the legislature, not the executive branch of government.[16] As a result, representatives of democratic states participating in the GA, ECOSOC, and the EXCOM do not have the authority to modify treaty obligations, even (or particularly not) when they concern issues that have far reaching domestic implications, such a refugee protection.[17] The larger point here is that UNHCR should assertively approach its supervisory function with the 1951 Convention as its mandatory guide, as opposed to taking its cues from government representatives in Geneva and New York participating in GA, ECOSOC, and EXCOM sessions. A failure to follow this principle does nothing less than to undermine the legitimacy of UNHCR itself.

Some may think this is a very naïve picture of the real world of international relations. However, those who think that international law and international organizations are vital means for addressing social problems in the world (and that their importance should be enhanced) must also be concerned with the legitimacy and actions of international organizations. For sure, their challengers, the "skeptics" and "realists" in international relations theory, are likely to dismiss such concerns as illusionary.[18] But then, they also harbor a fundamental doubt about the possibility of, or the ethics in, solving international social problems through the rule of law and, indeed, the potency of international organizations.

Of course, those who hold such views have every right to do so. However, it would be quite unsuitable for an international organization such as UNHCR to adopt such a position. It is beyond dispute that a core function of UNHCR is to promote and maintain the respect for the rule of law in a particular field—the refugee field. Clearly, UNHCR cannot promote this ideal by adopting a "skeptical," or "realistic," approach to international law. Perhaps the reality is that international law has little practical influence on refugee protection. The point is that it is the job of UNHCR to make it relevant.

What also follows from this is that the Office should not let speculations on what the "public opinion" in powerful donor countries may think on matters of refugee protection influence its statements on the content of the 1951 Convention and human rights generally. Laws govern these states, not polls. Notwithstanding how discouraging things might appear at times (such as the present), UNHCR should assume that as long as a state does not renounce the treaty, its government and its people feel committed to the principles established under it. UNHCR must focus on law as opposed to politics. Of course, governments may choose to ignore UNHCR's opinions. But then, UNHCR's role is not to help policy makers choose between law and politics, but to clarify legal issues. Still, pragmatic considerations must also be considered and we now turn to these.

Pragmatic Concerns

Thus far we have outlined what might appear to be a strict code of conduct that would not seem to allow for much flexibility to meet particular circumstances. Clearly, an organization like UNHCR must also be sensitive to context. And it should be recognized that the context UNHCR works within is politically charged—to say the least. However, real world circumstances do not give UNHCR a blank check to ignore legal and ethical principles. First, UNHCR must always strive to bring practice into greater conformity with principles. Second, even though there might be occasions where UNHCR feels it is forced to act pragmatically, the ends do not always justify the means. Instead, UNHCR needs to strike an appropriate balance between principles and pragmatism (but also recognizing and understanding that principles may well be pragmatic). Of course, such a balance must be formulated in reference to the ultimate goals and values that UNHCR should promote. To justify a departure from principles, UNHCR must have a sound basis for believing that the means employed will actually lead to a greater realization of the values that it should promote, or that the means employed are necessary to avert situations that cannot possibly be reconciled with these values.[19]

At some point contextual and pragmatic justifications tend to become mere rationalizations. For that reason, policies that purport or appear to be based on such considerations should not be accepted at face value but carefully scrutinized. For example, it is often claimed that supervision best occurs in the context of "constructive dialogue" with governments.[20] Obviously, there is nothing wrong (and much that is right) with mutual dialogue and the respect and perspective that this engenders. However, far too often this "constructive dialogue" has taken the form of secretive consultations between just a few players in UNHCR and the affected country, thereby leaving out of this "conversation" the democratic public at large. While there might be rare instances where secretive consultations are warranted, as a matter of principle this is not the way UNHCR ought to do business—especially with democratic states. But beyond this, since the whole idea behind international supervision is to facilitate public scrutiny of government policies, the expediency of such an approach needs to be questioned.[21]

Another doctrine that should be carefully scrutinized is the notion that the Office needs to soften criticism against larger donor states in order to ensure funding for protection elsewhere. As implied above, such a policy entails UNHCR giving something that it has no authorization to give. In addition to not following principle, it seems highly doubtful that such an approach is likely to generate a greater realization of the ends that UNHCR should promote (we return to this issue below).

What needs to be remembered in this context is that UNHCR does not implement refugee protection—states do. While UNHCR may play a role in the development of certain policies—such as how much funding should be spent on refugees or how many refugees a state is willing to admit—the Office is hardly ever determinative of the protection actually implemented. UNHCR's influence on refugee protection is indirect at best, and it is (or should be) aimed at the long-term rather than the exigencies of the moment. In light of the actual means UNHCR has to achieve the ends that the Office is directed to work towards, the most "pragmatic" approach that it can take is to act in accordance with principle (i.e., in accordance to the values set forth in the Statute, the 1951 Convention, and international human rights instruments).[22]

To conclude this section, it is important to discuss a particular problem pertaining to the issues of principles versus pragmatism, namely, the problem of appropriately separating organizational interests—the prosperity and well being of the public goals and its members as such—from functional goals—the public objectives that a particular organization should work towards. A responsible decision-maker of any public organization, national or international, must pay attention to organizational interests. The duty to do so may derive from the ethical duty to fulfill the organization's functional goals, or a duty to show concern for the fellow members of the organization. Apart from being influenced by such duties, members of an organization naturally tend to promote their organization's advancement out of concern for their own personal interests, such as their careers, salaries, status, or way of life.

Ordinarily, organizational interests, however motivated, are in full harmony with functional goals (an organization that is well funded, well organized and whose staff is highly motivated is more likely to accomplish its public goal than an organization that lacks these traits). Yet, in some situations, organizational interests and functional goals may conflict (the clearest example is when the goals of an organization are better advanced through downsizing rather than expanding the power of the organization in question). In case of such a conflict of interest, a conscientious decision maker should, as a rule, place the public interest that his/her organization is supposed to promote before institutional loyalties and personal interests. The problem is that such motivations may enter the decision-making process unconsciously, with the effect that the decision maker incorrectly conflates organizational interest with the organization's functional goals. In other words, the organization may rationalize that the protection of the organization is for the public good and that organizational interests are coterminous with the public good.

To achieve a proper balance between principles and pragmatism, it is essential that UNHCR establish an environment that promotes organizational accountability and which sorts out organizational ego and inappropriate personal interest from organizational goals. This consideration is of key importance because the Office is not subject to the same system of checks and balances that public organizations in modern states are. The risk that UNHCR incorrectly fuses organizational interests with organizational goals is probably greatest in the context of UNHCR's interactions with major donor states. Thus, it is particularly important that the Office critically scrutinizes such policies.[23]

The Human Rights Challenge in Europe

Human rights are based upon the notion that respect for basic human rights is imperative from a moral perspective and necessary in order to achieve sustainable world peace and prosperity.[24] In view of our increasingly interconnected world, where the effects of human rights abuses in one place oftentimes have a direct impact elsewhere, this rationale seems as compelling today as it did fifty years ago. If Northern states still believe in this philosophy, then there is a need for a clear and unambiguous commitment to human rights at all levels and in all areas.

Unfortunately, this has not been the case in Western Europe. On the one hand, these states are vigorous defenders of human rights. Indeed, all consider the promotion of human rights to be a primary foreign policy objective. This position has increasingly been implemented in practice, such as linking aid or trade relations to states' human rights records. Thus, Western European states not only view themselves as staunch defenders of human rights internally, but they have increasingly come to take on the role of dictating human rights norms to other states as well.

At the same time, however, there are serious human rights challenges in Europe that need to be addressed. The most urgent ones relate to the treatment of "foreigners" in the asylum and immigration sphere and the associated problem of rapidly growing racism and intolerance.[25]

There is a widespread sentiment that whatever rights noncitizens seeking admission may have, the paramount interest to restrict immigration surely supercedes this. This "non-rights" approach has a negative rhetorical effect. It deprives people of their humanity and dignity, which in turn legitimizes intolerance.[26] This not only affects people seeking admission, but the zeal in which mainstream politicians emphasize the need for tighter immigration control sends a clear message to the many millions of "non-white" European citizens and permanent residents that Europe is not for them.

Norms that would be rejected out of hand in other contexts on the basis of human rights suddenly seem "reasonable" and "realistic" in the immigration/ asylum realm. Notwithstanding the fact that all Western European states are multicultural, it is apparently perfectly acceptable to defend tighter immigration control on the basis of a limited capacity to absorb people of different ethnic origin than the majority population. At the same time, however, Western European states insist that people in places such as the Balkans, who in view of unimaginable atrocities may understandably feel some animosity towards "opposing" ethnic or religious groups, must abandon the "politics of ethnicity."[27]

The problem is that all debate on asylum and immigration issues in the North is permeated by a widespread and paralyzing "realism," that is to say that there is a decided tendency to accept the idea that in order to be taken seriously in this context one must take into account the present hostile sentiments against "foreigners"—and this is true even in the human rights community. The rationale of this norm is typified in the remarks of one prominent scholar: "[I]f the political leaders of the western world would work wholeheartedly towards the implementation of all applicable human rights standards in the immigration and refugee context, they would fail to be re-elected."[28]

What seems to be implied by this and similar arguments is that one must adopt a less rigid and more politically realistic or pragmatic approach to human rights—especially in the realm of refugee protection. This argument is paradoxical to say the least. The whole purpose behind the human rights regime is to contain intolerant impulses and trends that threaten the values underpinning it.

To conclude, because the North's commitments to human rights values that they promote in the South are truly put to the test in the refugee/immigration realm, it is vital to vigilantly insist on human rights principles in this sphere. Northern states will not be able to convince people in the South to refrain from intolerance, nationalism, and secessionist tendencies if our own democratic institutions cannot live up to these standards. The widespread perception that human rights are used as a means of preserving Northern hegemony should be noted in this context.[29] In addition, our failures to live up to international standards in the refugee and immigration realm can be used as a pretext for "other" governments to ignore human rights. Further, it is a mistake to believe that we in the North have once and for all eradicated the risk of widespread human rights abuse. In light of Europe's troubling past, the danger of ignoring the present xenophobic trend and its relation to immigration and refugee issues is apparent.[30]

Temporary Protection[31]

Background

The concept of temporary protection (TP) emerged in the context of the Civil War in the former Yugoslavia. In 1992, the High Commissioner formally requested that European states extend TP to persons fleeing the escalating crisis in Bosnia-Herzegovina. UNHCR's proposal for TP consisted of five main elements: (1) admission, (2) eligibility on a group basis, (3) emphasis on basic rights during stay,[32] (4) emphasis on return,[33] and (5) suspension of individual asylum applications.[34]

The way Western European states responded to the influx of refugees from the former Yugoslavia varied. Because there was no common understanding of what the concept entailed, it is somewhat misleading to state that governments implemented TP as a response to the refugee crises or because of UNHCR's call for such a response. Yet, there was a common pattern in states' responses, which had clear affinities with UNHCR's proposal for TP. In this way, UNHCR's proposal justified the various measures applied to refugees from the former Yugoslavia. Moreover, through time several governments chose to enact specific TP legislation or TP inspired legislation, and in this process directly referred to UNHCR's proposal.

By 1994–1995, the concept of TP had become less popular with governments primarily because no solution to the supposedly "temporary" conflict in the former Yugoslavia was in sight. TP enjoyed a revival of sorts following the Dayton Peace Accords after several governments started to repatriate refugees to Bosnia-Herzegovina and a number of these schemes were subsequently applied to refugee flows from Kosovo.[35]

Under the Treaty of Amsterdam, the Member States of the European Union committed themselves to work out "minimum standards for giving TP to displaced persons from third countries who cannot return to their country of origin and for persons who otherwise need international protection."[36] In 2001, the European Union Ministers of Justice and Home Affairs (JHA) adopted a directive to that effect. The directive entered into force on 7 August 2001 and applies to all EU Member States (MS) except for Denmark and Ireland.[37]

UNHCR's Analysis on TP and the 1951 Convention

A key element in UNHCR's proposal for TP was the notion that protection should last only as long as the refugees in question needed it. That is, admission and protection would be granted on the understanding that the refugees in question would return to their country of origin once conditions there had sufficiently improved. Still, it may be argued that the 1951 Convention already provides a legal framework for TP in the sense that it includes a right to admission but does not imply that protection is granted by permanent settlement. One of the great ironies (and inconsistencies) at work here is that UNHCR considered the vast majority of Bosnian asylum seekers to fall under the definition of a "refugee" under the 1951 Convention. This, then, raises the question why UNHCR did not simply encourage states to accept Bosnians as refugees and point to the possibilities of cessation of refugee status when the individuals concerned no longer required protection. In short, why was it necessary to create this new category of refugees?

The problem, according to UNHCR, was that Western governments feared that the application of some of the provisions of the 1951 Convention would encourage integration in the receiving states that, in turn, would hamper repatriation.

> Although refugee status under the 1951 Convention is always provisional, in the sense that the Convention ceases to apply if the circumstances which gave rise to refugee status cease to exist (Art.1c (5) and (6)), many of the provisions in Chapters III, IV and V of the Convention relating to employment, welfare and administrative measures, clearly help to facilitate refugees' integration in their country of asylum. The generous treatment accorded by many States, with the encouragement of UNHCR, to refugees recognized under the Convention is such that some of those States have expressed concern about extending these benefits to refugees in situations of large-scale influx lest they be deterred from repatriating when this becomes feasible.[38]

The integration "dilemma" described above has (or had) both an international and a national legal dimension. With respect to the international dimension, the question was whether the 1951 Convention obligated contracting states to apply to Bosnian refugees the provisions in the 1951 Convention that typically facilitated integration in the receiving state. As to the domestic dimension, the asylum law of most Western European states entitled refugees (or individuals admitted on a similar basis) to more generous rights than the 1951

Convention, and the question was whether these provisions also had to be extended to Bosnian refugees.

UNHCR's "solution" to this problem was as follows. First, UNHCR argued that the 1951 Convention allowed for a variation of rights depending on the nature of sojourn.

> The benefits provided under the various articles of the Convention have different levels of applicability depending on the nature of the refugee's sojourn or residence in the country: the most fundamental rights (Articles 3 and 33), and some others (see, e.g., Arts. 7(1), 8, 13) are extended to *all* refugees; other basic rights are applicable to any refugee present "within" the country (e.g. Arts. 2, 4, 20, 22, 27), even illegally (see Art. 31); other provisions apply to refugees "lawfully in" the country (Arts. 18, 26 and 32); while certain of the more generous benefits are to be accorded "to refugees lawfully staying [résidant régulièrement] in [the] territory" of the country concerned (Arts. 15, 17, 19, 21, 23, 24 and 28; see also Arts. 14, 16(2) and 25) . . . Although these gradations in treatment allowed by the 1951 Convention have not generally been explored, they would appear to be consistent with temporary protection, which would include admission, humane treatment and respect for basic rights, including non-refoulement, but would not give refugees whose stay was expected to be of short duration the full range of integration-oriented benefits accorded to those for whom asylum was also seen as the durable solution.[39]

Second, UNHCR suggested (or, perhaps more accurately, condoned) the practice of suspending asylum applications.[40] UNHCR argued that by suspending asylum applications, states would avoid strains on the asylum eligibility procedures. Yet, this policy also allowed states to block access to rights and remedies established under national law. While UNHCR did not explicitly address this matter, the Office certainly must have understood that this was a natural consequence of such practices. After all, one of the overriding goals of TP was to avoid rights that might work towards integrating refugees into receiving states.

Deficient Protection

The main problem with UNHCR's TP initative was the ambiguity it generated with respect to the status of Bosnian refugees and the relevance and content of the 1951 Convention. The Office did not describe in plain and consistent terms that TP was a means of affording protection under the 1951 Convention (read international law), but more in terms of a "pragmatic tool" not inconsistent with applicable international legal standards. On the one hand, the Office argued that the temporary element was already present in the 1951 Convention itself through the cessation clauses.[41] On the other hand, however, the particular circumstances in the Bosnian case were used as a justification for a "new approach." Furthermore, TP was presented as a means "to bridge the legal gap of international protection," that is, to provide protection to all persons in need of protection and not only to Convention refugees.[42] At the same time, UNHCR maintained the position that the vast majority of Bosnians from the former Yugoslavia were in fact Convention refugees.[43] Thus, as applied to Bosnians, the "legal gap" in international refugee law simply did not exist. Still, the High Commissioner felt it necessary to apply a new approach to this group of refugees. The confusion was further compounded by UNHCR's emphasis on the need for international guidelines on TP, which implied that there was a lack of applicable international *legal* standards to groups such as refugees from Bosnia.[44]

Another fundamental problem was that rather than enhancing individual rights, TP was designed for the conceived political interest of states. Underlying UNHCR's conception of TP was the idea that the preferred solution is for refugees to safely return to their country of origin. Since refugees can make up their own minds about what is in their best interest, the emphasis on repatriation essentially spoke to the presumed interest of receiving states to limit the number of foreigners (see below on the supposed pragmatic benefits of TP). In fact, by introducing TP, UNHCR went further than merely recognizing states' rights to determine whether or not to grant permanent settlement to refugees. Beyond this, a central idea underlying UNHCR's conception of TP was that if Bosnian refugees benefited from rights such as the right to work, family-reunification, freedom of movement, and so on, they might become "too integrated" into the receiving states and refuse to leave voluntarily when the situation in the former Yugoslavia had improved. In this way, TP was based on an underlying law enforcement objective—facilitating the enforcement of return policies.

This aspect of TP should not be seen in isolation. Rather, it must be viewed in the context of other solution-oriented concepts endorsed by UNHCR, such as "reception in the region of origin," "the right to return," "the right to remain," and "preventive protection." All of these concepts provided Western European states with a battery of excuses for keeping refugees away from their territories. The rationale so often employed is that it would be more efficient for these states to provide humanitarian assistance by some other means.

Although we think it was inappropriate for UNHCR to condone the practice of suspension of asylum applications, it is true that the 1951 Convention does not explicitly prohibit states from suspending asylum applications. However, what states are prohibited from doing is suspending rights under the 1951 Convention.[45] Since formal recognition as a refugee has a merely declaratory function,[46] and since Contracting States cannot know a priori whether there are 1951 Convention refugees in a particular group of asylum seekers, they must either treat *all* persons whose asylum applications they have suspended in accordance with the standards set out in the 1951 Convention, or else continue to process all claims.

Admittedly, UNHCR did not suggest that states should suspend *rights* under the 1951 Convention or under any other human rights treaty. What the Office did instead was to suggest that states could grant this group refugee protection against *refoulement* (for as long as they needed it), but that they did not have an obligation to extend *all* the benefits under the 1951 Convention to them. (In that way, the practice of suspending asylum applications, which in practice was equivalent to the suspension of benefits, was consistent with the 1951 Convention.) This strong emphasis on minimal rights under the 1951 Convention, coupled with the notion of suspension of asylum applications, obscured the fact that Bosnian refugees were entitled to protection under general human rights treaties.[47] Apart from this, UNHCR's legal reasoning in this context was unconvincing.

It is correct that the enjoyment of some of the 1951 Convention's provisions are conditioned by criteria such as "lawfully in" and "lawfully staying." At face value, these terms seem to refer back *exclusively* to the meaning that they have in Contracting States' domestic laws. This view, however, is misleading. A treaty is presumed to have an autonomous content. Instead, terms such as "lawfully in" and "lawfully staying" should be understood as having an autonomous international legal meaning that does not necessarily correspond to the meaning that identical or corresponding terms may have in the domestic law.[48] In other words, while national laws concerning the requirements for entry and stay should be taken into account in determining the scope of protection under the 1951 Convention, a categorization in the national legislation is not decisive in this regard. What matters is the actual relationship between the state and the individual or, more precisely, how the state's laws and procedure in effect treat the refugee in question.[49]

It follows that when a Contracting State, pursuant to its national laws and procedures, agrees to protect a refugee for as long as s/he needs protection—which was the whole point of TP—the refugee concerned is undoubtedly "lawfully in" and "lawfully staying in" the State Party. In such case, the Contracting State has a duty to grant the refugees in question all rights that lawfully staying refugees are entitled to under the 1951 Convention. This does not include a right to permanent residence. It does, however, include all the rights that, according to UNHCR, may "facilitate refugees' integration in their country of asylum." Whether the state in question has suspended a refugee's asylum application is immaterial in this respect as such a decision effectively incorporates a legal right to stay. The bottom line is that a state cannot circumvent the responsibilities under the 1951 Convention by creating new obscure classifications. Yet, UNHCR's TP proposal gave the impression that states could do just that.

It is also noteworthy that UNHCR failed to communicate that the terms "lawfully in" or "lawfully staying" must be read in light of a human rights based idea of the *qualities of law*. That is, the national laws that determine whether a particular refugee should be regarded and treated as merely present, lawfully, or lawfully staying, in a State Party must be consistent with the principles of the 1951 Convention and other human rights instruments. More specifically, such laws cannot be arbitrary and discriminatory. This, then, brings us to the more general question whether UNHCR's proposal for TP was in harmony with the principle of equality and non-discrimination.

By suggesting that Bosnian refugees be granted TP, UNHCR quite plainly suggested they could be treated differently than other refugees. What was the basis for this differentiation and was it justifiable? Before we examine this question it is useful to make a few remarks on how TP was implemented by states.

In practice, "beneficiaries" of TP schemes in Western Europe and other Northern states were denied a number of rights that they were entitled to, and which were enjoyed by other refugees.[50] For example, Article 26 of the 1951 Convention grants refugees "lawfully in the territory" of a contracting state the same freedom of movement as is applicable to aliens generally. Article 12(1) of the International Covenant on Civil and Political Rights (ICCPR) extends absolute freedom of movement to all persons lawfully within a state's territory, subject only to restrictions that are necessary to protect national security, public order, public health or morals, or the rights and freedoms of others. Yet, in some states entitlement to social assistance and housing benefits were expressly tied to residence in a particular municipality or reception center. Such restrictions did not apply to other groups of refugees. The 1951 Convention requires states to grant refugees the same access to employment as that provided to nationals of the most favored countries. Yet, several states either denied this right to beneficiaries of TP, or granted it on unequal terms compared to other groups of refugees (in some states the right to work was greatly limited in scope and only arose after a lengthy stay).

Many states also denied TP beneficiaries travel documents in violation of Article 26 of the 1951 Convention. Articles 17, 23, and 24 of the ICCPR prohibit arbitrary or unlawful interference by states with the families of non-citizens. Similarly, Article 10 of the 1951 Convention on the Rights of the Child urges the expeditious reunification of children with their parents. Yet, in several states beneficiaries of TP were, in contrast to recognized refugees, denied family-reunification, or else granted family reunification on unequal terms. Although these provisions do not establish a positive right to family-reunification, still, if states extend the right of family-reunification to some categories of refugees, it must do so on a non-discriminatory basis. Finally, compared to other groups of refugees, TP beneficiaries were denied an equal opportunity to integrate into, and an equal opportunity to permanently settle in, their host societies.[51]

There are several treaty provisions on equality and non-discrimination that have a bearing on UNHCR's conception of TP, including Article 3 of the 1951 Convention[52] and Article 26 of the ICCPR.[53] While the precise scope of these provisions varies, the concepts as such have some common features in international human rights law. Thus, it is generally accepted that the principle of non-discrimination does not require absolute equality or identical treatment, but recognizes relative equality, that is, different treatment proportionate to concrete individual circumstances. In general terms, a violation of the principle of non-discrimination is said to arise if there is (a) differential treatment of (b) similar cases (c) without there being an objective and reasonable justification, or if the benefit of the differential treatment (the government's interest in making a classification) is not proportional to the cost on those it affects and the degree to which it achieves it. Further, for a classification to be lawful it needs to pursue a legitimate end. Finally, a discriminatory motive is not a necessary component of a violation of the principle of equality, distinctions may be discriminatory also if they have the effect of nullifying or impairing equality of treatment.[54]

One of the rationales behind UNHCR's suggestion for TP was to save resources and prevent an overburdening of the asylum procedure in the face of a mass influx situation. However, among Western European states, only Germany experienced anything approaching a mass influx. In any case, asylum seekers from Bosnia did not impose a greater burden on the asylum procedures than an asylum seeker from, say, Somalia. The "difference" between the two, following UNHCR's line of reasoning, was that in the former case it could be assumed that the persons concerned were in need of protection whereas in the latter case that determination still had to be made on an individual basis.

Still, assuming that there was a genuine difference in this regard between Bosnians and other groups of refugees, this does not *justify* differential treatment between Bosnian refugees and other refugees in terms of the enjoyment of rights. The relevant difference, at least according to UNHCR, between Bosnians and other refugees in this regard was the presumed temporary nature of the conflict in the former Yugoslavia.

> In accordance with the principle of non-discrimination, any substantial differences in the standards of treatment of different groups of refugees should be related to genuine differences in their situation, such as, for example, the reasonable expectation that the stay of a particular group in the country of refuge was expected to be of short duration.[55]

Leaving aside the fact that this prediction ultimately proved to be terribly inaccurate, the legitimacy of the policy encouraged by UNHCR evidently required speculation on the likely duration of different conflicts.[56] Even if it were possible to predict with some level of certainty the outcome and length of a particular armed conflict, [57] which is rarely the case, it is impossible to draw any certain conclusion as to how the "outcome" is going to affect the protection needs of the individuals coming from that conflict. Which is to say that it is impossible to determine a priori the length of protection needs of individuals on a group basis. In short, this kind of irrefutable and speculative presumption can hardly justify any significant distinctions between different groups of refugees in terms of their enjoyment of rights under the 1951 Convention or other human rights treaties.

It has been argued that Bosnian refugees were actually placed in a privileged position vis-à-vis all other refugees on the grounds that they were not exposed to the risk of *refoulement* that might result from mistakes in the asylum determination process. While this could well be viewed as a decided plus, from a legal perspective it is difficult to reconcile the idea that Bosnian refugees were treated "better" than other refugees when they were simply granted what they were already entitled to—protection. Hence, this by no means counterweighs the negative effects that TP had on this group. Moreover, implicit in this line of reasoning is the idea that refugees who were from other parts of the world and who were not granted TP were exposed to a greater risk of *refoulement*. This, of course, raises the issue of discrimination, but now from the other perspective. Refugees who applied for asylum under the individual eligibility procedure were entitled to the same level of protection as refugees granted protection on a collective basis.

To be fair, the longer the conflict in the former Yugoslavia continued the more concerned UNHCR became with the continuation of some of these practices. However, UNHCR's concerns were raised too late, too timidly, and in the wrong forum (mainly in informal consultations with government representatives).[58] This overly cautious approach is understandable given UNHCR's own role in the development of these policies. If anything, UNHCR's slow and unsatisfactory awakening illustrates that what is easily destroyed is not necessarily easy to reconstitute. UNHCR recommended TP at a time when European states had already begun to restrict refugee protection. The Office must have understood that TP could be used to justify restrictions of refugee rights that went even further beyond those suggested by the Office.

TP and UNHCR's Role in Developing International Refugee Law

It might be argued that by initiating the concept of TP, UNHCR was simply fulfilling its role as a developer of international refugee law pursuant to Article 8(a) of the Statute. However, UNHCR never indicated that TP should be seen as a proposal for an amendment of international refugee law. The authority to propose amendments should be seen in light of UNHCR's treaty monitoring function, which encompasses the duty to clarify the content of refugee law—not to create it and certainly not to obscure it. In other words, the role that

UNHCR should play in this realm is to create the necessary conditions for informed public debate on refugee protection, more specifically, to elucidate on the human rights dimension of such issues. This, in turn, suggests that UNHCR must be clear on what it thinks the present status of international law is and what changes UNHCR thinks are needed. Stated plainly, UNHCR should clarify when it is proposing an amendment to international law and when it is merely "interpreting" relevant treaty law.

Further, the ability to propose amendments to refugee law does not give UNHCR a blank check. Article 8(a) cannot be understood to mean that the High Commissioner has the discretion to propose any kind of "amendments" to international law that have a bearing on those who fall under the High Commissioner's mandate. Simply stated, the human rights of refugees, asylum seekers, and even abusive asylum seekers are not something that UNHCR should open up for discussion. If states feel that the 1951 Convention is too burdensome, they have the right to unilaterally or collectively denounce the treaty or suggest a renegotiation of the obligations under it.[59] Yet, it is not the role of a UN agency like UNHCR to second-guess whether particular human rights treaties and provisions impose overly unpractical obligations on states. Rather, the direction UNHCR can go—the direction UNHCR must go—is to suggest ways of enhancing individual rights, not to suggest changes for some amorphous "greater good."

Perhaps one should see UNHCR's TP proposal not as an attempt to develop refugee law but as an attempt to "save" the 1951 Convention per se. This, however, begs the question whether it is acceptable for UNHCR to construe the 1951 Convention in ways that better correspond to the conceived political interests of states in order to ensure that they remain parties to it. The proponents of such a policy are willing to compromise the clarifying and normative force of the 1951 Convention—its raison d'être—to a degree that is impossible to reconcile with any meaningful notion of the rule of law, which, in turn, undercuts the whole rationale of their approach. For what exactly is it they want to rescue? The more this line of thinking gains acceptance, the greater the risk that treaties serve as apologies for dubious governmental practices instead of as means to restrain them. In addition, those who purport to stand for democratic values should be very skeptical about this train of thought. For what is really being argued is that the public should be shielded from the process of developing international law, which is indeed a very slippery slope.

Despite all the rhetoric and conflicting practices, Western states have not renounced the 1951 Convention. On the contrary, at the Ministerial meeting of States Parties to the 1951 Convention and/or its protocol relating to the status of refugees held in December 2001, representatives of Western European states, and other State Parties to the 1951 Convention, adopted a declaration in which they stressed the "relevance and resilience" and "enduring importance" of the 1951 treaty and its protocol and pledged their commitment to implement their obligations fully and effectively.[60] This "re-commitment" to the refugee convention was likely a welcome relief to many and was celebrated as a great success by UNHCR. While this reaction is understandable, it is also somewhat puzzling. States continue to be committed to the 1951 Convention as long as they remain parties to it. Of course, this re-commitment by state representatives may indicate that the states they represent intend to remain parties to the Convention. Yet, two questions arise in this context. The first question is: did this re-commitment stem from any meaningful public debates, or was this just another diplomatic triumph without much democratic foundation? The short answer to this question is no. The second question is: what did these states express a recommitment to?[61]

Given the present shape of international refugee law, it is debatable whether it would be such a great loss if Northern states would have denounced, or sought to renegotiate, the 1951 Convention. Arguably, such a development would contribute to more clarity in international relations. More importantly, perhaps, the public debate that would precede such a move would doubtlessly engage considerably more people around the world than all of UNHCR's informal consultations on TP or the ongoing Global Consultations on Refugee Protection. While there is a very real fear that an international reexamination of the 1951 Convention might lead to a regression in terms of refugee protection, a frank and open debate on the appropriateness of the 1951 Convention could place refugee issues within a broader human rights context—where they belong—and, at the same time, would go far in exposing Northern states' ambiguity towards human rights values. In our view, such a debate is long overdue.

The yardstick of success for international refugee *law* in Western European states, and Democratic states generally, is not these states' nominal participation in the 1951 Convention. Rather, it is the level of commitment that the populations of these states have to the underlying moral values of this Convention and human rights treaties, including the notion of the rule of law in this particular field. These values cannot be enhanced unless the public is fully confronted with the question whether it is important that their laws and practices fully conform to their international moral and legal obligations. For the same reason, the populations of such states must be allowed a fair opportunity to scrutinize any shift in paradigms of that law and the possible effects of such changes.

The "Trump" of Political Considerations— Did UNHCR's TP Initiative Save Lives?

UNHCR advanced the notion of TP because, in view of the restrictive trend in Europe, it was thought that this policy was likely to contribute to an overall enhancement in safety or refugees from Bosnia. Since it clearly did not lead to a general increase of substantive rights being afforded to refugees (see discussion above), this raises the question whether Western European states did in fact accept more Bosnian refugees because UNHCR made it easier for them to do so. Although no definitive answer is possible, there is scant empirical evidence of an increased generosity. For one thing, TP-inspired schemes were accompanied by the imposition of visa requirements for nationals from the former Yugoslavia (see below). Beyond this, because TP *mainly* applied to individuals who had already entered into Western European states, it is a peculiar argument to say that TP served to increase the flow of refugees.

This leaves two possible ways that TP might have enhanced refugee protection in Europe, although both explanations fail upon closer examination. The first one is the argument that unless UNHCR had devised TP, Western European states would have felt compelled to either accept Bosnian refugees on a permanent basis or to return them to persecution. Thus, by providing governments with an alternative solution (TP), UNHCR limited the risk of large-scale *refoulement*. At face value this may seem like a rational argument. The problem is that it erroneously assumes that governments felt limited to these two options. It assumes that states would not have devised TP type systems unless such schemes were initiated or validated by UNHCR, either because they did not possess the expertise to construct such schemes or because they did not want to act against the will of UNHCR. Unfortunately, governments have proven to be fully capable themselves of devising policies that they think suit their self-interest but that may not be in total harmony with international law.

The second argument runs along similar lines. By introducing the notion of TP, UNHCR intentionally provided European states with an apology for not recognizing Bosnians as Convention refugees. In exchange, government leaders made a promise that they would allow Bosnian refugees to stay for the (temporary) duration of the war. This argument begs the question why political leaders would be interested in receiving validation from UNHCR. The most plausible reason is that they feared that the opposite response—criticism that their refugee policies were inconsistent with international law—would enhance internal opposition against their refugee policies. Stated differently, it is likely governments welcomed UNHCR's proposal because it enabled them to afford refugees lesser rights at a lesser "public pressure" cost. Now, it is highly unlikely that elected political leaders would respond to increased political pressure to accept more refugees under better conditions by doing the exact opposite. Clearly, the external and internal pressure on governments would have increased had UNHCR openly and unambiguously declared that the Bosnians were entitled to protection under the 1951 Convention.

Implicit in the argument above is that European governments were not inclined to give refugee status to all refugees from the former Yugoslavia and that they were going to impose other forms of protection regardless of what UNHCR said. One might argue that European states took the initiative in the area of TP and UNHCR merely went along with it. To say that states introduced the notion of TP is inaccurate. Yet, it may be true that states would have moved in this direction on their own. However, had UNHCR not introduced this concept it would have retained the means of censuring such schemes if and when such policies violated the 1951 Convention. This is exactly the point we seek to make: by taking the initiative as it did, UNHCR in effect abandoned its supervisory role—its basic means to positively influence refugee protection.

Even worse, its initiative on this matter exacerbated public confusion, which almost certainly had a negative effect on the number of Bosnian refugees that these states received. The substitution of Convention status by TP status sent a signal that the 1951 Convention was no longer relevant because current problems were somewhat (and somehow) "different." The new status enabled governments to profess that most Bosnian refugees did not qualify for refugee status—but without having to confront this phony opinion head on. This position was, in turn, used as a moral justification for imposing and sustaining visa requirements on Bosnians. Indeed, the ambiguity created by UNHCR's TP scheme aided those who favored an extremely restrictive refugee policy. For one thing, it gave such forces a decided rhetorical advantage. They consistently pointed to the fact that Bosnians were not real refugees (because states did not grant them protection under the 1951 Convention) and thus that states did not have an obligation to assist them. Elected governments did not seek to correct this misconception (for obvious reasons) and UNHCR was strikingly absent from such "informed" national debates as well. Because of this, large segments of these liberal democratic states came away with the strong impression that they were being too generous when, in fact, they were anything but. At the end of the day, large numbers of people in Bosnia were slaughtered and Western European Governments—purportedly the standard-bearers of human rights—were able to take the position that there was no international legal obligation to help them. Moreover, these governments were allowed to argue that the ones who were allowed to stay, out of mere benevolence, should be given minimal rights so they could leave as quickly and as smoothly as possible. This moral discrepancy decidedly did not foster compassion and respect for human rights values in Western states, but fed into a growing anti-immigration and antirefugee sentiment.

The protection of Bosnian refugees in Western European states that did take place was a testament to the publics' and political leaders' (limited) willingness to assist people in need and (limited) concern for the integrity and credibility of international human rights and refugee law. UNHCR could have (and should have) done a better job of enhancing these inclinations—rather than promoting or endorsing policies that led in the very opposite direction.

Gains in the South?

While it is difficult to see in what way UNHCR's TP program enhanced protection in Western Europe, it may be argued that it was a necessary concession to ensure financial means from these states—which ultimately worked to the benefit of refugees in the South. Despite the fact that the work of the High Commissioner must be nonpolitical and unbiased, there seems to be widespread agreement among commentators that because UNHCR is dependent on voluntary contributions it is forced to adopt policies that reflect the interest and priorities of the major donor countries. For example, Gil Loescher has observed that in the past when UNHCR has criticized powerful donor states "the criticism was met with threats of cutting off funding. . . . In such situations in the past, UNHCR has often either become subservient to the policies of powerful western countries or become immobilized . . . thereby damaging its credibility as an effective and impartial advocate for refugees. . . ."[62]

There is no question that UNHCR's never-ending funding crisis severely hampers the organization's freedom of action. However, does this mean that it is unreasonable or unrealistic to demand consistency and impartiality from the High Commissioner?

First, the importance of UNHCR as a relief agency is not an end in itself. Although UNHCR has had a great deal of experience in dealing with large-scale displacements, it is important to acknowledge that there are other agencies that could assume this role without comprising their mandate. Or as Guy Goodwin-Gill expressed this: "UNHCR's mandate is not to provide food and relief to the needy, but to provide protection. . . . [T]here are, after all, other agencies capable of meeting human and material needs, and able to do so in complex situations without putting mandate responsibilities and constituents at risk."[63] If UNHCR is indeed faced with the harsh choice whether to succumb to Western interest or lose funding for relief efforts, the Office should arguably encourage that funding for relief efforts be gradually channeled through other agencies than the Office.

Second, when evaluating UNHCR's policies vis-à-vis the major donor states, one must also consider the nature of these states and their particular standing in the world. If UNHCR were (or was thought to be) subservient to the policies of Western states, it would align international refugee law with an unjust world order and thus greatly reduce its potency. Furthermore, there is a clear conflict between the ethical principles underlying a democratic society and the type of political concessions that some claim UNHCR is forced to make. Democratic accountability of decision makers dictates that the public has a right to know if their government's refugee policy is in conflict with international standards. If an elected government uses public funding as a threat to avoid criticism by an impartial supervisory organ (which specifically has been authorized by the state in question to monitor the government's refugee policy) it has—by any standard of democracy—committed an abuse of power. To soften criticism in such situations because it serves the purposes of elected politicians constitutes nothing less than an infringement on the democratic process itself. In the long run, this too erodes the credibility of the international legal system.

Third, how plausible is it that the major donor states would punish UNHCR because the Office has engaged in a public and principled debate on refugee protection, in other words, for fulfilling its mandate? Certainly, government representatives might threaten UNHCR to that effect. But the question is whether they would actually carry out such a threat. For one thing, such a policy would be difficult to explain to the public at large (remember, the presumption here is that UNHCR was engaged in a principled public debate). Further, it ignores the need that donor states may have for an international structure to dispense aid to refugees.

Fourth, and more importantly, how plausible is it that these states would punish refugees because UNHCR has criticized the refugee policies of elected governments? Certainly, such an approach would be even thornier to explain to the public.

To be sure, Western states have shown a remarkable disinclination to offer refugee protection. However, it seems somewhat far-fetched to argue that this limited compassion towards refugees would be further decreased because politicians are upset with UNHCR. After all, the financial resources attributed to UNHCR are resources already allocated from taxpayers specifically for humanitarian purposes. If these resources are not distributed to UNHCR, they may be channelled to refugees through other agencies. That such reallocation of resources will necessarily take place cannot be ascertained with certainty. But, importantly, neither can the reverse situation. The point is that the suppositions that (1) unless UNHCR is subservient to the policies of donor states their funding will be cut short and (2) unless refugees are given humanitarian assistance through UNHCR the total amount spent on them would decrease, are far too speculative to outweigh the predictable short and long-term costs that such policies will have, in Europe and elsewhere.

Still, for the sake of argument let us assume that by introducing TP UNHCR *did* enjoy some short-term gains, perhaps an increase in funding, or perhaps the Office avoided financial cutbacks. The question that needs to be asked is this: how likely is it that such gains are sustainable?

One inherent problem with this quid pro quo reasoning is that there are no guarantees that elected governments have the will, or the ability, to make good on their spoken or unspoken promises for a sustainable period of time. While it may be expected that Western states will assist refugees in situations where they have clear and tangible interests at stake—in Kosovo for example—the real problem facing UNHCR is to make sure that these states assist refugees everywhere and through time. That requires a greater commitment to human rights values on the part of the citizenry of donor states than that prevailing at the moment. Because in the final analysis, a state's commitment to refugee protection, both domestically and internationally, is linked inextricably with the citizenry's respect for the dignity of human beings regardless of their origin and their temporary location. A society inclined toward nationalistic anti-immigration sentiments is less likely to host refugees, or provide humanitarian relief for them elsewhere, than a society that is committed to human rights values and international solidarity. Only by promoting the values underlying human rights—both in countries of origin and in receiving countries—can refugee issues be effectively addressed. UNHCR's TP proposal did not work toward the realization of this objective.

4

Defining Persecution and Protection

The Cultural Relativism Debate and the Rights of Refugees

BONNY IBHAWOH

Until recently, the field of refugee studies was spared the contentious and polarized debate over universalism and cultural relativism that has dominated human rights discourse for so long. One reason for this is the fact that for decades there existed both in academic and policy-making circles a clear dichotomy between the human rights field and the refugee field. That line was represented by international borders. While the human rights field was primarily concerned with abuses of the rights of citizens by their own governments or institutions, the refugee field comes into play only after persons fleeing persecution have crossed international borders. Even the UN system clearly divided responsibilities for human rights distinctly from responsibilities for refugee protection. The refugee and human rights fields have therefore developed largely independently of each other, in spite of the obvious commonalties that underlie them both.[1]

However, the past few decades have witnessed a progressive blurring of the traditional lines between refugee studies and the human rights discourse. Academics, policy makers and the UN system have now crossed the line that once separated human rights and refugee issues. The admission of asylum seekers, their treatment, and the granting of refugee status have become crucial elements of the international system for the protection of human rights. One of the consequences of this trend toward the intermingling of both fields has been the extension of the debates that have underlined the human rights discourse about refugees. Perhaps the most prominent of these is the "universalism versus cultural relativism" debate. At the core of the debate is whether modern human rights conceptions are of universal character and applicability, or whether they are culturally relative—that is, dependent on socio-cultural contexts. In relation to refugee rights, the debate has focused on concerns that international refugee laws and national refugee policies in some Western countries are informed by cultural chauvinism and a lack of sensitivity toward non-Western cultures. This raises significant questions about the definition of persecution and protection as they relate to the rights of refugees.

This paper addresses the cultural relativism debate within the context of refugee rights. It examines the argument that contemporary international conceptions and instruments relating to refugee protection are, like the "universal" human rights regime, disproportionately skewed in favor of Western values and take inadequate consideration of non-Western perspectives. It explores the implications of these arguments both for the rights of refugees and the cross-cultural legitimacy of international and domestic refugee laws and policies. The broad objective here is to explore ways in which the protection of refugees can be offered in a truly universal manner. The chapter is divided into two main parts. The first part broadly reviews the cultural relativism debate in the human rights discourse, focusing on the African and Asian values debate. The second part examines the extension of this debate to the refugee field and its implications for refugee protection.

Human Rights and the Cultural Relativism Debate

The debate over whether, and to what extent, human rights conceptions are universal or culturally relative was the dominant feature of the global human rights discourse for the greater part of the last century. The debate proceeds partly from various international documents, particularly the United Nations instruments on human rights, which in spite of obvious Western influence declare their contents to be universal and inalienable. Also at the core of this debate is the conflict between collectivist thinkers who place the community above the individual and the individualists who place the individual above the community. It is not possible in this limited space to discuss in detail the varied and contending arguments that have been advanced for and against cultural relativism within the context of human rights. These themes have been adequately addressed elsewhere.[2] It is sufficient here to outline the major arguments in the cultural relativism debate and how they bear relevance to the rights of refugees.

Claims of cultural relativism in the human rights discourse have a great diversity of meaning and any evaluation of such claims must be sensitive to this diversity. In general however, proponents of the cultural relativity of human rights argue that human rights as conceived in the West are not necessarily applicable to "Third World" and non-Western societies, because their philosophical basis is not only different but indeed opposite. Whereas Western conceptions of rights are based on the notion of the autonomous individual, many non-Western conceptions do not know such individualism.[3] Proponents of cultural relativism have frequently stated that the classical "Western" liberal notions of human rights emphasize the primacy of individual, political, and civil rights.[4] On the other hand, most non-Western, Third World traditions place greater emphasis on the community basis of human rights and duties, on economic and social rights, and on the relative character of human rights. The complexities reflected in these categories have proved a vexing issue for those approaching the study of human rights from a global comparative perspective.

Proponents of the cultural relativism of human rights argue that the current formulation of "universal" human rights contains three elements that reflect Western values and makes them ill suited to some non-Western societies. First, the fundamental unit of the society is conceived as the individual, not the family. Second, the primary basis for securing human existence in society is through rights, not duties. Third, the primary method of securing rights is through adversary legalism, where rights are claimed and adjudicated upon, not through reconciliation, repentance, or education.[5] Other writers, however, have tempered the stridency of the cultural relativist position by arguing that while claims of universality and inalienability may be plausible for some specific rights, strong claims of universality and inalienability were not valid for many other rights.[6]

Arguments for cultural relativism in the human rights discourse have been categorized into *strong cultural relativism* and *weak cultural relativism*. Strong cultural relativism holds that culture is the principal source of the validity of a moral code or rule. The presumption is that rights and other social practices, values, and norms are culturally determined, but the universality of human nature and rights serves as a check on the potential excesses of relativism. Weak cultural relativism, on the other hand, holds that human rights are prima facie universal, but recognizes culture as an important source of exceptions in the interpretation of human rights.[7]

The position of most writers is that rather than a wholly universal approach, human rights discourse should apply "weak cultural relativism"—in other words, it should consider culture as an important consideration, without omitting the aspect of universality.[8] A related argument that has been advanced is that empirically there exists a core of universally applicable basic principles of rights that govern the relationship between the state and its citizens. To that extent, we can talk about some basic universal standards of human rights. At the same time, however, it is recognized that different human rights are considered important and fundamental at different points in time and under different circumstances.[9] Many of those who oppose arguments for the cultural relativism of human rights have based their criticism on a fear that a relativist position condones or even approves of social and cultural practices that violate individual rights. It is also feared that recognizing the legitimacy of the cultural relativity of human rights will undermine the entire universal human rights movement. These fears have largely informed the tension between the doctrine of cultural relativity and international human rights.

The debate on the universality or cultural relativity of human rights principles has centered, for the most part, on the Universal Declaration of Human Rights (UDHR) and other related international conventions such as the 1951

Refugee Convention. Perhaps the most famous argument for cultural relativism as it applies to the UDHR is the oft-quoted reaction of the American Anthropological Association to the draft proposal for the Universal Declaration of Human Rights in 1947. The Association argued that:

> Standards and values are relative to the culture from which they derive . . . [such] that what is held to be a human right in one society may be regarded as antisocial by another people . . . If the [Universal] Declaration must be of world wide applicability, it must embrace and recognize the validity of many different ways of life . . . The rights of man in the Twentieth Century *cannot be circumscribed by the standard of any single culture, or be dictated by the aspirations of any single people.*[10]

This position has since been echoed by other writers and continues to provide a reference point to which many writers anchor their arguments for cultural relativism in the human rights discourse.[11]

Non-Western Values and "Universal" Human Rights

The developing world has set its imprint on human rights thought, both by making human rights more socially oriented and also by questioning the focus on the individual that has characterized human rights discourse in the West. The arguments for "Asian values" and lately, "African values" in the conception and interpretation of human rights have been central to this trend.[12] The main themes in the African and Asian values debate have dwelt on the philosophical foundations of non-Western concepts of human rights and how these concepts contrast with western notions and institutions that were subsequently extended to other parts of the world through Western political and cultural imperialism.

In the African context, the approach to the discourse on the cultural relativism of human rights can be broadly divided into two schools. The first of these is the less radical approach, which is ideologically closer to the dominant universalist schools of the West. Proponents of this school, while arguing for the validity of a uniquely African concept of human rights, also recognize the universality of a basic core of human rights.[13] The second school stands in more radical opposition to the universalist approach. It seeks to fundamentally challenge Western-oriented state–individual thinking that otherwise dominates human rights. The main argument here is rooted in a belief in the distinctively different philosophical basis and worldviews of Western European and African societies, with a particular emphasis on the collectivist rather than individualistic nature of the concept of rights and duties in Africa.[14]

It is contended that in traditional Africa, the concept of rights was founded not on the individual but on the community, to which the individual related on the basis of obligations and duties. Rights in this context included, but were not limited, to the right to political representation, which was often guaranteed by the family, age groups, and the clan. The society developed certain central social features that tended to foster the promotion of both individual and collective rights. The dominant social orientations toward rights emphasized the group, sameness, and commonality, as well as a sense of cooperation, interdependence, and collective responsibility.[15] In these circumstances, the concept of human rights did not stand in isolation. It went with duties. Although certain rights were attached to the individual by virtue of birth and membership of the community, there were also corresponding communal duties and obligations. This matrix of entitlements and obligations, which fostered communal solidarity and sustained the kinship system, was the basis of the African conception of human rights. This communal philosophy has been made the cornerstone of the African Charter of Human and Peoples' Rights, which emphasizes the relationship between rights and duties as well as the collective rights of peoples.

The arguments for "Asian values" in the human rights discourse are similar to those that have been advanced for "African values." Leaders of East and Southeast Asian countries stress Asia's incommensurable differences from the West and demand special treatment of their human rights record by the international community. They reject outright the globalization of human rights and claim that Asia has a unique set of values, which, as Singapore's ambassador to the United Nations has urged, provide the basis for Asia's different understanding of human rights and justify the "exceptional" handling of rights by Asian governments.[16] According to this argument, the circumstances that prompted the institutionalization of human rights in the West do not exist in Asia. Besides, the importance of the community in Asian culture is incompatible with the primacy of the individual, upon which the Western notion of human rights rests. The relationship between individuals and communities constitutes the key difference between Asian and Western cultural values.

These arguments for peculiarly communal African or Asian values in the conception of human rights are confronted however with their own theoretical and empirical limitations in their relevance to contemporary African and Asian societies. Rather than the persistence of traditional cultural values in the face of modern incursions, the reality in much of contemporary Africa and Asia is a situation of disruptive and incomplete Westernization, "cultural confusion," or even the enthusiastic embrace of "Western" practices and values. The ideals of traditional culture and its community-centered values, advanced to justify arguments for the cultural relativism of human rights in the African or Asian context, far too often no longer exist.

It has been suggested that in asserting these values, leaders and elites in Africa and Asia find that they have a convenient tool to silence internal criticism and to fan anti-Western nationalist sentiments. At the same time, the concept is welcomed by cultural relativists, cultural supremacists, and isolationists alike as fresh evidence for their various positions against a political liberalism that defends universal human rights and democracy.[17] Some writers have even suggested that the picture of an idyllic communitarian society whether in the Asian or African context has been presented by rulers and elite to perpetuate patriarchy and the dominance of ruling groups as well as rationalize state violations of human rights.[18]

This is not the place to analyze the diverse criticisms that have been advanced against arguments for African and Asian values in the human rights discourse. It suffices here to point out that indeed, the extreme relativist argument for a distinctively Asian, African, or other concepts of human rights, which stands in contrast with the concepts and traditions of the "West," has its limitations. If anything, such notions of the absolute cultural relativism of human rights comes through as a misunderstanding inspired by cultural nationalism. What its proponents see as radically distinctive communitarian African or Asian traditions and conceptions also clearly possess ideals that are universal. However, while there may be a core of universal values that reflect inherent human worth in various societies, the broad expression of these values varies, not only in accordance with historical circumstances, but also from one social context to another. In order to find cross-cultural legitimacy, universal human rights necessarily have to be tempered by the specific cultural experiences of various societies. The challenge is how to strike the delicate balance between maintaining a core of basic universal human rights and yet allowing for some form of cultural expression and diversity.

Prioritizing and Categorizing Human Rights

The debate over the cultural relativism of human rights also extends to the question of the categorization and prioritization of rights. A number of attempts have been made to establish a hierarchy of human rights, or alternatively, a list of basic human rights that cannot be violated under any circumstances as opposed to human rights that are of secondary importance. The central question here is whether human rights are of equal importance or whether some rights take precedence over others.

Several writers have cataloged the emergence of a hierarchy of rights contained in the International Bill of Rights (the UDHR, ICCPR, and the ICESCR). First order rights are non-derogable under any circumstances and include the right to life, freedom from torture and other cruel, inhuman, or degrading punishment, as well as the freedom of thought, conscience, and religion. Second order rights include such rights as freedom from arbitrary arrests and detention, rights to fair trial, presumption of innocence, and freedom of expression and association. States may derogate from these rights during an officially proclaimed public emergency. Third order rights include the positive duties of the state to work towards the achievement of the rights to work, the right to education, social security, and medical care. These rights are unenforceable but states are required to undertake efforts within the limits of available resources to realize the goals in a non-discriminatory way.[19]

Some proponents of the cultural relativism of human rights disagree with this schema and have questioned the primacy of civil and political rights within the emerging universal human rights regime. They argue that unlike the West, where the dominant social orientation towards rigid and abstract individualism makes civil and political rights a priority, the priority in most non-Western societies is (or should be) the guarantee of a basic level of social and economic rights. They therefore stress the importance of basic social and economic rights over political and civil rights within certain social contexts. In some cases, this argument has been carried further, particularly by rulers in developing countries, to justify the curtailment of civil and political rights purportedly in the interest of the collective social and economic development. As one African ruler put it, "one man, one vote is meaningless unless accompanied by the principle of one man, one bread."[20] The same sentiments are echoed in China's 1991 White Paper, where it is stated that "[t]o eat their fill and dress warmly were the fundamental demands of the Chinese people who had long suffered cold and hunger."[21] Political and civil rights, in this view, do not make sense to poor and illiterate multitudes, as such rights are not meaningful under destitute and unstable conditions.

This disagreement over the prioritization of rights has been extended to the definition and interpretation of refugee rights. It has been suggested that the contemporary definition of a refugee has been informed by, and represents the Western liberal orientation of the preeminence of civil and political rights over economic and social rights. For instance, under the 1951 Refugee Convention, an asylum claimant must demonstrate that s/he fled because of a legitimate fear of persecution occasioned by his/her "race, religion, nationality, membership in a particular social group or political opinion." This legal construction of the 1951 Convention, which many Western countries have adopted, does not take adequate consideration of socio-economic concerns such as starvation, war, and environmental disasters as a basis for refugee status. This narrow definition of "refugee" reflects the Eurocentric liberal rights paradigm from which it emerged. As such, it focuses on the violation of liberal individual rights for which the state can be accountable. It is less concerned about violations of social and economic rights that may not necessarily be occasioned by the state.

Cultural Relativism and Refugee Rights

Criticisms of the definition of refugee rights and the international laws relating to these rights have not only centered on the point that they disproportionately reflect Western notions. Much of the critique has also focused on concerns about cultural chauvinism and cultural imperialism in the definition and interpretation of refugee rights. To what extent do international laws and domestic refugee policies offer protection to refugees in a truly objective and universal manner? Do the phrases "fear of *persecution*" and "*protection* of refugees" carry with them some implicit ethnocentrisms? These concerns have not only come from writers in the South but also from commentators in the North. Writers and policy makers in several Western countries have voiced concerns about cultural insensitivity or inadequate cultural consideration in the formulation of policies relating to refugees. One example of this is Canada, where questions have been raised about cultural chauvinism with regards to recent immigration and refugee policies in that country.

In 1993, Canada's Immigration and Refugee Board (IRB) issued a set of guidelines entitled *Women Refugee Claimants Fearing Gender Related Persecution*. The purpose of the guidelines was to provide the IRB decision-makers with a means of interpreting the legal definition of refugee in a gender sensitive manner. The guidelines were issued amid public outcry over several well publicized incidents regarding the plight of women who had made unsuccessful refugee claims based on gender related persecution. In one of such cases, a Saudi woman defied the law in her country by refusing to wear the mandatory veil. For this transgression, she claimed that she was publicly harassed and threatened by the unofficial "religious police" in Saudi Arabia.[22] The guidelines were therefore aimed at addressing such peculiar cases of refugee claims based on gender persecution.

Although the Canadian guidelines incorporate international norms in characterizing certain forms of culture-based discrimination and oppression as persecution, they go even further in that direction. The Canadian guidelines include extensive provisions for the protection of women fleeing culture-based persecution in their home countries. For instance, the guidelines stipulate that "a gender claim cannot be rejected simply because the claimant comes from a country where women face generalized oppression and violence and the claimant's fear of persecution is not identifiable to her on the basis of an individualized set of facts."[23] The guidelines also provide that "a woman who opposes institutionalized discrimination of women, or expresses views of independence from male social or cultural dominance in her society, may be found to fear persecution by reason of imputed political opinion."[24]

For the most part, the Canadian guidelines have been commended as a groundbreaking policy document that has facilitated significant advances in the protection of the rights of women refugees. Its provisions strengthen grounds on which women can be identified as a "particular social group" as a basis for proving persecution in a way that adheres to the definition of refugee under the 1951 Refugee Convention. This lead has been followed by other countries.[25] However, the guidelines have also been criticized by a few for going too far in judging other cultures by "Western" values. One Canadian official criticized the guidelines when they were introduced, wondering if by their terms Canada was not acting as an "imperialist country and impos[ing] its values on other countries around the world." He cautioned that Canada should not unilaterally try to impose its values on other countries through its refugee policies.[26]

This extension of cultural relativism to the realm of refugee rights, and specifically to Canadian refugee policies on women refugee claimants has been cautiously received. It has been suggested that what it asserts is that "the legal institutions of Canadian patriarchy ought to respect the patriarchal customs and laws of other states."[27] It has also been argued that no question of imposing Western values on other countries need arise at all in the realm of refugee rights because the recipient country plays a relatively minor role in asylum claims. Individuals arrive in the haven countries asking for admission, and that country simply says yes or no. A positive decision entails *no* consequences for the country of origin. A finding of refugee status does not reverberate in the official domain of international human rights law. At best, countries are embarrassed when their citizens are recognized as refugees elsewhere. Mostly, they are indifferent, dismissive, or disdainful.[28]

Indeed, concerns about cultural relativism may not have as much resonance and relevance with regards to refugees as in the field of international human rights. However, they have more consequences for countries and societies of origin than mere embarrassment. An international refugee law regime that is perceived as dominantly reflective of Western culture and disdainful of non-Western culture raises significant questions about the legitimacy of such laws and policies. While a finding of refugee status may not reverberate in the official domain of international human rights law, its effects on the country of origin are sometimes far-reaching when such findings are perceived as affronts on the legitimate cultures and institutions of the society of origin. This particularly arises when the refugee determination process and the Western media construct refugee claimants from non-Western societies as victims of a particular religion or culture. Such constructs influence official and public opinion in the countries of origin as to the legitimacy of international human rights and refugee laws. One example of this is the concern that has been raised in many Islamic societies about Western attitudes to Islamic tradition in relation to refugee claims. By categorizing such "innocuous"[29] Islamic traditions as those that require women to wear the veil as gender persecution, Western refugee policies exhibit insensitivity towards Islamic cultures. Related to this is the debate among feminist scholars about differences across cultures and the perils of imposing Western notions of feminism on the experiences of non-Western women.

The point here is not that discourses about cultural relativism or collective rights should be deployed in formulating refugees laws and policies to the detriment of the rights and welfare of individual asylum seekers. Indeed, the protection of individual refugee claimants must remain the central concern of international and national refugee laws and policies. However, protection

d, as much as possible, in a way that will enhance the interna-
cultural legitimacy of the refugee determination process. The
refugees both under international law and domestic policies
be offered in a truly universal and cross-culturally sensitive manner.
Some national processes for refugee determination have been sensitive to this
need. One example of this is a recent decision that generated widespread
media interest in Canada. It involved the successful claim by a Somali woman
and her two children that was based on "a well founded fear" of genital mutilation should they be returned to their native Somalia. In making the decision to
grant the claimant refugee status, the Refugee Board, sensitive to possible ac-
cusations of cultural insensitivity, used African sources in evaluating the practice of genital mutilation. It noted that "subjecting a young girl to Female
Genital Mutilation (FGM) is seen as a 'torturous custom' by women's rights
advocates in Africa who are campaigning to eradicate this practice."[30] It is significant that the Refugee Board sought to ground its decision on sources from
the claimant's own society rather than sources from Canada even when both
sources clearly point to the same conclusion. Such processes strengthen the
cross-cultural legitimacy and validity of the refugee determination process.
They also lend a universal character to the refugee determination and protection process.

"Cruel, Inhuman, or Degrading Treatment"

The protection against cruel, inhuman, or degrading treatment is central to
the contemporary universal human rights regime as reflected in the Universal
Declaration of Human Rights. Over the years, this provision has evolved in the
direction of enlarging and multiplying the possible fields of its application.
One of the most relevant results of this evolution has been the broadening of
refugee status requirements. The concept of "inhuman or degrading treatment," as inferred by both universal and regional treaties, is often taken into
account by national authorities when deciding to implement an order of expulsion or return of refugee climate to his or her country of origin.[31]

While there is relative agreement on the point that the infliction of cruel, inhuman, or degrading treatment constitutes persecution that may provide a
basis for granting refugee status, there is disagreement on what constitutes
cruel, inhuman, or degrading treatment. International human rights instruments simply stipulate that "no one shall be subjected to torture or to cruel, inhuman or degrading treatment or punishment."[32] There is, however, little
guidance from the history of these articles as to the precise meaning of cruel,
inhuman, or degrading punishment. In the course of drafting the ICCPR in
1952, the Philippines suggested that the word "unusual" should be intersected
between the words "inhuman" and "or degrading." While some delegates supported the addition, many others opposed it arguing that the term is vague and
relative, as what is unusual in one country may not be so in other countries.[33]

One writer wonders why the criticism of vagueness was not extended to the words "cruel, inhuman, or degrading," because what can be seen as "cruel and inhuman" in one culture may not be seen in the same light in another culture.[34]

To demonstrate this point, Abdullahi Ahmed An'Naim argues that in the majority of human societies today, corporal punishment is not regarded as necessarily cruel, inhuman, or degrading, yet in others it is viewed as a human rights violation. Similarly, the meaning of cruel and inhuman treatment or punishment in Islamic cultures may be significantly different from perceptions of the meaning of this clause in other parts of the world.[35] Definitions and interpretations of "cruel and degrading" treatment have also evolved with time and social contexts. In the earlier part of the last century, the League of Nations grouped polygamy in African and Islamic societies along with slavery as a gross abuse of the rights of women. Perceptions have since changed. All these show the dangers and difficulty of providing monolithic criteria for defining what constitutes cruel, inhuman, or degrading treatment. According to An'Naim:

> [t]he interpretation and practical application of the protection against cruel, inhuman, or degrading treatment or punishment in the context of a particular society should be determined by the moral standards of that society [although] there are many legitimate ways of influencing and informing the moral standards of a society. To dictate to a society is both unacceptable as a matter of principle and unlikely to succeed in practice.[36]

Indeed, while the infliction of torture necessarily entails subjection to inhuman and degrading treatment, it does not follow that inhuman treatment is necessarily also degrading. The absoluteness of the individual's rights to be treated in a humane manner has to be counterbalanced by the "justifiability" of the treatment in the particular situation. The general interest of the entire community on one hand and the threat to the social order, on the other hand, should be taken into account in determining whether a particular cruel or inhuman treatment is justified. As Alberta Fabbicotti categorically puts it, "the meaning of cruel, inhuman or degrading treatment is relative."[37]

These concerns that have been raised about the subjectivity in defining what constitutes cruel, inhuman, or degrading treatment logically translate to the realm of refugee rights when the phrase is deployed as a basis for determining whether claimants have demonstrated a "well founded fear of persecution." Within this context even the meaning of "persecution" becomes problematic. Persecution is not defined in the 1951 Refugee Convention, and some have suggested that its meaning is deliberately left vague in the UNHCR *Handbook on Procedures and Criteria for Determining Refugee Status*. The *Handbook* simply indicates that "a threat to life or freedom on account of race, religion, nationality, political opinion or membership of a particular social group is always persecution. Other serious violations of human rights—for the same reasons—would also constitute persecution."[38] However, persecution has been broadly defined as "sustained or systematic violation of basic rights demonstrative of a failure of state protection."[39]

Interpretations of what constitutes persecution have developed significantly in the past few years. For instance, in the realm of international refugee law, a growing number of judicial decisions have held that Female Genital Mutilation (FGM) amounts to inhuman and degrading treatment and constitutes persecution of women as a "particular social group." This precludes national authorities from expelling women to countries where they may be forced to undergo the practice.[40] But although FGM or female circumcision (depending on one's perspective)[41] has been generally recognized as a form of violence against women and a health hazard, there is an increasingly vocal group of writers (particularly women from the South) who disagree with this "labeling." They argue that the concerted international action against FGM stems from a lack of understanding and sensitivity towards non-Western cultures where female circumcision is practiced.[42]

These writers have raised significant questions about the neglect of salient cultural issues in international discourses and programs of action on FGM. Their point is not so much to dispute the established health risks and trauma associated with the practice but to draw attention to the stereotyped treatment and representation of the subject. According to Ifeyinwa Iweriebor:

> What is bothersome is not so much that people have a negative opinion of the practice, but that the issue is misrepresented as a form of child abuse or a tool of gender oppression. The language and the tone of the outcry in most cases reflect a total lack of respect for the culture of other peoples. Even more bothersome is the false portrayal: the falsification of statistics and a successful demonization of the practitioners.[43]

The point here is that whatever the benefits of including FGM as a form of gender persecution within the realm of refugee law and policies, such a move is inadequate if it is not sensitive to the cultural context of the practice. It is important, even in examining the human rights implications of FGM, to locate the discussion within the broad framework of the cultural dynamics that inform and affect the practice.

Criticism of the broadening of refugee status requirements to include FGM has also come from other quarters. While most legal scholars agree that female circumcision is indeed a legitimate ground for asylum,[44] some others have cautioned that this may not ultimately be in the interest of international human rights. They warn against an uncontrolled enlargement of human rights procedures, particularly as they relate to grounds for asylum. Although the enlargement of the application of the phrase "inhuman and degrading treatment" may be justified from a humanitarian point of view, it is questionable in so far as it raises the unprecedented result of progressively nullifying the very legal nature of asylum.[45]

Refugee Producers and Refugee Acceptors

An important feature of the refugee rights discourse that further highlights the debate over cultural relativism and the definition of persecution is the tendency towards the polarization of the world into categories of "refugee producers" and "refugee acceptors." In discussing this polarization, Audrey Macklin makes an interesting reference to the critique by contemporary postmodernist scholars of the parallel dichotomies that have been drawn along race and culture in the dominant discourses in the West—the Westernized or Northern Self versus the exotic Eastern or Southern Other. Within this schema of what Edward Said has described as "Orientalism," the exotic Southern or "oriental" Other is objectified and constitutes the reference point against which the West defines and asserts itself.[46]

This same critique also applies to the binary structure of the discourse on refugee rights. As with races and cultures, refugee discourse can be organized according to the binary opposites of self/other. In the refugee context, there are "refugee producers" and "refugee acceptors." The Western nations locate themselves firmly in the category of "refugee acceptors" and constitute themselves as distinctive and superior by reference to what they are not—that is states that "produce" refugees. To describe oneself as a refugee acceptor is to say that one is also a "non-refugee producer." This binary structure underlines the global refugee discourse.[47]

However, this categorization is problematic, particularly in relation to discrimination against women across the world. Consider the UNDP's conclusion that no country (not even the "non-refugee producers") treats its women as it treats its men, within the context of the assertion that severe discrimination on grounds of gender constitutes persecution.[48] Given that every country discriminates against women, how will the line be drawn between "mere" discrimination and discrimination so "severe" that it amounts to persecution? One concern is that the line may be drawn by reference to whatever Western (the non-refugee producing) countries do. As Macklin puts it:

> What "we" do is discrimination. The more the claimant state looks different from ours, the more what "they" do begins to look to "us" like persecution. In other words, the fear is that cultural difference may become the yardstick along which the shift from discrimination to persecution will be measured.[49]

The fear here is that notions of cultural superiority and inferiority may be employed to distinguish between those states that are "willing or unable" to protect women from domestic violence (non-democracies, current refugee producing states) and those Western states whose systems are simply "imperfect" and cannot be held accountable for an inability to protect each woman from individual human rights abuse. The practical consequence of this conception is that gender persecution tends to be more visible and identifiable as such only when it is committed by a cultural Other. For example, it seems that when some North American feminists want to make a pitch for granting asylum to victims of gender persecution elsewhere, they tend to be blind to the compelling evidence gathered by other North American feminists documenting local practices that might constitute gender persecution.

This is a concern that has been raised by "Third World" feminists who argue that because Western feminists are primarily concerned with themselves rather than the experiences of the non-Western woman "their conclusions are necessarily ethnocentric."[50] Others have questioned the cultural connotations often associated with the persecution of Third World women by Western feminists, arguing that discrimination against women is not derived from culture, but from power. As such, the answer to the global politics of power that seeks to control women across the world is to disarticulate "women" from "culture," deconstruct women as symbols, reconstruct them as human beings and problematize women's rights as human rights.[51]

At one level, the stance of Western superiority in the realm of gender relations seems innocuous, in that it is deployed in a discursive setting that is meant to benefit individual women seeking asylum. At another level, however, it bespeaks of a certain ethnocentrism that has been identified by many non-Western feminists.[52] This includes a tendency to posit Western women as the normative reference point against which the situations of Other women are evaluated and articulated. What this means in the refugee context is that the commonality of gender oppression across cultures is suppressed to ensure that what is done to women in non-Western societies looks fundamentally different from or worse than what is done to women in the West. This obscures an inherent contradiction in admitting women from non-Western societies as refugees in Western countries even when the lot of some women within these countries may not, in fact, be significantly better. The dichotomy between refugee-acceptors and refugee-producers, therefore, compels a parallel classification of Western women/Other women that serves to facilitate the admission of non-Western women fleeing gender persecution but does so in a way that remains politically and empirically problematic.[53]

Conclusion

Although the debate over the universality or cultural relativism of human rights continues among scholars, recent trends indicate that the discourse has gradually moved away from whether contemporary human rights are truly universal, and therefore cross-culturally applicable, to how the cross-cultural legitimacy of the emerging "universal" human rights regime may be enhanced.[54] One reality that has strengthened the need for the universalization of human rights is the trend toward rapid globalization in almost every sphere of human endeavor. The spread of the Western model of the state to other parts of the developing world has given rise to the need for constitutional and other legal guarantees of human rights. Thus, the modern concept of human rights, admittedly a product of the West, is increasingly becoming equally relevant in other parts of the world.

Besides, cultural relativism has been charged with neutralizing moral judgment and thereby impairing action against injustice.[55] Many writers are suspicious of what they see as a notion of cultural relativism that denies to individuals the moral right to make comparisons and to insist on universal standards of right and wrong. However, as An'Naim has argued, the merits of a reasonable degree of cultural relativism are obvious, especially when compared to claims of universality that are, in fact, based on the claimant's rigid and exclusive ethnocentricity. In an age of self-determination, sensitivity to cultural legitimacy is vital for the international protection of human rights. This does not preclude cross-cultural and moral judgment and action, but it provides a direction for the best ways of formulating and expressing judgment and undertaking action.[56]

Globalization and the universalization of human rights need not necessarily preclude attempts to temper the modern content of "universal" rights with the specific cultural experiences of various societies. In the refugee field, this calls for international and national refugee laws and policies founded on the basic universal human rights standards, but also informed by some level of cultural sensitivity. The present challenge is how to achieve this delicate balance. A first step in this direction would be for scholars and policy makers on all sides of the debate to accord more attention to the concerns of ethnocentricity and cultural chauvinism that have been voiced about international and national refugee laws and policies. So far this does not seem to be happening, as such voices are often dismissed as patriarchal, paternalistic, and perpetuating injustice. Yet, although these voices may not always represent the best ways of protecting the rights of individual asylum seekers, and in some cases may even be antithetical to these rights, they deserve close attention if the standards of international refugee protection are to be truly objective and universal. They also deserve attention if the humanistic philosophies that inform international refugee law and polices are not to be occluded by the perceived cultural biases and socio-economic inequities of the international world order.

3
Legal and Institutional
Protection of Refugees

5

Refugee Protection in Troubled Times:
Reflections on Institutional and Legal Developments at the Crossroads

BRIAN GORLICK*

There wasn't a racist bone or muscle in his body . . . But why, then? Why didn't he want a refugee in the family? Well, there was AIDS for a start . . . And then there was—it wasn't the poverty exactly—it was the hugeness of it, the Live Aid pictures, the thousands and thousands of people, the flies on their faces, the dead kids. Heartbreaking, but—what sort of society was that? What sort of people came out of a place like that? And all the civil wars—machetes and machine guns, and burning car tires draped around peoples necks, the savagery. Fair enough, the man was an accountant, but that was the place he came from. And why had he left? . . . They'd never know—it was too far away. It was too different; that was it. Too unknowable, and too frightening for his daughter.

Roddy Doyle, "The Dinner"

In the mid-1970s, about 80 million people—roughly 1.5 per cent of the world's population—were living outside the country of their birth. The figure is now closer to 150 million, according to the International Organization for Migration. It seems implausibly small, but the extent of human movement across borders is hard to monitor—and the figures are a mystery for those of us who have no idea how many people move in and out of our neighborhoods in a single day, or a year, or the course of a decade . . . Refugees are not necessarily poor, but by the time they have reached safety, the human trafficking organizations on which they de-

*Regional Protection Officer, UNHCR Regional Office for the Baltic and Nordic Countries, Stockholm. Many thanks to Charlotta Schlyter for her helpful comments on an earlier draft. The views expressed in this article are those of the author and do not necessarily reflect those of the United Nations or UNHCR.

pend have eaten up much of their capital. In the course of the excruciating journeys, mental and physical resources are also expended—some of them non-renewable.

Jeremy Harding, *The Uninvited: Refugees at the Rich Man's Gate*

The future of the international system of refugee protection is currently the subject of much debate. Increased numbers of asylum seekers and people on the move, largely from countries in the South, have led many Northern politicians and policy makers to call for increased control measures to deal with what are considered illegal migrants. Countries with strong traditions of receiving refugees and giving shape to the international regime of refugee protection advocate a rethinking of the very system they helped create. Despite the continuing value of international refugee law and asylum practices, many feel the system is not working, and international refugee law currently does not provide states with the means necessary to control irregular migration—while at the same time help identify those who are deserving of international protection.

Echoing these sentiments, former British Home Secretary Jack Straw proclaimed in 1999 that the 1951 Refugee Convention is "no longer working as its framers intended" and "the environment in which it is applied today is one that has changed almost out of all recognition from that of 1951." The Home Secretary noted that "numbers of asylum seekers have vastly increased." While not offering a ready formula for fixing the international system, he did identify the need to rectify the imbalance between the costs of processing asylum applications in developed countries and the provision of sufficient funds to make conditions in the regions of origin better for refugees.[1] Such initiatives, he proposed, "will reduce the pressure on refugees to travel further afield in search of protection." He went on to suggest that the EU set up a program "under which an agreed number of refugees—and possibly others in need of protection—would be identified in their own regions and brought to the EU for resettlement." The advantages of an enhanced resettlement scheme would be to reduce overall expenses to states while at the same time provide more orderly identification and reception of individuals deserving of refugee protection based on agreed criteria. Lastly, the Home Secretary suggested that "an EU or internationally-agreed list of safe countries or groups from which asylum applications would be ruled inadmissible or considered under a greatly accelerated process" would help reduce the phenomenon of so-called "asylum shopping."[2]

In fact, it is a refrain amongst some states not party to the international refugee instruments that the 1951 Refugee Convention and 1967 Protocol are outdated, euro-centric, and of limited relevance in dealing with refugee problems in less-developed countries. These countries argue there is little value in becoming party to the international refugee instruments. Such views were expressed by the former Indian permanent representative to the UN at the forty-eighth Session of the UNHCR Executive Committee:

> International refugee law is currently in a state of flux and it is evident that many of the provisions of the (1951 Refugee) Convention, particularly those which provide for individualised status determination and social security have little relevance to the circumstances of developing countries today who are mainly confronted with mass and mixed inflows. Moreover, the signing of the Convention is unlikely to improve in any practical manner the actual protection which has always been enjoyed and continues to be enjoyed by refugees in India. We therefore believe that the time has come for a fundamental reformulation of international refugee law to take into account the present day realities . . . it has to be recognised that refugees and mass movements are first and foremost a 'developing country' problem and that the biggest 'donors' are in reality developing countries who put at risk their fragile environment, economy and society to provide refuge to millions. An international system which does not address these concerns adequately cannot be sustained in the long run. . . .

The underlying theme in the above comments is the concern with increasing numbers of asylum seekers and refugees and the disproportionate burden on states. Related concerns about the security, economic, and environmental impact of involuntary movements of persons only fuels the debate in calling for new systems and methods to deal with and contain refugees and unwanted migrants, as some would have it, beyond one's borders.

This questioning of the founding legal instruments and principles of refugee protection has arisen due to a variety of factors including shifts in the global perspective of refugee problems particularly in the post–Cold War era. The powerful role of media attention (or lack thereof), in addition to ideological changes in refugee discourse have played a role in shifting the international response to refugee outflows.

This essay begins with a brief survey of the factors which have shifted the international debate on refugee protection and how this has influenced UNHCR. Measures states have taken to restrict unwanted movements of immigrants are then reviewed. This leads to an examination of the links with international human rights law and how the system of international human rights protection can be employed to complement gaps in the international refugee regime. This essay will also address some of the recent developments in international criminal law that have given shape to individual accountability for serious human rights violations. The final section will look at the current state of other accountability measures such as civil liability and compensation schemes for human rights violations. The conclusion argues that the emerging convergence of various aspects of international law is beneficial to strengthening the overall system of refugee protection.

Shifting Priorities, Attitudes and Institutional Change

Adam Roberts has written that the developments in the 1980s and 1990s "especially the increase in refugee numbers and the raising of barriers by states against inflows of immigrants" resulted in considerable changes "in the international handling of refugee issues." The "hardening of attitudes towards refugee influxes" coupled with intense media focus on select refugee crises has led to "major political and military consequences." According to Roberts such attention has contributed to the international community's sense of compulsion to take action to (ideally from a Western perspective) "tackle refugee issues in or near the country of origin."[3] The post–Cold War attitude towards refugees as having limited value as political pawns also explains the reluctance of powerful governments to provide military forces in conflict situations, which in the end serves to exacerbate refugee movements.

Gil Loescher has argued that "governments feel compelled to respond to refugee disasters, especially those covered extensively by the media, and therefore are likely to task the UNHCR and other international agencies to provide relief aid." Loescher further suggested that "the provision of humanitarian assistance is financially and politically a relatively low risk option for governments because it satisfies the demands of both the media and public opinion for some kind of action to alleviate human suffering . . . but it is also used by governments as an excuse for refusing to take more decisive forms of political and military intervention."[4]

As part of this global shift in the North's response to refugee crises, UNHCR has been pressured to play an increasingly expanded role. With no other international organization specifically mandated to deal with humanitarian crises that result in forced movements of individuals either within countries of origin or across international borders, UNHCR is seen as the agency with the closest responsibility to operationalize and coordinate large-scale humanitarian response, regardless of whether the victims of such displacement would formally come under the Office's mandate.[5] The fact that UNHCR maintains an extensive field presence and since the Gulf War has gained prominence as the lead UN agency in coordinating large-scale humanitarian operations also served to change the Office's perceived mandate and operational response.

During Sadako Ogata's ten-year tenure as High Commissioner for Refugees the Office found itself in uncharted territory that in some instances led to the deployment of civilian staff in environments riddled with conflict such as the former Yugoslavia, the former Zaire, or East Timor. Difficulties associated with providing protection to Rwandese refugees in the former Zaire and UNHCR's role in the former Yugoslavia have come under severe criticism as a distortion of the Office's mandate and a failure of commitment to protection principles by states. It has even been argued that humanitarian relief activities offered in a climate of armed conflict inevitably confuses the mandates of respective UN actors in the field, and in the extreme may result in a perpetuation of the conflict rather than an expedited peace.[6] Another legacy is that these operations will serve as tragic reminders of the risks humanitarian workers are exposed to in order to provide relief and protection to civilian victims.[7]

Some commentators argue that the evolution of UNHCR's mandate and operational priorities were unavoidable due to the changing nature of conflicts and the dynamics of displacement. It cannot be ignored, however, that the Office itself played a willing role to meet the demands of the international community. The corresponding increase in UNHCR's human and financial resources (with an annual budget almost exclusively reliant on voluntary donations from a handful of industrialized states) from $69 million in 1975 to a high of $1.4 billion in 1996 and some $1 billion in 1999; meanwhile, the number of persons of concern to the Office has jumped from 2.4 million persons in 1975 to approximately 23 million today also served to blur the categories of persons in need of international protection. Such rapid growth and unprecedented demands on UNHCR have not been without problems. The fact that during the height of the crises in the African great lakes region and the former Yugoslavia some 25 percent of UNHCR's annual budget went to these two operations is worth contemplating in the broader context of how limited resources are earmarked and spent.[8]

Furthermore, the demands on UNHCR and other humanitarian actors in the last few years to become involved in no-win situations have been problematic and have required the Office to become engaged in debates and negotiations on international security. Notwithstanding the inevitability of UNHCR assuming an expanded role, and the reality that UNHCR's work was never devoid of political implications, UNHCR and the refugee issue both have a different prominence today than when the Office was first established.[9]

B. S. Chimni has argued that a consequence of the UN Security Council and NATO's increasing involvement in refugee matters is that refugee protection will be "couched in the language of security." He identified three outcomes of this development. One, refugees are now clearly seen as threatening to host country's security which may lead to a lessening of adherence to fundamental rights such as the principle of *non-refoulement*; two, the use of the language of security may lead to justifying the use of force against a country of origin "even if, as was the case in Kosovo (and earlier in Iraq), the use of force actually accelerates refugee flows"; and three, the language of security "invades the world of humanitarianism and starts to displace it."[10] Chimni's critique and what has been offered by the analysis of international relations demonstrate that the development of linkages between the need to manage refugee flows and concerns of international security have resulted in de facto changes in UNHCR's mandate and practices. This in turn has led to the perception that new and exceptional responses to refugee problems must be developed.

The only falsehood in such thinking, in this commentator's view, is that changes in the international community's response to refugee crises have been shaped in reaction to exceptional and often high-profile operations as well as alarmist claims concerning increased numbers of asylum seekers.[11] What may be considered more traditional UNHCR operations geared towards facilitating asylum and securing basic protection and socio-economic rights for refugees, particularly in developing countries, have been largely ignored by the international media—and also it seems by many academic commentators. In the current climate, however, if a crisis is out of the eye of the media, funding and related difficulties commonly follow. The correlation between media attention and funding for refugee programs leading to selectivity in the international response is something UNHCR should guard against. Political expectations and precedents in operational responses, not to mention the development of "soft law" through countless resolutions adopted in international fora, have gone far beyond extending the mandate of UNHCR to categories of persons whom it assists.

According to Adam Roberts, UNHCR has been a victim of "force of circumstance" that cannot be wished away. In support of this conclusion Roberts cites the examples of Northern Iraq, the former Yugoslavia and Rwanda to explain UNHCR's pressured response to "prevent huge influxes (of refugees) to other countries, to try and feed and protect threatened people in their own countries, to arrange temporary rather than permanent asylum abroad, and to get those who have fled to return."[12] At the end of the day UNHCR may have been a victim of its own success. Whether UNHCR can or should sustain the reshaping of its protection mandate and operational response, or as some have argued return to "the basics of protection," are serious policy questions UNHCR has to address.

A final issue that deserves attention in contemplating the current state of international refugee affairs is the alarming impact of racism and xenophobia on popular culture in Western societies. Although it is difficult to pinpoint an increase in restrictive policies towards refugees as resulting from purely racist attitudes, the rise of right-wing movements, which in many instances have had considerable influence on the political mainstream is certainly cause for concern. This political dynamic is well summed up by Reg Whitaker:

> Governments increasingly find themselves pressured from opposite directions. Civil libertarians and immigrant communities on the one side demand more generous policies and decrying racism. Extreme right-wing xenophobic and nationalist movements on the other side demand more restrictive policies and assert the priority of the native born. Faced with this equation, most governments have opted to give more ground to the right, a decision perhaps dictated as much by the politicians' finely-tuned sense of where more votes can be found than by burning

racist convictions. The existence of racist influences on policy does not in itself demonstrate that policy is *determined* by racism. In the case of refugees, there are enough reasons to see why governments are becoming increasingly ungenerous, even obstructionist, without recourse to racism as a totalizing explanation.[13]

The fact that many European countries, including ones with strong human rights traditions such as the Nordic countries, have seen in some cases growing popularity in political parties which promote an anti-immigrant agenda has had a negative effect on the domestic refugee debate. Sweden, for example, which can rightly pride itself alongside the other Nordics as being a strong supporter of UNHCR and global human rights issues is grappling with its own extremist movements at home. Although Sweden's extremist movements have thus far been shunned by the political mainstream, they have had a disturbing impact in other ways. In 1999, the Swedish security police reported that 940 crimes had been committed by Swedish neo-Nazi groups. Many of these incidents involved violent assaults on immigrants and included the murders of two police officers and a well-known trade-union official who was shot after exposing a colleague as a neo-Nazi infiltrator. These murders were followed by serious threats and attacks on a number of others, including journalists and individuals working on behalf of anti-racist campaigns or with refugees. Many of these victims are now under police protection. Groups based in Sweden are amongst the most active in Europe in producing and disseminating white power music and racist propaganda via the Internet. The police have reported that the core group of neo-Nazis in Sweden consists of 1,500 people, but they have several thousand sympathizers. Tougher action against offenders has been demanded by some politicians and the public, but many are reluctant to surrender to growing demands to ban neo-Nazi groups, as this would conflict with laws and policies on freedom of expression.

Countering emerging political extremism, in addition to the broader objective of maintaining the international system of refugee protection based on the rule of law and equitable burden sharing are serious challenges facing the international community and UNHCR. To meet these challenges will now, more than ever, require sound policies and practices on the asylum front grounded in a firm commitment to human rights. Support in the form of financial and other economic contributions as well as inter-state cooperation and harmonization of asylum practices to high protection standards will also need to be achieved. The refugee problem is not getting any smaller or easier to deal with, nor will it go away. That the global refugee problem would somehow come to an end is what states thought, or perhaps wished to think, when UNHCR was created some fifty years ago. Regrettably, they were sorely mistaken.

Challenges to the System of International Refugee Protection

Many states which have subscribed to the international legal protection regime by voluntarily becoming party to the international refugee instruments are currently undertaking radical changes through legislative and inter-state arrangements which restrict access to asylum and the provision of legal rights to refugees. These restrictions include limiting access to refugee status determination procedures and employing an increasingly restrictive interpretation of the refugee definition. This trend has been described as "a pull back from the legal foundation on which effective protection rests."[14]

In order to avoid the related difficulties, expense and responsibility for protecting refugees on their own territory, one state temporarily introduced off-shore procedures for processing and granting temporary protection to asylum seekers, a practice which at the time was attractive to a number of European nations.[15] In the context of the former Yugoslavia and Northern Iraq the establishment of so-called "safe zones" offered a poor alternative to the practice of facilitating the access of persons seeking international protection to leave their countries of origin.[16]

More pedestrian, yet by no means less serious practices which may have the effect of deterring asylum seekers include: the use of administrative detention,[17] the misuse of readmission agreements,[18] the application of so-called "safe third country" principles,[19] the use of first country of asylum,[20] the imposition of carrier sanctions,[21] visa restrictions and inspection of travelers in foreign airports,[22] the absence of domestic refugee law or functioning determination procedures, restricting access to determination procedures including the right of appeal, the imposition of airport regulations,[23] and interdiction on the high seas.[24] These trends and practices have resulted in restricting the rights of refugees.[25] In the effort by states to control illegal migration, would-be refugees may find that they too are subject to these control measures.

These largely regressive approaches have found favor amongst traditional asylum countries that claim to be overburdened with asylum applicants arriving in large numbers. There is understandable concern that the arrival of increasing numbers of asylum applicants and the potential abuse of asylum procedures have resulted in a significant burden on some states, particularly in developing countries. However, it should be recalled that the system of international refugee protection could not have foreseen these unprecedented and wide-ranging developments to avoid state responsibility, nor were the international refugee instruments designed to address migration issues.

Although some states and academic commentators are calling for a new international legal framework or revised international refugee convention, it is unlikely that the international community would engage in reforming the current international legal regime with a view to making it more generous. In fact, revisiting the international legal instruments for the protection of refugees in the current political climate is considered a nonstarter by UNHCR.[26] Realizing that the international system of refugee protection is in disarray and could possibly face "fragmentation, or worse disintegration," in late-2000 UNHCR's Executive Committee endorsed the need to engage in global consultations aimed at revitalizing "the international protection regime and to discuss measures to ensure that international protection needs are properly recognised and met, while due account is also taken of the legitimate concerns of states, host communities and the international community generally."[27]

In addition to multilateral negotiations to seek common understanding on the future of international refugee protection, in circumstances where compliance by states with international legal obligations has proven ineffective[28] international human rights law provides a complementary protection framework for refugees. The following section will look at the records of the principal UN human rights mechanisms and how they are developing and strengthening the normative and operational framework for international refugee protection.

Refugee Protection and the Link to Human Rights

Approximately two-thirds of the world's countries are states parties to the 1951 Refugee Convention and its 1967 Protocol. These instruments remain the principal body of international law for the protection of refugees. Moreover, the refugee definition and a number of the rights provisions contained in these instruments have been widely incorporated into regional instruments and domestic legislation.[29] As concerns the human rights focus of the 1951 Refugee Convention, the direct line of descent from the UN Charter and the Universal Declaration of Human Rights is noted in its preamble. The 1951 Refugee Convention affirms "the principle that human beings shall enjoy fundamental rights and freedoms without discrimination." International refugee instruments codify a number of specific rights that states are obliged to provide to refugees. In view of rapid developments in the domain of human rights law which may complement and inform the interpretation of the refugee instruments it can be argued that the 1951 Convention is very much a living document which, despite its vintage, maintains its relevance in respect of providing a normative framework to address contemporary refugee problems.[30]

In addition to providing a definition of who is a refugee, international refugee law provides a full range of human rights to refugees.[31] What is considered the cornerstone principle of international protection, return from a potential asylum country at its frontiers or prohibition of expulsion or return of a refugee (*non-refoulement*), is found in Article 33. Also of importance is Article 5 which provides that nothing in the 1951 Refugee Convention shall be deemed to impair any additional rights and benefits granted by a contracting state.[32] Accordingly, the rights provisions in the 1951 Convention should be considered as minimum standards of treatment.

A review of the human rights standards contained in the 1951 Refugee Convention reveals that it is an extraordinary "Bill of Rights" for refugees. Many of the rights, such as enjoying non-discrimination and protection from persecution (i.e. denial of life, liberty, and personal security), are in one form or another enshrined in other international human rights treaties, such as the 1966 International Covenant on Civil and Political Rights (ICCPR), the 1966 International Covenant on Social, Economic and Cultural Rights (ICESCR), the 1984 Convention against Torture (CAT), and the 1989 Convention on the Rights of the Child (CRC). Under the Refugee Convention many of the rights are granted to refugees without restrictions, while certain provisions require that states parties provide treatment as favorable as that granted to other foreigners subject to the jurisdiction of the concerned state. Although the Convention provides an impressive array of rights to refugees, international human rights instruments such as the ICCPR and ICESCR may provide even broader legal protection. For example, in relation to housing rights and social security the Refugee Convention guarantees equality of treatment to refugees with other non-nationals, while the relevant international human rights instruments provide such guarantees *equally to all persons without restriction.*

Apart from variances of scope and application in the international treaties, as with any international human rights regime a continuous challenge is how to enforce this body of law. In the case of the principal UN human rights treaties there is commonly a system of treaty bodies that play a supervisory and enforcement role to ensure compliance by states parties with the treaty provisions. This is normally done through examination of state party reports submitted to the committee or treaty body established under a particular treaty. Depending on the agreement of individual states and the specific provisions of the human rights treaty, a committee may deal with inter-state and individual complaints as well as conduct field investigations on the human rights situation in a particular country. Notwithstanding the considerable authority, both real and symbolic, exercised by the treaty bodies as part of the broader system of international human rights protection, some have argued that the present procedures for ensuring compliance with international human rights standards is unsatisfactory and is in need of reform.[33]

The international refugee protection regime must also be considered as having great potential to ensure compliance with international standards, whether in states party to the refugee instruments or otherwise. The system of international refugee protection nevertheless differs from the international human rights regime in some significant ways. Firstly, to argue the limitations of the refugee protection system the following points should be acknowledged. Unlike international human rights law, there is no formal mechanism in international refugee law to receive individual or inter-state petitions or complaints or to examine state party reports or other information which can be used to formulate recommendations to states. In this regard, UNHCR has not given full effect to Article 35 of the 1951 Refugee Convention as a supervisory mechanism. A further observation is that the extent of UNHCR's involvement in protection and human rights issues concerning refugees largely depends on the scope and resources permitted to the Office to exercise its mandate in a particular country. A handicap in delivering on its protection mandate is limited human and financial resources. This means that field operations may be inadequately staffed and thereby addressing refugees' problems may be delayed or neglected.[34]

To argue the positive aspects of UNHCR's rights enforcement approach, a strong point remains the day-to-day presence of UNHCR protection officers in the field. This presence permits UNHCR to develop an appreciation of country conditions and potential solutions to refugee problems, as well as the likelihood of various approaches having favorable outcomes. A continuous field presence is extremely important for assessing and monitoring the human rights situation (which may impact on protecting or even producing refugees) in a particular region. It is also required for developing a strategy to take remedial action through intervening and working with government authorities, legal or national human rights institutions, and non-governmental organizations (NGOs). Along these lines UNHCR alone, or in conjunction with other actors, can develop assistance programs and protection initiatives geared towards safeguarding the human rights of refugees and other victims of forced displacement.[35]

As part of its sharpened focus on human rights issues, UNHCR has directly incorporated human rights principles and strategies in its policies and programs. Protection and human rights activities in countries of origin, working with states in the area of legal rehabilitation, institution building and law reform, enforcement of the rule of law, and developing specific protection guidelines for refugee women and children are relatively recent activities for UNHCR. These activities are supported by UNHCR's Executive Committee and have found shape in various policy directives and practices in the field. The involvement and success of UNHCR in such activities, as always, depends on the country conditions and the political commitment of governments to comply with international standards and cooperate with international agencies.

With regard to the promotion of human rights principles as part of its policies, operations, and related activities, in 1997 UNHCR adopted a policy paper on human rights. The paper constitutes the first time the Office addressed the interrelationship of human rights and refugee protection in a comprehensive manner. The paper states that in UNHCR's "goals, aims and objectives" the Office "must comply with international human rights standards." It notes that "not only must UNHCR staff be careful not to compromise fundamental protection principles and norms, but they must make program goals compatible with international human rights standards." Finally, UNHCR "must also try to enhance the observance of these [human rights] standards by [its] government and NGO partners."[36] In sum, the paper outlines how to incorporate human rights standards, information, and mechanisms in UNHCR's protection activities.[37]

Some commentators have suggested that this policy statement was long overdue and the absence for so many years of a specific directive on what is an obvious linkage between refugee and human rights protection reflected the ambivalence of UNHCR on human rights issues. Whatever the explanation, UNHCR has taken more determined steps to formalize a human rights approach on behalf of its particular group of beneficiaries. This is clearly an area in which the doctrine and practice of the Office should continue to mature.

International Legal Obligations

The idea of developing a system of human rights protection is not new. Indeed, many states have been established on the basis that individuals have certain inherent rights which must be respected by those governing.[38] The idea of establishing a system of human rights law at the international level is a more recent development and has taken shape through the United Nations itself. The UN Charter proclaims as one of the purposes and principles of the UN "promoting and encouraging respect for human rights and for fundamental freedoms for all without distinction as to race, sex, language or religion." Moreover, member states of the UN pledge themselves to take action in cooperation with the UN, and by consequence specific UN agencies, to achieve this purpose.[39]

Since the adoption of the UN Charter in 1945, the 1948 Universal Declaration of Human Rights and the Refugee Convention in 1951, a number of other international human rights treaties have been enacted, some which have been mentioned, for example the ICCPR and the ICESCR. In 1965, the UN adopted the Convention on the Elimination of Racial Discrimination (CERD); in 1979 the Convention on the Elimination of Discrimination Against Women (CEDAW); in 1984 the Convention against Torture and Other Cruel, Inhuman or Degrading Treatment or Punishment (CAT); and in 1989 the Convention on the Rights of the Child (CRC). In addition to the central foundational status of the Universal Declaration of Human Rights, more than 190 states have ratified or adhered to at least one (or in the majority of cases more) of the six principal human rights treaties, thus creating multilateral binding legal obligations of a continuing nature.[40]

These treaties have progressively developed the formation of international human rights standards as they employ precise and inclusive language.[41] Moreover, these treaties establish supervisory mechanisms that can adopt authoritative interpretations of the treaty provisions in addition to dealing with issues of state compliance and individual complaints. The scope and meaning of specific human rights obligations have also been developed by the UN treaty bodies, in particular the Human Rights Committee in its general comments[42] and during examination of state party reports.[43]

UN Human Rights Mechanisms and the Protection of Refugees

The development of jurisprudence coming out of the UN human rights mechanisms is encouraging and it provides a well-articulated legal foundation supportive of advocacy efforts on behalf of refugees. An NGO publication posed the following question: How can UN human rights mechanisms be used to enhance refugee protection?[44] Any response to this question will depend on a number of factors including the rights at stake and the mandate and effectiveness of a particular body. An added difficulty in making the international human rights system fully functional is that the UN machinery is complex and at times confusing. To make matters worse, although it would be wholly desirable that members of UN human rights bodies should act in an individual and independent capacity, the experience, competence, and objectivity of some members varies greatly. It must also be said that some UN human rights bodies are excessively politicised. An example is the Commission on Human Rights, which is the main UN forum dealing with human rights issues. The more than fifty members of the Commission are normally represented by government officials of UN member states; however, some states engage independent experts or academic advisors to attend as part of the national delegation. As a consequence of the general set-up of the commission a political bias is often reflected in the agenda, debates, and issues that are raised, or fail to be raised, at its annual sessions.

Although the main activities of the Commission on Human Rights have been in the areas of standard-setting and investigating violations of human rights relating to particular themes (for example, torture, detention, disappearances, violence against women) or individual countries,[45] it can propose that particular studies be undertaken and it can make recommendations and propose drafts of future international human rights instruments. The commission also has authority to recommend the establishment of specific procedures in the form of working groups and country and thematic rapporteurs. The commission has never given specific attention to the protection of refugees, and it has rarely considered cases of individuals whose human rights have been violated. It is equally uncommon for individual cases to be mentioned in a commission resolution. As part of its politicised make-up, an additional reason for the commission's failure to focus on refugee issues is that many states are understandably reluctant to allow any discussion by a prominent UN human rights body of their asylum policies. The fact that refugees are the responsibility of a specific UN agency also tends to keep refugee issues apart from the UN human rights program.

A function of the commission that serves to enhance refugee protection is its ability to highlight instances of human rights violations in various reports prepared by country and thematic rapporteurs and working groups. Not only does the information contained in commission reports bring to light or provide updates on the effects of human rights violations and the impact on displacement of individuals, but this information can help identify the causes of refugee flows and in some instances the scope and nature of the displacement problem. As a result of the presence at the commission of a number of governmental and non-governmental bodies and the media, this too can serve to notify the international community of particular problems as well as put pressure on an offending state to remedy a situation.

Attention to humanitarian crises publicized through the commission can also assist in soliciting support and resources for the work of humanitarian agencies involved in operational responses. Despite the mixed track record of the commission in addressing refugee issues, since the late-1980s UNHCR has taken a close interest in its work and the High Commissioner has addressed the Commission on Human Rights every year since 1992. In fact, the address to the commission is considered a major statement for the Office.

The Sub-Commission on Human Rights

The sub-commission is a subsidiary body of the Commission on Human Rights and is comprised of twenty-six members who are elected by the commission to serve in their individual capacities. The sub-commission generally operates in a politically less-charged atmosphere than the commission. Government representatives, NGOs, and international organizations are permitted to attend the sub-commission's annual four week session in Geneva as observers. The sub-commission's principal activity is to initiate studies on human rights questions that commonly lead to the development of new international standards. Similar to the commission, it can take up human rights issues in particular countries.

The sub-commission has no specific agenda item dealing with refugee protection issues. However, a number of country-specific resolutions of the sub-commission have made reference to specific violations of human rights of refugees. As an example, in a resolution on the situation of human rights in the Islamic Republic of Iran the sub-commission called upon the Iranian government to investigate the human rights violations in the country and stop violating the rights of Iranian refugees abroad.[46] The sub-commission also took account of the plight of Bhutanese refugees in Nepal and India and called for negotiations "in good faith" between Bhutan and Nepal to resolve this long-standing refugee problem. One would not normally expect such specificity being highlighted in resolutions coming out of the Commission on Human Rights.

The Work of the Treaty Bodies

The principal UN human rights conventions establish committees or treaty bodies to oversee and supervise the implementation of the provisions of a particular treaty. The authority of these treaty bodies varies depending on the convention, but in general they have two main functions: to examine periodic reports submitted by states parties which indicate the steps taken to implement the provisions of the convention; and receive and decide on petitions from individuals or states concerning specific violations of the treaty rights. In addition to these principal functions the work of the treaty bodies serves to publicize findings of human rights violations. During examination of state party reports government representatives may be called upon to explain why there are shortcomings in complying with international human rights standards and they are encouraged to remedy specific problems. The "observations and recommendations" prepared by the committees, as well as decisions on individual complaints, form an important source of country of origin information and international human rights jurisprudence.

Each of the treaty bodies has adopted "rules of procedure," apart from the specific procedural requirements contained in the relevant convention. These rules govern such matters as the form and content of state party reports, procedures for examination of state party reports, procedures for submitting individual or inter-state complaints, election of members of the committee, and establishment of pre-sessional working group meetings. Currently only the Human Rights Committee, the Committee against Torture, the Committee on the Elimination of Racial Discrimination and the Committee on the Elimination of Discrimination against Women have established procedures for considering individual complaints. The Committee on Economic, Social and Cultural Rights is in the process of developing a draft optional protocol which will provide for the establishment of procedures to permit receipt of individual petitions. States that ratify the optional protocol under the CEDAW recognize the competence of the committee to consider petitions from individual women or groups of women who claim their rights under the treaty have been violated. It also permits the committee to conduct inquiries into grave or systematic violations of the women's rights under the Convention. Some committees, such as those under the CAT and CRC, have also been involved in fact-finding missions.[47]

Individual complaints procedures available under some human rights conventions may be used as a legal remedy for refugees. In order to submit a complaint, the applicant (who must be the victim him or herself or someone with appropriate *locus standi*) must satisfy that he or she has exhausted all available domestic legal remedies and the matter is not being dealt with by another international procedure. However, individual complaints procedures are only available in respect of those states parties which have recognised the competence of a committee to deal with such petitions. Not surprisingly a large number of states have not recognised the competence of the respective treaty bodies to deal with such communications.[48]

In addition to the procedure to receive and decide upon individual petitions some international human rights treaties provide for an inter-state complaint procedure that permits states parties to lodge a complaint against another state party. In order to initiate an inter-state complaint it is necessary that both states recognize the competence of the committee to deal with such matters. Due to the sensitive nature of the inter-state complaints procedures they have never been engaged and are unlikely to be used in the future.

UNHCR has increasingly supported the work of the treaty bodies. UNHCR's involvement with these bodies has been to share information concerning refugee protection issues and follow and report on committee sessions during examination of state party reports. The concluding observations and recommendations of the committees, as well as published summaries of discussions and other reports, are used by UNHCR and in some instances complement strategies for discussing refugee protection issues with governments. Some committees, especially the Committee against Torture,[49] have developed extensive jurisprudence in cases involving asylum seekers which has proven helpful for expanding the scope of protection to refugees and other persons of concern to UNHCR.[50]

There are several advantages in using human rights law to highlight and reinforce refugee protection. One, the scope and application of many international human rights norms are broader and in some cases provide better sources of law on which to hold states accountable for specific violations. Two, many of the provisions of international human rights law are reflected in domestic constitutional provisions. Although some states require enacting legislation in order to formally adopt international treaty obligations, international human rights standards may inform the interpretation of human rights granted in national law. Three, the fact that many renowned legal experts are members of the UN-based treaty bodies is helpful in terms of garnering respect for their pronouncements, legal interpretations, and decisions. The wide geographical representation of the membership on the treaty bodies is also beneficial in bringing comparative expertise to their work. Four, despite limitations of financial resources, the treaty bodies have considerable success in securing legal, media, and other attention to their "conclusions and observations" as well as decisions in individual cases. Decisions arising out of individual complaints are especially important as they are legally binding on the concerned state party and they set precedents for other states parties. Five, the treaty bodies have been consistent in maintaining pressure on governments to remedy particular problems before they reappear before the same committee.

A final difference and strength of the work of the human rights treaty bodies is that they have broader mandates than UNHCR in respect of the scope of legal enquiry they can undertake. Although a few states have expressed dissatisfaction with the work and conclusions of some treaty bodies, and in some exceptional cases have denied access to Committee members to conduct field investigations[51] or have failed to comply with their decisions,[52] unlike UNHCR these bodies do not have to constantly tread the fine (and at times shifting) line between being diplomatic, pragmatic, and principled. Moreover, they are not financially reliant on the generosity of a handful of states, in a direct sense, as is UNHCR. As a result the work of these human rights bodies generally benefits from a greater degree of independence. Despite distinctions, differences, and advantages of both systems of law, a reasonable conclusion is that international refugee and human rights law needs to be seen as mutually reinforcing, not only in an interpretative sense, but in order to broaden and strengthen opportunities for enforcement.

Developments in International Criminal Law

Recent developments in international criminal law, such as the establishment and operation of the International Criminal Tribunals for the Former Yugoslavia (ICTY)[53] and Rwanda (ICTR)[54] and the adoption of the Rome Statute that created an International Criminal Court (ICC) in July 1998,[55] which is built on the historic work of the Nuremberg Trials, in addition to the developments that arose out of the arrest of Augusto Pinochet, have expanded the possibilities for holding individuals criminally responsible for serious violations of human rights. In the refugee context the work of the current international criminal tribunals, and eventually the ICC, is important as it can deter other violators. Furthermore, it is supportive of the reestablishment of the rule of law and it can help promote social reconciliation and the sense of confidence and rehabilitation required to give refugees reasons to choose to voluntarily return home.

The fact that renewed interest by the international community in this area of international law, in particular as regards universal jurisdiction and the absence of immunity for crimes against humanity, arose as a result of Pinochet's arrest and subsequent legal proceedings in the UK,[56] is bitterly ironic when one considers how his reign in Chile resulted in so many victims of human rights violations including thousands of persons who were forced to seek asylum. The Pinochet precedent has breathed a new urgency into the work of the international criminal tribunals, human rights organizations, and legal activists in an effort to bring other violators to justice. This has had a correlary effect in terms of pressuring national governments[57] to outlaw international crimes and bring criminal prosecutions against their own or other country's nationals who are alleged to have committed crimes against humanity[58] and war crimes.[59]

UNHCR has been a strong supporter of the establishment and work of the international criminal tribunals. As highlighted in its comments on the draft ICC statute, the Office drew on its own experiences in the former Yugoslavia and the African great lakes region to demonstrate that "criminal justice has an important part to play in reconciliation and peace-building." As an agency working in often risky field situations UNHCR's staff can "become witness to such crimes thereby exposing themselves to serious risk of reprisals."[60] The Office has accordingly sought the cooperation of the ICTY and ICTR, as well as the future ICC, to be sensitive to these concerns and provide "adequately for witness protection, non-disclosure, and inviolability of UN records." UNHCR has stated its commitment "to cooperate as much as possible with any future (international criminal) court in sharing information that may help to bring the perpetrators of such crimes to justice, as we have done with the existing Tribunals for the former Yugoslavia and Rwanda".[61]

As a result of UNHCR's extensive contact with refugees in the field, the work of the ICTY and ICTR and the related criminal standards they employ are also relevant to the application of the exclusion clauses under Article 1F of the 1951 Refugee Convention. As noted in UNHCR's comments on the draft ICC statute, the definition of crimes contained in the international refugee law instruments, to wit, a "crime against peace," "war crime" and "crime against humanity" is not restricted to those found in international instruments existing at the time of the creation of the 1951 Refugee Convention. The statutes of the ICTY and ICTR have provided guidance on the additional crimes which can be included within the scope of the exclusion clause. The court's criteria and decision to indict an individual also provides guidance to UNHCR for evaluating the "threshold for exclusion." In this context UNHCR has excluded asylum seekers from refugee status based on their indictment by the ICTR.[62]

Unlike the law of individual criminal responsibility that has been codified and operationalized in the form of international tribunals and related developments in domestic criminal law, an area of international criminal law that remains underdeveloped is that of state responsibility. Chaloka Beyani has suggested that a considerable difficulty arises in that "the law of state responsibility is not yet fully developed and is thus uncertain, despite ambitious attempts at codification," although as Beyani rightly notes, there is "a growing spectrum of respectable views on the subject of state responsibility and forced population displacement."[63] Article 25(4) of the ICC Statute specifically provides that "no provision in this Statute relating to individual criminal responsibility shall affect the responsibility of states under international law." Although several commentators have called for the ICC and the ICTR to have jurisdiction over states, the consensus on such an approach has not matured that far. It is noteworthy that international organizations, including UNHCR, have not expressed an opinion on the particular issue of state responsibility, notwithstanding that the concept of "state agents" is firmly grounded in international refugee law. As suggested by Jorgensen:

> An international criminal court would be the ideal venue for determining the responsibility of states accused of crimes, and would be the most effective way to achieve the desired connection between the substantive issues of the concept of state criminality and its procedural and institutional aspects. However, it remains to be seen to what extent states would be willing to commit themselves to this idea by signing a convention to

establish such a court and accepting its compulsory jurisdiction. For the time being it is conceivable that the International Court of Justice and other international tribunals will consider awarding punitive damages against states in appropriate circumstances, and perhaps once an international criminal court with jurisdiction over individuals has been up and running for some time, its jurisdiction could be extended to include states.[64]

Whether future developments in this area of international law will move in the direction of adopting the codification of criminal responsibility of states and thereby grant jurisdiction to deal with state crimes to an international court remains an open question. There are considerable obstacles to seeking further development and consensus of opinion in this area of international law. Not the least of these obstacles is the desire of many states, especially powerful states, to maintain an impenetrable shroud around concepts and practices relating to state sovereignty, national security, and how they conduct matters of foreign policy. At the end of the day, power politics may well remain the ultimate limiting factor.[65]

Reparation and Compensation

Article 75 of the ICC Statute recognizes the need to establish principles relating to reparations to victims including "restitution, compensation and rehabilitation." This provision further suggests that the Court may, on its own initiative or upon request, "determine the scope and extent of any damage, loss and injury to, or in respect of, victims and will state the principles on which it is acting." Reparations granted by the ICC may be made through the trust fund to be established under Article 79 of the ICC statute. Finally, Article 75(5) notes that "a state party shall give effect to a decision" by the Court in this regard, and sub-paragraph (6) notes that "Nothing in this article shall be interpreted as prejudicing the rights of victims under national or international law." These provisions of the ICC statute codify the possibility of victims of international crimes to seek redress and compensation from the Court. Outstanding questions of interpretation include whether the Court could choose to compensate victims ex post facto in the event that they fail to come forward, or are otherwise not identified during the course of criminal proceedings.

Apart from the ICC statute, there is a significant body of jurisprudence based on international civil liability and other international law which provides reparations and damages for injury to aliens and others as a result of losses due to wrongful acts by states.[66] In the refugee context there are a handful of historical examples of UNHCR administering indemnification funds to refugees who were victims of the German national socialist regime as well as to British citizens of Asian origin who were expelled from Uganda.[67] More recently, despite ongoing efforts by the Commission on Human Rights to develop the right to restitution, compensation, and rehabilitation for victims of gross violations of human rights and fundamental freedoms,[68] as well as sporadic development of regional principles,[69] there has been limited discussion in international fora, within UNHCR[70] or the academic community as to whether developing a universal scheme to provide reparation or compensation to refugees is desirable. In this context, although it is a distinct concept, the obligations of asylum states under international refugee law require that refugees be granted a wide range of rights that may result in considerable socio-economic and rehabilitative benefit to an individual.

The lack of initiative and interest on developing international standards for compensation and other restitution arrangements specifically for refugees may be partially explained by the issue being considered politically unfavorable and practically unattainable. Even if such a compensation scheme were in place, with the large number of refugees originating from developing countries being obliged to seek asylum in other developing countries it is doubtful whether individual refugees would be in a position to collect on the damages or other compensation from the state of origin.[71] The politically disadvantaged position of many of today's refugees is yet another factor in explaining the absence of political will to address this issue.

Conclusion

There is an emerging convergence between international human rights law, refugee law, and criminal and humanitarian law. The rapid developments that are underway in international human rights and criminal law complement the system of refugee protection. At a time when refugee law is under attack and its very foundations are being questioned, one must rely on other binding human rights norms and enforcement mechanisms to bolster the system of refugee protection.

The advantages of this convergence of international law and the use of complementary legal norms and mechanisms that may benefit refugee protection have been broadly surveyed in this essay. The perceived disadvantages, on the other hand, are that the specificity and strength of refugee law may be diminished if there is an overreliance on the human rights regime. Some academic commentators have argued that international refugee law can and should stand on its own as there is a downside in following an overly inclusive approach. Despite such reservations, when refugee law fails to provide protection to persons in need, the nonderogable legal standards found in international human rights instruments must be engaged. The language of human rights also provides a renewed strength to refugee discourse. To this end, the distinct advantages of embracing the international human rights regime in order to strengthen the system of refugee protection are worth pursuing.

The challenge of today, especially in Northern countries, is to ensure a strong commitment to basic principles of refugee protection that includes access to territory and the grant of asylum to deserving individuals. Where refugee law is not adequately applied, human rights principles can help in ensuring that minimum standards of treatment are met.

UNHCR must also ensure that it abides by existing and developing international legal standards. Although the Office has committed itself to using international human rights principles and practices as part of its policies and programs, it has been suggested that UNHCR "still remains largely unaccountable for the violation of its mandate." Brownlie and other commentators have rightly noted that a "correlative of international institutions possessing legal personality and rights (to offer humanitarian assistance, to advance claims, etc.) is responsibility in international law." Given the growing importance and role of international institutions it is "imperative that they be accountable for their actions."[72] Just as UNHCR must remain committed to the protection principles enshrined in international refugee law, so too should it respect and promote complementary principles and mechanisms in other fields of international law.

6
A Rare Opening in the Wall
The Growing Recognition of Gender-Based Persecution

EMILY COPELAND

The last two decades have been hard on persons seeking asylum in the industrialized world. Many states have turned toward utilizing increasingly restrictive interpretations of a "refugee" as defined in the 1951 UN Convention and 1967 Protocol. Moreover, states have streamlined their asylum processes and added new barriers that asylum seekers must overcome in order to just gain access to the system. One visible contradiction to this pattern of exclusion has been the growing acceptance of gender-based persecution as legitimate grounds for making an asylum claim. This apparent liberalization in the midst of rampant restrictionism raises some interesting questions: Are states accepting an expansion of the refugee definition? And, if so, why now? Have these developments improved the protection afforded to refugee women? How should advocates proceed in an effort to expand and deepen these measures to both improve protection and encompass more states?

In this chapter, I argue that international and state actions to date do represent a significant change in understanding the nature and scope of gender-based persecution and recognizing its existence. However, it would be premature to regard these developments as signifying a general acceptance for the expansion of the international definition of a refugee. Instead, the steps taken have primarily sought to clarify the meaning of the "social group" category cited in the 1951 UN refugee definition. For example, several states have recognized that the social group category can include cases in which women may have a well-founded fear of persecution based on their gender. They have also issued rulings or guidelines to help adjudicators make asylum determinations in cases concerning gender-based persecution. However, most have stopped short of advocating the use of "gender" as a sixth ground on which to base an asylum claim.

With regard to determining how advocates should proceed from here, it is useful to examine first the evolution of support for gender-based asylum claims in terms of the normative, social, and political forces supporting this process and then to compare this process with two historical attempts to expand formally first the scope and then the nature of international protection for refugees. As this chapter seeks to demonstrate, it is imperative that the support for expanding the definition of refugee in terms of gender-based persecution not be overestimated.

In order to make this case, I will first provide some general background on the efforts to improve protection to asylum seekers with gender-based claims. Then, I discuss the emergence of the issue of refugee women on the international agenda with a focus on the underlying forces that helped place it there. Next, I present two historical cases relating to the expansion of the refugee regime: first, the creation and acceptance of the 1967 Protocol and second, the failure of the 1977 Conference on Territorial Asylum. Finally, I offer some concluding remarks about what these cases might imply for the situation of today's refugees.

Gender-Based Persecution and International Protection

According to the 1951 UN Convention, a person is a refugee if:

> As a result of events occurring before 1 January 1951 and owing to a well-founded fear of being persecuted for reasons of race, religion, nationality, membership of a particular social group or political opinion, is outside the country of his nationality and is unable or, owing to such fear, is unwilling to avail himself of the protection of that country; or who, not having a nationality and being outside the country of his former habitual residence as a result of such events, is unable or, owing to such fear, is unwilling to return to it.[1]

Gender, as well as other potential grounds for persecution such as sexual orientation, is not expressly included as grounds for establishing a well-founded fear of persecution. Traditionally, claims based on gender were seen to have fallen within the category of "social group." Many legal commentators refer to the concept of social group as the "catch-all" category and the least well defined of the five grounds on which one can base a claim for asylum. Its origin in the 1951 UN Convention is the result of the Swedish delegate's proposal that the term "social group" be added to the definition since "experience had shown that certain refugees had been persecuted because they belonged to particular social groups."[2] It was accepted without much commentary or debate.

That gender issues were not at the forefront of decision makers concerns in the late 1940s and early 1950s should come as no surprise. Refugees, as a group, were fairly undifferentiated in terms of their social categories. Women clearly could be recognized as refugees in their own right in terms of racial, ethnic, or political persecution, and it was common knowledge for years that refugee women were targets for rape, abduction, and sexual exploitation. Still, until the late 1980s, the dominant approach was to label them as a "vulnerable group" along with the young, the elderly, and the infirm. Refugee women's claims were often viewed as "derivative"; that is they were perceived (not always inaccurately) as the spouses or close family members who were accompanying the "real" (i.e., male) refugee. In status determination hearings, for example, often only the head-of-household's case was examined, and a positive or negative decision on that case applied to all members of the household.

Gender-related persecution claims that were put forward under the "social group" category faced tremendous barriers. Gender alone was not recognized by states as being sufficient to constitute a social group. Instead, the asylum seeker had to show that gender, in combination with other characteristics, constituted a particular social group. Moreover, until recently, rape in the midst of conflict was viewed only as a criminal or private act and was not recognized as persecution or a political act. So too were the many human rights violations faced primarily by women that make up the bulk of gender-based persecution claims. Some of the more common forms of gender-based persecution include female genital mutilation (FGM), rape, sexual violence, physical violence, forced sterilization, oppressive morality codes, forced marriage, institutionalized gender discrimination, and prostitution. With the exception of FGM, these abuses can also affect men, but they are seen to affect women to a far greater degree.

Since the mid-1980s the needs and protection concerns of refugee women have been "discovered" by the international community, UNHCR, nongovernmental organizations (NGOs), and host countries.[3] During the UN Decade for Women (1975–1985), refugee women's issues were put on the international and UNHCR's agendas by a mobilized network consisting of government, NGO, and UN officials. Until 1985, the protection of refugee women did not even appear on the agenda of the Executive Committee of the UNHCR. Since 1988, however, protection concerns common to refugee women such as access to assistance, discrimination, safety, and sexual exploitation have been regularly discussed at the meetings of the Executive Committee of the UNHCR and the subject of several of its resolutions. In 1990, UNHCR issued a policy on refugee women that was followed in 1991 by a set of guidelines for UNHCR staff on "Improving the Protection of Refugee Women." While these guidelines focused mainly on the situation of refugee women in camps, they did address some issues of gender-related persecution and the asylum process as it affects women. Protection concerns regarding aspects of sexual violence against refugee women were raised in Conclusion No. 73 in 1993 and resulted in a new set of guidelines concerning sexual violence against refugee women. ExCom Conclusion No. 73 recommended the establishment of training programs to ensure that asylum adjudicators be sensitized to issues of gender and culture and noted that women who have been victims of sexual violence should be treated with particular sensitivity.

Specifically with regard to the concept of gender-based persecution, in Conclusion No. 39 the Executive Committee of the UNHCR noted that states could recognize women as constituting a particular social group as envisioned under the 1951 Convention when they faced harsh treatment due to having transgressed the social mores of the society in which they live. Individual states have moved forward to clarify their policy and provide guidance to the adjudicators in the area of gender-based claims.

Canada broke new ground in March 1993 by issuing formal "Guidelines on Women Refugee Claimants Fearing Gender-Related Persecution." While these guidelines are nonbinding, it was the first time that any state had instructed asylum adjudicators that women who fear persecution based on their gender can be recognized as refugees. The Canadian guidelines have served as a model for other states, and they were recently updated in 1996. Still, Canada was reluctant to use the general category of "women" as forming a social group; thus it is not all women, rather "women who fear persecution on the basis of their gender" who are included.

The United States followed suit in May 1995 with a memorandum to all U.S. asylum officers. Again, it does not introduce gender as a specific category; instead it basically instructs officers to be more sensitive to the plight of women and the difficulties they may face in putting forth their claims. Australia issued its own guidelines in July 1996. The Australian guidelines note that gender can influence the type of persecution or harm suffered by the refugee. Again, the guidelines do not advocate gender to be used as an additional ground for persecution in the 1951 Refugee Convention. A handful of additional states including New Zealand, South Africa (1999), and the United Kingdom (2000) have issued formal guidelines. The United Kingdom does not recognize a new category of persecution, but it did stress the inequality in the asylum procedures between men and women.[4]

What have these countries actually done on behalf of gender-related persecution claims? First, they have begun to recognize that there are cases where women, in conjunction with other characteristics, can have a well-founded fear of persecution based on their gender. Second, there is acceptance that these cases do meet the requirements of the "social group" category. Third, government officials are also becoming educated as to the ways in which gender inequality in the asylum process, in assistance and protection, and in societies in general can have serious consequences for women. This is an important shift; however, as academic and legal commentary has shown, the changes in attitudes and understanding are not reflected evenly in practice and still present many practical problems for women seeking refuge.[5]

Still, how can these changes in state policy be explained? Are states responding to international pressures, domestic interests, intellectual debates, or the development of new norms? In order to answer this question, I suggest we need to examine two separate but linked developments. First, there is the matter of how the "issue" of refugee women came to be placed on the international agenda and regarded as a topic of legitimate concern both within UNHCR and within states.[6] Second, there is the evolution of thinking on women's rights as they relate to the body of established international human rights laws.

The Emergence of Refugee Women's Issues

What brought refugee women's issues to the fore in the late 1970s was not a sudden shift in the demographic makeup of the refugee populations or, put differently, the emergence of a "new" problem. Rather, refugee women's specific needs and concerns had just never been systematically noticed by the powers that be. As UNHCR's former senior coordinator for refugee women, Ann Howarth-Wiles commented, "(w)omen were never deliberately marginalized, but our information came from the leaders of refugee committees that were exclusively male. Many aspects of daily life escaped us, such as a women's need for wood as fuel, or for cooking."[7] Elizabeth Ferris, a long-time NGO advocate for refugee women, has written: "Those in the positions of responsibility often do not *see* the problems or the resources of refugee women."[8] What was first required of UNHCR, as well as NGOs and states, to address the problems of refugee women was a shift of consciousness.

An important catalyst for shifting the consciousness was the UN Decade for Women (1976–1985). It created a supportive external environment for activities focusing on women. It provided a starting point and a focus for activity among NGOs, within states, and the within the UN system. As Elisabeth Prugl and Mary Meyer note, it created new bureaucratic and political spaces in which women's concerns on a wide range of issues could be placed squarely on the international agenda.[9] In some cases, events occurring as part of the UN Decade for Women generated concrete demands for UNHCR to respond to a broader set of UN-sponsored initiatives on women.

Mobilizing around the timeframe and events set by the UN Decade for Women was a transnational network composed of NGO, UNHCR, and state officials who took an interest in the issue of refugee women. They worked to generate "new" information on the needs and protection issues facing refugee women and to educate actors on the nature and extent of these concerns. These efforts extended beyond the end of the UN Decade for Women and really started to bear results in the early 1990s with the development of UNHCR policies and guidelines on refugee women.

A third and critical factor in sustaining pressure on UNHCR was the action of first Canada and then the United States. Within UNHCR's Executive Committee in the late 1980s, Canada consistently pressed the topic and called for change. According to Gene Dewey, then UNHCR's second highest ranking official, while there was a great deal of NGO pressure and support for the topic of refugee women, it was the incessant prodding of the Canadian Government that spurred many of the activities within UNHCR.[10] "At every meeting of the Executive Committee or in informal discussions, the Canadians would ask what are you [UNHCR] doing on the refugee women's issue and then would press us [UNHCR] to do more. The U.S. government also supported the issue, but the lead was taken by the Canadians."[11] Moreover, Canada supported its call for reform with funding for UNHCR earmarked for that purpose. Combined, these three forces created an "external push" that was then used by sympathetic insiders to propel policy change within the organization.

Supporting each of these events in turn are societal changes. The movers and shakers behind the UN Decade for Women were mainly women working on women's issues. For several decades, women had been breaking down barriers in their own societies, in the workplace, courts, academia, and so on. As a result, by the 1980s, there were now women in mid- to senior-level positions working within NGOs, governments, universities, international organizations, and so on. It was mainly women who led the charge to address refugee women's issues within UNHCR.

Yet, how can one explain Canada's pursuit of refugee women's concerns within UNHCR? In response to the question, "Why did Canada select the issue of refugee women as one of its key policy interests within UNHCR?" Michael Malloy, Canada's then representative to ExCom, remarked that at the time pushing women's issues in Canada and in development work overseas was an important focus for the Canadian government. Thus, taking on refugee women's issues at UNHCR fit within the Canadian government's existing focus. He explained the Canadian government's general policy orientation as the result of domestic factors at play within Canada. There was domestic pressure to focus on women's issues and support for this effort within the Canadian NGO community.[12]

Thus one can speculate that credit is, in part, due to domestic factors that are themselves partly shaped by long-term social movements. In time, the push for women's rights within Canada and the United States, for example, changed these societies in important ways. The rise of feminism, gradual societal acceptance for new roles for women, equality in the workplace, and public identities other than wives and mothers helped to prepare the domestic groundwork to push for changes at the international level.

Evolution of Thinking in Human Rights Law

Over the past two decades, critics have charged that existing human rights laws are biased with regards to women. With regards to women's issues, the 1979 CEDAW Convention on the Elimination of All Forms of Discrimination against Women is the most comprehensive human rights treaty. States are not only forbidden to undertake discriminatory actions but are also required to take affirmative steps to eliminate discriminatory treatment of women. However, the general critique is that human rights abuses that occur in the public sphere (such as torture) are condemned under international human rights law, but other issues such as rape or domestic abuse are relegated to the private sphere and thus are not protected under international agreements. The slogan "Women's Rights are Human Rights" attempted to focus attention on the types of human rights abuses affecting mainly women that were neglected under more general human rights instruments.

The evolution of the protection agenda illustrates the debates and developments within the human rights field. In 1993, the World Conference on Human Rights and the UN Declaration on the Elimination of Violence Against Women were enacted. Human rights scholars became increasingly aware that while "persecution on account of gender is now being recognized by human rights advocates, the ability to seek refuge from persecution on account of gender has failed to develop accordingly. While part of this lack of development reflects a more general failure within the human rights discourse to adequately reflect the persecution of women, it also in part results from archaic ideas of who a refugee is."[13]

Within the refugee advocacy community, there was recognition that the 1991 guidelines had neglected the issue of sexual violence. That recognition, combined with news coverage of rape campaigns in Bosnia, focused attention on issues of refugee protection and sexual violence. The *Kasinga* case in the United States was a watershed in raising awareness about female genital mutilation. Moreover, as the lawyer for Kassindja, Karen Musala has written, the case became a cause celebre just as Congress was debating the 1996 Illegal Immigration Reform and Immigrant Responsibility Act (IIRIRA). The publicity and the conditions of her detention generated a lot of public sympathy for Kassindja at a time when public opinion appeared to be strongly anti-immigrant.[14]

Thus, an interesting development is the strong convergence of the debates in the refugee protection field and in general human rights law over what constitutes gender-based persecution. Given the constraints in international refugee law, advocates are using human rights law and commentary in pursuing asylum claims for gender-based persecution. Human rights law, with its focus on the individual, offers a counterweight to state's emphasis on sovereign rights. These two approaches bring into focus the embedded tension regarding whether the needs of individual protection trump the concerns of states regarding control.

Nor are human rights analysts shy in suggesting ways in which the law ought to evolve. Part of states' resistance to adopting an unrestricted concept of "gender" as a social group is due to the fear that it would result in a "flood" of asylum claims from women. Receiving countries are less focused on providing adequate protection to all those in need than they are on ensuring their *control* over the "floods" of people claiming refugee status, particularly those asylum seekers who appear at the borders. From the advocate's perspective, the prioritization of control over protection is hard to justify. It is difficult to estimate the actual, much less the potential, number of asylum seekers who invoke gender as a basis for a well-founded fear. Stephen Knight at the Hastings

Center reports that "INS has been saying that there are about 1,000 gender cases annually at most," but Knight questions whether or not the INS really knows this with any certainty.[15] In Canada in 1994, 304 women applied under the new guidelines; of this number 195 were granted refugee status.[16] It could be that more time and better data are needed before it can be proven that allowing claims based on gender does not "overburden" states.

Given this situation, how should advocates proceed if they want to strengthen the protection provided for victims of gender-based persecution? One approach might argue for a continuation of advocacy activities to date, such as working on individual states to develop progressive approaches toward evaluating gender-based claims. Individual states could adopt domestic legislation recognizing gender as a basis for claiming persecution.[17] An alternative approach is one that argues that a new "protocol" is needed; one based along the model of the 1967 Protocol that would explicitly add "gender" to the definition of a refugee.[18] In evaluating the potential of success for each approach, I argue that two historical examples may be illuminating.

Expanding the Scope of International Protection: The Adoption of the 1967 Protocol

The only formal international expansion of the 1951 UN Convention to date has been the adoption of the 1967 Protocol. The 1967 Protocol was significant in that it not only removed the time and geographical limitations from the definition of a refugee, but it also committed states to apply the protections contained in the 1951 Convention.[19] The need for such a protocol had become apparent since the mid-1950s as it became more and more difficult for new, emerging refugee flows to trace their origins to "events occurring before 1 January 1951" as the 1951 Convention required. While such an extension was plausible in the case of the Hungarian exodus in 1956, it was not sustainable for the Algerian refugee flows in 1958. Thus, the UN General Assembly had to adopt an ad hoc solution and authorize UNHCR to use its "good offices" to aid the Algerian refugee flow.

UNHCR officials and others recognized that the Algerian refugee flow was only the tip of the iceberg. New large refugee populations were emerging from the struggles for national independence in many parts of the world. Approximately two-thirds of the members of the Organization of African Unity (OAU) won their independence during the 1960s. By the end of that decade, the decolonialization process had created over one million refugees in need of assistance and protection. One of the first initiatives of the OAU was to signal its intent to draft a convention covering refugee flows in Africa. Clearly, those states, organizations and individuals who wanted to protect and assist refugees through the auspices of the UNHCR faced new challenges.

In 1964, with funding from the Carnegie Endowment for International Peace and the Swiss government, UNHCR organized a colloquium on ways to resolve the growing discrepancy between refugee groups that were covered by the 1951 Convention and those included under the more universal definition found in UNHCR's statute. The increasing reliance on ad hoc mechanisms such as the use of UNHCR's "good offices" highlighted this gap in protection. The participants at the colloquium suggested creating a protocol to the 1951 Convention. They then proceeded to draft a text that included the removal of the time and geographical limitations found in the 1951 definition of a refugee. UNHCR next prepared a revised version of the draft protocol; this was circulated to governments and then considered by the Executive Committee in October 1965. By May 1966, nineteen generally favorable replies had been received and this number increased to thirty-two by October 1966. After six months of revision, the Protocol was opened for signature. Within seven months, fifty-two states had acceded to the instrument. Even the United States, which had chosen not to sign the 1951 Convention, ratified the Protocol in October 1968.

While the process appears to have been extremely smooth, the support for the expansion of international protection should not be taken as a given. During the drafting of the 1951 Convention, there were clear efforts made by the United States but also European states to restrict the scope of international protection agreed to in the 1951 Convention as well as the life of UNHCR. The 1951 Convention required almost three years to obtain the necessary number of signatures for it to enter into force. In contrast, the 1967 Protocol entered into force only six months after it was ratified. What were the forces supporting the creation and implementation of the 1967 Protocol? Given the United States' opposition in 1951 to creating a global refugee regime, it is worthwhile to focus on the factors that supported the change in U.S. policy.

The U.S. ratification of the 1967 Protocol was an easy and non-controversial process. In a lobbying campaign on behalf of the Protocol, more than eighty-six voluntary agencies expressed their support for ratification; this signaled to the Senate a sound basis of domestic support for the action. The State Department also lobbied in favor of ratification. The arguments brought in favor of ratification included:

1. The treaty articles did not conflict with U.S. laws and practices such as allowing for the freedom of movement within the country.[20]
2. The principal articles followed the line of the most favored treatment clauses commonly used in treaties of friendship and commerce such as the treaty of Friendship and Commerce and Navigation between the United States and the Federal Republic of Germany signed on October 19, 1954.
3. The treaty covered only protection and not material assistance.
4. The treaty did not commit the United States to enlarging its immigration measures for refugees.[21]

The then acting director of the Office for Refugee And Migration Affairs, Laurence Dawson, attributed U.S. acceptance of the 1967 Protocol to two factors: first, no new legislation was needed, and second there was the "overwhelming petition of the voluntary agencies . . . They were getting their constituents activated to petition Congress."[22] The more general conditions supporting the acceptance of the 1967 Protocol are discussed below.

The Failure of the 1977 Conference on Territorial Asylum to Codify an Individual's Right to Asylum

The story of the failure to codify an individual's right to asylum is complex one spanning over thirty years.[23] It is beyond the scope of this paper to retell it in exacting detail. In brief the story goes as follows.

The term "right to asylum" has traditionally referred to a state's right *to grant* asylum as one of its sovereign powers. In the immediate post–World War II period during the discussions on what would become the 1948 UN Declaration of Human Rights, the Human Rights Commission adopted as the original text of Article 14(1), "Everyone has the right to seek and *to be granted* asylum from persecution" (emphasis added).[24] The text was altered at the suggestion of the UK delegate to read ". . . to seek and to enjoy asylum . . ." This change was made in order to clarify that the individual does not have the right to be granted asylum.[25] While accepting the change, the Commission on Human Rights decided to examine the "right to asylum" issue at an early opportunity.

After adopting the 1948 Declaration, the Commission on Human Rights then sought to turn it into a legally binding treaty. The first draft text of the Covenant on Civil and Political Rights did not include a right to asylum. Several states and the then Director-General of the International Refugee Organization made proposals supporting the inclusion of a right to asylum in the draft covenant, but there was also much disagreement on the issue. According to Paul Weis, a former director of the Legal Division of UNHCR, the attempt to include a right to asylum in the 1966 Covenant on Civil and Political Rights failed due to the opposition of states who did not believe that the right to asylum constituted a basic right and the inability of Western and Socialist states to agree on the scope of the definition of who should be granted (as well as excluded from) the right to asylum.[26]

Supporters of the right of asylum then tried to create a nonbinding declaration in support of the right of asylum. In 1957, the French representative Rene Cassin submitted a draft "Declaration on the Right of Asylum." Again, however, no clear consensus existed. There was a sizable group of states that supported the creation of an obligation for states regarding the right of asylum for persecuted individuals. They included: Austria, Ceylon, Federal Republic of Germany, France, Haiti, Iran, Israel, Japan, Netherlands, Peru, Spain, Sweden, and Switzerland. Nineteen states had adopted such as policy in their municipal laws or aliens legislation.[27] A second group was willing to support a declaration setting out principles on the need to act in a humanitarian manner toward asylum seekers. A third group steadfastly maintained the asylum was not a right of individuals but rather a right of states.

When the "UN Declaration on Territorial Asylum" finally passed ten years later in 1967, it contained no right to asylum. To quote Paul Weis:

> Great pains were taken to make it clear that asylum was not a right of the individual but the right of States to grant asylum, first, by deleting the word 'right' from the title of the Declaration, and also by declaring in Article 1(1): Asylum granted by a States, *in the exercise of its sovereignty*...[28]

Once the Declaration on Territorial Asylum was approved, work then began to turn the declaration into a binding convention.[29] In 1971 the Carnegie Endowment, in consultation with the UNHCR, convened a "Colloquium on Territorial Asylum and the Protection of Refugees in International Law." As was the case with the 1967 Protocol, the group of experts prepared a set of articles for inclusion into a draft convention on territorial asylum. The draft went through the Executive Committee and then to the UN General Assembly. After two years of debate, the General Assembly established a group of experts on the Convention. In revising the convention, the group of experts restricted the benefits to asylum seekers in several ways and weakened the commitment of states regarding *non-refoulement*. However, it was felt that the revised draft convention represented a degree of consensus among states, so the General Assembly requested the Secretary-General to convene a conference of plenipotentiaries on territorial asylum in 1977.

UNHCR and many NGOs were very dissatisfied with the work of the group of experts. Thus, two additional efforts were made to create alternative texts for states. The NGOs drafted an alternate convention in 1976, and a Nansen Symposium was organized by a private committee under the honorary presidency of Ambassador Schnyder, the former UN High Commissioner, and the executive chairmanship of Professor Atle Grahl-Madsen. According to the participants of the Nansen Symposium, the purpose of the "progressive development of humanitarian law" was to create more favorable conditions for the refugees and asylum seekers. The symposium report states:

> It is better to have a good convention, which may not be ratified because it would impose too stringent obligations on Contracting States, than to have a weak Convention, which is not ratified, because it is felt that it does not represent any progressive development of international humanitarian law.[30]

In early 1977, the Conference on Territorial Asylum met to discuss the draft convention prepared by the group of experts; the meeting attracted ninety-two states. Five general coalitions formed, mainly along regional lines; four of these groups were not inclined toward establishing a right to asylum.[31] The strongest opposition came from Communist countries. In addition, large numbers of developing states in Africa and Asia were concerned with the ramifications of such a convention on countries faced with mass influxes. A third group, composed mainly of Arab states along with a few African ones, was concerned with national liberation movements. Primarily Western and Latin American states formed the fourth group, which was in favor of creating a quasi-right to asylum. And the fifth group consisted of only a few Western European states that advocated a strong obligation. Another complicating factor was the strong opposition expressed by a coalition of Eastern European, Asian, and Arab countries regarding the participation of NGOs. NGOs were ultimately not allowed to participate as observers with the possibility of submitting written and oral comments. During the course of the meeting, several retrograde steps concerning refugee protection were actually proposed. The drafting committee soon ceased its work as it became clear that very few of the articles would have managed to secure the necessary two-thirds majority support.

Thus, the effort to develop progressively international refugee law by creating a right to asylum failed dramatically in 1977. The group that drafted the original text was seeking to improve existing conditions in favor of the refugees. It if had passed in its original form it would have represented a substantial liberalization in the entry component of the refugee regime for a large number of states. More generally, states, aside from the few that had already established a quasi-right to asylum, were not amenable to expanding the protection. Perhaps, the originators of the effort did not envision that their efforts could possibly result in worse conditions being established. Yet, this was almost the case; the supportive states ended up having to fight a rear guard action just to maintain the existing standards. Atle Grahl-Madsen places the failure to establish a right to asylum on the insufficient preparation of the draft text that was sent to the United Nations. He also notes that:

> It was probably naïve to set the costly machinery of the United Nations in motion on such a weak basis. Perhaps we were blinded by the success of the Refugee Protocol, 1967. On the other hand, the United Nations was not the same in 1972 and in 1977. I think we have to admit that the climate has become much tougher and that it was not possible in 1972 to foresee all the difficulties, which would arise.[32]

Implications for Gender-Based Protection from Persecution

What do these two cases—the adoption of the 1967 Protocol and the failure of the 1977 Conference on Territorial Asylum—imply for the progressive development of international protection for asylum seekers with gender-based claims? Perhaps the discussion of the 1967 Protocol should provide grounds for optimism. Here there is a case where UNHCR, in cooperation with non-state actors and sympathetic governments, took the lead to create a narrowly drafted protocol with broad implications. By merely removing the time and geographical limitations, this opened up the possibility of protection for large numbers of people. So too, some commentators urge, would be the effect of adopting a narrow protocol that added gender as the sixth ground on which to base an asylum claim. One could envision progressive implementation; those states that were willing and able could immediately adopt the Protocol, while others could wait and would still be bound by the 1951/1967 treaties.

However, a closer analysis of the forces supporting the 1967 Protocol and the events undermining the 1977 Conference on Territorial Asylum provide some grounds for caution in pursuing this approach. The 1967 Protocol was not creating "new norms" it was merely expanding the application of existing ones to people who were not covered under the 1951 Convention. More generally, states had had sixteen years of experience with the obligations embedded in the 1951 Convention. The passing of time had also reassured states that the obligations were neither excessive nor unreasonable. One should recall that the primary reason for the time limitation (as well as the geographical limitation) in the 1951 Convention was to reassure states that the commitments embedded in the treaty were neither indefinite nor undefined. Many states had taken advantage of this limitation. By 1964, the geographic limitation had been invoked by no less than fifteen signatories not all of which were European states. By 1967, many of the earlier anxieties had proven groundless and the problems manageable. Moreover, since 1951 there had always been some basis of support for a universal approach. This is evidenced by the success of the United Kingdom's efforts to have the UNHCR's Statute include a universal definition of a refugee.

Thus when UNCHR took the initiative in the early 1960s to remove the time limit, most signatory states were generally supportive. Three interrelated problems were of concern to UNHCR and states. First, the majority of UN member states felt the new refugee flows should receive international attention, and these flows were emerging outside the context that was covered by the 1951 Convention. Thus, there was a pressing problem facing states that needed a response. Second, UNHCR was the agency best suited to become involved, but it was at a disadvantage in the new situations due to a lack of an applicable international agreement. Third, OAU states were moving to create their own agreement applicable to African refugee flows. This last aspect worried UNHCR and refugee advocates because it might introduce a different standard of protection and undermine UNHCR's claim to universality. UNHCR acted as the catalyst in order to suppress the emerging regional challenge to its role, help address the problems raised by new refugee populations, and ensure the universality of the refugee regime. It was able to do so based on the exiting support of governments and the absence of a veto from strong states.

In contrast, the efforts supporting the draft Convention on Territorial Asylum were an explicit attempt to expand progressively the nature of protection provided to refugees. While the "right to asylum" was not a new norm per se, it was not a widely established one. Only those states that already recognized a right to asylum strongly supported the effort to create an international right to asylum. Most states felt that this norm had important, mainly negative, implications for their exercise of sovereignty. Moreover, some states, particularly those in the developing world that were facing massive refugee flows, worried that the development of this norm could add significantly to their burdens.

The time periods and domestic/international environments in which the ratification of the 1967 Protocol occurred were different than the atmosphere faced by supporters in the late 1970s (and one could argue today as well). The immediate post–World War II period was conducive to the recognition of human rights and the creation of human rights norms. The mid-1960s was a positive period for refugee protection. For example, the success of the civil rights movement in the United States also undermined exclusionary attitudes based on race in immigration and refugee laws. The process of decolonialization generated new states that wished to be included in the refugee regime and a desire of existing states to assist them. Since most of the major refugee flows in the 1960s were taking place in the developing world, it was easier for industrialized states to be generous. Thus, the cost of supporting the 1967 Protocol seemed minimal. Finally, there was no major opposition to the 1967 Protocol from influential states. Together, these factors created a favorable environment for non-state actors and concerned governments to push the agenda of refugee protection.

This was less true in the 1970s. In the 1970s, the supporters did not perhaps adequately assess the international environment when pushing for consideration of the new convention. Supporters saw the need to create the convention in light of the gaps of protection but did not focus on trying to understand the forces that supported continuing or even expanding the limits to protection.

Today, unfortunately, I would argue that the international environment facing refugee advocates is not conducive and is even hostile regarding a new, narrowly drafted protocol that would adopt "gender" as a sixth category. To be sure, there is the growing understanding of gender-based persecution and increasing acceptance of the idea that one's gender could be the basis for persecution. Thus, we find some general consensus in the conclusions of the Executive Committee of the UNHCR. More importantly, we have steps taken by individual states to improve protection for gender-based persecution claims. However, the main actions of states to date have been to clarify of how gender-based persecution fits into the preexisting social group category. Thus, commentary on gender-based persecution by practitioners and academics has served to educate government officials on the nature and forms of gender-based persecution and to explain how gender ought to be taken seriously as the basis of a claim for asylum. In an important sense, the effort has not been one of new norm creation but rather one of reinterpretation of existing norms. This has made it easier for states to adapt existing policies to take a new understanding of gender-based persecution in to account.

Support for these new practices as well as our understanding of gender-based persecution has been aided by a convergence of attention paid to women's human rights issues, protection of refugee women, and a rise in feminist scholarship. These have combined in the creation of transnational networks, information sharing, and institutional cooperation. Still, these processes have been strong and influential in a relatively small number of countries; many other states, while having to deal with these issues internationally, face much weaker domestic pressures.

Given the discussion of the evolution of support for gender-based claims, as well as an analysis of the adoption of the 1967 Protocol and the failure of the 1977 Convention on Territorial Asylum, I argue that there are strong grounds for caution in pushing for a protocol. To this analyst, it appears that, although changing, the societal and political grounds are not yet firm enough to support efforts akin to a new, formal protocol. However, it is encouraging to note the results to date by focusing on changing the domestic legislation, municipal law, guidelines, regulations, and practice in states so that acceptance of the legitimacy of gender-based persecution claims becomes the norm instead of the exception. At that point, the likelihood of achieving a formal protocol to the convention is increased.

It is also productive to encourage development of women's rights within the general framework of human rights law as that is another mechanism to make protection levels stronger. If there is a force that can work on the progressive development of refugee law it is likely human rights law. Thus, while in some cases, it makes more strategic sense to use the international level in order to develop the domestic level, in this case, I argue that a strategy, which targets domestic level changes using human rights law, could be the most effective in advancing the cause of protecting women from gender-based persecution.

The Role of Non-Governmental Organizations in the International Refugee Regime

ELIZABETH G. FERRIS

Non-governmental organizations (NGOs) have a long history of providing assistance to refugees and other displaced people.[1] However, in recent years, they have also become increasingly involved in protection of refugees, a task mandated to the United Nations High Commissioner for Refugees (UNHCR). This growing NGO involvement in refugee protection is a consequence of both the international community's inability to protect uprooted people and the increasingly active role which NGOs are playing in international political and economic issues. Following a brief historical overview of NGO involvement with refugees, this paper examines the current context of NGO activity and the roles that they are playing in the international refugee regime.

A Bit of History

Long before international efforts were developed to respond to the needs of people uprooted by war and persecution, individuals and private groups provided immediate assistance to those forced from their homes. With the emergence of organized voluntary associations in the middle of the nineteenth century, organizational capabilities were in place—capabilities that were channeled into relief activities in the early decades of the twentieth century.

These early NGOs responded to emergency situations without much assistance or coordination from governments, by mobilizing funds, sending personnel, and extending immediate material assistance. These early attempts are remarkable in part because of the amount of funds generated and the scope of relief activities carried out at a time when logistical difficulties were enormous. During the interwar period, voluntary agencies took the lead in responding to famine in the Soviet Union, war victims in the Balkans, and genocide in Armenia. In the latter case, a consortium of agencies organized the Armenian Committee for Relief in the Near East, known as Near East Relief, which raised $20 million, sent relief teams into affected areas, fed an average of 300,000 people per day, established and administered all hospital services for Armenia, and took charge of over 75,000 orphans.[2]

But the activities of the early NGOs were not limited to the charitable provision of relief assistance. From the beginning, many were also involved in lobbying and advocacy activities. For example, in 1911, the American Jewish Committee lobbied the U.S. government on Russian treatment of U.S. Jews applying for Russian visas.[3] This action forced the U.S. Congress to overturn an eighty-year old treaty regulating U.S. commercial ties to Russia. Moreover, their assistance activities brought issues to the public's attention, stimulated international awareness, and created pressures for governmental response. Michael Marrus describes how hundreds of thousands of refugees were kept alive by NGOs in the period between the end of World War I and the establishment of the League of Nations High Commissioner for Refugees in 1921 and "[b]y keeping so many alive, the private organizations helped to maintain the pressure of refugee crises. In the long run, this activity helped to elicit a response from governments and from the international agencies set in place after the First World War."[4]

During the decades between the establishment of the first international instrument for refugee relief and the creation of UNHCR in 1951, NGOs were involved, not only in providing relief, but also in lobbying for the creation of strong international organizations. The early efforts at international institutions were cooperative ventures between NGOs and incipient global structures. The League of Nations appointed a High Commissioner for Russian Refugees, Fridtjof Nansen, as a result of a conference of NGOs which was convened by the Red Cross, and "it was in response to the invitation of that conference that the Council had set up an office of High Commissioner for Refugees."[5] In 1924, the Permanent International Conference of Private Organizations for the Protection of Migrants was formed in Geneva and worked closely with Nansen in the formative years of his organization.

During the years preceding World War II when Western governments imposed ever-more restrictive provisions to keep the victims of Nazism out of their countries, NGOs worked together to press for a more humane response toward those seeking to flee from their countries.[6] More than sixty NGOs (including ten international NGOs and national societies from twelve different countries) participated in the operations of the United Nations Relief and Reconstruction Agency (UNRRA) from 1943–47. NGOs provided a range of services and support to UNRRA, including seconding personnel, developing supplemental projects in countries receiving UNRRA aid, contributing supplies directly to UNRRA, and establishing joint planning committees between NGOs, UNRRA, and governments in countries receiving UNRRA aid.[7] But when UNRRA came to an end in 1947, there were still 2 million refugees. NGOs then played a crucial role in lobbying for the formation of the International Refugee Organization (IRO) and when it too came to an end in 1949, in pushing for its replacement.[8] NGO involvement in refugee assistance was part of a larger movement of NGOs to influence the development of international law and the United Nations in the immediate postwar period. Over 1200 NGOs attended the San Francisco Conference that finalized the UN charter. "Some authors claim that the NGOs were directly responsible for the existence of the Charter's provisions on human rights."[9]

At the national level, coordination mechanisms for NGOs were established in North America and Europe. In June 1948, the Standing Committee of Voluntary Agencies (SCVA) was formed on the international level with thirty-seven national and international agencies "to provide for joint representation in discussions with competent organizations or governments on refugee problems" and to facilitate joint consultation among the voluntary agencies concerning needs of refugees, conditions of work, and so on.[10]

The relationship between governments, NGOs, and international organizations became more formalized under the International Refugee Organization (IRO). In January 1949, the Director-General of the IRO held a Working Conference of IRO and Associated Voluntary Agencies with 104 representatives from IRO and 100 representatives of forty-nine voluntary agencies from thirteen countries. The Conference discussed operational issues and ways to facilitate future planning when IRO's mandate expired. The idea was that the international agency should provide for legal protection and tracing while NGOs provided assistance to the "residual group" of refugees. But SCVA in October 1949 wrote to the IRO noting that voluntary agencies were ancillary to international agencies and needed a strong international organization.[11] In other words the NGOs were unwilling and unable to assume the functions abandoned by the IRO.

The nature of relationship between the NGOs and the international organization charged with assisting and protecting refugees changed with the creation of the Office of the United Nations High Commissioner for Refugees (UNHCR) in 1951. UNHCR was to be the spokesperson for refugees and to provide legal protection to refugees while care and assistance was to be left to voluntary agencies. In other words, UNHCR was not intended to be operational, but rather to work with and through NGOs. In its initial year of operation, the budget of UNHCR was only $300,000 at a time when 1.25 million refugees fell within its mandate. Moreover, UNHCR was not authorized to spend any of its funds on direct assistance to refugees. The budgets of many NGOs at this time were considerably larger than UNHCR's operational budget. In the 1950s, the Ford Foundation gave $3 million to a number of voluntary agencies with the stipulation that UNHCR administer the funds—a move which strengthened the interdependence of UNHCR and NGOs. NGOs needed a strong UNHCR to provide protection for refugees and UNHCR was dependent on NGOs for provision of assistance.

During the 1950s and 1960s, NGOs, particularly religious agencies, continued to provide substantial relief and were essential to the functioning of the refugee regime. One 1953 analysis found that fully 90 percent of postwar relief was provided by the religious agencies.[12] But NGOs also took the lead in lobbying for resettlement opportunities and in providing the resources needed for resettlement of the hundreds of thousands of Hungarian refugees fleeing Soviet intervention in 1956.

In 1962, the International Council of Voluntary Agencies (ICVA) was formed and by 1965, sixty-five agencies had become members of ICVA (by 2000, the number had increased to eighty, most of which were coalitions or umbrella organizations themselves). From the early 1960s to the early 1980s, NGOs grew in size and range of activities but their expansion did not keep up with the growth in intergovernmental organizations, particularly with UNHCR. The steady expansion of UNHCR's mandate, particularly with the adoption of the 1967 Protocol removing the geographical restriction, meant that UNHCR could now act in situations from which it had previously been excluded. The growing number of refugees in Africa and Asia increased the cost of relief. Governments devoted more resources to bilateral refugee aid, some of which were channeled through NGOs. More government funds meant an increase in NGOs' organizational capacities but also a potential weakening of their independence.

By the 1980s the proliferation of NGOs, the growth of indigenous NGOs in the developing countries, and changing understandings of development meant that Northern NGOs came under increasing pressure to decrease their direct involvement in provision of service abroad and to support the development of local institutions. Institution-building and empowerment replaced concepts of community organizing—community organizing that had largely been carried out by expatriate staff in the 1960s and 1970s. The impact of dependency theorists and the extrapolation that foreign aid agencies were perpetuating dependency in another, albeit "altruistic" form meant that agencies began to change their mode of operation. More emphasis was placed on capacity-building of local NGOs.

Another impetus for change in Northern NGOs working with refugees came from the increasing numbers of asylum seekers arriving at the borders of Western countries. In the United States, the Mariel exodus and the arrival of large numbers of Central American asylum-seekers in the early 1980s challenged NGOs that had previously been involved with refugees through overseas assistance and through resettlement of government-approved refugees arriving in the United States. These NGOs had worked closely with the U.S. government in providing services to resettled refugees in return for substantial funding. But with the arrival of large numbers of Central Americans and the rise of Central American solidarity groups, the NGOs were challenged to act in new ways. For many of the traditional U.S. agencies, relationships with the U.S. government underwent considerable change. From negotiating contracts and administering projects in close cooperation with the U.S. State Department, the NGOs found themselves embroiled over protection issues with both the Immigration and

Naturalization Service (INS) and the State Department, agencies whose advisory opinions were crucial in asylum determination proceedings.

Although not as closely involved with resettlement, most European NGOs working with refugees had enjoyed close relationships with their governments in administering their overseas refugee assistance programs. The major national refugee councils (Norwegian Refugee Council, Danish Refugee Council, Swiss Refugee Council, etc.) had been involved in either small-scale refugee integration projects at home or in major refugee assistance projects abroad (or both) when the number of asylum seekers increased dramatically in their own countries. In some of the countries, the NGOs took the lead in opposing their governments' restrictive policies to new arrivals. In other countries, new NGOs emerged as the large established refugee NGOs either reacted timidly or could not act. In Canada, relations between the Canadian Council for Refugees (formerly known as the Standing Conference of Canadian NGOs working with Refugees) and the Canadian government deteriorated sharply in the late 1980s as the government introduced much more restrictive asylum legislation. Canadian NGOs were sharply critical of their government; they brought their concerns to international fora such as the UN Human Rights Commission and brought court cases against the government.

While changes were taking place in northern NGOs serving refugees, even more dramatic changes were taking place in the development of NGOs in the South. By the year 2000, NGOs were major actors in their own countries and on the international scene.

The Blossoming of Civil Society

Proliferation of NGOs

The growth of NGOs worldwide in the past two decades has been phenomenal. As *The Economist* summarizes, "[t]he end of communism, the spread of democracy in poor countries, technological change and economic integration—globalization, in short—has created fertile soil for the rise of NGOs."[13] With the fall of the Berlin wall in 1989, a new emphasis on development of democratic institutions was accompanied by the belief that a strong and vibrant civil society was essential to the success of democracy. Civil society—including NGOs, trade unions, business and popular organizations, religious groups, and professional associations—was formally encouraged by development donors and lauded by political leaders of all stripes. The triumph of "people power" in the Philippines in 1989, the movement against impunity in Latin America, the global campaign against landmines, and the environmental movement were all manifestations of the power of civil society. In more recent times, strong NGOs and grassroots initiatives are protesting against the negative consequences of globalization as evidenced in the now-common sight of protesters at meetings of international financial institutions. It is within the context of the broader civil society that the number of NGOs has increased.

According to the *Yearbook of International Organizations,* there are now 26,000 international NGOs, compared with 6,000 in 1990. The U.S. alone has about 2 million NGOs, 70 percent of which are more than thirty years old. India has about 1 million grassroots groups while more than 100,000 NGOs sprang up in Eastern Europe between 1989 and 1995. "As a group, NGOs now deliver more aid than the whole United Nations system."[14] Some observers estimate that the total funding channeled through NGOs worldwide is in excess of $8.5 billion per year.[15]

The proliferation of NGOs makes generalizations impossible. Refugee-serving NGOs include small organizations staffed by volunteers and housed in church basements to organizations with annual budgets close to $1 billion per year—about the same as UNHCR's. Some NGOs, particularly religious organizations, have large constituencies numbering in the hundreds of millions. Others are membership organizations whose members contribute funds and volunteer their time. As the number of NGOs increases, so too does competition between them. Vanessa Houlder observes in regard to the growth of environmental groups, "[t]he number of groups is estimated to have quadrupled to 20,000 over the past three decades, but their expansion has not been matched by a growth in volunteers' time and resources."[16]

Growing Public Funding and an Emphasis on Emergencies

Financial support from the international community for the South has shifted from primarily development assistance (with occasional emergency programs) to increasing percentages of assistance going to emergencies. And in emergency assistance, in particular, the proportion of overseas development assistance being channeled through NGOs has increased dramatically in the past fifteen years. The 1990s saw the biggest increase in the number, size, operational capacities, and resources of NGOs. In 1994 UNHCR reports that there were over 100 NGOs operating in Rwandan camps in then-Zaire, 150 in Mozambique, 170 in Rwanda, and some 250 in Bosnia and Herzegovina. "It is governments, rather than individual donors, that are most responsible for the recent increase in NGO funding. In 1970, public sector funding accounted for a mere 1.5 percent of NGO budgets. By the mid-1990s, it had risen to 40 percent and was still increasing."[17] This increasing reliance on government funding raises questions about the extent to which NGOs are really non-governmental. Some large international NGOs receive over 90 percent of their funding from government sources; others have imposed limits on the percentage of governments funds which they will accept. In many Southern countries, governments have set up their own NGOs to channel resources. And the close relationships of many national Red Cross and Red Crescent national societies with their governments raise questions about how independent they are.[18] Jan Pronk, former head of the Dutch bilateral aid programme said fourteen years ago:

> The corruption of NGOs will be the political game in the years ahead—
> and it is already being played today . . . NGOs have created a huge bu-
> reaucracy, employment is at stake and contacts in the developing world
> are also at stake. It will become impossible for them to criticize govern-
> ments for decreasing the quality of the overall aid program. NGOs will
> lose in the years ahead . . . they will be corrupted in the process, because
> they will receive enough money for their own projects but the rest of the
> aid program will suffer.[19]

Many international NGOs maintain that their independence and integrity
have not been compromised by reliance on government funds and that their
close relationships with governments give them the access needed to conduct
effective advocacy on policy issues. But trends in governmental funding of
NGO work are a cause for concern for many in the NGO community.

The impact of increasing governmental resources, the shift toward emergency response, the expanding role of the media in shaping humanitarian response, and the proliferation of NGOs has increased competition between
NGOs. The emergence of new NGOs in response to a particular emergency situation (including the so-called "briefcase NGOs") make it difficult to general-
ize about NGO activities. Many large international NGOs feel a need to be
present and visible in emergency situations covered by the media in order to
attract more funds from the public. Horror stories abound of international
NGOs rushing to the scene of refugee emergencies with camera crews in tow so
that video clips of "our man in the field" can be immediately transmitted back
home. The need to demonstrate a visible presence in emergencies hinders coordination among agencies. For example, when it became possible for NGOs to
return to Cambodia in the early 1990s, many international NGOs staked out
their own "territories" and "sectors" with little regard for the needs of the country as a whole or for their own capacity to deliver promised assistance.

Governments of Southern countries sometimes find themselves unable to
control these NGOs. Hanlon demonstrates that the NGOs in Mozambique
were much better-resourced than the Mozambican government and that the
government was virtually powerless to control the expansion of NGO activity
in the country. The long-term effects of this, Joseph Hanlon argues, is that the
Mozambican government was disempowered to govern the country because of
the NGOs.[20]

The so-called "CNN effect" in which humanitarian response is shaped by
media coverage of particular emergencies, coupled with competition among
NGOs to raise funds, has meant an imbalance in the international community's response to refugee situations. This is true of governments, UN agencies,
and NGOs. The figure most often cited is that of Kosovo where UNHCR spent
an average of US$1.50 per refugee per day where the equivalent with respect to
figure Sierra Leone was 11 cents.[21] To be sure, NGOs continue to provide

needed services in dozens of refugee situations outside the public eye, but the pressure to respond—and to be seen to be responding—in the high media coverage emergencies is substantial.

International NGOs, Indigenous NGOs

Within the NGO world, the difference between local (or indigenous or national or Southern) NGOs, which operate in only one country, and international NGOs is particularly important. Many international NGOs have long-term commitments to the countries in which they are working through their development, human rights, or capacity-building projects. But emergency situations pose particular problems. The fact is that while many international NGOs have the capacity and the willingness to respond immediately, visibly, and often effectively to large-scale refugee emergencies, most of them will leave the country or significantly reduce their operations once the immediate crisis is past. They will move on to the next large-scale media emergency. But the indigenous NGOs will remain in the country for the long-term. In recognition of this and as part of a commitment to building civil society, Northern NGOs are increasingly working through local NGOs, providing funds and training to them to carry on their work.[22] The process around the international conference on the Commonwealth of Independent States (CIS) led to the establishment of hundreds of new NGOs in the republics of the former Soviet Union.[23]

Brian Smith notes that the role of Northern NGOs acting as intermediaries between indigenous NGOs and donor governments has been an important asset to Northern NGOs. "[I]t has been these partners in the South that have made it possible for international NGOs to establish their reputation as having a comparative advantage over bilateral and multilateral agencies in reaching and aiding the hard-core poor in the South with cost-effective strategies tailored to meet their basic needs."[24] But today's donor governments are raising questions about why they are channeling funds to local NGOs through international NGOs instead of directly to the local NGOs themselves. In some cases, local NGOs are now competing directly for funds from Northern governments with international NGOs. This phenomenon produces strange rhetoric with international NGOs often defending local NGOs at the same time that they argue that international NGOs are best-placed to channel funds to indigenous groups. Nor are donor governments consistent in their policies. The stringent reporting requirements of many donor governments and intergovernmental bodies, such as the European Union, deter indigenous NGOs from participating in the funding. And often NGOs do not see the priority for detailed reporting, given the urgency of responding to needs on the ground. Moreover, many donor governments and European Union funding programs require an expatriate presence as a condition of assistance. Thus, even in projects to build local capacities, a foreigner is needed to assure quality control of the project.

A Drive toward Professionalism and Accountability

Another consequence of the growing reliance of NGOs, and particularly international NGOs, on government funding is the need to become more professional and accountable. Coupled with growing media reports on NGO activity and multi-donor evaluations (such as that carried out on Rwanda) pressure has increased for NGOs to become more accountable for their activities. NGOs have always had standards for their work, ranging from anecdotal means of evaluation to sophisticated agency-specific criteria, although it is probably fair to say that most NGOs did not have systematic evaluation systems in place by the mid-1990s.[25] But perhaps partly in anticipation of the imposition of common standards by donor governments, NGOs have worked hard in the past decade to develop and implement standards based on their own experiences. In 1997, the Humanitarian Charter and the Minimum Standards in Disaster Response, known as the Sphere Project, was launched with the aim of increasing the effectiveness of humanitarian assistance and make the humanitarian agencies more accountable. This initiative, spearheaded by the Steering Committee on Humanitarian Response and InterAction, is the result of the combined efforts of over 200 organizations, including NGOs, the International Red Cross and Red Crescent Movement, academic institutions, the UN (including UNHCR), and government agencies. Sphere has developed standards in five areas: water supply and sanitation, nutrition, food aid, shelter and site planning, and health services. Sphere has also launched a comprehensive training program to make the standards and the rights-based Humanitarian Charter widely known in the field.[26] These standards are now becoming generally accepted in the broader international community, as evidenced by their endorsement by the Inter-Agency Standing Committee.

In addition to these standards, each NGO has its own criteria for assessing and evaluating its work. While there has been broad (but not easy!) agreement on the minimum standards, it has been much more difficult to establish compliance or oversight mechanisms. NGOs are still reluctant to give authority to another body to judge their own performance.

A newly initiated project, the Humanitarian Accountability Project (formerly known as the Omsbudsman project) seeks to take the question of accountability a step further by including beneficiaries in the process of evaluating delivery of humanitarian assistance. The project has received considerable interest—and criticism—from NGOs; presently the project is beginning to test three pilot projects in different parts of the world.

UNHCR-NGO Relationships

In 1999, UNHCR channeled $295 million through 544 NGO implementing partners. Some 50 percent of all UNHCR programs are now implemented by international NGOs, 34 of these NGOs receiving more than $2 million each.[27] However, UNHCR has tried to work more intentionally with indigenous

NGOs and by 1999, 395 national NGOs were working in partnership with UNHCR, three times the number five years earlier. In 1999, these national NGOs implemented nearly 20 percent of UNHCR's projects. During the Bosnian crisis, more than 90 percent of UNHCR's humanitarian assistance was distributed by local organizations such as Merhamet, Caritas, and local Red Cross branches.[28]

Receiving funds from UNHCR enables NGOs to expand their activities and is cost-efficient for UNHCR. But dependency on UNHCR funding, like dependency on government funding, has its drawbacks. When UNHCR withdraws its support—because of budget difficulties or because it is not satisfied with the NGO—the NGO may go out of business. Indigenous NGOs are particularly vulnerable in this regard; thus when UNHCR cut programs in Bolivia, a long-standing refugee program, the Centro de Estudios Especializados sobre Migración (CESEM), was forced to close. UNHCR's sudden budget cuts at the end of 2000, in many cases after programs had been begun, left many NGOs holding the bag. "What can we do?" one international NGO staff person lamented, "we'd spent our own money in good faith that the UNHCR contract would be honored. But now UNHCR comes and says 'sorry, we'll have to cut our budget, please return 10 percent of the funds you've already received.' We didn't have any choice—if we wanted to work with UNHCR in the future. We lost a lot of money last year, but at least we're a large organization and will survive. A lot of the smaller ones won't."[29]

The impact of UNHCR budget cuts has affected NGO abilities to deliver needed services. According to UNHCR, "an NGO responsible for 6,500 refugees in Jembe camp [Sierra Leone] announced in mid-October 2002 the cessation of all activities in view of UNHCR's incapacity to honour its financial commitments," and in the Democratic Republic of Congo, "implementing partner staff have been laid off in health, water, sanitation and psychosocial programmes."[30]

At one level, the UNHCR–NGO relationship is thus marked by the inevitable tensions of a donor-recipient relationship. In 1994, UNHCR convened a major international NGO conference in Oslo, Norway, Partnership in Action, known by its acronym PARinAC. Since then regular meetings have been held at the national and regional levels to stimulate relationships between UNHCR and indigenous NGOs. National and regional NGO focal points have been identified to facilitate relations. In some regions, relationships have been strengthened both within the NGO community and between NGOs and UNHCR. In other regions, cooperation remains difficult. In all regions, the lack of resources for NGOs to meet on their own on a regional basis remains a problem.

UNHCR–NGO relationships in the area of protection have always been difficult and occasionally antagonistic, as spelled out in the section below on NGO involvement with protection. But some of these tensions are the result of the deteriorating protection situation for refugees in most parts of the world.

The Crisis in International Refugee Protection

Many studies point to the crisis in international refugee protection.[31] As Rachel Reilly points out "[u]nlike most other areas of human rights where it is possible to chart progress over the last decades, states have largely regressed in their commitment towards protecting refugees over the past fifty years."[32]

Refugee Protection and the Nature of Warfare

As many have written, today's conflicts are characterized by an increasing number of civilian casualties, fueled by an arms trade of unprecedented proportions, and largely carried out by private armies and warlords. Far from being the unintended victims of warfare, civilian populations have increasingly become the targets of military action. In conflicts in which enemies are demonized, villages and entire populations have become the targets of military action in which children and women suffer disproportionately. Millions of children have been killed, maimed, uprooted, sexually abused, and traumatized by today's wars.[33]

In Afghanistan, Sierra Leone, Chechnya, Angola, the Great Lakes, and many other situations, warlords fight with each other for territory and for control of natural resources. Armed movements today are rapidly fragmenting and "the criminal exploitation of local resources, as well as direct predation on civilians, makes these conflicts very unstable."[34] The nature of these self-financed conflicts means not only that wars drag on for years, but that humanitarian assistance becomes extraordinarily difficult. Humanitarian aid itself becomes a resource over which armed groups struggle, refugees are frequently caught in the middle. Jean-Christophe Rufin refers to *indirect* assistance provided to armed movements under cover of "humanitarian aid."

> The pretext of relief, morally impossible to contest as long as civilians could be shown to be victims, enabled so-called "humanitarian sanctuaries" to be set up. Huge refugee camps along international borders—effective protection against the retaliation of government armies—were used as safe bases by many guerrilla movements (in Afghanistan, El Salvador, Cambodia, Mozambique, etc.) In such bases, guerrillas could mingle with civilian refugees, control a large influx of international aid and, in some cases (Eritrea, the Polisario Front, El Salvador), build up a kind of shadow state.[35]

Provision of humanitarian assistance in Somalia, Bosnia, and Rwanda fundamentally changed the perceptions of humanitarian actors, including NGOs, about the impact of their assistance on conflicts.[36] These experiences marked the "end of innocence" on the part of humanitarian organizations. Humanitarian aid could be used—and was used—to prolong the wars.

Moreover, in the past, it was difficult but possible in some situations for humanitarian actors to negotiate with opposing armed factions for the provision of relief. This was the case, for example, with Operation Lifeline Sudan. But in situations where competing private armies struggle for power and resources, such negotiations become more difficult, and more dangerous. Current efforts by the UN High Commissioner for Refugees to negotiate a safe corridor for the return of Sierra Leonean refugees from Guinea are extraordinarily difficult.

In the context of conflict in the world today, the protection of refugees and displaced people has taken on troubling dimensions. Governments of host countries are understandably reluctant to provide refuge to people uprooted from conflicts in a neighboring conflict as they do not want the violence to spill over into their countries. The international community finds it increasingly difficult to mobilize resources for refugees who may remain in exile for years, or even decades. Without the assurance that international support will be forthcoming, host governments are further discouraged from accepting refugees. And physically protecting refugees in situations where warlords have the power—and who are indifferent to international humanitarian law or the neutrality of humanitarian workers—is increasingly dangerous. In the past few years, the murders of UNHCR, ICRC, and WFP staff in East Timor, Sierra Leone, Chechnya, and Burundi has led to intensive soul-searching debates over staff security and the limits of acceptable risk. Many NGO staff have also been victims of the violence inherent in trying to provide relief in situations of armed conflict. It is increasingly difficult to protect refugees and displaced people in all regions of the world.[37]

Protection and assistance are, of course, closely linked. If refugees do not receive the assistance they need to survive, they will seek it elsewhere. Women will turn to prostitution to feed their families, young people will be recruited to join rebel forces when there are no educational or other opportunities in refugee camps, and refugees may turn to crime—which often brings reprisals.

While protection in the regions from which refugees come is deteriorating, it is also being eroded in Western countries through increasingly restrictive policies on asylum. An excerpt from Human Rights Watch's recent report on UNHCR at 50 summarizes the manifestations of the erosion of asylum in Western countries:

> . . . many of the policies introduced by Western European governments have systematically obstructed the right to seek and enjoy asylum and have made it very difficult for those in fear of their lives to leave their country of origin freely and seek asylum elsewhere. . . . Western European countries have sought to shift responsibility for providing protection to refugees on to other countries. . . . Western European governments have

progressively diluted and undermined their obligations under the Refugee Convention over the past years with seriously detrimental consequences for those in need of international protection . . . the growing barriers to legal entry into EU countries has meant that asylum seekers and migrants are increasingly turning to the services of opportunistic, corrupt and dangerous human trafficking and smuggling syndicates who are able to circumvent routine migration controls . . . the restrictive policies described above are implemented within a climate of hostility and xenophobia towards refugees, asylum seekers and migrants. Politicians and the media have shamelessly manipulated xenophobic and racist fears in order to muster political support.[38]

Recent proposals by the governments of the United Kingdom and Australia to fundamentally change the 1951 Refugee Convention raise serious questions about the future of refugee protection. The trends noted above—growing difficulties of protecting refugees and displaced people in the regions from which they come and more restrictions on asylum-seekers coming to the West—are related. As the Australian Minister of Immigration, Philip Ruddock, stated at the UNHCR Executive Committee meeting in 2000, Western governments currently spend an estimated $10 billion on asylum seekers—more than ten times the budget of UNHCR which is caring for twenty times as many refugees and displaced people. While NGOs have questioned whether funds freed up by admitting fewer asylum seekers would be directed towards meeting UNHCR's budget, governments are clearly drawing the connection. And UNHCR continues to experience difficulties in funding its programs, particularly in regions which do not receive much media coverage.

NGO Involvement in Refugee Protection

The crisis in refugee protection and the corresponding inability of UNHCR to protect refugees in all situations have led to increasing NGO activity in the area of protection of refugees. While this is not a role that most NGOs have sought—or for that they have been trained—the on-the-ground reality is such that NGOs are often compelled to play a protection role. This "privatization of refugee protection" is a worrying sign of the international community's inability to protect people forced to flee their countries. Given current global trends and UNHCR budgetary shortfalls, it is likely to continue. There are many ways in which NGOs are involved in protection.

NGOs Sounding the Alarm

In contexts where protection is becoming more elusive for refugees, asylum seekers, and internally displaced people, NGOs play an important role in drawing attention to unmet protection needs in specific situations and in identifying global trends. Their research, visits, lobbying activities, and public statements have warned of the crisis in refugee protection for at least the past decade.[39]

Reports from the field often serve as early warning of potential refugee crises, although they are rarely given the attention they warrant. For example, in 1983, Dutch Interchurch Aid warned of a coming famine in Ethiopia. Over the course of the next year, the NGO became increasingly alarmed at deteriorating conditions and organized visits to the capitals of seven European countries urging early action to prevent a large-scale tragedy. No action was taken until the famine reached catastrophic proportions—and a large-scale response was not mobilized until the BBC broadcast a shocking report in late 1984.

Within the international NGO community, traditionally a sharp difference has been seen in the roles played by human rights and humanitarian NGOs. Human rights NGOs seek to protect refugees by denouncing human rights violations, monitoring on-going situations, and publicly naming governments that do not protect refugees and displaced people. Traditionally, humanitarian NGOs have seen their primary role as assisting refugees and have been reluctant to publicly denounce human rights violations for fear of having their assistance activities curtailed. An NGO denouncing incursions by Thai soldiers into the refugee camps on the Cambodian border in the late 1970s, for example, could risk expulsion by the Thai government. Rather, humanitarian NGOs maintain that they use quiet interventions as appropriate to raise the concerns with relevant public officials or armed groups.[40] Although differences do exist between these two types of NGOs, in practice the lines have always been blurred. Some international NGOs, including most of the religious ones, engage in both human rights and humanitarian work. Informal arrangements for sharing information have always existed between agencies that are operational in a given area and others that have more freedom to denounce human rights abuses. Umbrella organizations may speak out in cases where refugees' protection is being violated based on information received by one of their members. For example, ICVA engaged in a long process of consultation in Central America in the late 1980s in which its international umbrella provided a space for indigenous and international human rights NGOs to speak freely of the shortcomings in protection of refugees. ICVA, composed of many international NGOs as well as indigenous ones, was in a better position to publicly denounce these violations than the local agencies. The work of NGOs in placing the issue of internally displaced people on the international agenda in the late 1980s was the combined effort of humanitarian NGOs with direct experience in the field about the needs of internally displaced people and human rights organizations.

The differences between human rights and humanitarian NGOs are also narrowing as humanitarian NGOs are increasingly involved in protecting refugees in the field. UNHCR, in cooperation with NGOs, recently published *Protecting Refugees: A Field Guide for NGOs* (1999) in recognition of this increasing role. This field guide provides concrete suggestions for enhancing

NGO work in refugee protection in program design and implementation and in advocacy with relevant authorities.

Protection through NGO Assistance and Presence

As mentioned above, protection and assistance are related. In many parts of the world, the assistance provided by NGOs serves to protect people who would otherwise find themselves facing protection problems. Urban refugees and asylum seekers not recognized as refugees are particularly vulnerable to exploitation or violence. In Egypt, the Joint Relief Ministry not only provides Sudanese refugees with medical and educational assistance, but also registers the Sudanese and provides them with identity cards. Although neither the registration nor the identity card has any legal validity, there have been many cases where the refugees have extricated themselves from difficult situations with Egyptian authorities by producing the official-looking card.

NGOs who are providing traditional assistance, such as delivering food, may be drawn into providing protection in a more direct fashion. For example, the International Catholic Migration Commission was tasked with providing assistance to vulnerable groups in Kosovo after the NATO intervention. Most of the vulnerable refugees were Serbs, many of whom were isolated and were afraid to go out of their barricaded homes. ICMC staff found themselves not only delivering food, but also escorting the Serbs to doctors, informing KFOR forces about their presence and trying to secure necessary protection to prevent attacks on their homes.

The presence of international NGO staff in refugee camps and refugee situations can provide another form of protection. In some places, UNHCR does not have sufficient staff to remain in camps overnight or to be a continuous presence; in these situations, NGO presence may be a powerful force for protection. Indigenous NGO staff may also provide protection to detained asylum seekers or rejected asylum seekers by their presence. Thus in Lebanon, the Middle East Council of Churches regularly visits detained refugees (including those recognized by UNHCR) and migrants. These regular visits are intended not only to provide assistance to the detainees, but also to remind prison officials that there are organizations that are observing the treatment of detained migrants and refugees.

Indigenous NGOs may be the only providers of protection in war-torn countries when the international community withdraws. In East Timor, the withdrawal of the international community in the face of escalating violence following the referendum for independence, meant that local NGOs and particularly churches were the only bodies providing protection to endangered people. People fled to churches and convents and in some cases, remained hidden there for weeks. The withdrawal of the international community from Sierra Leone in 2000 largely abandoned the population to competing armed groups. But indigenous NGOs, churches, inter-religious groupings, and the Red Cross remained behind.

In Western countries, NGOs have long provided legal assistance and counseling to asylum seekers. Increasingly NGO lawyers are assisting with asylum claims and appeals in seeking to obtain legal protection for asylum-seekers. In Germany, Sweden, and other European countries, a sanctuary movement has grown up to shelter asylum seekers who have been rejected by the government.

In all of these cases, NGOs are providing protection to refugees and other uprooted people—protection that would not be otherwise provided by UNHCR or other international bodies.

NGOs and Awareness-Raising

Many NGOs are engaged in public education efforts to raise awareness of the refugee situation and its causes with important domestic constituencies. These activities run the gamut from African celebrations of "Refugee Sundays" to sophisticated campaigns on particular refugee crises, as in the U.S. Committee for Refugees' 1998–99 "Voices for Colombia" campaign. These activities serve to mobilize popular support for refugees and for the agencies working with them. By increasing the visibility of the issue, they can also be important in fund-raising for the NGO. And perhaps most importantly, they can help build a constituency to support advocacy efforts.

NGOs and Advocacy

As noted above, NGOs have been involved in advocacy on behalf of refugees since the beginning of the modern international refugee regime. But in recent years, this advocacy has become both more widespread and more sophisticated. By providing expert background and policy alternatives, NGOs are recognized in Northern countries as major players in decision-making. In the United States, the Refugee Council-USA has launched major advocacy campaigns around specific legislative issues. Thus in the year 2000, NGOs were able to mobilize large numbers of constituents to reinstate funds cut from the government's emergency refugee response account. In Europe, the European Council on Refugees and Exiles (ECRE) has brought its considerable expertise to bear not only on efforts to influence national legislation, but increasingly to play a proactive role in the formation of asylum and immigration policy at the European Union (EU) level. While European NGOs have long seen the need for close cooperation in response to the EU, NGOs from other countries are also increasingly seeking transnational cooperation. Thus, U.S. and Canadian churches worked together to oppose a proposed U.S.–Canadian Memorandum of Understanding that would have prevented asylum seekers denied by U.S. authorities from receiving refugee status in Canada.

Global networks, such as those supported by umbrella organizations such as ICVA, the World Council of Churches, and Caritas Internationalis, also provide an opportunity for coordinated advocacy at the national and international level. ICVA plays an invaluable role in distributing information to a broad range of NGOs in the South as well as the North and in facilitating the participation of Southern NGO representatives in international meetings. ICVA facilitates NGO input into important UNHCR meetings through drafting of common NGO statements and providing a forum where NGOs can agree about which NGO will speak on which agenda item. This is particularly important in meetings of UNHCR's Standing Committee and the Global Consultations on Refugee Protection where NGO input is limited to one intervention per agenda item. As important as the statements and meetings are ICVA's efforts to provide necessary information to NGOs about the issues to be discussed at UNHCR meetings—information that NGOs can use to lobby their national governments before the UNHCR meeting.

Church networks are also able to catalyze inter-regional collaboration in advocacy. A January 2001 meeting between churches in Southern Europe and the Middle East, for example, led to an agreement that both regions would focus their advocacy on efforts to facilitate voluntary repatriation to the Middle East.[41]

NGOs also play a vital role in advocacy vis-à-vis the international system of humanitarian response. Thus, three NGO networks (ICVA, InterAction, and SCHR) participate regularly in the Inter-Agency Standing Committee and in many of its working groups seeking improve coordination within the international humanitarian community in emergency response. NGOs are working closely with the IASC's Senior Network on Internal Displacement and have participated in the network's missions to the field. The Norwegian Refugee Council's Global IDP project provides both an invaluable database and a means of mobilizing NGO expertise for international policy discussions on internally displaced people.

NGOs and Conflict-Resolution

Many NGOs are involved in efforts to address the fundamental causes which uproot people—whether by working to reduce human rights violations, to organize sanctions against trade in natural resources (such as diamonds) that are financing conflicts, or to reform the international financial system. Increasingly humanitarian organizations are becoming involved in these issues. Thus the Steering Committee for Humanitarian Response, which brings together nine of the largest humanitarian assistance NGOs, is working on issues such as small arms trade. Given their work with the victims of small arms, diamond trade, and human rights violations, humanitarian organizations bring a unique perspective to advocacy on these issues.

For the most part, the NGOs involved in conflict-resolution and reconciliation have been different NGOs than those working to assist and protect refugees. However, humanitarian NGOs are increasingly seeking to tailor their programs in ways that support the lasting resolution of conflicts. Experiences in Somalia, Bosnia, and Rwanda have raised awareness of the fact that humanitarian assistance can actually exacerbate conflicts. But NGOs are less certain about how to ensure that their programs make a positive difference in the community, particularly given the neutrality implicit in humanitarian assistance. International NGO staff in particular may arrive in a given conflict situation with ideas of bringing different ethnic groups together but find themselves losing community support in the process. People who have been victimized by another ethnic group need time before they can engage in processes of reconciliation.

NGOs have been more active in refugee repatriation, rehabilitation, and reconstruction programs in post-conflict situations. These programs are intended not only to heal the damage caused by the conflicts, but also to prevent the resurgence of further violence. But this means that humanitarian professionals are likely to find themselves concerned with a broad range of tasks, including community-based peace making, supporting the revival of a judiciary, and the creation of national police forces.[42] The demands placed on NGO staff are thus increasing, not only must they be experts on specific issues such as sanitation or health care, but they must also be prepared to protect returnees, to foster cultures of tolerance, and to support efforts to rebuild civil society.

Ethical questions abound with regard to humanitarian assistance in the present day: Should NGOs continue to provide assistance to individuals known to have participated in violence? If not, what are the implications for their civilian relatives? Should NGOs turn over information they receive about people involved in the violence to relevant international legal bodies? Should NGOs call for UN peacekeeping troops or for the armed intervention of other bodies? To what extent should NGOs cooperate with military forces in the provision of humanitarian assistance? These are difficult questions for NGOs who often see themselves as nonpartisan providers of relief and for the international community generally. As Hugo Slim says "[r]elief agencies have problems with their identity and position within today's wars because they are trying to do something which is intrinsically difficult: they invariably find themselves trying to represent the values of humanity and peace within societies which are currently dominated by the values of inhumanity and violence. More often than not therefore, they are swimming against the current of that society, or certainly of its leadership. They are representatives of views which are often seen as a threat by leaders and peoples committed to violence and war."[43] Unfortunately there are few fora where such issues can be openly and self-critically discussed.

UNHCR–NGO Collaboration in Protection

In March 1999, UNHCR convened a meeting in New York on "Strengthening Collaboration with Humanitarian and Human Rights NGOs in Support of the

International Refugee Protection System."[44] The meeting brought together senior NGO and UNHCR officials to identify the roles which NGOs can play in protecting refugees. The meeting made a number of concrete recommendations and named a Steering Committee to follow up on the recommendations. The Steering Committee, jointly chaired by UNHCR and NGOs, met five times over a two year period and translated the more than forty recommendations made at the New York meeting into five task forces charged with creating concrete projects and ideas. These task forces considered:

- Sharing and use of sensitive information between humanitarian and human rights actors
- Operationalizing protection by providing for NGO training in the field of protection
- Capacity-building and collaboration with national NGOs on protection identify the specific types of capacity-building needed
- Standard-setting processes to consider ways of strengthening NGO participation in UNHCR meetings
- Accessions to and compliance with the 1951 Convention and advocacy.

Work continues in all of these areas, with perhaps the most concrete results being achieved in the area of NGO training where a project has been developed, staff hired, and an ambitious training program set up. The training will be carried out by NGOs, with UNHCR support, for NGO staff working in the field on refugee protection.

The Reach-Out process formally came to an end in the fall of 2000 with agreement that necessary follow-up would be carried out by ICVA. NGO participants in the Reach-Out process felt that it had been successful in increasing collaboration between human rights and humanitarian NGOs and that it had provided a constructive forum for discussions on protection with UNHCR. UNHCR's convening of the Global Consultations on Refugee Protection in 2001 is presently serving as a catalyst for NGOs to organize more strategically on specific issues to be discussed at the consultations.

In discussions on NGO involvement in refugee protection, NGOs constantly live with the tension between their increasing involvement with refugee protection in the field and their fear that by doing so, they are abetting the erosion of UNHCR and governmental responsibility for this protection. So, on the one hand they press UNHCR to be more assertive in exercising its protection mandate and urge governments to give UNHCR the resources it needs and on the other hand, they provide protection in places where UNHCR or governments are unwilling or unable to do so.

Relations between UNHCR and NGOs on protection issues are often contentious. UNHCR sometimes perceives NGOs as one-sided, inflammatory, and not appreciative of the political complexities and restrictions under which UNHCR operates. UNHCR staff sometimes feel personally attacked when an

NGO releases a report or a press release denouncing UNHCR's activities in a particular region—particularly when the report or press release comes as a surprise. NGOs sometimes see themselves as the true champions of refugee protection and see UNHCR as overly acquiescent to governments seeking to limit refugee protection. And NGOs sometimes speak out too quickly or react on the basis of inadequate information. In the past there have been fora for NGOs and UNHCR to come together in nonconfrontational, off-the-record settings to share information on protection concerns and to grapple together with the difficulties in increasing refugee protection in concrete cases. Unfortunately, those fora have disappeared and most NGO–UNHCR interaction at the international level either occurs through informal individual conversations (which are usually productive) and more formal large-scale meetings where questions are publicly raised in large plenary halls in the Palais des Nations.

The Need for Strengthened Partnerships

The issues around refugee assistance and protection today are serious and strengthened partnerships are needed between NGOs, between UNHCR and NGOs, and between governments and NGOs. NGOs have a great deal of expertise to contribute to contemporary policy debates, but many problems remain in effectively channeling these contributions. The revitalization of ICVA, coupled with the growth of NGO networks and coordinating bodies in all regions of the world, offer some hope that NGO coordination will improve. The growth of electronic communication has enabled timely information to be shared broadly among NGOs. It is now possible with a few clicks of the mouse to learn how dozens of international NGOs are responding to particular refugee situations and to receive action alerts from many more. Although Southern NGOs have been slower (in some cases) to acquire the technology, communications have expanded dramatically both within the South and between Southern and Northern NGOs within the last decade. These advances in communication are increasing the ability of NGOs to advocate for refugees in a timely fashion and to participate in many of the international policy debates. However, the continued competition between NGOs for funding, the complexity and pace of events, and the fact that NGOs are so busy "doing" that they have little time to reflect are limitations to NGOs' ability to work collectively on refugee protection issues.

Both the PARINAC and the UNHCR–NGO Reach-Out processes demonstrate the common interest of UNHCR and NGOs in strengthening NGO involvement in refugee protection. Building on these positive experiences to develop appropriate fora for UNHCR–NGO discussions, particularly on sensitive areas of refugee protection, would be useful. For example, issues of the asylum/migration nexus, staff security, and reform of present inter-agency coordinating structures are all of vital interest to both UNHCR and NGOs. Informal, off-the-record meetings between UNHCR and concerned NGOs could provide not only some substantive insights on these issues, but also some potential strategies for making real progress. The model currently being followed for NGO participation in the UNHCR Global Consultations on Refugee Protection is an interesting one that may lead to more intensive NGO engagement in UNHCR processes. ICVA has a staff person charged with following the consultations, sending out information, organizing NGO pre-meetings, and coordinating NGO input into the consultations. At the same time, UNHCR has hired an NGO-seconded staff working in its Department of International Protection to ensure that NGO input is taken seriously in its own internal processes.

NGO relations with governments on issues of refugee protection have generally focused on either lobbying governments to change their national policies or seeking their support (including financial support) for specific protection initiatives. There have, of course, been many other forms of collaboration as in the close relationships between InterAction's Disaster Response Committee and the U.S. government on issues of training of field personnel, the Sphere guidelines, and civilian-military cooperation on humanitarian issues. Some of the most effective NGO advocacy has been done when NGOs agree on common action points with the actual advocacy carried out by NGOs in national capitols. The clearest example of this in the broader international arena is the success of the International Campaign to Ban Landmines in which NGOs were able to mobilize widespread political support for a new international treaty in a short period of time. Recent years have not witnessed this kind of dramatic success story with respect to refugee protection, but the possibilities remain open. Presently, there are indications that NGOs are more willing to meet with government representatives informally to talk about UNHCR-related issues. And some governments include NGO representatives in their delegations to UNHCR's Executive Committee. There are also many successful cases in which NGOs advocated with governments for specific UNHCR programs (e.g. refugee children, refugee women).

NGOs have been active participants in the international refugee regime for many years and it is likely that they will become even more active, particularly in the area of refugee protection, in the years to come.

4
Policy Implications
of Refugee Protection

8

Changing Priorities
in Refugee Protection

The Rwandan Repatriation from Tanzania

BETH ELISE WHITAKER

On December 5, 1996, the Tanzanian government and the Office of the United Nations High Commissioner for Refugees (UNHCR) issued a joint statement that read, in part, "all Rwandese refugees in Tanzania are expected to return home by 31 December 1996."[1] That same day, UNHCR distributed information sheets to refugees about the repatriation exercise, including the immediate suspension of economic and agricultural activities in the camps. The camps had been home to more than half a million Rwandan refugees since 1994, when they fled civil war and an advancing rebel army at home. They were eventually joined in Tanzania by nearly 500,000 refugees from Burundi and Zaire.[2] As a haven of peace in a troubled region, Tanzania had long hosted refugees from neighboring countries. By December 1996, however, patience seemed to have run out.[3]

Upon receiving the repatriation announcement, many refugees wanted extra time to see how the integration of returnees from Zaire would unfold within Rwanda.[4] Several wrote a letter to Tanzanian President Benjamin Mkapa requesting him to reconsider the December 31 deadline. As the government's position became clear, though, Rwandans sought other methods to avoid repatriation. On the evening of December 6,[5] refugees started fleeing camps in Karagwe district. Nearly 10,000 refugees hiked toward Uganda and Kenya, where they hoped to get asylum. When questioned about their decision to flee, many said, "Death is death"; they would rather face the possibility of death in Tanzania than what they perceived to be certain death upon return to Rwanda. UNHCR sought to calm the situation by holding regular food distributions in the camps, which brought some refugees back from the woods. Those who did not return were rounded up a week later, when UNHCR sent trucks to bring them back to the camps.

Despite this experience in Karagwe, aid workers were seemingly surprised when Rwandans also began to leave the massive camps in Ngara district further south. During the night of December 11, more than 35,000 refugees suddenly fled the Ngara camps and headed east, away from Rwanda. As the exodus continued the following day, heavily armed Tanzanian troops surrounded the area. On December 13, the army set up roadblocks 70 kilometers east of Ngara, forcing as many as 200,000 fleeing refugees to turn around and retrace their steps. Meanwhile, the camps were closed and their entrances were blocked. All Rwandan refugees were herded down the road toward the border. On December 14, the first group of refugees crossed into Rwanda. *Operesheni Rudisha Wakimbizi* (Operation Return Refugees) had officially begun.

During the repatriation exercise, UNHCR provided both financial and logistical assistance to the Tanzanian government. It gave the Ministry of Home Affairs more than $1.5 million for extra equipment and personnel expenses associated with the operation.[6] Way stations were established along the road to distribute high-energy biscuits and water to the departing refugees. On December 19, after more than 400,000 Rwandans had been cleared out of Ngara, the army moved north to Karagwe district. Early the following morning, Tanzanian troops cleared out the camps and the long march to the border began. The only officially recognized border-crossing point was at Rusumo in Ngara district, an average of 160 kilometers from the Karagwe camps. Trucks were provided by UNHCR to transport vulnerable groups (pregnant women, children, elderly people), but most refugees traveled the largest part of the journey by foot. Finally, on December 28, 1996, officials announced that the massive repatriation exercise to Rwanda was finished.

The Rwandan repatriation from Tanzania in December 1996 can hardly be described as voluntary. For this reason, it is notable that UNHCR, as the international body with a mandate for refugee protection, was so closely involved in planning and implementing the operation. This paper examines the reasons behind the mass expulsion of Rwandan refugees from Tanzania, and particularly the involvement of UNHCR in that process. The first section discusses the increasing influence of political and security concerns on refugee protection decisions in recent years. The second section focuses more specifically on the Tanzanian context and the decision to send the Rwandan refugees home. In addition to UNHCR, the role of other international organizations is also explored. The third section describes the skewed logic of refugee protection that emerged from the particular dynamics of the Rwandan situation. Finally, the conclusion examines the implications of this shift in priorities and questions whether the increasing contextualization of refugee protection decisions is necessarily problematic.

The Changing Nature of Refugee Protection

In the mid-1990s, the forced repatriation of Rwandan refugees from Tanzania was not unique. It was representative of a broader international trend toward more restrictive refugee policies and declining protection standards. In 1996 alone, more than twenty countries expelled refugees from their territories.[7] In the face of complex refugee crises around the world, international organizations were increasingly caught between their humanitarian missions and geopolitical dynamics. Often, concerns about refugee protection and the principle of *non-refoulement* came into direct conflict with political and security priorities, forcing aid workers to make difficult decisions. In most cases, as then U.N. High Commissioner for Refugees Sadako Ogata explained in April 1997, the best they could do was pursue the "least worse" option.[8] In addition to the situation in central Africa, humanitarian groups faced similarly complicated dynamics in Somalia, Angola, Liberia, Sierra Leone, Sudan, Chechnya, Afghanistan, and the Balkans.

In many of these situations throughout the 1990s, UNHCR was confronted with dilemmas in which it was obliged to choose between "a limited number of options, none of which is fully consistent with the principles which the organization is mandated to uphold."[9] In 1991, for example, Turkey refused to admit a large number of Kurdish refugees fleeing northern Iraq. The United States and its Gulf War allies claimed to have avoided both *refoulement* and the provision of asylum by establishing and protecting "safe havens" within Iraq. Despite concerns about pushing refugees back at the border, UNHCR had little choice but to participate in the operation and assist the Kurds within their country of origin. The option for the refugees to stay in Iraq was not matched by a similar option of asylum elsewhere,[10] so the only other approach would have been to not assist the Kurds at all.

UNHCR also faced a dilemma in 1992 in the former Yugoslavia, where its assistance in evacuating people from situations of danger indirectly facilitated the process of ethnic cleansing. In 1993, UNHCR participated in the repatriation of Rohingyas from Bangladesh, where they were under attack, back to Myanmar, where human rights violations continued to be a problem. In all of these situations, including the Rwandan repatriation from Tanzania examined below, UNHCR faced a choice between its humanitarian mandate to protect refugees and political dynamics on the ground. These two sets of concerns, while often in conflict, were very much interrelated, as regional and international politics had important implications for refugees and their security. In each case, UNHCR claims that it "ultimately decided to . . . proceed with a course of action which, while far from optimal in terms of protection standards, nevertheless appeared to be in the best interests of the refugees concerned."[11]

According to Myron Weiner, "many of the policy dilemmas that have confronted UNHCR and other humanitarian institutions in recent years are the consequence of having to choose among conflicting norms."[12] The various goals of humanitarian intervention often compete with one another, forcing aid agencies to choose between them. As a result, "monistic humanitarianism"—the determination of policies based solely on human rights principles—is giving way to "instrumental humanitarianism," which requires decision makers to assess the likely consequences of alternative policies. In much the same way as economists, humanitarians must conduct cost-benefit analyses and make trade-offs among conflicting values. Through this process, a strategic approach to humanitarian assistance is emerging in which political and security considerations have an increasing influence on refugee protection decisions.

Many observers argue that this shift toward instrumental humanitarianism is relatively new, emerging basically since the early 1990s. It would be wrong to suggest, however, that refugee protection decisions have only recently started to be affected by political considerations. Refugee situations are inherently political, and refugee policies are "governed more often than not by politics and ideology, rather than ethics."[13] UNHCR faced a number of dilemmas in previous decades similar to the ones described above. In the early 1980s, for example, UNHCR worked with the governments of Djibouti and Ethiopia to encourage the repatriation of roughly 40,000 Ethiopians from Djibouti, most of whom did not want to leave. When Djibouti authorities forcibly repatriated several hundred refugees, UNHCR officials did little to increase protection for the remaining refugees. They told unsuccessful applicants for refugee status to flee because their protection could not be guaranteed. UNHCR was cautious in its approach to refugee protection in Djibouti in part because it feared that, "if the government were pushed too hard, it would simply . . . deport the Ethiopians *en masse*."[14] The organization was clearly forced to choose between competing priorities even at that time.

Nevertheless, such dilemmas in refugee protection have become increasingly complex and more frequent in recent years. Several factors explain this shift. First, and most important, is the end of the Cold War. In 1951, UNHCR was established in response to refugee flows caused by World War II. The body was generally concerned with protecting individual refugees from the new communist regimes in Eastern Europe. In the 1960s, focus shifted to the developing world, where independence struggles and decolonization led to large-scale but often temporary refugee flows. During the 1970s and early 1980s, as the Cold War manifested itself in conflicts around the world, refugees were seen as defectors from communism and victims of the superpower struggle. Until 1980, in fact, the U.S. limited its definition of refugees to people fleeing communism. Throughout the Cold War, UNHCR operations were supported in large part by Western donors seeking to win over allies and discredit communist regimes.

With the warming of relations between the Soviet Union and the United States, however, the situation changed. Wars that were fueled by Cold War tensions came to an end, only to be replaced by new and more complicated conflicts involving issues of identity, nationalism, and ultimately power. Refugees were no longer perceived as victims of broader geopolitical conflicts, but rather as actors in the conflicts. As support from Western allies declined, host countries in the developing world increasingly viewed refugees as a source of instability and an economic burden. Countries in the West feared a massive influx from Eastern Europe and operated under the assumption that anyone seeking asylum was doing so primarily for economic rather than political reasons. As attitudes toward refugees changed, discussions about their protection were no longer framed solely in the language of human rights. Instead, various other political and regional security considerations were taken into account.

A second but related reason for the recent increase in refugee protection dilemmas is the decline in the availability of durable solutions. Due to the nature of the Cold War, repatriation was not generally perceived as a viable option during that period. Instead, integration and third country resettlement were pursued as the long-term solutions to refugee situations. Starting in the mid-1980s, however, resettlement and integration became less desirable as attitudes toward refugees changed and the magnitude of refugee flows increased. During this period, UNHCR "transmogrified from the international community's lead agency for protecting refugees into its spearhead for containing or reversing refugee flows."[15] An early demonstration of this new approach came in 1987, when UNHCR assisted in the controversial repatriation of Sri Lankan refugees from India.[16] The organization declared the 1990s the decade of repatriation and turned its attention to evaluating conditions in the refugees' countries of origin.

The emphasis at first was on voluntary repatriation.[17] Refugees were encouraged to return to their home countries, which was assumed to be what they wanted. With the crisis in the former Yugoslavia in the early 1990s, however, it was argued that the 1951 UN Refugee Convention required only that states ensure "safe return," not that repatriation be voluntary. International efforts to resolve the conflict focused largely on creating conditions that would allow refugees to return home. This was an important component of the 1995 Dayton Peace Accord. European countries granted temporary protection to Bosnian refugees and the UN created "safe areas" within Bosnia to prevent people from fleeing in the first place. In 1999, faced with the massive Kosovo refugee crisis, NATO even went to war to create conditions that would allow for a safe return.[18]

In contrast, of course, the international community did relatively little to seek a long-lasting peace, and with it a permanent resolution to the refugee situation, in central Africa. As Sadako Ogata argued in 1998, "the international community has yet to engage in an intensive and comprehensive effort to resolve the dangerous political and ethnic tensions that have caused . . . the controversial refugee exodus."[19] In the absence of the political will necessary to create conditions for a safe return, UNHCR developed what B. S. Chimni calls "the doctrine of imposed return."[20] In September 1996, Dennis McNamara, the Director of UNHCR's Division of International Protection, stated that refugees may be sent back to "less than optimal conditions in their home country" against their will.[21] It was this latest approach to pursuing repatriation as the only durable solution that came into play just a few weeks later during the forced repatriation from Tanzania.

A third reason for the recent shift toward instrumental humanitarianism is the changing nature of refugee populations themselves. As mentioned earlier, in most regions, refugees are no longer perceived exclusively as victims of conflict, but instead as active participants in the conflicts. Many refugee communities are heavily armed and are organizing returns to their home countries by force. This situation sours relations between the host government and the country of origin, and heightens security concerns along the border. Of course, the existence of "refugee-warrior" communities is not new.[22] Throughout the 1970s and 1980s, refugees from Namibia, Zimbabwe, Afghanistan, Nicaragua, and Eritrea, to name just a few, conducted military training and launched incursions across the border from bases in host countries. In the setting of the Cold War, these groups were often armed and supported by international allies. In recent years, though, yesterday's "freedom fighters" have become today's refugee warriors. In the absence of external support for their military causes, they have integrated themselves with civilian refugee populations and exploited humanitarian assistance to further their own goals. In some cases, they have taken control of the camps themselves, further complicating refugee protection decisions for the host government and the international community.

In the context of these various changes in the 1990s, international assistance efforts shifted from strict humanitarianism toward a more deliberate analysis of the potential outcomes of various policy alternatives. This approach requires that refugee protection decisions be contextualized, taking into account the specific dynamics of each situation. Policies appropriate in one situation may not be suited to another. In the case of the Rwandan repatriation from Tanzania, according to a senior UNHCR official, the organization's involvement was "a compromise" and a bow to "new realities."[23] In order to understand these realities, it is necessary to examine more carefully the context in which the repatriation took place. The next section of this paper focuses on the reasons that the Tanzanian government decided to repatriate the Rwandan refugees from its territory. As political and security considerations became increasingly important, UNHCR once again found it necessary to choose among conflicting priorities.

The Context of Refugee Repatriation in Western Tanzania

Although Tanzania had experienced frequent refugee influxes from the countries along its western border, the 1994 influx from Rwanda was different because of its sheer magnitude. In late April, more than 170,000 people crossed a narrow bridge into Tanzania within 48 hours. By early 1995, northwestern Tanzania was host to nearly 600,000 Rwandan refugees—fifty percent more refugees than the entire country had received in the previous three decades (1961–1993). Instead of dividing them into scattered agricultural settlements, the Tanzanian government concentrated these new refugees in densely populated camps close to the border and discouraged agricultural production. The idea, according to one official, was to make their stay in Tanzania as temporary as possible. UNHCR and international non-governmental organizations (NGOs) flocked to the massive camps, where they established relief programs to address the needs of refugees and, in some cases, local hosts.

As regional refugee flows continued, Tanzanian policy shifted markedly. Authorities stepped up their efforts to discourage agricultural activity and placed restrictions on refugee movement among camps. Faced with a further influx of Rwandan refugees from camps in Burundi, Tanzania closed its western border in March 1995. The border remained officially closed for several months, although many refugees managed to cross anyway. In January 1996, the border was reopened in response to international pressure and an escalation of violence in Burundi. The December 1996 decision to repatriate the Rwandan refugees, therefore, was part of a broader shift in Tanzanian refugee policy. Although it came at a time when the country was undergoing a process of political liberalization, democratic pressures had little influence on refugee policy making.[24] Instead, the decision was based on an interrelated set of factors involving regional security, Rwandan politics, and international funding levels. This was the context in which the Tanzanian government and UNHCR issued their joint statement.

The Rwandan Patriotic Front (RPF) government that came to power in Rwanda in July 1994 regarded the massive refugee camps along its borders as a significant security threat. Many of its military opponents in the civil war, including people implicated in the genocide of more than 800,000 Tutsi and moderate Hutu, were organizing a forceful return to Rwanda from the camps in Zaire and Tanzania. These hard-line refugees were reportedly intimidating their neighbors and preventing them from returning to Rwanda voluntarily. Regional agreements in January 1995, February 1995, and November 1995 all stressed the importance of separating the suspected *génocidaires* and intimidators from "innocent refugees" in order to facilitate mass repatriation. International assistance to separate the groups was not forthcoming, however, and repatriation efforts failed.

By 1996, the Rwandan government made clear that if the international community were unable to resolve the security problem, the RPF would take action itself to eliminate the threat along its borders.[25] Rwanda did exactly that in October and November 1996 with attacks on camps in eastern Zaire that sent hundreds of thousands of refugees running. In a period of just a few days, the violence forced roughly 600,000 refugees back into Rwanda, where the RPF government could more easily control them. Another 300,000, including suspected *génocidaires*, headed west into the dense forests of central Zaire, where many were massacred by advancing rebel and Rwandan troops.[26] As these events unfolded, it became clear that the strategy of the RPF government was to create a buffer zone along its borders from which it would be safe from rebel attacks.

When a Rwandan envoy visited Dar es Salaam on November 21, 1996, therefore, Tanzanian authorities had every reason to believe any sort of explicit or implicit threat that the Rwandan government was prepared to take similar action to clear out the refugee camps in western Tanzania.[27] Although no details about the meeting were released, people close to the situation said that the envoy expressed Rwandan readiness to receive the refugees, even without the separation of intimidators, and assured Tanzanian authorities that the refugees would not be killed upon returning home. Rather than risking a military attack into its territory, or at least continued tension along the western border, Tanzanian officials decided to send the refugees home, where Rwandan authorities could deal with them directly. In many ways, the government decision was driven by the desire to avoid drawing Tanzania into a growing regional conflict.

A second factor behind the repatriation operation was the adoption by policy makers of the view that the security situation within Rwanda had improved. Based on this line of argument, Rwandans no longer had a legitimate claim to refugee status because the disturbances to public order at home had ended. This was the basis upon which Rwandans entered Tanzania as refugees in 1994. According to the 1969 Organization of African Unity (OAU) Convention, refugee status is extended to persons fleeing "external aggression, occupation, foreign domination, or events seriously disturbing public order." This represented an expansion of the 1951 UN Refugee Convention, which granted protection to individuals living outside their own countries due to a "well-founded fear of persecution." Under the expanded definition, governments could offer protection en masse to people fleeing civil war and violence without requiring them to be individually screened. A legitimate question arose, however, when the situation that led to the granting of refugee status no longer existed.[28]

With the exception of France, a close ally of the former Rwandan government, the international community largely accepted the argument that peace and stability had been restored to Rwanda, and thus that it was safe for the refugees to return home. This view was pushed strongly by the new Rwandan government, which was somewhat embarrassed that the refugees were not repatriating on their own. In order to claim legitimacy as a government and to start the process of reconstruction, the RPF regime in Kigali needed the refugees—representing roughly one-sixth of the country's population—to return. By adopting the RPF view that there was relative peace in Rwanda, therefore, the Tanzanian government further improved its relations with Rwanda while providing additional justification for the repatriation operation. According to its joint statement with UNHCR in early December 1996, the government had decided that "all Rwandese refugees can now return to their country in safety."

A third but related element underlying the December 1996 repatriation was the declining availability of funding to support Rwandan refugee programs.[29] To some extent, this factor may have been even more important than regional security issues, particularly in explaining UNHCR's involvement.[30] Unlike some bodies of the United Nations, UNHCR is entirely dependent upon voluntary contributions from member states for its field operations. By 1996, UNHCR was finding it increasingly difficult to raise the necessary funds to support the refugee operation in the Great Lakes region. The international spotlight had shifted its focus to humanitarian emergencies in Bosnia and elsewhere, and the situation in central Africa moved into its shadows.[31] The two primary donors for Great Lakes operation—the United States and the European Union—were hesitant to pump more money into the refugee camps when the situation in Rwanda appeared safe for their return. Western governments were also aware of the broader geopolitical picture that was beginning to play itself out in the region.

Funding concerns became particularly apparent at a roundtable meeting with donors in Geneva at the end of June 1996. According to Bonaventure Rutinwa, a leading Tanzanian scholar, this is when the repatriation operation really began.[32] The meeting revealed a significant split between the two most important Western players in central Africa: the United States and France. While France favored continued donor support to the refugee camps in Zaire and Tanzania, the U.S. held that aid funds would be better spent on long-term reconstruction efforts within Rwanda rather than short-term refugee relief outside of the country. Due in part to lingering concerns over French interests in Rwanda,[33] the U.S. perspective prevailed. The Tanzanian government had long made clear its position on the necessity of international burden sharing; donor representatives in Geneva were therefore aware that the withdrawal of funding for the Rwandan relief operation would eventually lead to repatriation—forced or otherwise.

Thus, it was a combination of these three factors—regional security concerns, perceptions of stability in Rwanda, and declining funding levels—that formed the basis for the decision to repatriate the Rwandan refugees in late 1996. To that end, UNHCR signed a memorandum of understanding with the Tanzanian government requiring all Rwandan refugees to leave the country by the end of December. According to subsequent public relations reports, the organization did so based on assurances from Tanzanian authorities, including the president himself, that force would not be used. The eventual use of force during the operation was perceived as an unforeseen consequence of the refugees' attempt to flee eastward, which triggered a military reaction. Nevertheless, UNHCR continued to provide logistical and other forms of support for the repatriation exercise even after it became clear that the military was to be involved (and largely in control). The organization only sought to disassociate itself from the forced nature of the repatriation after being criticized for its own role.

While UNHCR as an organization facilitated the repatriation exercise, individual field staff continued to be strong voices for refugee protection. Several

UNHCR expatriate staff members were ordered off the road during the repatriation for challenging the army's conduct of the operation, and at least one was expelled from the country altogether. "UNHCR was split," one observer argued. "The decision was approved by Geneva but the field staff were still following the rule book." In the end, the official UNHCR position seemed to be to support the massive return of refugees to Rwanda while questioning, if not fully criticizing, the government's use of the military. In January 1997, a letter was drafted from the High Commissioner to the Tanzanian president expressing concern about the use of force during the operation; under pressure from the Tanzanian foreign minister, however, the letter was never sent.[34]

UNHCR was not the only member of the international community that was complicit in the repatriation of Rwandan refugees from Tanzania. During and following the exercise, no foreign government voiced an official objection to the military operation. The U.S. and other Western powers essentially accepted the Rwandan view of regional security and supported the goals that repatriation was designed to meet. International NGOs were also largely silent about the operation. Privately, aid workers expressed concern about possible human rights violations, but publicly their organizations said little. Most international NGOs working in western Tanzania had development projects in other areas of the country for which they needed to maintain good relations with the government. In addition, at the international headquarters level, many NGOs were split. While staff in Tanzania expressed concern about the repatriation operation, staff in Rwanda wondered why the refugees had not been forced to return home sooner. Given these pulls and pushes, international NGOs seemingly decided that silent cooperation was the best response to the repatriation exercise.

In contrast to the silence of international governments and operational NGOs active in the region, several human rights organizations strongly condemned the repatriation operation, attacking the Tanzanian government and especially UNHCR for its role. Amnesty International criticized the repatriation operations from both Zaire and Tanzania, arguing that they reflected "a shocking disregard for the rights, dignity and safety of refugees."[35] On behalf of Amnesty International, a Canadian official met later with President Mkapa to express concerns about the repatriation process. Human Rights Watch similarly accused UNHCR of having "shamefully abandoned its responsibility to protect refugees" by assisting the repatriation operations, and derided international governments for their tacit approval: "The international community has barely disguised its satisfaction at seeing the refugee camps around Rwanda forcibly disbanded."[36] Human rights groups were quite critical of the repatriation operation, though their influence on policy makers was limited.

The international community on the whole thus did little to prevent a forced repatriation of Rwandan refugees from Tanzania, and may have pushed the government further in that direction. Western donors in particular hastened the move toward repatriation by withdrawing their support for the relief operation. UNHCR provided both funding and logistical assistance for the repatriation exercise. Interestingly, when Tanzania avoided international criticism for the operation, the government saw an opportunity to impose more restrictions on refugees still living within the country.[37] Starting in early 1997, there were frequent military operations to round up refugees who had been living in Tanzanian villages since the 1960s and 1970s and move them to camps with the more recent arrivals. Although UNHCR joined human rights groups this time in criticizing the round-up operation, the organization's authority on refugee protection in Tanzania had already been somewhat compromised.

Skewing the Logic of Refugee Protection

During the December 1996 repatriation operation, not all of the Rwandan refugees living in Tanzania were forced back to their home country. Individual refugees who were likely to be killed or arrested upon returning to Rwanda could approach the Tanzanian government and request asylum. In many ways, this was a shift back to the traditional definition from the 1951 UN Refugee Convention in which asylum status was based on an individual fear of persecution. The Rwandan refugees had initially been admitted to Tanzania based instead on the expanded 1969 OAU definition, which included persons fleeing serious disturbances to public order. The requirement that Rwandans now meet the more restrictive definition in order to receive asylum was designed to limit the number of people eligible for protection. Even so, it suggested that the Tanzanian government was somewhat wary of forcing back refugees who might be killed. The peculiarity of this case was that refugees who could claim a legitimate fear of persecution upon return to Rwanda were those who had participated in the 1994 genocide.

The question of guilt pervaded the Rwandan refugee operation in Tanzania from the beginning. Local hosts, government officials, international aid workers, and even the media had a different attitude toward Rwandans than other groups because many of the refugees had blood on their hands. There was general frustration with the refugees' continued presence in Tanzania, where they were seen as hiding from justice. UNHCR estimated that 90,000 out of approximately one million Rwandan refugees in Tanzania and Zaire were suspected *génocidaires*.[38] According to one Tanzanian official, however, "As time went on, they were all seen as killers." This was in part because the refugees rallied around their leaders and protected neighbors whenever Tanzanian authorities tried to arrest suspects in the camps. Many aid workers struggled with the thought that their humanitarian efforts were supporting killers and were allowing militia to re-group and organize a forceful return. In many ways, the Rwandan refugees were perceived as having cloaked themselves in a "facade of victimhood"[39] to secure international assistance and further their own political and military objectives.[40]

During the December 1996 repatriation, refugees with blood on their hands thus had the most to fear from returning to Rwanda. They were likely to be arrested and punished for their crimes, perhaps even executed. Although Tanzanian authorities wanted to see suspected *génocidaires* brought to justice,[41] they worried about the possibility of refugees being summarily killed as soon as they crossed the border into Rwanda. Such an incident would spark international criticism for the repatriation and would tarnish Tanzania's reputation on refugee issues. Tanzanian officials were so concerned about this possibility that President Mkapa reportedly did not grant an audience to the envoy from Rwanda in late November 1996 until assurances were provided that returning refugees would not be killed. As additional protection against such a situation, the Tanzanian government gave Rwandans the opportunity to present themselves to authorities if they had legitimate reason to believe that they would be killed upon returning to Rwanda. In December 1996, roughly 150 to 200 Rwandans took advantage of this offer, choosing to stay behind and seek asylum in Tanzania.

In the end, this created a disturbing situation in which "innocent" refugees were sent home, often against their will, and *génocidaires* continued to receive protection in Tanzania. People who confessed to participating in the genocide were moved to a new prison camp further away from the Rwandan border that was supported by UNHCR and the international community. The majority of refugees who were not guilty of murder, however, were forced back across the border into Rwanda. As Rutinwa argued, "Tanzania has skewed the logic of refugee protection. They only protect the killers. If you haven't killed anyone, then you are sent home."[42] In addition, the few international organizations that publicly criticized the forced repatriation from Tanzania were seen in some circles as having sided with the *génocidaires*. Thus, the issue of guilt that had complicated the Rwandan refugee situation from the beginning continued to have a distorting effect even during the repatriation operation.

Conclusion

In the end, political and security considerations in western Tanzania outweighed protection priorities with respect to the Rwandan refugees. The decision to repatriate roughly half a million refugees in December 1996 was based primarily on the threat of attack from Rwanda, the widespread perception of stability in that country, and the related decline in funding available to support the relief operation. At the same time, Tanzania's lingering concern about the possibility that returning refugees would be killed led to a disturbing situation in which those who feared arrest and punishment in Rwanda continued to receive protection on the other side of the border. The forced nature of the repatriation operation was regrettable, but the underlying reasons for the decision were in many ways quite understandable.

The Rwandan repatriation operation was designed at least in part to prevent Tanzania from being drawn into broader regional conflicts. Although observers at the time may not have believed Tanzania was really at risk, subsequent events in central Africa suggest otherwise. After attacking the refugee camps in eastern Zaire in late 1996, Rwanda and its Ugandan allies marched west toward Kinshasa, helping Laurent Kabila come to power in May 1997. But when Kabila failed to protect his eastern neighbors from attacks by rebel groups operating out of eastern Congo, Rwanda and Uganda once again supported rebel movements there. In response, Kabila's new allies, including Namibia, Angola, and Zimbabwe, sent troops to his defense. By September 1998, more than ten regional governments and rebel armies were involved in the conflict, which continued into 2001. Despite various threats[43] and the continued presence of refugees, Tanzania has largely managed to stay out of the regional conflict. It is not clear that Tanzania would have been able to do so if the Rwandan refugees had not been sent home.

In a sense, then, the decision to repatriate the Rwandan refugees could be seen as a strategy of conflict prevention or avoidance. This in itself is an important priority, along with refugee protection. As the central Africa case illustrates, though, these two priorities may at times conflict with one another, forcing aid workers to make a difficult choice. In Tanzania, UNHCR apparently determined that conflict prevention was more important than refugee protection. The High Commissioner herself explained: "When refugee outflows and prolonged stay in asylum countries risk spreading conflict to neighboring states, policies aimed at early repatriation can be considered as serving prevention.... [This is] what motivated ... UNHCR's policy of encouraging repatriation from Zaire and Tanzania to Rwanda, even though human rights concerns in Rwanda never disappeared."[44] This argument reflects an emerging perspective that violations of refugee protections such as freedom of movement and *non-refoulement* can at times be justified as conflict prevention strategies.

Human rights advocates have been sharply critical of this approach in central Africa, charging that it is a "renunciation of principle to *realpolitik*."[45] They are particularly concerned about the willingness of UNHCR, NGOs, and donors to abandon long-standing refugee protection standards in the face of short-term political imperatives. As one critic argues, "The absolute values of international humanitarian law would now seem to be largely replaced by relative 'conflict management' objectives designed to achieve a strategically or economically favourable peace."[46] While these are legitimate critiques, the implicit assumption that refugee policies can be deduced directly from human rights principles without regard to conflicting political and security concerns overlooks the importance of these factors in determining the patterns of refugee migration in the first place.

The only clear way to resolve the growing number of refugee protection dilemmas would be to devise approaches limiting the extent to which various objectives come into conflict. This may require mechanisms to reduce the importance of political and security considerations in refugee policy making. An increase in the amount of non-earmarked funding available to UNHCR, for example, may reduce its dependence on key donors and allow it to make discretionary decisions.[47] Clarification of the theoretical and organizational distinctions between UNHCR's two primary roles—humanitarian assistance and refugee protection—may ensure that protection issues receive more sufficient attention.[48] The international provision of security in refugee situations through the establishment of safe areas or other means may lessen the likelihood that refugee populations will become targets of further attacks.

In the long run, though, policy priorities will inevitably come into conflict—be they refugee protection and conflict prevention or other important objectives. This is particularly true in the post–Cold War era, when geopolitical dynamics no longer structure decisions in such a way as to prioritize some objectives over others. Increasingly, in this changing world, refugee protection dilemmas will require careful analysis of the likely consequences of various policy alternatives. The contextualization of policy decisions may result in the declining universality of protection standards, but it may also allow for the development of policies that are more appropriately tailored to address the needs and priorities of the situation at hand.

9

The Marginalization
of Palestinian Refugees

Thus, unlike any other group or category of refugees in the world, Palestinians are singled out for exceptional restrictions in all the main international legal instruments which govern the rights and obligations of states towards refugees. Over 5 million Palestinian refugees are currently denied access to their right to international protection.[2]

Palestinians constitute the largest refugee population in the world,[3] and their exile is one of the longest in contemporary history, spanning over half a century. However, the international community has treated Palestinian refugees with ambiguity, neglect and, more significantly, has left them without international protection. This chapter will examine the historical and legal origins of the international protection gap and its impact on refugees, and it will suggest policy and institutional changes that are necessary to redress this situation in the Palestinian case.

A key element to any durable solution begins when the two sides of a conflict begin to interpret the past in similar if not concurring ways, which allows for admission of and responsibility for wrongdoing, and upon which solutions such as repatriation, compensation, restitution, and reparation may be envisioned. As Guy Goodwin-Gill has posited: "In international law, the obligation to make a reparation is premised on liability, that is, the attribution of imputability of an internationally wrongful act to the responsible State. In the present case [the Palestinian case], the wrong done comprises flight or expulsion, followed by dispossession."[4]

Palestinians and Israelis view the historical juncture of 1948 in contradictory terms. The official Israeli historiography is premised on the politics of negation that denies a historical and national existence of a Palestinian people. Golda Meir stated in 1969 that Palestinians did not exist, whereas the late Prime Minister Rabin, while still a general in the army, referred to the "so-called Palestinians," and Menachim Begin called them the "Arabs of Eretz Israel" (land of Israel).[5] The official Israeli interpretation of this past is reflected in their denial of any responsibility in creating the Palestinian refugee problem.[6]

Since its establishment, the Israeli state has maintained a consistent position that the right of return, as well as issues relating to compensation and restitution for Palestinian refugees, infringe on Israel's "right to self-determination" and that the return of refugees would be an "act of suicide on her part."[7] In other words, the Israelis reject the principle of the right of return, claiming that the return of refugees to their homes will compromise its character as a *Jewish* state.[8] Consequently, there has been no 'attribution of imputability of an internationally wrongful act' to the Israeli state. It is only in the last two decades that the "New Israeli Historians"[9] have begun to challenge the official foundational myth of the state to reveal the violence inflicted upon the indigenous Palestinian population by Jewish militias as they "cleared them" out of their villages and towns.

Nonetheless, the New Historians remain few and their impact marginal when compared to the dominance of Israeli historiography in the public arena and in Western societies. Israel, as the embodiment of the European Zionist movement, emerged as the victorious side in the 1948 war, and in the process, the congruity and continuity in the Palestinian worldviews of history, geography, and demography have been vanquished. Over five million Palestinian refugees are the living witness of this war, scattered in various countries, the majority living in poverty. One-third languish in refugee camps. Since their displacement, refugees have been awaiting the implementation of UN Resolutions, primarily those that relate to their right of return (including the related rights of restitution and compensation, as enumerated in General Assembly Resolution 194, paragraph 11, which will be discussed later in the chapter) and self-determination.

The United Nations Relief and Works Agency (UNRWA) provides humanitarian assistance exclusively to Palestinian refugees. However, UNRWA has no protection mandate. Although the United Nations Conciliation Commission for Palestine (UNCCP)[10] was mandated to provide Palestinian refugees with international protection, it became dysfunctional only a few years after its establishment. Neither UNHCR nor any other international body has stepped in to fill the vacuum. "Protection" in this chapter is used in its broader meaning to include "durable solutions," "human rights protection," and "diplomatic protection."

This lack of international protection has a direct and detrimental impact on the lives of refugees. Israeli armed attacks on civilians and refugees in Gaza and the West Bank, including attacks on camps that fall within the territories under the Palestine Authority, prompted the UN Commission on Human Rights (CHR) to send an Inquiry Commission.[11] The Commission submitted its report in March 2001, calling for an international presence to monitor and report on compliance with human rights. Nevertheless, no significant pressure has been placed upon Israel to abide by international law, and in most votes before the Security Council, the United States either votes against resolutions condemning Israel's violations of humanitarian, refugee, or human rights laws, or vetoes these recommendations.[12]

In Arab host countries, Palestinians have been vulnerable to armed conflict, expulsions, and other violations of human rights—and this situation has existed for more than five decades. This chapter will take an interdisciplinary approach to examine how this state of affairs arose, how it has been left to fester as it has, and finally, examine possible alternatives and institutional arrangements that might be implemented to fill the protection gap. In particular, this chapter addresses the question of whether the UNHCR should now involve itself with the Palestinian crisis and the manner in which this might be accomplished.

International Responsibility: A Historical Legacy

As the Ottoman Empire began to crumble towards the end of World War I, western powers vied for control over the Middle East. Between July 1915 and March 1916, the British Commissioner in Cairo, Sir Henry McMahon, corresponded with Sherif Hussein of Mecca, promising that Great Britain would recognize and support the independence of the Arabs if they revolted against the Ottomans.[13] However, the British government was secretly negotiating with France and Russia to partition the Ottoman provinces among them. The Sykes-Picot Agreement,[14] signed in May 1916, accorded France the territories that later emerged as Syria and Lebanon, while Britain took control of the area that became Iraq and Transjordan. Palestine was to be placed under international administration, the form of which was to be decided after agreements were made with Russia, the other Allies, and the representatives of the Sherif of Mecca. The agreement also stated that "there shall be accorded to Great Britain the Ports of Haifa and Acre." Nevertheless, at the peace conference after the War, the Balfour Declaration took the place of the international agreement.[15] However, following the Bolshevik Revolution in 1917, Russia withdrew from the war and divulged the secret to the world, shocking the Arabs who were still fulfilling their part of the McMahon-Hussein correspondence.

Less than a year after the Sykes-Picot agreement was signed, the British Foreign Secretary, Arthur James Balfour, sent a letter dated November 2, 1917 to the British Zionist leader Lord Lionel Rothschild that stated that:

His Majesty's Government views with favour the establishment in Palestine of a national home for the Jewish people, and will use their best endeavours to facilitate the achievement of this object, it being clearly understood that nothing shall be done which may prejudice the civil and religious rights of existing non-Jewish communities in Palestine, or the rights and political status enjoyed by Jews in any other country.[16]

As Arthur Koestler describes the Balfour Declaration, it was an "illegal act of one nation (Britain) to give to another (Jews), the country of a third (Palestinians)."[17] According to Mallison, the Palestinians were a people de facto as the inhabitants of Palestine long before the twentieth century. The Palestinians, along with other Arab peoples, fell under the rule of the Ottoman Empire until the First World War. With the defeat of the Ottoman Empire, the League of Nations designated Britain as the mandatory power under the League of Nations Mandate for Palestine. Moreover, the Covenant of the League of Nations recognized "provisionally" the "existence as independent nations" of the communities, which were formerly parts of the Turkish Empire, and this included provisional recognition of the Palestinians. The British Mandate at the time acted as a 'custodian' which, consistent with the requirements of Article 22 of the Covenant, was designed to lead the people who were "not yet able to stand by themselves" to independence. Consequently, it "contained an implicit recognition of Palestinian national identity."[18]

However, when the League of Nations issued the British Mandate on July 24, 1922, it incorporated the Balfour Declaration in its articles without ascertaining whether it was consistent with the Covenant of the League of Nations.[19] This act on the part of the League of Nations was *ultra vires*, a violation of its principles as stated in its Covenant in Article 22 (4). The incorporation of the Balfour Declaration, which replaced the International Administration envisioned by the Sykes-Picot agreement, ran counter to prior recognition by the League of Nations of Palestine's provisional existence as an independent sovereign nation as recognized in the 1919 Covenant and contradicted the promises made by the British to Sherif Hussein in Mecca. In other words, the inclusion of the Balfour Declaration in the articles of the British Mandate, particularly Articles 2, 4, 6 and 7 (see Annex I), which referred to the cooperation between the British government and Zionist institutions, went beyond the scope of what had already been stipulated in the Covenant to be the terms of the various mandates. In additon, legal experts argue that the recognition of the de jure rights of Palestinians as a people with national rights was also recognized by the United Nations when it authorized them to establish an "Arab state" in the Partition Plan (UNGA Resolution 181) in November 1947.[20]

It is important to examine the Sykes-Picot Agreement, the Balfour Declaration and the British Mandate period because of their far-reaching consequences on refugees and the related pivotal elements of: (a) nationality (the issue of Palestinian national identity); (b) sovereignty (self-determination, including the establishment of a state); and, (c) territory (land issues pertaining to Jewish settlement on Palestinian land and the Palestinian right of return).

In light of the above, it will be observed that the Balfour Declaration did not refer to the population in Palestine, either as Arabs or as Palestinians, but rather, as the 'existing non-Jewish population of Palestine.' In other words, those who constituted then more than 92 percent of the population were not regarded as a national community with sovereignty rights over Palestinian territory. According to Khalidi, this was not a coincidental omission, while Abu-Lughod describes the omission as the "politics of negation" of Palestinian national and territorial rights.[21] Consistent with the spirit of the Balfour Declaration, the British mandate in its official documents also did not refer to the "Palestinians," rather, to confessional affiliation, namely, Muslims, Christians, and Druze; only rarely did the British refer to Arabs. Today, Israeli official classifications also do not refer to the "Palestinians" within Israel, but use confessional affiliation, or the terms "non-Jews," and "minorities."

In light of its commitment to the Zionist project, the British mandatory authorities in Palestine provided the Jewish settlers with political, military, economic, and logistical support, including facilitating Jewish immigration to Palestine.[22] In the thirties, Jewish immigration to Palestine increased, especially following the rise of fascism in Europe. Between 1931 and 1944, the number of Jews in Palestine increased from 174,606 to 528,702 settlers.[23] This factor, combined with discriminatory British laws against the indigenous inhabitants, such as the Emergency Laws that prohibited Palestinians (but not Jews) from forming political organizations, or obtaining weapons to defend themselves, fuelled anger and resistance against the Zionist–British collaboration and against what Palestinians recognized by then as their impending dispossession.

In November 1947, the United Nations General Assembly (UNGA), in an attempt to bring an end to the escalating violence, passed Resolution 181, proposing to partition Palestine into an Arab and a Jewish state. According to the plan, a Jewish minority with clear colonial objectives would have been allocated the larger territorial base upon which to establish a state, while the Palestinian majority would have been allocated the rest, with the exception of Jerusalem, which was to be administered internationally.[24] However, rather than quelling the conflict, the Partition Plan sparked further unrest, and Zionist Jewish paramilitary organizations, primarily the Haganah,[25] which had been preparing and arming with British and Western support, proceeded to expel Palestinians, who despite the increase in the number of Jews due to immigration constituted more than two-thirds of the population.[26]

The Palestinians were no match against the Jewish paramilitary organizations. The Arab armies were not only poorly equipped and lacking coordination, but they were drawn into the conflict too late and thus were incapable of reversing the military situation.[27] On May 15, 1948, Israel declared the establishment of the "Jewish State," thereby fulfilling the objective of the Zionist movement. As for the Palestinian Arabs, whose uninterrupted presence in Palestine as the majority population dates back at least for a millennium and a half, 1948 marks the beginning of their protracted exile and diaspora. By the end of *al-Nakbah*, or "the Catastrophe," the term Palestinians use to describe the 1948 war, over 530 villages were devastated and depopulated, and hundreds of thousands of Palestinians living in villages and urban centers were forced out.[28] The moveable and immovable assets of indigenous inhabitants were seized by the nascent Jewish State and its citizens, including vast areas of land, banks, schools, and homes. More significantly, between 700,000–900,000 Palestinians were forced to flee.[29]

UN General Assembly Resolution 194 (III)

As was the case with the League of Nations in its incorporation of the Balfour Declaration into the articles of the British Mandate, the United Nations, upon its establishment, also became embroiled in the conflict. This occurred when it proposed to partition Palestine in November 1947 (UNGA Resolution 181), and again, when the UN admitted Israel as a member state on 11 May 1949, in UNGA Resolution 273. The condition for the acceptance of Israel at the UN was that it "unreservedly accepts the obligations of the UN Charter and undertakes to honour them from the day when it becomes a member of the UN."[30] However, since its establishment, Israel's official position has been noncompliance with the right of return as reaffirmed in UN Resolution 194 (III),[31] and the international community has taken no steps to enforce compliance.

On the 16th of September 1948, the UN Mediator, Count Folke Bernadotte,[32] submitted a Progress Report on the events in Palestine in which he outlined his recommendations to the UNGA.[33] Based on his report, the widely quoted UNGA Resolution 194 (III) was passed on the 11 December 1948, including paragraph 11:

> 11. Resolves that the refugees wishing to return to their homes and live at peace with their neighbours should be permitted to do so at the earliest practicable date, and that compensation should be paid for the property of those choosing not to return and for loss of or damage to property which, under principles of international law or in equity, should be made good by the Governments or authorities responsible;

> Instructs the Conciliation Commission to facilitate the repatriation, resettlement and economic and social rehabilitation of the refugees and the payment of compensation, and to maintain close relations with the Director of the United Nations Relief for Palestine Refugees and, through him, with the appropriate organs and agencies of the United Nations.[34]

It is important to highlight here the relationship between the protection issue and Resolution 194 (III). The protection mandate for Palestinian refugees was established through the creation of the United Nations Conciliation Commission (UNCCP), outlined in the second paragraph of UN Resolution 194 (III). The UNCCP's mandate as expressed in Resolution 194 (III) was to "facilitate the repatriation, resettlement and economic and social rehabilitation of the refugees and the payment of compensation." According to Boling, the emphasis on repatriation as the preferred solution for Palestinian refugees reflects several principles that had become customary norms of international law by 1948. The aforementioned principles include the right of displaced persons to return to their homes, as well as the prohibitions against arbitrary denationalization and mass expulsion.[35]

However, within four years after its creation, the UNCCP reached a stalemate and became practically dysfunctional. The failure of the UNCCP can be attributed to several factors.[36] The first is Israel's noncompliance with the resolution and its longstanding rejection of the right of return. On June 5, 1948, Joseph Weitz, director of the Jewish National Fund, met with David Ben-Gurion, Israel's first Prime Minister, and suggested a plan for preventing the return of refugees to their homes.[37] The rejection of the right of return was formalized and adopted by the Israeli cabinet on June 16th of the same year.[38]

Secondly, Palestinian refugees refused to abandon their right of return and Arab states rejected UN proposals and plans for integrating refugees into host societies. This became apparent during the ad hoc Committee meeting that was held in August 1950 in Geneva to finalize the drafting process of the statute of UNHCR. The draft contained a provision to the effect that "persons falling under the competence of the High Commissioner's Office for Refugees, shall be those defined in Article 1 of the Convention Relating to the Status of Refugees."[39] During the discussions in Geneva, the representatives of Egypt, Lebanon, and Saudi Arabia put forth an amendment to distinguish Palestinians from other refugees. The amendment was introduced because, as the Lebanese delegate observed, other persons became refugees due to actions taken contrary to UN principles. In the Palestinian case, however: "The existence of the Palestine refugees . . . was the direct result of a decision taken by the United Nations itself, with full knowledge of the consequences."[40]

The third factor underlying the failure of the UNCCP was the lack of political will on the part of the international community to support the UNCCP in achieving its objectives. Moreover, the UN merged the role of international protection with the larger conflict, which has had grave consequences for Palestinian refugees. As Rempel writes:

> The decision by the UN General Assembly to merge the role of international protection for the refugees with the larger task of Arab-Israeli conciliation . . . ultimately compromised the ability of the UNCCP to protect and promote the basic legal rights afforded to refugees under international refugee law and under the wider body of international human rights law. . . . In the midst of all the other outstanding issues on the agenda, the rights of the refugees were, in effect, displaced in the search for a resolution of the entire conflict itself.[41]

The United Nations Relief and Works Agency

Having failed to repatriate refugees, the UN established an economic survey mission (ESM) in August 1949 that would examine integration programs in neighbouring Arab countries as part of its overall objectives. It is interesting to note that the first head of the ESM was Gordon Clapp, chairman of the U.S. Tennessee Valley Authority. The ESM aimed at applying a model of development and integration in the region, namely, the Jordan Valley water development project, similar to the economic projects in the U.S. that followed the economic crisis of the 1920s. However, refugees and Arab states opposed these large-scale economic schemes and they eventually failed.[42]

Based upon the recommendations of the Economic Survey Mission, the United Nations Relief and Works Agency (UNRWA) was established by UNGA Resolution 302 (IV) on December 8, 1949 (see Annex II). The Agency began its operations in May 1950, providing relief and basic services to refugees in Jordan, Gaza, Syria, and Lebanon, and until 1952 to refugees within Israel.[43] However, UNRWA's mandate as outlined by the UN was to be strictly humanitarian.

The term *Works* in the name United Nations Relief and Works Agency betrays its raison d'etre, which is essentially to integrate refugees in the host countries. This was particularly the case in the 1950s and in the words of the Advisory Commission Chairman John Blandford Jr., these works projects were to encourage "the antithesis of camp life and idleness."[44] Western powers hoped that such projects would lead to integration, contrary to Palestinian aspirations for repatriation. However, the underlying political objectives were clear to the Palestinian refugees and Arab states. Over the years, refugees have resisted the reduction of their predicament to a "humanitarian cause," and as Benjamin Schiff rightly noted, despite the passage of decades, this huge bureaucracy (UNRWA) was unable to pacify refugees or subdue their national struggle.[45]

In the fifties and sixties, refugees called for the "burning of ration cards," and intensive politicization of the humanitarian classifications, sites, and experiences foiled any implicit or explicit policies to assimilate or settle refugees in second or third countries of refuge.[46] UNRWA itself, despite all attempts at steering away from the political quagmire, has often been pulled into it by the empirical realities on the ground. In some cases such a 'pull' was positive, especially during the first *Intifada* (Palestinian uprising) in 1987 when it skillfully maneuvered around Israeli opposition and, in a manner of speaking, trespassed its humanitarian mission for adopting a protection role.

Between 1988–1994, UNRWA established the Refugee Affairs Officers Programme (RAOs) that played an important, if limited, role in defusing the confrontation between Palestinians and the Israeli occupation forces during the *Intifada*, or uprising, which had begun in 1987. The RAOs' functions included visiting refugee camps, reporting on disruptions of the agency's operations, and facilitating the delivery of food and emergency relief. Legal officers at UNRWA prepared reports, including allegations on human rights violations, which were passed on to Israeli military commanders, but also to higher ministry levels. "Protection by publicity" was implemented by public information officers, who used statistics and information gathered by the RAOs to publicize violations committed against the refugee population.[47] This was a unique and positive experience in the agency's history. The RAO program indicated that the agency has the potential to play a more proactive role in the Palestinian refugee problem and possibly play a part in filling the protection gap, on the condition that there is international support and a more expansive mandate.

UNRWA's diminished capabilities, attributed in the agency's publications to "donor-fatigue" and budget cuts,[48] have affected basic services to refugees, both in terms of quantity as well as quality, in the areas of education, health, and social and relief services. Although increasing poverty is a significant aspect in refugee demands for the expansion and improvement of the agency's services, there is also a strong political message being sent by refugees to the agency and the international community against solutions that abrogate their political and legal rights. Indeed, Palestinian refugees see a clear link between UNRWA's continued presence and their political rights.[49]

UNRWA's mandate as instituted by the UN General Assembly is to provide services for Palestinian refugees until a political (durable) resolution to the refugee problem has been reached. With the Declaration of Principles on Interim Self-Government Arrangements of September 13, 1993, signed in Washington, D.C. between Israel and the Palestinians, the possibility of a political solution to the Palestinian–Israeli question—as envisioned by the PLO leadership, Israeli leaders, and the United States—began to take shape. However, the Declaration of Principles and following agreements (known as the Oslo agreements) have marginalized Palestinian refugees since these agreements were not anchored on the basis of UN resolutions, specifically Resolution 194 (III). Thus, any move to dismantle UNRWA in the current political context and within the Oslo framework for peace would have far-reaching economic and political ramifications for refugees and for the region.

The "Exclusionary" Clauses: UNHCR and the 1951 Refugee Convention

To facilitate the functioning of the agency, UNRWA developed its own working definition, which states that a Palestine refugee:

> [S]hall mean any person whose normal place of residence was Palestine during the period 1 June 1946 to 15 May 1948 and who lost both home and means of livelihood as a result of the 1948 conflict.[50]

As Takkenberg observes, it is rather perplexing that the discussions on Palestinian refugees as a "special case" and in the deliberations of UNGA Resolution

302 (IV), which established the agency, no definition was included for a "Palestine refugee" under the mandate of UNRWA. In fact, the General Assembly had never formally approved the definition developed by the agency, although it had accepted it tacitly.[51]

UNRWA's definition has no legal bearing in international law and is meant to facilitate management requirements of the bureaucracy itself. The definition was initially inherited from its predecessors (mainly NGOs working under the umbrella of the United Nations Relief for Palestine Refugees), and it has evolved and changed over the years.[52] Moreover, this definition does not include all Palestinian refugees, rather a subset that UNRWA has defined as eligible for assistance. Consequently, Palestinian negotiators in the Refugee Working Group and the Quadripartite Committee (established during the political negotiations within the Oslo framework to deal with the refugees and displaced persons)[53] have used UNRWA's definition only as a base, but have proposed an expanded definition to be more inclusive of many other categories of refugees that UNRWA's definition excludes, such as the non-registered refugees.

The establishment of UNRWA a few days before the UNHCR Statute took effect and prior to the 1951 Refugee Convention resulted in the "temporary exclusionary" clause. In Article 1D of the 1951 Refugee Convention, the "exclusionary" clause states that:

> This Convention shall not apply to persons who are at present receiving from organs or agencies of the United Nations other then the United Nations High Commissioner for Refugees protection or assistance. When such protection or assistance has ceased for any reason, without the position of such persons being definitively settled in accordance with the relevant resolutions adopted by the General Assembly of the United Nations, these persons shall *ipso facto* be entitled to the benefits of this Convention.

Similarly, paragraph 7 (c) in the UNHCR Statute states:

> Exclusion under this clause applies to any person who is in receipt of protection or assistance from organs or agencies of the United Nations, other than the UNHCR. Such protection or assistance was previously given by the former United Nations Korean Reconstruction Agency and is currently given by UNRWA . . . there could be other situations in the future.

According to Takkenberg, Article 1D of the 1951 Refugee Convention and paragraph 7 (c) of the UNHCR Statute were both included with Palestinian refugees in mind and with the intention of "excluding" them. However, based on the discussions on the Article in the UNHCR: "It may, therefore, be more appropriate, as Grahl-Madsen suggests, to consider Article 1D as a 'suspensive clause' rather than an 'exclusion clause.'"54

The ambiguity created by the above-mentioned clause in the 1951 Refugee Convention and the UNHCR Statute has become a source of legal complications for Palestinians. As Takkenberg observes, Article 1D of the Convention has proven to be an obstacle to refugees who were residing in one of UNRWA's areas of operations and have attempted to seek asylum or protection as refugees in third party countries.55

Here two issues need to be emphasized. The first is that the international community considered refugees as a special and important case. Consequently, the inclusion of Article 1D in the Refugee Convention, along with the earlier establishment of the UNCCP, were undertaken as a form of *heightened* protection and precautionary measures to ensure that they received protection and assistance at all times until their situation was resolved according to international law.56 This interpretation, which views Article 1D in the 1951 Convention as a guarantee of protection, is supported by the second paragraph which states that should assistance or protection cease, refugees will "*ipso facto be entitled to the benefits of this Convention.*"

Thus, rather than being treated as an "exclusion cause," Article 1D should be viewed—and in the term used by Susan Akram and Guy Goodwin-Gill—as a "contingent inclusion clause."57 A key term to emphasize in the Article is *ipso facto,* which means that Palestinian refugees should have been provided with international protection as soon as the UNCCP became dysfunctional in the early 1950s; and, when assistance or protection fail, they do not need new screening to become entitled to the benefits of the Convention.58 Consequently, the issue of whether Palestinian refugees fall under coverage of the 1951 Refugee Convention is related to the activation of the inclusion clause of Article 1D.

The aforementioned interpretation has been recently reestablished by Akram and Goodwin-Gill, who in a *Brief Amicus Curiae* concluded that:

> Article 1D's plain language, drafting history and applicable canons of treaty construction all allow for only one interpretation of its meaning. Article 1D, as a contingent inclusion clause is the only interpretation consistent with the protective scheme envisioned for the world's refugees in general, and for Palestinians in particular, under the 1951 Refugee Convention and its 1967 Protocol.59

The second point regarding Article 1D of the Convention and paragraph 7 (c) of the UNHCR Statute is that the interpretation of these clauses varies from one country to another. Within UNHCR itself (probably due to the self-imposed distancing from the Palestinian case), there is also no consensus. One of the obvious indications of the uncertain relationship between UNHCR and Palestinian refugees is UNHCR's statistical recording and reports on refugees.

In recent publications, Afghan refugees are cited as the largest refugee group, underscoring that Palestinian refugees (who *are* the largest group) do not fall under its mandate, and thus, are therefore not of direct concern to UNHCR.[60]

UNHCR has been wary of seeming too intrusive on the sovereignty of states, and it has intervened only in an ad hoc manner in determining the refugee status of Palestinian applicants. As an example, during 1994–1995 a Palestinian refugee expelled from Libya found his way to Malta, where he attempted to apply for a student visa to the UK. His application was rejected several times on the grounds that he carried a Refugee Document[61] with no residency permit in any country. Consequently, he was forced to seek asylum through UNHCR. However, his application was refused because he was told that he is an "UNRWA-refugee." Employing informal channels and people with political influence, further attempts were made until he obtained a visa into the UK, as well as asylum in Malta. His visa to the UK was granted through the assistance of an UNHCR staff member who manipulated the guidelines and helped him acquire a document stating he had a job in Malta to which he could return upon completion of his education in the UK.[62] This scenario is not unusual. I have interviewed a number of individuals who have been shuffled between UNHCR and UNRWA offices, each considering the other as the appropriate agency for handling Palestinian refugee cases.

Further complications for Palestinian refugees occur as a consequence of the diverse interpretations of Article 1D and 7 (c) in the UNHCR Statute by states. In Canada, for example, determination of refugee status is based on the definition of a "Convention refugee" as embodied in subsection 2, paragraph 1 of the Immigration Act. In Switzerland, on the other hand, determination of refugee status is based on the Swiss Asylum Law, which does not contain a clause similar to Article 1D of the 1951 Refugee Convention.[63] The problems for Palestinian refugees are thus related to the interpretation of the Article, including the phrases '*for any reason,*' and '*ceases to exist*' in the same sentence, for example, whether it applies to *all* Palestinian refugees or to the particular applicant. Finally, the ambiguity is compounded by the incorrect interpretation of UNRWA's mandate, mainly, the wrong assumption that falling under UNRWA's mandate requires that the refugee is living in one of its areas of operation, or, that he or she is registered with the agency. However, as Takkenberg clarifies:

> What counts is whether the individual concerned falls under UNRWA's mandate, that is, that that individual has the *possibility* of requesting the services provided by that organization if so required and taking into consideration the applicable procedures and criteria. This possibility not only exists for those actually residing in UNRWA's area of operations, but also for those who have left the area, as long as they are able to return.[64]

The confusion surrounding Article 1D and Paragraph 7 (c) prompted the legal unit at BADIL, a non-governmental organization (NGO) working on Palestinian residency and refugee rights, to distribute a questionnaire directed to practitioners in the field of refugee and asylum law. The questionnaire, dated April 2001, is a *Request for Assistance in Locating UNHCR Opinions and National Domestic Law Cases Interpreting the "Palestinian Clauses" in Certain Statutes & Conventions, as Well as Host State Obligations towards Palestinian Refugees.* The questions are directed to acquire better understanding as to how these various institutions interpret and apply Article 1D of the 1951 Refugee Convention, Paragraph 7 (C) of the UNHCR Statute and the 1961 Convention on the Reduction of Statelessness, Article 11.[65]

An Expanded and More Visible UNRWA?

The UNRWA-Refugee Relationship

UNRWA is one of the largest and oldest bureaucracies in the United Nations system. Therefore, it is rather odd that it does not have international visibility and clout equivalent to that of UNHCR or other international agencies. The agency has over 20,000 employees, the vast majority of whom are Palestinian refugees. At the top of its hierarchy are the international staff, numbering around one hundred employees, who nevertheless occupy key positions and are closely linked to donors and Western powers. Thus, the boundaries between UNRWA and registered refugees are porous, rendering the agency as a site for contestation by different actors and often with conflicting agendas. With tentacles reaching out to the international community, yet very rooted in Palestinian refugee communities and their history, UNRWA's presence has become a political symbol of Palestinian political and legal rights, as well as a provider of basic humanitarian and social services not matched by host governments.

There are many advantages to maintaining UNRWA as an institution with an expanded and more visible role in the international arena, which would indirectly support its ability to provide some level of protection. Here, it is important to point out that the suggestion is not that UNRWA should carry the sole or primary responsibility for granting such protection, rather, that it should play a more proactive role in this arena in conjunction with other international organizations, primarily UNHCR and the International Committee of the Red Cross (ICRC).

An important element that renders the agency a significant institution is its organizational culture and history. UNRWA has coexisted with the Palestinian refugee problem for over half a century and its institutional memory and experience are indispensable. For over half a decade, the agency acted as the welfare state-in-exile for Palestinian refugees, primarily for the most economically disadvantaged segments. The agency is both a service provider and an employer, which means it is a source of steady income for a significant number of refugee households. Although the agency did not create Palestinian nationalism, nevertheless, over the years refugees, both as beneficiaries and employees, mapped out a Palestinian identity onto its various sites and spaces.

Any political initiative to dissolve UNRWA at this critical stage in the region will signal to refugees that they have been "sold out" by the international community. The possibility of the dismantling of the Agency is not far-fetched. In 1993 following the signing of the Declaration of Principles, UNRWA announced that it was preparing to "hand-over" its services, that is, planning its own dissolution and handing over its assistance program to other institutions.[66] Almost immediately, funding was made available for a Peace Implementation Programme (PIP),[67] aimed at improving the "living conditions" of refugees and helping the Palestinian Authority in building an infrastructure.

The PIP, established by the agency and applied to the territories under the Palestinian Authority only, was conceived as a developmental model as opposed to simply a short-term relief program. Therefore, the PIP may be viewed as a form of politicization in the agency's mandate. The agency's declaration of support of the Oslo *political* peace process, and undertaking practical steps in helping the Palestinian Authority build state institutions *prior* to the resolution of the refugee problem, should be questioned. Since the Oslo peace framework regarding the refugee problem is not based on UNGA Resolution 194 (III) to which UNRWA is bound as a UN body, it may be argued in this case that the agency has crossed its "purely humanitarian" boundaries into the political arena, neglecting, if not violating, its commitments to UN resolutions. Moreover, refugees in the Diaspora criticize the Agency for having redirected a major bulk of its resources to the PIP, perceived as one of the reasons for the dramatic reductions of much needed humanitarian services for refugees living in surrounding countries, especially in Lebanon.

However, the peace initiative encountered serious impediments: Oslo has failed in bringing about an end to the conflict, the establishment of a Palestinian state, or the resolution of the refugee problem. The collapse of Oslo meant the continued existence of UNRWA which—at least for the time being—abated the fears of refugees and employees of an imminent dissolution of their agency, although there is a great deal of concern and insecurity regarding the decrease in the quantity and quality of services.

UNRWA: Assistance and Informal Protection?

Beginning at the end of March 2001, UNRWA initiated a new program called the Operation Support Officer Programme (OSO). The OSO program works informally to facilitate the delivery of humanitarian assistance to the refugee population and is indirectly providing some measure of protection to refugees, currently under extreme vulnerability due to Israeli violations of human rights, refugee law, and humanitarian law. The informal nature of the program is due to the fact that UNRWA has no protection mandate as such, but in emergency situations it is often able to adapt some of its programs to respond to the crisis at hand. In addition, the informal and low-key operation minimizes Israeli objections, namely, that UNRWA has violated its humanitarian mandate by providing protection. Simple practices such as driving around in a UN car to check whether food rations have been delivered or reporting on Israeli violations can make a difference on the ground, albeit on a small scale and not sufficient to enforce an end to the occupation, or to Israeli violations.[68]

Although relatively new, the OSO has the potential to emulate the Refugee Affairs Officer program implemented by UNRWA during the first *Intifada* in 1987. However, it is limited in scope and confined to the West Bank and Gaza, hence, it does not include the majority of refugees who reside in neighboring countries, nor does it provide international protection for internally displaced Palestinians who have been subjected to various forms of discriminatory laws and practices. Here it is important to mention that the internally displaced Palestinians, or Palestinian citizens of Israel, have also been barred from returning to their lands from which they were displaced during the 1948 conflict. Israel has subsequently confiscated all their land. This has rendered the 'internally displaced' economically vulnerable to Israel's state policies.[69] Nevertheless, such temporary programs (the RAOs and OSOs) provide a practical example of how international protection could actually become more effective in the Palestinian context.

In the past few months and following the Israeli military incursion on the West Bank and Gaza, Peter Hansen, UNRWA's Commissioner-General, condemned Israel's responses to UNRWA's humanitarian activities, including the rejection of the Israeli Defense Forces to allow ambulances and relief workers into camps, and their use of UNRWA schools as military posts and Israeli armed attacks on UNRWA vehicles, clinics, schools, and personnel that led to the death and injury of a number of UNRWA employees. Hansen's criticism of the Israeli attacks triggered a number of articles accusing the agency of turning a blind eye to "terrorist activities." Alan Baker, the Israeli foreign ministry's legal adviser flew to Washington in June 2002 to meet with U.S. lawmakers and State Department officials to put pressure on the U.S., and to reiterate Israeli concerns about what he called "anti-Israeli" bias by some UN officials, including, comments made by Kofi Annan's Special Middle East envoy Terje Roed-Larsen and UNRWA's Commissioner-General Peter Hansen. Baker said that one of the primary goals of his visit was to press for a requirement that the Agency notify the United Nations if and when it became aware of 'any misuse' of the refugee camps.[70] Thus, while the agency's attempt to provide some semblance of protection to Palestinian refugees has been criticized by Israel as a violation of its "humanitarian mandate,"[71] in this case, the agency is being requested by the same government to trespass its mandate by providing information regarding political activities in refugee camps.

Although Baker rejected suggestions that such a move would give UNRWA precisely the political role Israel did not want it to have,[72] still, the recent Israeli criticisms and pressure on the U.S. to cut its funding for the agency raises serious questions regarding the ability of the agency to continue its humanitarian services. This is especially the case in the territories under Israeli occupation: long curfews and the inability of UNRWA to distribute food, medicine, and relief to refugees, except intermittently and when allowed by the Israeli authorities, means that UNRWA is easily constrained by the Israeli state, even when delivering basic humanitarian aid. This betrays the fact that it is not only refugees that are vulnerable to the political turmoil, but also their agency, which lacks the necessary international clout to withstand political pressures. In fact, the Israeli media blitz against UNRWA had willing ears in the United States. Tom Lantos, the ranking Democrat on the House International Relations Committee, and Tom Delay, the Majority Whip, supported the Israeli criticism and suggested the ending of U.S. funding to UNRWA.[73]

Protection Needs

In light of the aforementioned discussion, it might seem that one possible solution to the international protection gap is to officially grant a protection mandate exclusively to UNRWA to fill the gap left by the UNCCP. At first glance this might seem like a feasible solution due to the agency's organizational and historical position in Palestinian society. However, a deeper examination will reveal that this solution would be counterproductive.

Currently, UNRWA functions with relative flexibility among refugees because it does not have a mandate to intervene politically and is not perceived as a threat to host states. In fact, UNRWA has carried the burden of providing many services, otherwise the responsibility of host states. In addition, the agency's skill in avoiding or navigating (if not always successfully) around the political domain has given it relative autonomy and fostered a close relationship with the refugee population. In some cases, the agency provided individual refugees with "protection" from governments in large part because it has been seen as a neutral and harmless organization that has no effective impact on sovereign states, or at the international level.

Consequently, in the unlikely event that the United Nations General Assembly were to officially and exclusively grant UNRWA a protection mandate, the agency would lose its current flexibility. Granting an official mandate of protection to UNRWA, thereby allowing it to intervene with host states on behalf of refugees, would alarm Israel and Arab states and subject UNRWA to closer scrutiny and intrusion in regards to its activities and employees, thereby hindering its ability to function with its current flexibility in the refugee community.

Moreover, refugees themselves, who coexisted with the agency for over half a century, might become suspicious of a sudden change in the agency's mandate in a charged political environment. In fact, the relationship between refugees and the agency has fluctuated over the years and can be described as a love-hate relationship, depending on the political context. On the one hand, refugees blame the agency for its attempt to contain the revolutionary zeal of the Palestinians, while on the other its much-needed services and its association with their political right of return render it indispensable. Hence, a fundamental change in its organizational policy and practice might sound the alarm bells that the agency is once again attempting to integrate refugees, as was the case in the early fifties. Consequently, the porous boundaries between the agency and refugees would harden and the trust established between UNRWA and refugees would be jeopardized.

The UNHCR and Palestinian Refugees

The debates in the drafting histories surrounding the mandates of UNRWA and the UNHCR reveal that the exclusion of Palestinians, then represented mainly by Arab governments, occurred precisely because of the dramatic scale of displacement and the creation of a stateless population in which the international community was directly involved. The justification at the time to exclude particular populations to avoid an overlap in the mandates of two UN bodies was reinforced by the position of Arab states. The representatives of Arab governments feared that should Palestinian refugees fall under the umbrella of UNHCR, the urgency of their case might be diluted. Moreover, Arab states did not want to carry the burden—financial or otherwise—of a calamity they did not create, and were anxious that the decision of defining Palestinians as Convention Refugees might provide Israel with an excuse not to repatriate them.[74]

The problem, however, is that millions of Palestinian refugees have been left with little, if any, protection. Thus, it is time to reconsider the role of UNHCR. What is envisioned is a division of labor: an international *protection* mandate to be provided by UNHCR, without dismantling UNRWA or diminishing its role as a provider of humanitarian *assistance*. Consequently, the most feasible solution to the protection gap is a structure that will involve both UNRWA and UNHCR, whereby the former maintains its flexible *assistance* mandate, while the latter would intervene to provide international *protection*. On this point, it is important that UNHCR—if it assumes a protection mandate (i.e., durable solutions)—understands and incorporates strategies based on the legal constraints attached to the Palestinian refugee case that do not necessarily govern other refugee cases.

The most salient legal constraint that UNHCR may encounter in the case of Palestinian refugees is embedded in Article 1D, which refers to relevant resolutions of the UN, namely UN General Assembly Resolution 194 (III), which would act as a break on the option of resettlement. In other words, if Israel continues to refuse to allow refugees to return, UNHCR would not have a mandate to attempt resettlement because the host state refuses to allow refugees to return.[75]

Another important point to consider relates to the structures of, and boundaries between, the protection and the assistance mandates of both UN bodies (UNHCR and UNRWA). In light of the fragmentation of the Palestinian refugee population in the various host countries and the need for UNRWA in emergency situations to respond immediately, the boundaries between assistance and protection must be flexible. This approach to the international protection gap might present a feasible scenario. For such an arrangement to succeed, consultations with the relevant UN bodies will be necessary. However, what is even more necessary is an international *will* to provide protection to Palestinian refugees, guided by ethical and moral principles based on the universal—and not selective—applicability of international law.

It is possible to envisage other scenarios, such as the reactivation of the UNCCP. The latter has existed for over fifty years, it has since been dysfunctional. Moreover, the members who formed the UNCCP upon its establishment were Turkey, the U.S., and France. In the current political climate, such a structure and membership would be unproductive. Consequently, the revival of the UNCCP would have to entail a redefinition of its role in a way that conforms to the current political and historical context, as well as a restructuring of the Commission that ensures impartial intervention. This latter point is important, particularly due to the fact that the United States, as a member of the UNCCP, has a long record at the UN and in other international forums that testify to its biased support and protection of Israel.

Nevertheless, the fact that the UNCCP has recorded Palestinian property losses in the first few years renders it an important source for refugee claims to be filed against the state of Israel for property and land confiscated under domestic Israeli laws, but which violate international law. The filing of claims is an important part of any durable solution in the Palestinian refugee case, and as such, the UNCCP has an important role to play. Another alternative, which also emerged in some of the writings of legal scholars, is "temporary protection."[76] In the Palestinian case, according to the proponents of this solution, temporary protection might pose the best of both worlds in that it would assuage the fear of refugees and Arab states of any permanent settlement scheme in host countries, while providing basic human rights to refugees. In other words, it will ensure that the right of return and self-determination are not being compromised by the provision of citizenship or permanent residency to refugees.

However, the question remains as to the legal standing of temporary protection, and at least in some Arab countries this has been the de facto situation for refugees. For example, refugees have been granted civil and economic rights in Syria, while still being able to maintain their national identity; that is, Syria did not give them Syrian passports. The advantage of temporary protection status is that it offers a solution for many of the residency and asylum appeals of Palestinian refugees and stateless persons, who are ensnared by conflicting mandates and policies of the UNHCR, UNRWA, and the various domestic refugee/asylum laws of nation-states around the world. However, it is quite possible that formalizing temporary protection for Palestinian refugees will further delay the active intervention of an international body to facilitate the implementation of a *durable* rather than a *temporary* solution—which is more than half a century overdue.

Conclusion

The marginalization of Palestinian refugees must be seen as the failure of the international community, both in its direct responsibility in the creation of the Palestinian refugee problem and in failing to grant Palestinians international protection and a mechanism through which to end their protracted exile. It is ironic that Article 1D, initially meant to provide Palestinian refugees with *heightened* protection, resulted in *negligible* attention. However, the marginalization of Palestinian refugees could be avoided if the inclusion clause, that is, the second paragraph of Article 1D, is triggered. The application of the inclusion clause will grant Palestinian refugees at least the same level of protection from the international community that is available to all other refugees, by virtue of automatic coverage under the 1951 Refugee Convention.

Given the historical involvement of the international community in producing and perpetuating the Palestine refugee problem, a concerted effort must be made to extend international protection to refugees who have been rendered vulnerable for decades. As Richard Falk has noted:

> The clarity of international law and morality, as pertaining to Palestinian refugees, is beyond any serious question. It needs to be appreciated that the obstacles to implementation are *exclusively* political—the resistance of Israel and the unwillingness of the international community, especially the Western liberal democracies, to exert significant pressure in support of these Palestinian refugee rights.[77]

New initiatives to provide Palestinian refugees with international protection must be based on the application of international law and the various UN Resolutions. UNRWA is a central institution with a vast pool of experience, not to mention its historical archival material on Palestinian refugees. Any political move to hand over the agency's services and archives to other institutions, such as the Palestine National Authority or Arab host states, prior to finding a durable political solution to the refugee problem will cause further instability and will represent a violation of UNRWA's mandate. The agency should form part of a consultative structure that includes the UNCCP and UNHCR as well as other existing and relevant UN bodies, including the Office of UNCHR and the ICRC, in order to activate immediate international protection for Palestinian refugees. Continued failure to grant Palestinian refugees international protection constitutes a form of discrimination against one group of refugees based on national origin. This discriminatory policy by UN bodies contradicts Article 26 of the International Covenant of Civil and Political Rights, which stipulates that all persons are entitled without any discrimination to the equal protection of the law.

ANNEX I
The Palestine Mandate
The Council of the League
of Nations

July 24, 1922 (Excerpts)

Whereas the Principal Allied Powers have agreed, for the purpose of giving effect to the provisions of Article 22 of the Covenant of the League of Nations, to entrust to a Mandatory selected by the said Powers the administration of the territory of Palestine, which formerly belonged to the Turkish Empire, within such boundaries as may be fixed by them; and

Whereas the Principal Allied Powers have also agreed that the Mandatory should be responsible for putting into effect the declaration originally made on November 2nd, 1917, by the Government of His Britannic Majesty, and adopted by the said Powers, in favour of the establishment in Palestine of a national home for the Jewish people, it being clearly understood that nothing should be done which might prejudice the civil and religious rights of existing non-Jewish communities in Palestine, or the rights and political status enjoyed by Jews in any other country; and

Whereas recognition has thereby been given to the historical connection of the Jewish people with Palestine and to the grounds for reconstituting their national home in that country; and

Whereas the Principal Allied Powers have selected His Britannic Majesty as the Mandatory for Palestine; and

Whereas the mandate in respect of Palestine has been formulated in the following terms and submitted to the Council of the League for approval; and

Whereas His Britannic Majesty has accepted the mandate in respect of Palestine and undertaken to exercise it on behalf of the League of Nations in conformity with the following provisions; and

Whereas by the afore-mentioned Article 22 (paragraph 8), it is provided that the degree of authority, control or administration to be exercised by the Mandatory, not having been previously agreed upon by the Members of the League, shall be explicitly defined by the Council of the League Of Nations; confirming the said Mandate, defines its terms as follows:

ART. 2. The Mandatory shall be responsible for placing the country under such political, administrative and economic conditions as will secure the establishment of the Jewish national home, as laid down in the preamble, and the development of self-governing institutions, and also for safeguarding the civil and religious rights of all the inhabitants of Palestine, irrespective of race and religion.

ART. 4. An appropriate Jewish agency shall be recognised as a public body for the purpose of advising and co-operating with the Administration of Palestine in such economic, social and other matters as may affect the establishment of the Jewish national home and the interests of the Jewish population in Palestine, and, subject always to the control of the Administration to assist and take part in the development of the country.

The Zionist organization, so long as its organization and constitution are in the opinion of the Mandatory appropriate, shall be recognised as such agency. It shall take steps in consultation with His Britannic Majesty's Government to secure the co-operation of all Jews who are willing to assist in the establishment of the Jewish national home.

ART. 6. The Administration of Palestine, while ensuring that the rights and position of other sections of the population are not prejudiced, shall facilitate Jewish immigration under suitable conditions and shall encourage, in co-operation with the Jewish agency referred to in Article 4, close settlement by Jews on the land, including State lands and waste lands not required for public purposes.

ART. 7. The Administration of Palestine shall be responsible for enacting a nationality law. There shall be included in this law provisions framed so as to facilitate the acquisition of Palestinian citizenship by Jews who take up their permanent residence in Palestine.

Done at London the twenty-fourth day of July, one thousand nine hundred and twenty-two.

ANNEX II
United Nations General Assembly Resolution 302 (excerpts) December 8, 1949

302 (IV). Assistance to Palestine Refugees
The General Assembly,
Recalling its resolutions 212 (III) 2/ of 19 November 1948 and 194 (III) 3/ of 11 December 1948, affirming in particular the provisions of paragraph 11 of the latter resolutions,
Having examined with appreciation the first interim report 4 of the United Nations Economic Survey Mission for the Middle East and the report 5/ of the Secretary-General on assistance to Palestine refugees, . . .
7. Establishes the United Nations Relief and Works Agency for Palestine Refugees in the Near East:
   (a) To carry out in collaboration with local governments the direct relief and works programmes as recommended by the Economic Survey Mission;
   (b) To consult with the interested Near Eastern Governments concerning measures to be taken by them preparatory to the time when international assistance for relief and works projects is no longer available;
8. Establishes an Advisory Commission consisting of representatives of France, Turkey, the United Kingdom of Great Britain and Northern Ireland and the United States of America, with power to add not more than three additional members from contributing Governments, to advise and assist the Director of the United Nations Relief and Works Agency for Palestine Refugees in the Near East in the execution of the programme; the Director and the Advisory Commission shall consult with each near Eastern Government concerned in the selection, planning and execution of projects; . . .
20. Directs the United Nations Relief and Works Agency for Palestine Refugees in the Near East to consult with the United Nations Conciliation Commission for Palestine in the best interests of their respective tasks, with particular reference to paragraph 11 of General Assembly resolution 194 (III) of 11 December 1948;
21. Requests the Director to submit to the General Assembly of the United Nations an annual report on the work of the United Nations Relief and Works

Agency for Palestine Refugees in the Near East, including an audit of funds, and invites him to submit to the Secretary-General such other reports as the United Nations Relief and Works Agency for Palestine Refugees in the Near East may wish to bring to the attention of Members of the United Nations, or its appropriate organs;

22. Instructs the United Nations Conciliation Commission for Palestine to transmit the final report of the Economic Survey Mission, with such comments as it may wish to make, to the Secretary-General for transmission to the Members of the United Nations and to the United Nations Relief and Works Agency for Palestine Refugees in the Near East.

10
Arguing about Asylum
The Complexity of Refugee Debates in Europe

NIKLAUS STEINER

Few issues in Europe today are as controversial as the granting of asylum. While the general ideal that politically persecuted people ought to receive asylum is widely accepted, the source of the controversy lies in the details. What precisely constitutes "political persecution?" How can an asylum application be judged fairly? To what extent should domestic constraints influence asylum decisions?—these are all difficult questions that bring to light the complex mix of political, cultural, moral, legal, economic, and ideological motives that shape asylum policies in Europe.

Asylum in Europe has not always been this way. Until the late 1970s, the issue caused little controversy because few people applied for asylum. Those who did were usually well-educated Eastern Europeans who were economically and ideologically useful. Asylum in Europe changed dramatically from the late 1970s to the mid-1990s as the world's refugee population soared from 2 million to 15 million.[1] Better communication and transportation links helped people from all over the world reach Europe where they have been applying for asylum in unprecedented numbers. Within a decade, annual asylum applicants in Europe increased ten-fold, from 60,000 to 600,000, with the majority of these applicants coming from countries as diverse as the former Yugoslavia, Romania, Turkey, Sri Lanka, Iran, Lebanon, Zaire, Pakistan, and India. This rise in the number of asylum seekers, their diverse countries of origin, and the decline of communism have all led to making asylum such a highly controversial issue in Europe today.

Yet, despite being at the forefront of contemporary European politics, asylum has received only scant attention from political scientists. This oversight is regrettable because asylum is intimately linked to other controversial European issues including the rise of far-right parties, the restructuring of the welfare state, and the integration of Europe into the European Union. Not only has political science in general overlooked asylum in Europe, but so has its sub-field of international relations, despite the obvious links between asylum and issues that are integral to the field such as sovereignty, foreign policy, and legitimacy. This gap in the literature must be filled because, as Myron Weiner has written, "migration and refugee issues, no longer the sole concern of ministries of labor or of immigration, are now matters of high international politics, engaging the attention of heads of states, cabinets, and key ministries involved in defense, internal security, and external relations."[2]

Studying asylum also demonstrates weaknesses in the dominant international relations paradigms that seek to explain state behavior on the basis of their rational pursuit of assumed national interests.[3] While it is of course uncontroversial to argue that states consider their interests when setting asylum policies, this issue demonstrates the difficulty of objectifying national interests. In his discussion of asylum, Andrew Shacknove subdivides "national interests" shaping asylum into *political stability, economic stability,* and *foreign policy concerns.*[4] While it may be tempting to assume that asylum policies are simply the outcome of a rational cost/benefit analysis of these three interests, objectively determining refugees' effects on a country's politics, economy, and foreign policy is not easy. Regarding *political stability,* one might argue for a restrictive asylum policy because cultural homogeneity promotes political stability or alternatively for an open policy because foreigners contribute to political stability.[5] Regarding culture, does cultural heterogeneity enrich a society, as Alan Dowty argues, or does it dilute national culture and identity, as Patrick Buchanan, Jean-Marie Le Pen, and Jörg Heider argue?[6]

Regarding *foreign policy,* granting asylum to a refugee is an explicit critique of another state's treatment of its citizens, so states are often quick to accept refugees from foes, but hesitant to accept them from friends. Such an asylum policy was common during the Cold War, but in many cases outside of the Cold War context asylum policies cannot simply be explained as the result of relations between sending and receiving countries.[7] Many sending countries such as Sri Lanka, Ghana, or Nigeria are difficult to categorize as either friends or foes. Even more perplexing from a foreign policy viewpoint is that a country such as Germany accepts significant numbers of Kurds from Turkey, a NATO ally. Clearly in the last two decades (and especially since the end of the Cold War), the distinction between "good" refugees and "bad" refugees has virtually disappeared, and Europe now simply faces people who seek its protection.

Regarding *economic stability,* I have found little work that considers the economic impact of refugees on receiving countries. The debate over the economic impact of *immigrants,* however, is still unresolved. Furthermore, there are conflicting opinions about whether economic stagnation causes resentment toward foreigners (whether refugees or immigrants). On the one hand, Daniéle Joly and Zig Layton-Henry stress the importance of economic hardships to explain the tension over asylum in Europe. On the other hand, in her study of Germany, Britain, Canada, and the United States, Marilyn Hoskin found that, except in the United States, public opinion toward immigrants was weakly related or unrelated to economic variables of any kind, and she concludes that immigration, like many issues, stirs up both rational and irrational sentiments that defy easy prediction.[8] Theories that are fixated on rational states pursuing objective national interests are clearly insufficient for understanding asylum in Europe today and we must broaden our lens to consider other motives.

The limited number of scholars who do focus on asylum generally agree that asylum is shaped by a complex configuration of national interests, international norms, and morality. Gil Loescher, for example, believes "The formulation of refugee policy involves a complex interplay of domestic and international factors at the policy-making level and illustrates the conflict between international humanitarian norms and the sometimes narrow self-interest calculations of sovereign nation states." Sarah Collinson writes "A moral, legal or humanitarian obligation to offer protection to refugees will, in practice, always be balanced against the political and economic interests and concerns of potential asylum states." Similarly, Shacknove argues "Refugee policy has always been at least one part State interest and at most one part compassion. Appeals based solely upon compassion, solidarity or rights are only occasionally successful." And Joly concludes "[Ethical factors] generally play some part when supranational values are accorded sufficient importance or when a particular conjuncture allows the refugees' interest to coincide with other interests at stake in the variegated fabric of national and international factors at play."[9] This literature then generally assumes that asylum policies are the result of a tug-of-war between international norms and morality loosening asylum on the one hand and national interests tightening it on the other. While intuitively sound, I have found little work that systematically explores this struggle, so this chapter is a step toward exploring this alleged tug-of-war that shapes asylum in Europe.

It must be clear that this article deals with *refugees* not *immigrants*, and this distinction is crucial to make.[10] While both may be considered a subset of international migration, an *immigrant* is an individual who voluntarily migrates from one country to another, usually for economic betterment. The difficulty of defining a *refugee* has long been a focus of refugee scholars and needs not detain us here. Instead, it is important to understand how the three states under consideration define a refugee. In assessing whether an individual is a refugee and therefore deserves asylum, Switzerland, Germany, and Britain all use the criteria laid down by Article 1 of the 1951 UNHCR Refugee Convention. Accordingly, all three states consider refugees to be individuals who face persecution because of their *race, religion, nationality,* or their *membership of a particular social group,* or *political opinion.* The asylum controversy in Europe revolves around the fact that economic hardship is *not* a criterion for being recognized as a refugee. The crux of the matter is that European states claim that the vast majority of those seeking asylum today are in fact not persecuted refugees but are opportunistic immigrants who abuse the asylum process with illegitimate claims. This charge is vehemently denied by those who believe Europe is becoming a fortress and turning its back on people who deserve protection.[11]

While I separate *national interests, international norms,* and *morality* for analytical purposes, I am fully aware that in practice these motives are significantly entangled because we tend to design our actions so that our self-interests and our non self-interests coincide. Such an entanglement of motives is quite common in asylum where accepting refugees can grant legitimacy, strengthen democracy, express humanitarian sentiments, mollify religious concerns, grow the economy, enhance security, bolster international law, and satisfy public demands. Explaining away this complexity as mere reflections of national interests is dubious at best.

When referring to *international norms,* the asylum literature cites numerous explicit international and regional agreements that prescribe the establishment of an asylum process, the definition of a refugee, the principle of *non-refoulement,*[12] and the link between asylum and human rights. For Germany, Switzerland and Britain, the most important international refugee norms are the 1951 United Nations Convention Relating to the Status of Refugees and its 1967 Protocol, the 1948 Universal Declaration of Human Rights, and the European Human Rights Convention. As of 1995, 128 states has become party to the 1951 Convention and/or 1967 Protocol, including Britain, Germany, and Switzerland.[13]

I use the term *morality* to mean the capacity to distinguish between right and wrong and the willingness to act upon what is right. In other words, a moral argument has a reflective and an active component.[14] In asylum debates, moral arguments not only claim to know what is right, but they also claim to actively promote it. In pointing out moral obligations to grant asylum, the asylum literature most often stresses either religious or philosophical foundations, specifically Judeo-Christian ideals or the central tenets of Liberalism.[15] We must be careful to differentiate between *norms* and *morality.* Certainly there is a great deal of confluence between norms and morality; respecting the principle of *non-refoulement,* for example, conforms not only to an international norm but also satisfies moral principles. Yet, it is a mistake to use norms and morality interchangeably because norms can also be amoral or immoral, that is they may either not involve moral principles or they may contradict them.

To probe the struggle between national interests, international norms, and morality in asylum, I explore the arguments made by Swiss, German, and British parliamentarians when drawing up asylum legislation between the late 1970s and the mid 1990s. As a source of analysis, parliamentary debates offer the most accessible and clear articulation of politicians' arguments within a formal political institution. Members of parliament use this forum to argue their positions, to shape the political discourse, and to impress the public. The public, in turn, evaluates these arguments and reacts to them in the next election. Parliamentary debates, then, play an important role in the open exchange of ideas between representatives and the public, and this exchange is fundamental to liberal democracies.

This chapter covers the period from the late 1970s, when asylum was just beginning to cause political ripples, to the mid-1990s, when it had become one of the dominant issues in Europe. Germany, Britain, and Switzerland offer a wide variation in European asylum policies: Germany's policy has been among the most generous, Britain's has been among the most restrictive, and Switzerland's has been in between. Given the spatial and temporal variation in the asylum policies of these three countries, parliamentary debates capture a whole range of arguments built upon concerns for national interests, international norms, and morality, and this range nicely demonstrates the complexity of asylum.

I should finally note that my intention is not to offer a causal explanation for the variation in asylum policy outcomes. Instead, I offer a better understanding of asylum by considering the complex interaction of national interests, international norms, and morality in asylum debates.[16] By offering a better understanding of asylum, I hope to lay the groundwork for future research that can offer causal explanations, but such research is currently hampered by our oversimplified view of asylum.

Parliamentary Asylum Debates in Germany, Switzerland, and Britain

This research reveals that the arguments of parliamentarians differ significantly from what the literature had predicted.[17] Their choices are often counterintuitive and they represent a complex interplay of national interests, international norms, and morality. While I keep these three categories of arguments separate for analytical purposes, in practice they are quite entangled as parliamentarians on both sides of the issue usually work hard to combine them by arguing that their position serves national interests, conforms to international norms and fulfills a moral good.

Regarding the *national interests* addressed earlier by Shacknove, parliamentarians rarely defended their positions on the grounds of *foreign policy* interests. This was true even during the Cold War. Only in the 1993 German debate did foreign policy arise to any significant extent: supporters of that tighter asylum legislation argued that it would further Germany's foreign policy goal of European unity by promoting the harmonization of European asylum laws, while opponents of the tighter legislation complained that it would dump Germany's asylum problems on its newly democratized eastern neighbors and thereby strain relations.

Even more remarkable was the near absence of arguments over *economic* interests. Not a single supporter of tighter asylum in any of these debates argued that asylum should be tightened because of threats to labor markets or to the economy as a whole. At most, some complained of the financial burden that a loose policy placed on the asylum process and (especially in Germany) of housing shortages brought on by the rising number of asylum seekers. Meanwhile, opponents of tighter asylum were completely silent about the positive economic impact of asylum seekers and refugees.

Furthermore, neither side addressed to any significant extent the effect asylum-seekers and refugees had on the host society's *cultural* interests. Only in the 1979 Swiss debate that loosened asylum did supporters of looser asylum refer to their *positive* cultural impact, but even then they spoke only of refugees of the distant past, not of those coming presently. And only in the 1994 Swiss debate did supporters of tighter asylum refer to any significant extent to a *negative* cultural impact, namely the increased drug trade in Zürich that they largely attributed to asylum seekers.

Instead, when relying on national interests, parliamentarians on both sides appealed mainly to the political interests of *internal harmony* and *effective governance*. Cross-nationally and cross-temporally, parliamentarians remained remarkably consistent in focusing on these two national interests, but they differed sharply in their interpretations of how to further these interests. Supporters of tighter asylum consistently made the following argument: tighter legislation is needed to fight asylum abuse that is increasingly irritating citizens who demand such legislation. In the 1987 British debate, Stokes (Conservative) asked Home Secretary Hurd (Conservative) "Is my right hon. Friend aware that the vast majority of people in this country are thankful for the steps that he is taking to deal with bogus immigration? Is he further aware that the attitude that we have heard from the Opposition is quite untypical of the vast majority of all classes of people living in this country?"[18] This argument was especially stressed in the 1993 German debate that followed a year of significant far-right wing violence against foreigners. Schäuble (Christian Democrat) argued that by fighting abuse, this tighter asylum legislation would "provide the necessary foundation for tolerance and harmony between Germans and foreigners."[19] Solms (Free Democrat) pointed out that 90 percent of the Germans supported the tighter legislation and he warned "A failure [to pass it] would have dramatic consequences. The trust in politics would be severely damaged. The trust in the democratic parties would be further weakened. Not only the democratic parties but the entire democratic system would begin to teeter."[20] Likewise, Klose (Social Democrat) warned that inaction on this matter "threatens the stability of our democracy, especially because the temptation is great to exploit politically these problems and fears. We democratic parties have nothing to gain from this situation that only helps the pied-pipers of the right [*Rattenfängern von rechts*]."[21] Marschewski (Christian Democrat) made this argument most dramatically by drawing a historical parallel: "If history can teach us anything, then the 1920s and the early 1930s are revealing: Weimar failed because the democrats could not agree. We must prove ourselves by demonstrating that we are capable of resolving these problems."[22] In other words, supporters of tighter asylum legislation argued that such legislation would effectively fight abuse, combat racism, and carry out the will of the people.

Opponents of tighter asylum tended simply to reverse this main argument of the supporters: tighter legislation was ineffective in fighting abuse, it fueled racism, and it violated democratic principles. In the 1993 German debate, for example, Weiß (Bündnis 90/Die Grünen) warned of the "oppressive madness of the nationalists" and said "It is a shame that such a proposal is even being discussed in the German parliament, because this proposal was negotiated in the back-rooms among political tacticians who sought to cater to the lowest populist sentiment."[23] Similarly, in the 1987 British debate, Meadowcroft (Liberal) complained that the Government was not fulfilling its democratic role because "the Government are seeking to follow their Back Benchers instead of endeavouring to lead and initiate."[24] The Shadow Home Secretary Kaufman (Labour) argued "The Bill is about having a shoddy little debate in which racism can be stirred up in hope of winning a few votes. At every general election, Tory Members cannot resist playing the race card."[25] In the 1994 Swiss debate, Goll (Social Democrat) complained that the government was scapegoating foreigners for deep societal problems and she argued "This legislation will simply bring new problems instead of solving old ones. So, [Federal Councilor] Koller, quit constantly shifting problems around, which only brings an escalation on all fronts."[26]

With regard to national interests, then, both sides avoided foreign policy, economic, and cultural arguments and instead consistently stressed that asylum legislation had to satisfy the political interest of being effective, anti-racist, and democratic. That legislation should be effective, anti-racist, and democratic is, of course, a rather bland and unrevealing assertion about national interests. The controversy is not *what* the interests are, but *how* to achieve them. Supporters of tighter asylum legislation argued that such legislation would effectively fight the abuse that had come to irritate citizens who demanded action. Opponents argued that such legislation was an ineffective way to fight the abuse and that it merely pandered to xenophobic pressures from citizens and thus violated democratic principles. These contradictory arguments raise nagging questions. Can tighter asylum legislation effectively fight abuse or do the problems lie elsewhere? Does tighter asylum legislation reassure citizens and reduce their racism or does it cater to the existing racism and justify it? Is it in the national interest for parliamentarians to follow the will of the people or to lead it? These are difficult questions and they illustrate that national interests are not objective truths that are discoverable, but are in fact subjective claims that are contestable and that can pull asylum in opposite directions.

These asylum debates further reveal that *international norms*, too, can pull in opposite directions. International asylum norms have been explicitly expressed and supported in scores of national, regional, and international agreements. The two most important international refugee norms put forth by international conventions are the definition of a refugee and the principle of *non-refoulement*. It is crucial to note that none of the tighter asylum legislation introduced in any of these debates proposed changing either of these two international norms. In fact, many supporters of tighter asylum legislation, especially cabinet representatives, stressed that such legislation conformed to international norms and that international norms in fact enabled them to tighten asylum. Essentially, they argued that international norms are good and that their tighter legislation conformed to international norms and therefore they, too, were good.

Some supporters of tighter legislation, especially members of the far right, however, wanted to tighten asylum even further and complained that international norms constrained them from doing so. In the 1994 Swiss debate, Keller (Swiss Democrat), for example, scorned the European Human Rights Convention for protecting foreigners whom he accused of dealing drugs in Switzerland. He said "Ladies and gentlemen of the Left, try telling the many schoolchildren in the plagued neighborhoods of Zürich that these few hundred criminal foreigners are entitled to human rights. You argue that this so-called Human Rights Convention should protect such people. That brings tears to my eyes!"[27] Such supporters of tighter asylum thus argued that international norms were wrong and that parliamentarians should ignore them and tighten asylum as they please.

It was precisely this constraining role of international norms that some opponents of tighter asylum also stressed, but for the exact opposite reason. They argued that tighter legislation had to be rejected because it violated international norms. Weder (Independent) argued in the 1994 Swiss debate that this tighter legislation violated not only the European Human Rights Convention and the 1951 Refugee Convention, but also the Anti-Racism Convention and the UN Children's Convention. In the 1993 German debate, Hirsch (Free Democrat) argued that the tighter legislation was not compatible with Germany's obligation to international law that stems from the UNHCR Convention, and in the 1986 British debate the Shadow Home Secretary Kaufman (Labour) argued that the tighter legislation irrefutably violated Article 31 of the 1951 Convention. And if not violating the *letter* of international norms, some opponents of tighter asylum legislation argued that such legislation certainly violated the *spirit* of these norms. Rechsteiner (Social Democrat), for example, complained that the deliberate effort made by the tighter 1986 legislation to treat asylum seekers who entered Switzerland illegally worse than those who came legally violated "the sense and spirit of our asylum law and the Refugee Convention."[28] Similarly, Meadowcroft (Liberal) said "To say that we shall take unilateral action despite what might happen elsewhere, and to excuse doing so on the ground that someone can travel on properly with documents, seems to go against the spirit of the international attitude that we should advance. If we do not play our part in coping with the problems of the world's refugees, how can we expect others to do so?"[29] In other words, these opponents of tighter asylum argued that international norms are good and should be upheld, that tighter asylum legislation violated at least the spirit of these norms, and therefore such legislation should be rejected.

Finally, other opponents of tighter asylum legislation conceded that such legislation conformed to international norms and complained that these norms enabled parliament to pass them. In the 1994 Swiss debate Plattner (Social Democrat) said "I know that this legislation conforms to the European Human Rights Convention. That, however, does not speak for the legislation, but rather against the Convention. This legislation contradicts my moral sensitivity [*Rechtsempfinden*]."[30] While this argument rejected international norms because they violated *ethical concerns,* another argument claimed that international norms violated *sovereignty.* Allen (Labour), for example, argued against EU norms that he feared would enable Britain to tighten asylum. He warned of delivering the British parliament to the Schengen and Trevi groups and to a "Masonic college of European committees."[31] These opponents of tighter asylum, then, argued that international norms were flawed and that parliamentarians should ignore them and reject tighter asylum legislation for other reasons, including sovereignty and morality.

From this complex role that international norms played in these asylum debates, we derive a 2 × 2 table taken from the 1994 Swiss debate.

The Multifarious Roles of International Norms in Asylum Debates

		Attitude toward International Norms	
		Positive	Negative
Attitude	**Tighter**	Koller	Keller
toward	**Looser**	Weder	Plattner
Asylum			

Koller stressed international norms because he believed they enabled Switzerland to tighten asylum. Weder stressed that international norms constrained Switzerland from tightening asylum. Plattner complained that international norms enabled Switzerland to tighten asylum. Keller complained that international norms constrained Switzerland from tightening asylum further. This 2 × 2 table clearly belies the simplistic assumptions about international norms in much of the asylum literature.

With regard to *morality,* parliamentarians on both sides of the issue stressed the moral obligation to grant asylum to refugees. Contrary to expectations stemming from the asylum literature, however, these moral arguments were rarely religiously based. And when religious arguments were made at all, they tended to be made by opponents of tighter asylum who argued not so much that a Judeo-Christian obligation exists to grant asylum, but rather that members of Christian-based parties who supported tighter asylum were not living up to their parties' ideals. In other words, the argument was not *I am a Christian and therefore I support looser asylum* but rather *You claim to be a Christian and yet you support tighter asylum.*

The best example of this backhanded religious argument came in the 1993 German debate when Gysi (Party of Democratic Socialism) leveled it against the Christian Democrats. He began "A glance at the Bible makes it perfectly clear that the Christian Democratic Union and the Christian Social Union should renounce the term 'Christian'." He then quoted several Bible passages and reminded the chamber that Jesus considers only those people just who feed the hungry and accept strangers. His sermon caused an extraordinary commotion in parliament, partly because of the irony of Gysi citing the Bible. Marschewski (Christian Democrat) yelled "It also says 'The sanctimonious go to hell'" and "The fifth commandment says 'Thou shall not lie'." Other Christian Democrats called "It also says 'You shall not bear false witness'" and "A misuse of the Bible." At this point Gysi asked President Süssmuth to restore order and she said "The speaker asks for silence although he demands a great deal of us" which was applauded by the Christian Democrats, Free Democrats, and Social Democrats. Gysi answered "It is news to me, Ms. President, that the Bible is considered impudent in the German parliament" to which Rüttgers (Christian Democrat) shouted "What a prankster!" and Feilcke (Christian Democrat) responded "He's not a prankster! He's crazy! (*Das ist keine Witzfigur! Der spinnt!*)."[32]

Moral arguments based on the central tenets of Liberalism also did not pan out as expected. While Liberals in the literature stress that *equality* promotes cosmopolitanism and a (more) open world and that *liberty* demands free(er) movement of people and less state power, most opponents of tighter asylum were unwilling to argue their case so strongly. Instead, they limited themselves to arguing that the concept of liberty had to protect their own citizens from poorly conceived and unjust legislation. In other words, this liberal argument was less concerned with granting asylum to refugees and more concerned with protecting citizens from an intrusive state. This argument was most extensively made in the 1994 Swiss debate in the aftermath of numerous government scandals in the previous years. Fankhauser (Social Democrat) said the tighter legislation was "absolutely out of proportion and irresponsible. Our constitutional state, which protects every citizen from unnecessary state interference, may not be toyed with so lightly."[33] Tschäppät (Social Democrat) warned "The mere suspicion that you are hiding asylum-seekers who received an initial negative decision would now be grounds enough for your house to be searched. Be aware: this measure is not aimed at foreigners, this measure is aimed at Swiss houses, churches and parsonages—that is hard to believe."[34]

Less prominent in the asylum literature is a third moral position that claims events of the World War II era now pose a moral obligation to grant asylum to refugees. This argument had a noteworthy resonance in these debates, although it varied significantly across time and place. In Britain, supporters of tighter asylum explicitly rejected any suggestion that Britain's poor refugee policy during that era now posed a moral obligation.[35] British opponents of tighter asylum also did not stress the faults of that policy, but instead claimed that if the tighter legislation currently being debated had been in place during the war, then fewer refugees would have been able to enter Britain. In other words, British opponents of tighter asylum did not argue that Britain's poor refugee policy during that era now posed an obligation, but rather that Britain's policy had been relatively good and that tighter legislation would now betray that record.

This *World War II* argument played out differently in Switzerland. In the first Swiss debate that loosened asylum, numerous parliamentarians stressed the moral obligation stemming from Switzerland's abysmal refugee policy during the war. This argument, however, faded over the years and played almost no role in either the 1986 or the 1994 debates, as if some kind of statute of limitations on moral guilt had run out. One might have expected the opposite to happen: as the war generation was replaced by a younger, more critical generation, Switzerland's role during the war would be increasingly questioned. However, that was not the case. In fact, only in the past few years has Switzerland's role during the war come under heavy attack and only because of pressure from abroad regarding Swiss banks still holding Nazi gold and accounts of Jews who perished in the Holocaust.

In Germany, not surprisingly, World War II played a prominent role in each of the debates, and numerous parliamentarians on both sides of the issue spoke of an obligation toward today's refugees because of the Nazi era. Bühling (Social Democrat), for example, spoke of Germany's liberal policy stemming from "the bitter experiences of the Nazi time, during which many Germans had to flee abroad and could consider themselves lucky if they found asylum there."[36] Olderog (Christian Democrat) opened the 1986 debate in the Bundestag by declaring "During the Nazi period, many thousands of politically persecuted Germans received asylum in other countries. Therefore, today and in the future, we vigorously emphasizes not only the legal but also the moral obligation to offer protection to the politically persecuted from other countries."[37] Ströbele (Greens) explained "For us, this past represents an obligation. We think that since 600,000 Germans were accepted by other countries during the Nazi period, then that means we have an obligation today to do all that we can to pay humanity back."[38]

If read carefully, all these statements reveal a curious twist. The focus is on "Nazi" persecution and on how "Germans" suffered under it. In other words, the argument was not (as might be expected) *We Germans made others suffer during that period so we now have an obligation to grant asylum to those who suffer*. Instead, the argument was consistently *We Germans suffered during that period so we now have an obligation to grant asylum to those who suffer*. In all of these German debates, in fact, only a single parliamentarian, Ulrich Briefs (unaffiliated, formerly of the Party of Democratic Socialism, successor to the old Communist Party of East Germany), spoke of "German crimes" and of "monstrous historical German guilt."[39]

While not a single parliamentarian in any of these debates rejected the abstract moral principle of "helping refugees," putting this principle into practice was highly contentious. How, for example, does one best fight asylum abuse, which most parliamentarians agreed was a problem? It is important to note that many supporters of *tighter* asylum argued that tighter legislation was, in fact, moral because they helped "real" refugees by weeding out asylum abuse committed by "undeserving" ones. If sincere, this moral argument belies the simple tug-of-war image often presented in the asylum literature that has morality only pulling for looser asylum. The Swiss Justice Minister Koller (Christian Democrat) was typical in making this moral argument when, in 1994, he said "Only if we succeed in tackling the obvious asylum abuses efficiently . . . do we have a chance to uphold our humanitarian tradition of granting asylum to persecuted people."[40] While such apparent concern for refugees was widely denounced as hypocritical and self-serving by opponents of tighter asylum, one must wonder what the best way is to fight asylum abuse whose existence is widely acknowledged.

Another difficult moral issue is the obligation parliamentarians have toward their own citizens. Ward (Conservative), who supported tightening British asylum, spoke of the duty "to maintain the way of life which people already living in this country want and to provide the social and welfare services for which they have paid and which they expect to receive. We should be failing in our duty if we allowed an overload of new people to destroy that way of life."[41] These moral obligations toward citizens can be at odds with moral obligations toward refugees and it is not always clear how to balance the two.

Some supporters of tighter asylum also suggested that it is unclear whether granting asylum to refugees is even the best way to help them. They argued that it might be better to help refugees in their own region rather than granting them asylum in Europe. Aware that such an argument would meet skepticism, Lüchinger (Free Democrat) in the 1986 Swiss debate said "You may claim that this suggestion is a sign of a guilty conscience. But it is my firm conviction that we can better help refugees (but also economic migrants) from far away countries by supporting them in their own culture instead of trying to accept them at any cost in our culture that to them is strange and unfortunately also sometimes hostile."[42] So, while all parliamentarians accept the moral obligation to help refugees, they bitterly disagree about both the quantity and the quality of this obligation, and this disagreement pulls asylum in opposite directions.

Conclusion

Using an historically based, contextual analysis of German, Swiss, and British parliamentary debates, this chapter explored the complex and often counterintuitive roles national interests, international norms, and morality play in shaping asylum legislation. Contrary to the tug-of-war image commonly found in the literature, my findings expose the subjective nature of national interests by demonstrating that parliamentarians on both sides claim to promote national interests. Furthermore, international norms set a desirable standard for some parliamentarians on both sides, but are rejected by others who find them either too constraining or too lax. Finally, all parliamentarians (even extremists) accept the moral obligation to help refugees, but they sharply disagree on how to fulfill this obligation. In other words, while parliamentarians are always able to tie national interests and moral obligations into their arguments, they find international norms less flexible and therefore sometimes bothersome.

By focusing on asylum in Europe, this chapter engages an intensely controversial issue that has not received enough attention from political scientists. It challenges the central assumptions of conventional international relations theories that seek to explain a country's behavior on the basis of objective national interests; such an approach inadequately explains asylum policies because such policies are also significantly influenced by international norms and morality. While the limited asylum literature does address this influence, it tends to assume that national interests tighten asylum and international norms and morality loosen it. By studying the complexity of asylum, my work fills a void in one literature, and challenges the central assumption of another.

When studying these asylum debates, it is intriguing to note not only what parliamentarians say but also what they do not say. When considering this negative, one is struck that parliamentarians did not argue that granting asylum to refugees serves national interests. They only debated whether specific asylum laws served national interests, but none of them claimed that the general principle of asylum promotes such interests. This begs the obvious question: *Why is asylum maintained if no parliamentarian believes it serves national interests?* Put another way: why not simply abolish this principle that has led to so much controversy in each of these three countries over the past two decades?

While this chapter is an inadequate format for answering this question, I would like to suggest a possible direction for future research. A number of scholars have also been weighing this question of why states admit "unwanted immigrants," although much of this work focuses on immigration and not asylum. In both cases, this scholarship addresses the question by focusing either on international or on domestic constraints that states face in controlling such admission.[43]

Those scholars focusing on international constraints generally argue that globalization and the rise of an international human rights regime are constraining states' abilities to control their borders, thereby forcing them to accept unwanted foreigners.[44] They speak of a decline in sovereignty and of a decrease in the capacity of states to keep such foreigners out. In short, states admit unwanted foreigners because there is increasingly little they can do to prevent it. This perspective seems heavily influenced by the situation in Europe in the early 1990s—those of us who were following this issue at the time certainly remember the stark maps of Europe overlaid with big, bold, arrows pointing from east to west that warned ominously of the potential for millions of people flowing out of the East Bloc and the former Soviet Union.

As the parliamentary asylum debates in this chapter show, the international norms and moral sensibility that are enmeshed in an international regime can indeed constrain a state's ability to control its asylum process. This constraint is especially evident in the inability or unwillingness of a state to carry out deportations of rejected asylum seekers if these may violate the principle of *non-refoulement.* What these asylum debates also make clear, however, is that international norms and morality can enable a state to tighten asylum. The calls to harmonize asylum in Europe, to uphold the UNHCR definition of a refugee, and to fight asylum abuse for the sake of "real refugees" are excellent examples of a state's ability to tighten control over asylum and to limit the number of people it accepts as refugees. Scholarship that only sees asylum and human rights regimes as constraints misses a great deal of asylum's complexity.

Regarding the claim that globalization constrains a state's ability to control borders, it is certainly true that economic restructuring has uprooted vast numbers of people across the globe and that this restructuring has forced (or enabled) an increasing number of them to reach Europe. Furthermore, it is true that Switzerland, Germany, and Britain can do very little to control the outflow of people from Sri Lanka, Turkey, Nigeria, Ghana, Lebanon, and so on who arrive at their borders seeking entry. Irrespective of the parliamentarians who argue that more ought to be done to help people in their own countries so they are not compelled to leave in the first place, it is hard to imagine any short- or medium-term actions that European governments (alone or together) can undertake to fundamentally alter the current unequal distribution of wealth, which drives many poor people to migrate. This globalization argument, however, only helps to explain why people are on the move, but not why states continue to accept them. In fact, as Gary Freeman argues convincingly, European states have increased, not decreased, control over their borders,[45] and such control over borders could continue to increase significantly if European states would be willing to make such an expansion of their infrastructure a priority as, for example, the East bloc did in constructing the Iron Curtain. Of course, they will not take it so far, and to understand why not, we need to shift our focus away from international constraints to domestic constraints.[46]

In his analysis of border control, Freeman focuses on the domestic constraints imposed by political dynamics.[47] He writes that the primary obstacles to immigration control are political, not economic, demographic, or technical, and he specifically focuses on the lobbying process that occurs on behalf of immigrants to counter tighter laws. He argues that this pro-immigration lobby is often successful because those who stand to benefit from admitting foreigners are more concentrated and more easily organized than those who may be harmed by it. While convincing in the case of immigration in the United States and the guest workers programs in Europe, this explanation is less strong for asylum. For as we see in these asylum debates, parliamentarians do not speak of the benefits that refugees bring to their countries. Indeed, it is rather remarkable that even those parliamentarians most adamantly opposed to tighter asylum laws did not lobby for refugees, but rather lobbied against the laws—a perhaps subtle but crucial distinction.

Also focusing on domestic constraints is Christian Joppke, who generally agrees with Freeman but adds a legal dimension.[48] Joppke argues that the legal process is less prone than the political one to the swings of populist antiforeigner sentiments, and this stability is an important factor in explaining why European states accept unwanted foreigners. He writes that, especially in Germany, an activist judiciary has aggressively and expansively defended the rights of foreigners, despite the political rhetoric.

The evidence from these parliamentary asylum debates suggests adding to these domestic constraints an ideological dimension, and this proposition dovetails with Freeman's discussion of "anti-populist norms" and Joppke's emphasis on liberal values.[49] It must be remembered that these debates never considered abandoning asylum, and there seems to be an unequivocal acceptance in Switzerland, Germany, and Britain to grant asylum to refugees despite articulating no benefits. The acceptance of this norm, I suggest, is a function of the identity of liberal democracies. In making the argument that liberal democracies maintain asylum because the asylum principle constitutes an important part of their liberal identity, I share Joppke's wariness of stating a tautology.[50]

To understand this link between identity and asylum, we turn to the distinction between *constitutive* and *regulative* norms. In some situations, norms are constitutive in that they help define an actor's identity by providing the proper behavior for assuming that identity, while in other situations norms are regulative in that they prescribe the proper behavior for an actor's established identity. A norm can therefore either shape identity or prescribe behavior, or it can do both simultaneously. In analyzing these parliamentary asylum debates, the focus was on regulative norms, but to understand this identity–asylum link, we need to shift our attention to the constitutive norm of granting asylum to refugees.

For in all of these debates, parliamentarians, regardless of country, party or position, claimed that granting asylum to refugees constitutes an important part of the identity of a liberal democracy. Swiss and British parliamentarians argued that, as democracies, their countries have been granting asylum for centuries, and German parliamentarians argued that asylum has been fundamental to the rebirth of Germany after 1945. All these parliamentarians would agree with Wolfgramm (German Free Democrat) who said, "It is one of the noblest humanitarian duties of liberal democracies to grant asylum to the politically persecuted," with Wheeler (British Conservative) who said that maintaining the tradition of asylum "must remain an important part of our government and culture," and with Furgler (Swiss Christian Democrat) who argued that granting asylum was essential to Switzerland's national character (*Wesensgehalt dieses Staatsvolkes*).[51]

Importantly, both supporters and opponents of tighter asylum stressed the role of identity, as exemplified by the following remarks from the 1987 British debate. Lawler (Conservative) argued that passing a tighter asylum law would strengthen Britain's tradition of granting asylum: "Many speakers have pointed out that the country has had a long history of accepting genuine political asylum seekers. I hope that that tradition will continue. It will continue as long as the threat of abuse is minimised and prevented. For that reason I give the Bill my strong support." Dubs (Labour) opposed the tighter asylum law and said, "I regret that we could not continue with our normal tradition of tolerance and welcome for all asylum seekers who seek refuge here. That tradition is many centuries old, and tonight the Government have closed the door on it."[52]

Having concluded my analysis that asylum is shaped by a complex configuration of national interests, international norms, and morality, it is worth noting that *identity* encompasses this entire configuration. For how parliamentarians see themselves and their countries and how others see them is a function of what they want (interests), fulfilling expectations (norms), and doing good (morality). Because political debates are expressions of identity, parliamentarians usually work hard to combine all three types of arguments in defense of their position. This tripartite configuration is especially evident in the argument that asylum laws must be effective, democratic, and anti-racist. For analytical purposes, I labeled these goals as national interests because of the standard use of this term. However, if we loosen the analytical restraints, we see that in fact these goals are also norms that democracies abide by, and they do so in large part because they believe these goals serve moral ends. This entanglement is seen in Solms' (Free Democrat) summary of why the tighter 1993 German asylum law is needed: "We do this out of responsibility to the politically persecuted. We do this out of responsibility to the security of the constitution state. We do this out of responsibility to the stability of the democratic order. Last but not least, we do it out of responsibility to the coalescence of Europe."[53] More than just expressing concern for national interests, international norms, and morality, Solms is expressing how he sees himself, his party, and his country, and he is inviting others to see this identity as well. Arguing about asylum is more than just arguing about interests, norms, or morality. It is arguing about identity.

Ultimately, it is identity that maintains asylum in Europe today. Not a single parliamentarian, not even those of the far-right, argued that asylum should be abolished. And it will not be. Despite the controversy, none of these countries will abandon this principle. While they will almost certainly continue to tighten their asylum laws, interpret their refugee definitions more narrowly, and coordinate new international norms to make access to the asylum process tougher, they will not declare themselves unwilling to grant asylum to refugees. They will maintain this principle because of the way they see themselves and the way others see them. Parliamentarians in Switzerland, Germany, and Britain cling to this identity, however controversial it may be.

11

Post-Conflict Reintegration and Reconstruction
*Doing It Right Takes a While**

PATRICIA WEISS FAGEN

Conflict undermines the ability of states to protect and serve the needs of their citizens. War-to-peace transitions imply social, economic, and political transformations to bring about citizen security, rule of law, more equitable distribution of resources, functioning markets, responsive and effective governance, an active civil society, and basic trust. These are the building blocks of durable peace and development. Under the best conditions, this kind of rebuilding in a society torn by war requires a decade or more. The "best conditions" mean that governments and society share a political will for peace and change. As will be shown in the cases that follow, political will is more likely than not to be frayed, if not wholly lacking following long periods of war and violence. International support can and must contribute to peace building and social integration, but donors and international agencies still have much to learn about how to do so following civil conflict.

The Challenges of Peace Building

The notion of furnishing humanitarian relief to assist nations to recover after wars is long accepted. The best known and most ambitious example of post-war assistance, the Marshall Plan, involved the U.S. in a long-term commitment to restore European prosperity. Going well beyond the notion of recovery, the Marshall Plan brought U.S. financial and investment resources to Europe so that the post-war European leadership could put it to use in rebuilding the formerly vibrant economies. Although this example is still invoked with regard to aid projects in war-torn countries, it is clear that today's Third World nations battered by decades of civil strife are facing fundamentally different situations than did Europe after the Second World War. In Europe, aid was channeled through strong and tested institutions and experi-

---

*The research for this paper was funded with a grant from the United States Institute for Peace.

enced government bureaucracies. Projects were planned and executed in reasonably transparent and politically acceptable fashion so as to produce sustainable results. The rebuilding process rested on already existing structures of democratic governance, law, and market mechanisms.

By contrast, the civil conflicts during and after the Cold War not only have left regions and countries physically devastated—as was Europe after World War II—but also plagued by external involvements, weak political and economic institutions, and torn social fabric. Even with stable political institutions and ample resources, the challenge of addressing, simultaneously, demobilization, landmine removal, refugee and internally displaced persons returns, macro-economic requirements, and election preparation—the standard post-conflict menu—would be daunting. In reality, since the Cold War, rebuilding in virtually every case has been hampered by forms of continued violence and injustice and by governments that neither fully enjoy the trust of their people nor prove able to address the seemingly intractable poverty in which the majority of citizens live. Relief efforts may be required for a number of years while development strategies are being pursued.

To sustain a war-to-peace transition beyond relief, the international community has sought to use resources for two overlapping purposes: (1) programs aimed at building the structural bases for durable peace, usually in the form of projects to enhance security, justice, dispute resolution, reconciliation, gender equality, and good governance; and (2) policies and programs meant to promote national capacities for managing and sustaining broadly based economic development.

The projects in the first category aim to strengthen institutions that support civil society. Because the international agencies presently undertaking such efforts have been doing so for less than two decades, there are few historical precedents and a still insufficient understanding about how to use international resources most effectively to these ends over the long term. Expectations of what can be achieved remain unrealistic with regard to transferring "democratic" capacities, estimating the time it will take to realize goals, and determining when it is appropriate for external agencies to phase down or withdraw. International donors whose funds support UN agencies and numerous non-government organizations (NGOs) working in war-to-peace transitions face a daunting challenge of formulating policies and mobilizing and channeling resources to tasks that encompass several sectors.

Promoting economic development is even more challenging. Although international support for economic development in poor countries has been ongoing for over 50 years, the development agencies now undertaking projects in post-conflict war-torn countries are on unfamiliar ground. First, to define development progress in contexts where there are massive and urgent needs related to emergency relief can be problematic. Second, it is yet more daunting to achieve development goals where the psychology of war and distrust still prevail, and where security, justice, and human rights (the institution building components) have yet to be adequately addressed.

There are certain assumptions on which most development experts agree. Without elaborating in detail, it has been abundantly demonstrated that the requisites of development depend on political and social as well as on economic factors—on humanitarian development and human rights.[1] The noneconomic factors are essential, among other reasons, because development strategies invariably require cooperation, sacrifices, and willingness to accept postponement of benefits. Moreover, the changes, however productive, almost always entail significant losses to certain established economic sectors.

The demands for sacrifice and postponement of benefits are hard to justify following war and crisis when people already have experienced extreme hardships, have fled their homes, and lost property and means of sustenance, but expect the end of conflict to yield, finally, a peace dividend. It is difficult to persuade battered and impoverished populations to trust investments leading to future rather than present benefits when war has taught them that survival depends on taking everything one can from what is immediately available. A related problem is to reign in the avarice of those who have found ways to benefit from the economy of war, and who stand to lose wealth and power as rule of law and institutional integrity take root.

In designing and implementing relevant programs, the broad array of international entities currently involved both in relief and development activities have been obliged to reexamine their mandates, staffing, and funding patterns. None of the agencies of the United Nations system is well designed or organized for steering political and social reform in countries with weak institutions, and still plagued by the hostilities and distrust of war. Yet, nearly all have demonstrated that they have something to contribute.

Steps and Sequences

As international actors have learned, the steps taken in the early stages of a war-to-peace transition can determine whether peace will be sustained or conflict renewed. The effectiveness of international programs often depends on whether and how peace dividends reach the populations that have participated in and suffered from conflict. Likewise, post conflict reconciliation may either be enhanced or threatened depending on whether the return of refugees and persons displaced by war can be seen as contributing community well being.

International agencies have notably improved their ability to bring resources to the local level. When one asks about successful peace building efforts, it is common to be told of how projects have been designed both to generate income and promote reconciliation in communities that were torn apart; about projects that empowered vulnerable groups such as widows or landmine victims; and about how small amounts of international funding have supported local creativity and innovation in areas of education, health, and local justice. International and non-governmental agencies are justly proud of the ways their funding has served to strengthen civil society, which usually refers either to local organizations with an orientation toward peace or to traditional forms of mutual assistance, justice, and conflict resolution. Attempts to integrate projects and programs across several communities and to extend promising community development innovations to a regional level have been less successful. Because they have been less successful, the donor initiated community projects often prove unsustainable after international funding and oversight are withdrawn.

The most discouraging results of international assistance have come from attempts at the national level to effect the political changes that will enable sustainability in post-conflict peace building, that is, the initiatives aimed at establishing good governance and effective and responsive institutions. Institution strengthening at all levels is an essential element in peace building. Yet, international projects intended to reform justice systems that are dysfunctional and corrupt, to avoid politicizing the use of aid, and to replace corrupt and over-centralized public administration with transparent and responsive structures often have little to show for the investments. Nor have attempts to condition international assistance to donor priorities proved particularly effective.[2] As will be elaborated below, it is important to look critically at the effects of international funding patterns, budgetary and bureaucratic separation between relief and development aid, of projects isolated from instead of broader programs, and the problematic relationship of donor programs to local, regional, and national government priorities.

Defining Roles in Post-Conflict Rebuilding

Before the end of the Cold War, the roles of the bilateral donors, the UN proper, and the various international agencies in recovery and reconstruction were fairly easy to define. UNHCR repatriated refugees and only refugees, and assisted them with a modest package of necessities meant to carry them over for a short time until they could support themselves. The UNDP helped governments design and implement development plans and to obtain needed funding for development projects. The World Bank focused on macro-economic policies and practices in developing countries, and approved development loans to be executed by their governments. UNICEF's projects focused on the particular problems faced by children and, by extension, on supporting the needs of their mothers. Relief agencies specialized in rescue and rebuilding, and at bringing food items and vital needs to victims of war and natural disasters.

Today, by contrast, it is extremely difficult to sort out roles and mandates among the players. The present approach to rebuilding war-torn societies is to insist that foundations of development can and should be built during humanitarian emergencies, including actual conflict. A recent UNDP evaluation affirms its post-conflict roles by stating, "every stage of crisis and post-conflict has a development dimension."[3] This means both that relief agencies and development agencies are to work side by side from the start, and boundaries between relief and development to become institutionally and operationally more flexible. In practice, the agencies that once maintained fairly narrowly defined mandates with regard to relief and reconstruction are now adopting more ambitious programs that have longer-range goals. And the development agencies that once eschewed any involvement with early hands-on economic, political and social rebuilding initiatives as "pre-development," now seek to contribute their skills at the earliest possible phase and at grass roots levels. These tendencies occur both among UN agencies and international NGOs.

While relief and development agencies have effectively cooperated in some situations, sustained inter-agency or multi-donor coordination is rare, even where there is a consensus about objectives. Projects aimed at reintegrating persons uprooted by war illustrate the problem. The agendas of nearly every agency and donor working in war-torn countries necessarily includes programs and services related to reintegration: assisting repatriated refugees, returning or resettling internally displaced persons, integrating former combatants into civil society, generally assisting war-affected populations, and bringing resources to areas emptied and impoverished by war. Reintegration, therefore, should be an area in which cooperation and coordination are maintained. This is not the case.

Reintegrating War Uprooted Populations: A Shared Responsibility

At a minimum, UNHCR repatriates refugees and lays the legal and economic foundations for their reintegration. Increasingly, UNHCR has been initiating reintegration projects that extend benefits beyond refugee-returnees to other war-affected populations. Upon UNHCR's departure, however, its initiatives are rarely incorporated—or are amenable to incorporation—into the development programs underway. UNDP inherits caseloads of demobilized soldiers and is charged to help them become reincorporated into civil society. More often than not they go to the same communities where refugees are returning. But, the programs for reintegrating former combatants are not necessarily coordinated with UNHCR community based projects or integrated into broader development strategies, even when UNDP is active in designing these strategies. Internally displaced persons may be included in UNHCR community based programs, but if the internally displaced persons return to areas where there are few returning refugees, neither UNHCR nor other agencies may be present. OCHA mobilizes humanitarian agencies to assist IDPs in camps. Although it is widely known that, as a consequence of war, large numbers of internally displaced persons swell the populations of medium and large cities, the development organizations that address the problems of urban sprawl rarely take into account the special needs of the displaced.

Since the early 1990s, UNHCR has been extending its presence in countries of origin following repatriation. Over the past years the refugee agency has expressed the concern that difficulties in bringing about desired handovers of repatriation programs sometimes leads it to "maintain its involvement longer than it sensibly should."[4] Funding has been shrinking across the board for extended programs on behalf of repatriates. Consequently, as will be illustrated below, the agency is phasing out its operations in some countries where its contributions are still needed. Most recently, in Afghanistan, UNHCR has fallen short of funding needed to support the ongoing repatriation, with little prospect of further support for reintegration and development activities.

There has been a lively controversy regarding the value of the short-term programs UNHCR offers to returnees. At issue are the quick impact projects, (QIPS)[5] that UNHCR made a major component of reintegration programs in Central America and has continued to put in place where large numbers of refugees have returned to war-torn communities (Cambodia, Mozambique, Tajikistan, Bosnia). QIPs moved UNHCR beyond traditional repatriation practices both because they encompassed collective assistance to communities heavily populated by diverse returnees rather than to individual repatriate families, and because they were intended to lay foundations for future development. Few of the tens of thousands of QIPs have proven sustainable, however, because they are not monitored, and are not or cannot be maintained by local and national entities. As a review of UNHCR activities in Mozambique noted:

> The short-term engagement of UNHCR in Mozambique with rapidly implemented initial rehabilitation of community infrastructure is closely linked to the broader recovery and poverty alleviation efforts which in turn cannot do without a growth economy, prudent management of the public finances, sustained donor commitments and an effective use of declining development aid.[6]

These conditions were not abundantly present in Mozambique and rarely occur anywhere in the years immediately following the end of armed conflict. While they are inadequate vehicles for development, however, QIPs have served important functions such as reconciliation and confidence building. Moreover, they have brought resources that governments could not or would not furnish to affected communities.

There is a better than even chance that QIPs and other form of micro projects will be sustainable if, first, local and national entities can execute them and, second, if they reinforce government priorities. Project sustainability is directly tied to building and preserving national capacities at all levels for planning and execution. UNHCR has recognized that reintegration (and therefore, its exit strategies) depend on "progressive assumption of responsibilities by national counterparts and/or development agencies." Its documents maintain that capacity building is "a regular feature of UNHCR operations, from emergency through to durable solutions."[7] While both relief and development agencies claim, in similar terms, that they are committed to capacity building, evidence indicates that practice lags far behind rhetoric. Capacity building is a time-consuming and staff intensive activity, hence especially problematic for humanitarian relief agencies. It implies not only training local residents, but also supporting the national institutions that must continue to employ them. Unfortunately, efforts directed at capacity building are likely to be sacrificed as donors demand exit strategies and complain about "mandate creep."[8]

Every country that has received international assistance has experienced setbacks, distortions and outright failures when major humanitarian entities have scaled down programs prematurely and left behind half-completed projects. Presumably well-meaning agencies regularly over-fund activities at the outset of a process when local absorption capacities are still low, then scale down after local capacities have been artificially built up to meet demand. Or, they create local partner agencies that cannot support themselves independently. Although development agencies remain in place after the relief community departs, the projects they oversee are constrained, like those of the relief agencies, by demands for early results, and resistance to perceptions of open-ended commitments.

All development processes demand continual balancing and bridge building between achieving short-term results and preparing for long-term goals. Being cumulative, the impacts of international programs are likely to be difficult to measure. They are all the more so, because reconstruction, reintegration, and security may be distorted for years by legacies of war. The lion's share of donor resources for humanitarian assistance following civil conflict has gone to emergency response mechanisms, leaving far less with which to achieve medium and long-term post-conflict outcomes. This is certainly shortsighted. Coordination, planning, and commitment remain equally important well beyond the emergency phase. Virtually all war-to-peace transitions are uneven over time. New and ever more complicated decisions about relief, rehabilitation, development, security and national capacities continue to arise as peace is secured, refugees return, and normal economic activities resume.

The examples that follow elaborate how long-term goals have been frustrated to varying degrees by lack of common purpose, unrealistic expectations with regard to what can be achieved, serious underestimations of the length of time required to produce visible results, precipitous judgments of what has been achieved, and funding patterns that promote fragmentation and dependence and discourage coordination and comprehensive planning.

Defining Purposes: Contrasting the Experiences of El Salvador and Rwanda

El Salvador, 1991–1994

The first requisite for working effectively and coordinating efforts is to share a common view of the goals to be pursued. Conflicts in El Salvador, Guatemala, and Nicaragua during the 1980s not only had brought vast destruction and severely weakened the national economies of the warring countries, but also had generated hundreds of thousands of refugees and threatened security throughout the region. The three civil conflicts were cast in Cold War ideological tones, but fought in order to redress social and economic injustices and political repression. In all three, but especially in El Salvador, both the peace process and post-conflict rebuilding were greatly assisted by regional initiatives. From the late 1980s, Central American political leaders and opposition groups sought a comprehensive plan for regional reconstruction that envisioned peace and development as part of the same process.

The major donors agreed to channel humanitarian assistance funds to the diverse populations uprooted by war through a program, CIREFCA,[9] jointly operated by UNHCR and UNDP. Beyond serving as a channel for humanitarian assistance, CIREFCA was designed as a forum of reconciliation and cooperation among national leaders, between and among opposing groups, between former refugees and governments, and between governments and non-government organizations. Within the CIREFCA framework, an Italian funded project under the UNDP, PRODERE,[10] executed projects promoting regional cooperation and inter-agency collaboration in former conflict areas.

The twelve-year conflict in El Salvador was brought to a close at the beginning of 1992 thanks to a United Nations-brokered peace agreement. Having successfully negotiated the agreement and taken charge of overseeing its compliance, the United Nations enhanced its reputation and relevance, and established its position as a major institutional player in peace making. The peace negotiations came about thanks both to the end of the Cold War and to the political will the part of government and the opposition forces of the FMLN[11] to end a conflict that neither side could win. The agreement was encouraged and strengthened by the concerted thrust for peace throughout Central America.

While donor coordination was sporadic and rarely went beyond information sharing, the Salvadoran peace accords were sufficiently detailed to give donors, international agencies, NGOs, and the Salvadoran population a "map" to follow and a means of gauging achievements. The donor community, sharply divided during the conflict, drew together and channeled considerable support toward the goals defined by the peace agreements. The donors' commitment to the peace process was strengthened by the fact that the United States, which had been the primary supporter of the Salvadoran government and military, turned its considerable influence toward moving the government in the direction, first of the peace agreement and then of compliance with the measures therein. The process was rocky from the start, and there were frequent disagreements among The United Nations Mission for El Salvador (ONUSAL) and other international actors as to priorities and what constituted compliance, but the overall goals and general direction were never in question.

El Salvador then became something of a laboratory for peace building in which United Nations and other international actors learned what was and was not possible to achieve by means of their influence and presence. The two sides had reached specific agreements addressing the major concerns that divided them: new security structures, political institutions, land titles for former combatants and returned refugees/IDPs, human rights, a truth commission, elections, and socio-economic change. There were timetables for completion and provisions for United Nations oversight. ONUSAL, had—for that time—an unusually strong mandate; it was adequately funded and well staffed.

In El Salvador, the war affected populations encompassed the refugees, the majority of whom returned while the war was still being fought, internally displaced persons many of whom returned at the same time and to the same areas, and the demobilized combatants. Under the auspices of CIREFCA, both UNHCR and UNDP could and did join in projects that benefited war affected populations collectively in their communities. Both agencies worked closely with ONUSAL. While competition and overlapping roles and relations created some problems,[12] the UN bodies cooperated in important ways. UNHCR phased down its operations during 1994–1995. The returnees had achieved the security of full citizen rights, and reestablished themselves as political and economic participants in the nation.

The UN presence in El Salvador and the continuing interest of several donors in the peace building process were critical to opening El Salvador politically and establishing national institutions charged to protect citizen security, human rights, and national dialogue.[13] Unlike most subsequent UN missions, ONUSAL withdrew in accordance with evidence of compliance with the peace measures, rather than with an exit tied to a specific date or event.[14] The mission phased down and closed its doors formally at the end of 1996. By that time progress toward the goals of the peace process was being driven by internal dynamics not external initiatives. Nevertheless, ten years after the peace accords, there are many disappointments: the effectiveness of the new Civilian Police Force, a politically diverse and professionally trained force that was a cornerstone of the peace accords, has been marred,[15] and a severe crime wave overwhelms its capacity to provide security. Many aspects of the Salvadoran judicial system were significantly improved after the war thanks to internationally funded projects, but major failings persist to this day.[16] The specifically peace related institutions mandated by the accords remain fragile. Resolution of the complicated and sensitive land issues, only vaguely framed in the accords, is still open to question. One of the most intractable of these land issues derives from the establishment of repatriate communities on land vacated by its owners during the war. The international presence did not and could not significantly change the socio-economic injustice and inequities that continue to plague El Salvador. That task remains to be addressed by political leaders within the country who now, for the first time in its history, represent wide political diversity.

Critics have pointed to numerous areas in which international initiatives could have been clearer, better implemented, or more comprehensive. Nevertheless, this early test of international capacities in peace building yielded a number of durable achievements. Compared to subsequent peace building efforts, El Salvador proved to be a fairly "easy" case for the UN peace mission and the other international entities that made common cause with the peace agenda. The clear framework for action, the donor unity regarding that framework, and the linking of exit strategies to completion of tasks were fundamental in this regard.

Rwanda, 1994–2001

The contrast with Rwanda is dramatic. The long war in El Salvador was destructive of economy, society, and infrastructure, but in Rwanda, the few months of genocide (April–July 1994), following on years of intermittent conflict and repression,[17] left the country seriously damaged physically and the society traumatized. Some 800,000 persons were slaughtered. During the 1990s, Rwanda continued to experience armed incursions and was embroiled in regional conflicts. Refugee flight, return, and new arrivals from other countries are still ongoing, and the government is promoting controversial programs of internal resettlement. The setting for international peace building was less conducive in Rwanda than in El Salvador for the following reasons:

1. While the peace process in El Salvador was part of a regional peace effort that involved partnerships among national governments, international organizations, donors, and NGOs, Rwanda has struggled to maintain peace in the midst of continuing regional conflict, within which it was a major player until 2002.
2. While in El Salvador humanitarian assistance was a fundamental element in buttressing political will for regional peace, humanitarian assistance has been a factor accentuating tensions throughout the Great Lakes region—and nowhere more than in Rwanda. The Rwandan government's relationship with the international community began

with an inherent distrust of the latter's motives, due to the individual and collective roles of the UN and the major powers prior to and during the genocide and the subsequent support for Hutu refugees.

3. Fulfilling the measures in the Salvadoran peace accords entailed continuing negotiations and compromises between the two former adversaries who shared a political will for peace and had previously agreed to steps that needed to be taken. By contrast, the Rwandan government came to power through military victory in an ethnic conflict. There was no peace accord and no agreed-upon guidelines for the now dominant group to redefine the nation and reintegrate the returning refugees from the majority ethnic group, which had recently been seeking its elimination.

Rwanda was not well governed in the past, and the country has long suffered from extreme poverty and land shortages. Past policies of international investment and assistance exacerbated rather than improved ethnic relations and the levels of poverty for the majority. From April through July 1994, some 800,000 Rwandans, one out of every ten citizens—overwhelmingly Tutsis but also moderate Hutus—were slaughtered. Extremist Hutus orchestrated the genocide, having advertised their intentions and publicly organized fellow Hutus throughout the country to join. UN peacekeepers were withdrawn rather than augmented, and no serious effort was made internationally to prevent or forcibly halt the massacres. Rather, the genocide was brought to a close by an effective invasion of Rwanda led by the Rwandan Patriotic Forces (RPF) from its exile positions in Uganda. By July 1994, the RPF had gained effective control of the country, whereupon close to 2 million Hutus took flight. Belatedly, the major powers and the United Nations acknowledged a measure of their respective shares of responsibility for opening the way for the Rwanda genocide. But, there was little consensus among the various international actors as to the roles they should play in the context of the genocide and its aftermath and, in the opinion of this writer, too little understanding in some quarters that the impacts of genocide, fear, and distrust could not quickly be dissipated.

From the Rwandan perspective, the two earliest and most visible international initiatives related to the genocide benefited the groups that had initiated it: In June 1994, the French created a safe zone in the southwest of the country (Zone Turquoise) to protect fleeing Hutu officials, soldiers, and citizens, and to provide humanitarian assistance. From July 1994 through the following year, UNHCR with multiple humanitarian partners and massive funding oversaw humanitarian assistance to the refugee camps in Zaire (now Democratic Republic of Congo) and Tanzania. The refugee camps were established to respond to a genuine refugee emergency, while the French effort was dubiously humanitarian. In both the Zone Turquoise and in the camps, protection and assistance were provided to the innocent as well as the guilty. There were

civilians who did not participate in genocide but fled in fear, as well as innocent family members. Among the refugees were many who had directly participated in the bloody events and, more importantly, the *interhamwe* leaders
who organized the slaughter. From the protective cover of refugee camps, the
leadership continued to organize incursions and intermittent guerrilla activity
inside Rwanda long after the RPF had formed a government and was striving
to rebuild the country.

Following the genocide, the bulk of the substantial international humanitarian assistance—amounting to about $400,000 a day—was for the maintenance
of Hutu refugee camps rather than for national recovery and reconstruction.[18]
The Rwandan government strongly resented the international community and
UNHCR in particular for what it believed was direct support for the group
commonly referred to as *génocidaires*. In November 1996, when Zaire's (Con-
golese) rebel army with the RPF forcibly closed the camps, and drove its residents either back to Rwanda or deeper into the countryside, many among the
major international human rights organizations accused these armies of killing
or causing the deaths of thousands of fleeing refugees. Tanzania cooperated
with Rwanda and sent the refugees back, en masse at the end of 1996.

The refugee, returnee, and related integration programs inside Rwanda that
began in mid-1994 have variously served the competing needs of returnees
and internally displaced persons: the approximately 2 million (cumulative) returning Hutus mainly from the Zairian and Tanzanian camps, some 800,000
"old case" Tutsi returnees from Uganda, Burundi, Congo and elsewhere,[19] and
the genocide victims who remained in the country.

By the end of 1994, a host of NGO relief organizations were disbursing generous amounts of emergency assistance inside Rwanda, but doing so with little
coordination among themselves or with the government.[20] Significantly less
funding was channeled to support the RPF led government's development
plans than had been pledged to it at the beginning of 1995[21] and was very
slowly disbursed. Although the government insisted that most funding should
go directly to the newly organized ministries for their priority programs and
capacity building objectives, donors preferred to channel their humanitarian
assistance through the UN and foreign NGOs. Donors variously cited the government's limited capacities and suspected political agenda for this preference.
From the start, the government and key donors (primarily the French and Bel-
gians) distrusted each other and suspected political motives to be governing
decisions. During 1995 the government expelled thirty-eight NGOs, terminat-
ing the programs of another eighteen.[22]

The country faced overwhelming needs in rebuilding infrastructure and
restoring basic services and these needs increased dramatically at the close of
1996 when about 600,000 Hutu refugees returned en masse from the camps in
Zaire and 500,000 from Tanzania to a country lacking shelter, land, and the
means to provide for the livelihood of its population. The genocide and its af-

termath also made it abundantly clear that mechanisms for conflict resolution and human rights protection and an effective judicial/penal system were fundamental to Rwanda's future. Donor funds were drawn preferentially to the latter set of issues, but largely without needed linkages among their respective projects and sometimes with contradictory objectives.

Underlying donor decisions are differing political assessments of the Rwandan government's achievements. There have been no national level elections since the present regime seized control.[23] Early on the government's overriding concern with security raised skepticism regarding its stated commitments to civil society development and its military was deeply implicated in human rights violations. On the other hand, the government has promoted reconciliation and national unity, includes Hutu officials at all levels, and has facilitated the return of hundreds of thousands of Hutu refugees. Finally, it is the undisputed central authority in the nation.

The most salient issues have been:

Finding Solutions for the Prisons and Prisoners

Of particular concern are the approximately 120–130,000 prisoners accused of genocide packed into jails where conditions are grim and overcrowding is unacceptable. (Fear of arrest was a major deterrent to refugee return until the camps were emptied forcibly.) As of 2000, up to 40,000 prisoners had not yet been charged and those charged were being judged at an agonizingly slow pace. Donors' concerns included the methods of detention, the conditions in the jails—especially those in rural areas—and the overall legal standards and procedures being used. Although of immense humanitarian importance, they rejected the allocation of major funding to improve prison conditions when the real need was for an overall process to permit the release of the majority of prisoners and to sentence the remainder. The government reduced the prisoner population—although far from inadequately—first, with the release of all minors. Then, in June 2001, the Rwanda government initiated a traditional community mechanism, *gacaca*, in which judges preside over local level courts that determine the guilt or innocence of genocide suspects. *Gacaca* courts not only resolve genocide cases more speedily than regular judicial trials, they permit a range of punishments not necessarily involving long jail terms.[24] Since their initiation, they have been resolving cases at a fairly rapid rate. While the mechanism has been criticized in human rights arenas as leading to uneven justice and opening the way to vengeance, the Special Representative for Human Rights and other major human rights agencies are, nonetheless, sympathetic to the need for *gacaca* and are reserving judgment.[25]

Judicial Reforms More Broadly Defined

In view of the prison logjam, donors identified judicial reform as a key priority. The government itself has recognized that structural, material, and human resource gaps in the judicial system have impeded its ability to judge those accused of genocide. Several donors funded judicial modernization and training projects which, although badly needed, are recognized in retrospect to have lacked clear definition and common objectives. The cumulative impacts have been disappointing. Funding has also gone to the creation of the International Criminal Tribunal for Rwanda, which Rwandans at first disparaged, but which they now agree seems to be operating more effectively. The multiple projects to improve the delivery of justice have not been accompanied by similar levels of attention to broader issues of governance and development.[26]

Land, Shelter, and New Communities (Villagization)

The return of about a million Hutus from the refugee camps, combined with the prior return of over 100,000 old caseload Tutsi exiles, accentuated an already dramatic problem of land and shelter.[27] Returnees from the latter group often had occupied the abandoned houses and land of the former, until the Hutus returned en masse and sought to recover their property. The outcome in a surprising number of instances was a temporary sharing arrangement between the two. UNHCR embarked on massive program to provide new housing and to repair damaged buildings between 1994 and 1999.[28] At this writing in 2002, as UNHCR is being phased out, the country still requires an extensive shelter program to accommodate released prisoners, the continuing refugee returns, and the still large number of landless and homeless Rwandans.

The government's solution is a program to relocate some 650,000 displaced persons from both new and old caseload refugees to new communities in underdeveloped regions in the country. The program, called *imidugudu*, proposes the relocation of large numbers of Rwandans to clusters of settlements in sparsely populated areas. It is controversial among potential donors, both because the degree to which relocation is voluntary is held in doubt, and because many suspect the primary motive to be national security rather than the well being of the relocated population. Consequently, donors have not met government requests for assistance in providing services, sanitation, and needed infrastructure. The government, nonetheless, has proceeded with the plan, which it maintains is the only reasonable way to ease land pressures, to accommodate the homeless population and to relieve pressures in overcrowded and underproductive communities.[29] The program lacks adequate funding to be massively implemented, but where it is being put in place, the predictable result is a self-fulfilling prophecy: given the poor conditions and lack of services in the new communities, few Rwandans are eager to go, and the relocations are less than voluntary in many cases. The controversy over new communities is likely to grow sharper as local demand for shelter grows more acute.[30]

Rwanda's Role in the Congo War

Incursions from Hutu militants based in the Congo resulted in numerous deaths and seriously threatened Rwandan security. The members of the UN

Security Council recognized this threat, condemned the armed actions, and did not push for premature demobilization in Rwanda.[31] There was far less sympathy for Rwanda's military involvement in Congo, where the army was fighting in a general regional war against the Kabila government from 1998 to 2002. During these years Rwanda and other participating countries ignored pleas from the UN Security Council to leave. With the peace agreements signed in 2000, the various neighboring countries are withdrawing troops. Rwanda, however, conditions the withdrawal of its troops to security guarantees regarding control over *Interhamwe* forces still in Congo. A Congolese-Rwanda agreement signed in 2002 may satisfy these conditions.

International agencies have made impressive contributions to rebuilding and reintegration in Rwanda, but have expressed disappointment with what they perceived to be limited progress in priority programs: justice reform, economic revitalization, building a representative and democratic government, national capacity building, and so on. By and large, donor agencies have cited a lack of political will as a major—if not the major—factor. In reality, it is also the near absence of planning for common goals either among agencies or in coordination with government priorities that has limited the collective achievements and the sustainability of individual agency efforts.[32]

In fact, the Rwandan government and the donors have not disagreed with regard to priorities, but rather process. The donors came to Rwanda with projects in support of peace and channeled funding for them through international NGOs. The government, with its own peace agenda, wanted donors to channel funds for that agenda through government institutions. In order to shape the direction of international efforts, therefore, it put mechanisms in place to direct donor contributions through the Finance Ministry toward budget needs and, at the same time, required NGOs to register their projects with local Community Development Councils wherever they planned to work. Donors and NGOs, at first, complained of the politicization of funding and maintained that the councils were far from autonomous. Nevertheless, in complying, they have contributed to greater community vitality.

The difficulties related to governance and humanitarian projects have been far less evident in the development and financial areas. The development agencies have been amenable to working with the Rwandan government to improve the economy overall. Relations between the government and the IFIs and UNDP have been fairly positive, at least since 1996.[33] The World Bank has made funding and balance of payments credits available to Rwanda, and directly supports some community development through municipal authorities. The government has complied satisfactorily with the requisite policy reforms.[34] Rwanda has received an important debt relief package to help it cope with effects of a recent drought. In 2001, two inter-agency missions took place with UNHCR, UNDP, and the World Bank,[35] and the completion of a joint donor and government paper for a Poverty Reduction Support Program.[36]

Not surprisingly, the missions concluded that for development to proceed, effective reintegration would be essential. As the donor participants in the study missions and Poverty Reduction maintained:

> (T)he most visible conflict related after-affects of the genocide and the victory of the RPF are the issues of human resettlement and reintegration.[37]

And the study further noted:

> The lack of response to the resettlement needs appears to be a traditional funding gap as a result of the institutional financing structures. The aid agencies keenest to work with the government focus on the long term perspective. Reintegration, ostensibly a short-term problem, may not be encompassed in the . . . strategies of development cooperation.[38]

Today, one can see progress in Rwanda on a number of priority objectives. After having long insisted that reconciliation would have to await justice for those guilty of genocide, the government in 2000 established a National Commission for Unity and Reconciliation, and defined reconciliation as a national goal.[39] A Commission on Human Rights and a Constitutional Commission, established in late 1999, is drafting the country's first constitution since colonial rule. In local elections in March 2001, some eight different political parties participated—belying the notion that the nation is divided solely into two ethnic groups. Citizens voted for municipal officials that previously had been appointed. During 2000–2001, a few thousand of the large number refugees from Congo assumed to have perished in the army invasion of the camps in 1996 and its aftermath began to return to Rwanda.[40]

That it is now possible to move forward on a number of political initiatives—human rights and reconciliation, decentralization and political activity—is related to the government's growing sense of security. Resolving of the war in the Congo and removing the threat of attack from Hutu extremists are key to continued improvement.

The agencies involved in the early rebuilding and reintegration efforts have phased down or left. UNHCR is phasing out in terms of its assistance to Rwandan returnees, although it remains in Rwanda due to the presence of refugees from Burundi. It is not clear whether others will support UNHCR projects, ranging from shelter construction to an innovative Rwandan Women's Initiative. In any case, its assistance to the newly repatriating Hutu refugees from the Congo is minimal. The problems of phasing out were foreseen: In 1998, UNDP and UNHCR had created a joint Reintegration Planning Unit (JPRU) to plan and monitor reintegration activities. It produced disappointing results and received little donor support.

Unrealistic Expectations and Sequences:
Minority Returns to Bosnia and Herzegovina

As in El Salvador, a detailed peace accord in Bosnia and Herzegovina (BiH) elaborated the measures to be taken to establish a durable peace. In BiH, however, important sectors of the national leadership and population opposed the agreement and refused to implement it. Contrary to Rwanda, the members of the international community were prepared to work toward the common goals defined in the Dayton agreement, but coordination has remained a serious problem throughout. Donors failed to understand the cumulative impacts and linkages among separate programs, underestimated the length of time that would be required to achieve desired ends and, as will be shown below, they defined expectations more in terms of their own national and institutional interests than with reference to the realities on the ground.

The murderous conflict from 1992–1995 in Bosnia and Herzegovina and Croatia, formerly part of Yugoslavia, dramatically altered the pre-war demography. Serbian aggression was intended to achieve ethnic uniformity by forcibly displacing the non-Serb—primarily Muslim—population. In Bosnia and Herzegovina, the war produced approximately 1.8 million refugees, at least the same number or more internally displaced persons, and 200,000 deaths, from an initial population of about 4.4 million.[41] The population fell by about a half between 1991 and 1995 and, of those remaining, more than half of the population was displaced from their original areas.[42] By the time the war was brought to a close in December 1995, Bosnian cities, towns and rural communities were sharply segregated along ethnic lines. Additionally, following the war, the once moderately prosperous Bosnia was physically in ruins. Close to two-thirds of the housing had been wholly or partially destroyed; factories, schools, medical facilities, and communications networks were in ruins. The GDP in Bosnia had declined some 75 percent between 1991 and 1995.[43] Billions of dollars were necessary to rebuild and restore the economy.

The General Framework for Peace in Bosnia and Herzegovina (GFAP), commonly known as the Dayton peace agreement, recognized the de facto creation of two separate ethnically defined entities: the Federation of Bosnia and Herzegovina and the Rebublika Srpska. Bosnians, Muslims, and Croats uneasily shared the former, and the latter's population was almost exclusively Serb. This division accepted the reality that decentralized ethnic authority was a sine qua non for the parties' acceptance of the accords.

The specific measures comprising the Dayton agreements, to the contrary, were aimed at undoing the ethnic separation caused by the war and, thereby, reversing what had been the motor force of the conflict. Annex 7 of the Dayton agreement states the parties' agreement to respect the right of refugees and internally displaced persons, and to permit them to return to the places in which they had lived prior to the war without "harassment, intimidation, persecution, or discrimination, particularly on account of their ethnic origin, religious belief or political opinion."[44] UNHCR was given the leading role in repatriating refugees and promoting the right of return for internally displaced persons, as well as general oversight over humanitarian assistance and reintegration activities. Nearly all donors designed their aid packages to facilitate return, reconciliation, and reintegration. The European governments' commitment to reversing ethnic cleansing has been buttressed by their eagerness to make repatriation a viable option for the hundreds of thousands or refugees within their borders.

The Dayton accords established a structure, still largely intact at this writing, that gives ample space for international interventions in every sphere. The NATO Stabilization Force (SFOR) has been charged with security, the Office of the High Representative (OHR) with oversight for international programs, the Organization of Security and Cooperation in Europe (OSCE) and the United Nations Mission with oversight for other aspects of the Dayton accords. The OHR with UNHCR assume responsibility for return of refugees and internally displaced persons. In addition, virtually all donors have targeted their assistance in some fashion to promoting return and to enhancing political will to receive returnees.

Until the end of 1999, however, the efforts to induce *minority* returns—that is, the return to areas in which one's ethnicity was in the minority—produced discouraging results. In retrospect, the reasons both for the initial failures and for the now greater success of these efforts are fairly clear.

The political conditions following the Dayton Accord were anything but conducive to minority returns. The parties to Dayton who steadfastly opposed the efforts of minorities to return were able initially to restrict freedom of movement. In addition to the extensive destruction of homes and infrastructure and scarcity of employment, ethnic minority refugees and internally displaced persons faced local hostility and officially sanctioned legal obstacles to reclaiming property and rights. Local officials and elements in the local population frequently threatened the lives of former residents from minority families who sought to reclaim homes and property. Minorities seeking to return were often physically harassed, and subjected to practices such as the levy of so-called war taxes, a requirement of special visas, discriminatory distribution of public assistance, and onerous registration requirements.[45]

Thus, in 1996 most returnees were limited to the elderly and families whose reintegration was not complicated either by ethnic factors or major war damage to homes. From 1996–1998, countries of Western Europe and the former Yugoslavia began to suspended temporary protection for refugees, causing the return of over 150,000 refugees to BiH during 1997–1998.[46] These returns were not voluntary and did not repopulate minority areas. The vast majority of the returnees were Muslims and Croats who had left the country after having been ethnically cleansed from home districts. Inside BiH, they could be secure only in selected Federation communities. The Federation, therefore, became increasingly crowded with a population of internally displaced persons, many of whom lived in collective centers and were entirely dependent on international assistance.

During 1997 and 1998, the donors' strategy was to use resources as incentives to induce ethnic minorities to return to their homes. The initiatives, designed for maximum demonstration effects, took a two pronged approach: there were rewards for Bosnian municipalities and communities that were willing to collaborate, and cash and other incentives for those willing to return. Overall, OHR and UNHCR worked to remove the physical and economic obstacles to return. Attracting minority returns with economic incentives, however, was insufficient so long as security issues and legal rights remained unresolved.

Prior to 1998, proponents of minority returns looked in vain to the international forces of NATO (SFOR) to take more forceful measures against Dayton's opponents, but not until December 1998 did the SFOR depart from it previous pattern of ignoring war criminals and begin to arrest some of the major figures among these criminals.[47] Until that time, war criminals could be found living openly in their communities. Thereafter a number of strong measures from the Office of the High Representative demonstrated a new international will to impose rather than simply persuade adherence to the Dayton Accord. Actions in such areas as economic transparency, judicial reform, control of borders, control of the mass media, anti-corruption measures, human rights, and electoral reforms were initiated in rapid succession, all aimed at further unifying the territory and diminishing the power of the extreme nationalists. Moreover, The Dayton agreement received a boost and the ultra-nationalists in BiH suffered an unanticipated setback with the changes of government in both Croatia and the former Yugoslavia during 2000.

As political extremists lost ground, the inability of property owners and renters to reclaim their homes or to evict those illegally inhabiting these homes still loomed as a major impediment to return. Post-war property legislation in both entities created virtually insurmountable obstacles for owners wishing to evict squatters and recover the property from which they had fled.[48] After many attempts to convince or induce the entities to repeal discriminatory property legislation in favor of a legal framework in keeping with the Dayton agreement, finally, on October 27 1999, the High Representative took decisive action. He issued decisions that brought together all property legislation in force in both entities, harmonized legislation of the Republika Srpska with that of the Federation in accordance with Annex 7, and established a coherent strategy for securing implementation of the new property laws. Although various municipalities have found ways to limit or delay property recovery, implementation of the property laws showed significant improvement between 2000 and 2001.[49] The fact that a nationwide property law is in place seems to be driving home the reality that people cannot continue indefinitely to illegally occupy other peoples' apartments and houses.

Taken together, improved security enforcement and property legislation significantly changed the situation and, perhaps more importantly, perceptions about security and authority. In consequence minority returns at last showed an upswing. Although refugee returns still lag,[50] in 2000 many among the displaced persons living in the Federation set out to recover their original homes in Republika Srpska and in some Croat dominated areas within the Federation. The number of UNHCR registered minority refugee returns in Bosnia and Herzegovina during the first quarter of 2000 more than quadrupled the number for the same period during 1999, and by the end of the year, returns reach about 60,000, or 50 percent more than the 1999 return level.[51] In the first half of 2002 alone, 50,000 Bosnians returned to prewar homes.[52] This said, it is important to note urban returnees still find it difficult to surmount the bureaucratic hurdles to property recovery. The returnees are primarily from rural villages formerly inhabited by ethnic minority groups, and subsequently destroyed by the dominant ethnic majority. The *sine qua non* for the continuing repopulation of rural areas, therefore, is assistance for rebuilding homes and social infrastructure.

The unprecedented opportunity notwithstanding, donors since 2000 have displayed a clear trend to reduce contributions to BiH relief and assistance operations, and to the Balkans generally. Over the past two years the total United Nations Consolidated Appeal Process (CAP) has considered progressively lower requests for assistance for UN agency projects. But donor responses have declined yet more precipitously than the amount of the requests. In 2002 the U.S. Bureau for Population, Refugees and Migration, a major donor to ethnic minority reintegration efforts throughout the period, cut its funding in half, limiting it to NGO projects.[53]

Since 2000, as funding for its programs has declined precipitously, the need for UNHCR's assistance has been rising due to a modestly increasing caseload of refugee returns and a faster growing caseload of minority non-refugee returns. The badly needed housing construction is lagging in the rural villages that were destroyed, and important programs that furnish legal advice, information and short-term income generation are in jeopardy. Meanwhile, approximately 5,700 in Bosnia alone (55,000 counting all the entities affected by the war) still live in are called "Collective Centers," and are dependent on international assistance. Vigorous support for housing construction and for other initiatives could solve this problem, but little support has been forthcoming.[54] In terms of protection, as more people return to areas difficult to access, they will need security that—in the short run at least—only the international forces and police can furnish, as well as reconstruction assistance. But in the U.S. and in other national capitals, political leaders are contemplating serious reductions in the international forces.

There is virtually unanimity among analysts and field workers that BiH needs long-term programs that strengthen institutions and provide economic bases for reconciliation; overall, a stronger emphasis on the development end of the relief-to-development spectrum. Meanwhile, however, the case for continuing support for construction and reconstruction of housing and protection for at least the next few years is equally compelling. Logically, as more people return to remote and impoverished areas destroyed by war, both financial assistance and protection are essential. Reductions in funding for activities that are considered to be within the sphere of relief should not automatically follow decisions to embark on longer-term development. The donors in this case, in effect, are punishing the minority returnees for not having returned when they (the donors) made funding available—in 1997 and 1998. Yet, it is evident that conditions did not permit a safe return during those years—at least in part because the same international community had not yet taken the necessary steps to make them safe. Greater support for programs of institutional strengthening and economic restructuring will contribute to the security and well being of all groups, but those who are now rebuilding their lives in their places of origin need immediate assistance.

Incorporating Reintegration and Peace Building into the National Agenda: Mozambique

UNHCR's dilemmas underscore the problem faced by relief entities generally: the agency takes on a range of tasks that are needed in order for returnees to be able to reintegrate under the difficult conditions found in war-torn countries. In consequence, the agency becomes engaged in an ever-expanding range of projects,often including activities that are both unfamiliar and impossible to complete within the timeframe that donors will support. The line between meeting the short term needs essential for returnees to become rooted again in their countries of origin, and becoming involved in long-term development processes proves difficult to define. Moving beyond the former is frequently unavoidable when refugees, along with other war-affected populations, return to areas lacking access, services and economic options, but doing so also raises expectations that UNHCR cannot hope to meet.

The peace process in Mozambique shared some of the advantages of El Salvador. In both countries the peace accords marked a clear end to the armed conflicts and acceptance by the former armed parties[55] that a peace process would involve important changes in politics and society. In both countries, long negotiating processes were facilitated and encouraged by outside entities and regional political events. Both countries ended their respected conflict with greater political stability than is usually the case following long internal war. The UN fielded well-funded missions to both countries, ONUSAL in El Salvador and ONUMOZ in Mozambique. These missions took on a full range of military, political, electoral, and humanitarian activities intended to consolidate the measures elaborated in the peace agreements. Human rights oversight played a more important role in El Salvador, while the organization of elections was more important in Mozambique. In both cases UNHCR was deeply involved in reintegration efforts.

In Mozambique, large areas of the country emptied during sixteen years of war were repopulated within two years after peace was reestablished. Some 1.7 million refugees returned from six countries, and perhaps double the number of internally displaced persons either went back to their home districts or settled elsewhere in the country. They returned to a landscape almost empty of infrastructure, homes, or production. Of the more than a million refugees repatriated to Mozambique in less than two years, most returned without UNHCR assistance. UNHCR's activities in Mozambique were primarily devoted to reintegration. The challenge was how to determine priorities "of a limited and temporary assistance in an environment with seemingly endless needs."[56] It operated at first within the framework established by the UN Mission, ONUMOZ and its Office for Humanitarian Coordination, ONUHAC, created in December 1992, two months after the peace agreement. Two years later, however, following elections, ONOMOZ/ONUHAC departed the country, leaving UNHCR, UNDP, and other agencies to complete the wide range of activities it had initiated. At about the same time, (belatedly) UNHCR finally formalized its own reintegration strategy. That strategy called for a community based approach that encompassed internally displaced persons as well as returning refugees and launched an extensive program combining relief, recovery, and restoration of social infrastructure.[57]

The "lessons learned" in the Mozambican case offer considerable insight into the problems related to the so-called "relief to development gap." The program was one of the largest UNHCR had ever undertaken. It included 1,575 QIPs, placed in every war-affected district. Relations with the government were good throughout the process.[58] UNHCR also developed close working relations with the two principal development agencies: UNDP and the World Bank, and the respective representatives facilitated one another's projects. UNHCR was able to leave a legacy of visible social infrastructure: schools, clinics, wells, and access roads, none of which would otherwise have been there for the repatriates.

In an effort to achieve as much as possible and to bring benefits to all the areas affected by war and refugee return, UNHCR sought to maximize efficiency, and devoted relatively little time for capacity building or development of local resources. If local people lacked requisite skills, non-local staff would be used. If building materials were of better quality and more easily obtained from non-local sources, they were purchased from outside the country. Decisions as to where to place projects were made quickly and involved limited local participation. Today, some of the multiple schools, health clinics, and water and sanitation projects that UNHCR left behind are staffed with teachers and nurses, and maintained by local governments. Reportedly many others have fallen into decay. A Mozambican who worked for an international agency reported having seen structures in Tete intended as schools being used instead to house goats, two years after UNHCR's departure because the community had not been consulted as to the appropriate location for a school building.[59]

Acknowledging that it was unrealistic to expect the development agencies to assume UNHCR's reintegration agenda without prior familiarity with the latter's operations, UNHCR and UNDP, with the participation of the Mozambican authorities and the World Bank, undertook a joint situation analysis of UNHCR operations at the end of 1995. They produced what was called District Development Mapping. The purpose was to provide essential information to the development partners and government agencies as to the conditions in several war-torn districts where UNHCR was working but soon would leave. This exercise was useful both in helping to identify ongoing and future development needs, and in facilitating UNDP's access to the field. But, as later recognized, it would have been considerably more helpful had it been undertaken earlier and updated periodically, and had it encompassed the whole country.[60]

UNHCR left Mozambique at the end of 1996. Within the next two years, the majority of UN relief agencies and the extremely (many would say excessively) large number of NGOs who had come to Mozambique to contribute to post-conflict rebuilding had left as well. Mozambique remains largely dependent on external assistance to this day, its dependence having been exacerbated by disastrous floods in 2000 and 2001. The government, therefore, has been hard-pressed to assume financial and oversight responsibilities for the multiple peace projects left in its hands. Some examples:

Donor expertise and funding made possible the elections and electoral mechanisms put in place in 1994. These mechanisms involved expensive imported technology, which the government has been hard pressed to maintain since then with far less external electoral support. Similarly, funds from USAID, the European Union, DANIDA, and UNDP have supported capacity building and modernization of the National Assembly, but the government has not devoted money from its own budget to sustain these activities. Nor have the donors insisted on government commitments to do so. Despite numerous projects, there is little to show in the way of judicial improvement. When donors cut back on support for handling cases in the Maputo and provincial courts, no government funding replaced the lost revenues, and the backlogs of cases have only grown.[61] Nor have government funds maintained the buildings, libraries, or prisons the donors paid to build. A fairly new police reform and reorganization is now underway, and it remains to be seen the extent to which it will be sustained.[62] The government is impoverished.

What is troubling is that in Mozambique—as in El Salvador—the government perceives peace building and reintegration projects as the donors' rather than its own responsibility. This is not what was intended, but donors both inadequately involved the government at the outset and/or did not establish the kinds of mechanisms and organizational structures that a poor country could easily sustain. The majority of projects were selected with little or no government involvement, and were implemented directly by foreign agencies that hired local staff, or through international NGOs.

The majority of refugees and IDPs returned to areas in the central and northern parts of the country that at some point had been under the control of the opposition RENAMO. RENAMO—now a political party—is a strong political competitor, and the FRELIMO government understands the political importance of channeling its own or—preferably—donor resources to these areas. Today there is something of a patchwork of projects funded alternatively by donor and government sources. Local and national officials have tried, but not always succeeded, to maintain the community services—health, education, water—that UNHCR and other donors put into place during the emergency. These projects survive only where there is either continuing external support or compelling political reasons to sustain them.[63]

Conclusion

The reintegration of refugees, IDPs, and former combatants is vital to any transformation from war to peace. War-to-peace transitions, in turn, depend on government and citizens' embrace of the peace agenda, and institutional bases on which state and society are being reconstructed. International assistance and outside agencies cannot pull societies together, enforce good governance, or oblige citizens to reconcile. Nevertheless, external involvement is essential at every stage to move the process forward. Financial resources, technical expertise, and the cumulative effects of capacity and institution building efforts buttress governmental and non-governmental sectors committed to a peace agenda.

Progress invariably occurs more slowly in some sectors than in others. The cases of Bosnia and Rwanda illustrate how national commitments to peace, reconciliation, and democratic values can evolve over time toward desired ends. In such cases, international programs that achieved disappointing results at an early stage may become essential and effective at a later stage. The idea of "staying the course" means allowing realities on the ground determine the nature and timing of international interventions and the funding for these interventions. In Mozambique, where government and society were committed to durable peace, benefits of donor programs were less sustainable than might have been the case had more time and resources been devoted to building local capacities and nurturing local resources.

What has been learned that can and will be carried over to Afghanistan, Angola, and Congo, the major countries now embarking on war-to-peace transitions? Two very clear messages now emanate from the capitals of donor countries and headquarters of major international agencies with regard to the most politically visible of these, Afghanistan: first, the need to "stay the course" until the country can sustain peace and embark on development; second, the importance of building local capacities from the outset. Prospects in Afghanistan are marred by poor security, lack of law and order, and an extremely adverse economic situation. But, the prospects are bright in terms of the will and capacities of Afghan citizens. On the donor side, the commitment to stay the course and build capacities will obviously depend on a continued flow of funding aimed simultaneously at relief and development. The challenges will be for governments to find a way to make this happen bureaucratically and financially and to work toward shared objectives and realistic goals. At this writing UNHCR has repatriated well over one million people, but is not planning major reintegration projects, for which it lacks funding. UN and NGOs are contributing to short-term reintegration efforts as they can, in the face of very difficult access to returnees who reside outside of the major cities. The international commitment to longer-term reintegration remains to be defined.

Donors have advocated coordination and common planning but, to date, have not practiced it very much among themselves. Internally, most of the major donor countries still maintain separate—often competing—budgets for relief and development activities, despite the essential and well understood links between the two. While donors regularly meet along regional and thematic lines, for example, members of the European Union, the Nordic group, the UN system, to promote democracy, electoral processes, health, and so on, such meetings are limited to informal cooperation and exchange of information. Coordination at the international level is nonbinding. The Development Assistance Committee has produced guidelines for working in conflict and post conflict situations,[64] to which the majority of donors have subscribed, but not often followed. The World Bank's consultative groups also have established long-term goals in several countries, most of which remain under funded.

Nor has there been adequate donor support for UN proposals that might bring better planning, coherence, and coordination. UNDP has spearheaded what appears to be a useful initiative to achieve more coherent planning for long-term goals: the common country assessment (CCA) and subsequent development action framework (UNDAF). An initial joint assessment brings together all relevant national and international actors to assess all aspects of the country situation. The resulting common framework is meant to bring about actions that are both complementary and relevant to national needs. Among the participating countries—few of which are in the post-conflict category—are Mozambique and Rwanda. Nevertheless, implementing the projects and programs that comprise the UNDAF depends on donor support, for which the latter have no obligation.

In 2000, UNHCR engaged the World Bank and UNDP in an attempt to reach commonly formulated and agreed operational responses that would span the relief to development transition in post-conflict societies. The initiative was coolly received and abandoned.

At a time of diminishing funding for international assistance across the board, and especially for UNHCR, the cases reported here are meant to show the importance of continuing support following prolonged conflict. International actors have undertaken to improve conditions brought on by war and violence, to establish institutions able to govern fairly and effectively, and to lay the foundations for economic development. In all the countries discussed here, it can be said that the international community actors have been committed and serious about supporting desired changes. It is tragic that efforts that have *not* failed are brought to a close due to premature judgments and minor funding shortages. In the future, based on clear understandings of what can and cannot be achieved, donors should be prepared to lend their support toward what inevitably are slowly and unevenly evolving results.

5
Refugee Protection Post–September 11

12

Securing Refuge from Terror
Refugee Protection in East Africa after September 11

MONICA KATHINA JUMA and PETER MWANGI KAGWANJA

In the wake of the terrorist attack on the United States of America and the global war against terrorism after September 11, 2001, refugee protection in East Africa poses renewed challenges both to states and humanitarian agencies, particularly the Office of the United Nations High Commissioner for Refugees (UNHCR). Relatively stable, the three East African Countries of Kenya, Uganda, and Tanzania have gained renewed salience in the world's geopolitics. Because of its strategic importance and location in a volatile and violent Greater Horn of Africa, which is characterized by weak and collapsing states, East Africa is poised to become a key anchor in the anti-terrorist campaign.[1] This region is both a theater and victim of terrorist activities. On the one hand, Sudan and Somalia, both ravaged by decades of civil wars in neighboring East Africa, are perceived as havens and sponsors of terrorism.[2] In the same vein, al-Qaeda fighters are said to have military bases and allies in Somalia. On the other hand, Kenya and Tanzania have been and are possible targets of terrorist attacks.[3] Kenya is particularly coming under the spotlight because of an alleged link between al-Qaeda and the Somalia-based al-Itihaad. Among the first groups suspected of being connected to Osama bin Laden, the al-Itihaad movement and Somalia are possible targets of global counter-terrorism activities. Wary that it could be a possible target, Uganda, which neighbors Islamic Sudan and has its own large Muslim population, has remained on high security alert.

It is our contention that the emerging coalition with East Africa will change the character of refuge and the prospects for refugee protection. Any war will, no doubt, trigger new refugee flows and complicate the protection of refugees in the region. Undergoing political transitions to democracy and faced with poverty and fiscal difficulties, East African governments have readily embraced the global coalition against terrorism in the hope that Western countries will support incumbent regimes and intervene favorably with the international financial institutions.[4] In this configuration, refugees, generally perceived as a liability, are likely to become pawns in a wider geopolitical game in which they are redefined as agents of insecurity and terrorism.

We argue in this chapter that refugee protection in the aftermath of September 11 will be shaped by three broad factors. These are: the history of state resistance to refugee protection, declining capacity of humanitarian actors, particularly the UNHCR, and the changing nature and characteristics of refugee populations in East Africa. In discussing these factors we explore the prospects of enhancing refugee protection in the light of changing internal dynamics within East Africa, especially the democratization process, and the global war against terrorism.

States and Refugee Protection

The anti-terrorist campaign in East Africa is unfolding against the background of mounting state insensitivity and hostility to the plight of refugees and aliens. Over the years, shortage of land; swelling numbers of refugees; growing xenophobia, racism and ethnicity; declining economies; and rising unemployment have cumulatively led to restrictive legal and administrative policies and reluctance to host refugees. Refugee protection in East Africa has changed from relatively tolerant and hospitable regimes of the 1970s and 1980s to open hostility and resistance to refugees in the post-1990s. More and more, the refugee phenomenon has come to be seen as a force of national and regional insecurity and instability. Consequently, refugee policies and administrative structures are geared towards keeping refugees and asylum seekers out by closing borders, preventing entry, denying them asylum, and sending them back home, even forcefully. For instance, Tanzania closed its borders ostensibly because the international community refused to provide it with assistance to deal with Rwandese influx following the 1994 genocide. Within East Africa, refugees face a wide array of human rights abuses, including arbitrary arrests, prolonged detention, brutality, harassment, and extortion by state security agents.[5] States are presenting images of refugees as threats to security, economic burdens, and environmental degraders. To deal with this "menace," the three countries have sanctioned a wide plethora of policies that confine refugees to remote camps and settlement areas, severely restricting their freedoms of movement and right to work and exposing them to insecurity related to banditry, militia, and rebel groups.[6]

To varying degrees, all the three states have systematically abdicated their responsibilities to refugees. In the mid-1990s Tanzania signed an agreement with donors allowing UNHCR to be the sole conduit through which all aid for refugees would be channeled and left refugee protection and assistance to the agency, only participating minimally in status determination. Similarly, following a steady refugee influx throughout the 1990s, Uganda allowed humanitarian actors, particularly the UNHCR, untrammeled sway in refugee affairs. To elicit the support of the state and its functionaries, UNHCR paid incentives to, and raised the salaries of, government officers, supported security forces, and set up desk offices in all refugee hosting areas.[7] While many analysts lament the marginalization of the state in the relief sector by humanitarian agencies and non-state actors, it is clear that the problem of refugee protection has much to do with a deliberate decision by the state to withdraw from the refugee arena and to abdicate its responsibilities as stipulated in international refugee law.[8]

Furthermore, the problem of refugee protection is accentuated by the current crisis of governance in the region. More specifically, deteriorating domestic politics, endemic corruption, a burgeoning HIV/AIDS pandemic, and humanitarian crises stemming from natural and man-made factors have continued to erode refugee protection in East Africa. The democratization process in the 1990s increased domestic fragility and instability as tensions within and between the ruling party/movement and the opposition mounted, party alliances shifted, and as competition for political space increased. Refugees were caught in the political crossfire. In Northern Kenya, Somali refugees became key determinants of electoral outcomes as they were recruited and registered as voters for the incumbents.[9] In some cases, parliamentary and civic candidates aligned to refugees lost in elections. This aroused the ire of the host population, heightened anti-refugee sentiments, xenophobia and violence, and agitation for equal privileges, assistance, and protection as refugees.[10]

Declining refugee protection in East Africa is also connected to state suspicion and resistance to radical Islamic ideology among sections of refugees. Even before September 11, 2001 the nexus between Islam and asylum was manifest in East Africa. The vast majority of national leaders have viewed Islam from a security prism. From Zanzibar, Pemba, to North Eastern and Coastal Kenya, radical Islam is linked to separatism and ethno-nationalism. The protection of refugees associated with the Islamic faith such as Somalis stems from the state's desire to stave off militant nationalism and irredentism, which are inspired and often supported by global pan-Islamic groups. This is the case in Kenya where response to Somali refugees is heavily influenced by negative perceptions and fears. Since independence Kenya has harbored deep-seated suspicion of the role of radical Islam in fueling pan-Somali nationalism, secessionist tendencies, hardline opposition politics among its Somali population and their kith and kin in the Horn of Africa.[11] Thus, although the settling of Somali refugees among their Kenyan kith and kin has facilitated their integration and protection of certain rights, these refugees are saddled with a heavy baggage of enduring prejudice, marginalization, and colonial-style punitive expeditions against their Kenyan counterparts.[12] Besides state repression, the profiling of Somali refugees for security reasons is a common feature in Kenya and beyond.

The effect of state prejudices is accentuated by the lack of adequate legal and administrative capacity at the national and regional levels. At the national level, states have either failed to enact laws protecting refugees or simply passed acts that are hostile to them. Since 1992, Kenya has procrastinated in enacting a refugee bill, forcing humanitarian agencies to operate in a legal void. Refugee affairs are, therefore, regulated by hostile and often contradictory acts, such as the Immigration Act, the Kenya Citizenship Act, the Registered Lands Act, the Aliens Registration Act, and Restriction of Aliens Act, most of which have a long pedigree in colonialism.[13] A draft bill (2001), to be debated in parliament, requires criminal procedures such as fingerprinting and photographing refugees as part of the identification procedures. On their part, Uganda and Tanzania have passed hostile refugee acts. Once defined as a resettling state, Uganda's new law requires refugees to be in the country for two decades before they can be considered for naturalization.

Refugee Protection and Regional Security

Beyond the national level, refugee protection in East Africa is also compromised by the changing dynamics of regional conflict and insecurity in the Greater Horn and Great Lakes regions of Africa. These regions, which have experienced drastic regional spread of internal conflicts in such countries as Rwanda, Somalia, Burundi, Sudan, Ethiopia, and Democratic Republic of Congo, have forced refugees to flee to the relatively stable East African countries. The presence of such refugees has influenced both inter-state relations and state response to refugee protection and assistance.

In most cases, refugees are viewed as diplomatic burdens, political irritant, and embarrassment to East African countries, all of which consider themselves as neutral in these conflicts. For instance, relations between Tanzania and Burundi have been souring since 1995, as Burundi consistently accuses Tanzania of aiding and providing Burundian refugees with training facilities and shelter after they attack their home country. Refugees in northern Uganda are pawns in the conflict between the government and the Lord's Resistance Army (LRA). Alleged to support the Sudanese People Liberation Army, refugees have been subject to several attacks by insurgent groups supported by the Khartoum government.[14]

The presence in East Africa of refugees drawn from the former elite including professors, government officials, businessmen, and professionals, poses two related challenges. Often perceived as threats to incumbent regimes at home, this category of refugees is under constant threat of assassination, abduction, and disappearances by agents of their home governments, seeking to eliminate political rivals. For instance, approximately 3,500 Rwandese who fled to Nairobi after the 1994 genocide live in perpetual fear of various forms of reprisals including elimination by the post-genocide regime in Rwanda. Conversely, hosting states perceive such refugees as potential threats to good relations with refugee-generating neighbors and, therefore, as diplomatic embarrassments. The implications of this for human rights protection include failure to give special protection to high profile refugees. Oromo refugees from Ethiopia in Kenya make repeated claims of increasing insecurity and lack of protection from the host government. One Oromo refugee expresses the degree of insecurity suffered as follows:

> We live an insecure life. . . . We fear not only the Kenyan police but also threats from Ethiopians acting for the government. Recently a refugee was attacked by masked men, stabbed in the chest and left for dead. . . . We cannot expect to get any help from the Kenyan police. . . .[15]

This state of insecurity has made refugee camps unpopular to those who consider themselves at the risk of abduction, assassination, and disappearance by security agents of home governments exploiting insecurity in camps and their environs. The decision to remain in urban areas means these refugees fall outside of UNHCR relief and protection nets, remain vulnerable and join the endangered category of refugees and other illegal aliens.

Regionally, the three East African countries are yet to develop a common legal framework for dealing with refugees. In the EAC Treaty, refugee issues are lumped together with security and defense matters but the mechanisms for dealing with them are underdeveloped. The deficiency of capacity within the EAC to deal with refugees was exposed when no less than 2,000 refugees from the Islands of Zanzibar and Pemba, Tanzania fled to Kenya following civil unrest in January 2001.[16] Eager not to endanger the rapport among partner states, the EAC chose to remain silent and to do nothing about this test case.

The regional mood within East Africa has been one of restricting rather than expanding refugee rights. Attempts by officers in charge of refugee matters to harmonize policies and practices in all three countries have so far failed. In the mid-1990s, East African leaders, echoing the Schengen experience with the creation of a "Fortress Europe" in the early 1990s, agreed on the "approximation" of policies and practices instead of harmonizing legal and administrative frameworks for dealing with refugees. Thus, in terms of protection, nation-states cannot look to the regional framework for higher standards of treatment of refugees.

In a region where refugee policy has long been intricately bound with security concerns, the war against terrorism is thrusting state security to the fore to the detriment of refugee rights and protection. Further, the war against terrorism is likely to thrive on the existing prejudices against refugees in general and Somali and Muslim refugees in particular. Ultimately, the effects of the absence of enabling legal frameworks, crisis of governance, and heightening insensitivity of states to refugees on refugee protection are compounded by the declining capacity of humanitarian agencies.

Declining Capacity of Humanitarian Agencies

The rolling back and marginalization of the state in the refugee sector in the 1990s shifted the entire burden of refugee protection and assistance in East Africa to humanitarian actors, especially UNHCR. For instance, defining itself as a transit state, Kenya conceives refugees as "UNHCR's problem." Besides complicating UNHCR's responsibility to advise governments, monitor assistance and protection standards, set the norms for other actors, and mobilize resources, this attitude burdens the UNHCR with new responsibilities abandoned by the governments.

To begin with, hostility from the state coupled with the absence of refugee bills or restrictive municipal law, suspension or weakening of eligibility, and status determination committees make it difficult for the UNHCR to forge useful partnerships, benefit from state structures dealing with refugees, and deprives it of a domestic legal and policy framework for refugee protection. Paradoxically, efforts by UNHCR to confront challenges precipitated by a policy and legal vacuum have accentuated the crisis of protection. For instance, its attempts to contract a non-governmental organization in Kenya to determine the status of refugees on its behalf put it in the contradictory role of determining eligibility claims as well as protecting refugees and asylum seekers. Another initiative that backfired is the agency's attempt to establish a reception center in Nairobi aimed at separating criminal elements or *génocidaires* from bona fide refugees and enforcing the exclusion clause (Art. 33) of the 1951 UN Convention on the Status of Refugees. Most refugees, especially Rwandese, fearing victimization, went underground and exited the protective umbrella of UNHCR.

Across the three countries, UNHCR has had to deal with shrinking resources. Over time, the general program budget of UNHCR has declined. For instance, in Kenya its budget has declined from US$58 million in 1992/93 to approximately US$13 million since 1997.[17] Such budgetary constraints have forced UNHCR to size down its staff, to reduce the number of NGO partners, and to concentrate more on relief than supervision of the standards of treatment of refugees. Accordingly, UNHCR has been censured for privileging relief over the importance of human rights protection.[18]

In terms of durable solutions, chances for integration have dwindled as possibilities for repatriation in safety and dignity have declined, leaving resettlement to third countries as the only desirable option for refugees. However, opportunities for resettlement, especially to Western countries, have also shrunk with the few available openings reserved for vulnerable and special cases such as persecuted ethnic minorities, women, and minors.[19] To qualify, therefore, refugees have reconstructed identities to fit the narrow criteria of resettlement by projecting themselves as persecuted minorities. The resultant competition for resettlement chances has led to scandalous cases of corruption involving UNHCR officials, some of whom have been charged in Kenyan courts for receiving bribes to influence the outcome of applications for asylum and resettlement. This has eroded the image of UNHCR as an incorruptible and just protector of refugees and hurt its credibility regionally. The cumulative effect of these developments has been the abuse of the asylum and protection system by both UNHCR officials and refugees. To correct the situation, UNHCR Headquarters in Geneva sent a team comprised of international investigators to look into these and other mismanagement allegations in 2001.[20]

The location of refugee camps in remote areas presents serious challenges to protection. Unable to gain work and in some cases to engage in agriculture or keep animals to supplement relief, most refugees have become virtually dependent on relief handouts provided by agencies. Further, the absence of modern infrastructure of justice, including law courts and magistrates, in addition to the inefficiency of mobile courts that the government, at the behest of UNHCR, has set up,[21] has forced UNHCR to sanction traditional systems of justice such as *maslaha* courts in camps. While many studies underscore the importance and popularity of these traditional systems of justice, these customary structures often violate human rights.[22] Moreover, owing partly to inadequate personnel to facilitate the running of refugee camps, UNHCR has relied on traditional systems of governance to maintain law and order. However, these systems have been unable to resolve human rights problems arising from abduction of young girls, forced marriages, female circumcision, wife beating, and illegal incarceration.[23]

Beyond the camps, there is limited capacity to protect the human rights of urban refugees, the vast majority of whom fall outside of the UNHCR protection system. Except for the newly launched Refugee Consortium of Kenya and the Refugee Law Project in Uganda, no other human rights NGOs focus exclusively on the protection issues of urban refugees in East Africa. It is this vacuum that makes urban refugees, a largely forgotten group as far as international attention is concerned, an extremely vulnerable category.

Changing Dynamics of the Refugee Population

Over and above the vulnerability wrought by the lack of humanitarian capacity, the changing nature and character of refugee populations has undermined their protection in East Africa. A majority of the current refugees are fleeing escalating conflicts relating to crisis of democratization, human rights abuses, and civil wars in the Horn and Great Lakes regions. The spread of the anti-terrorist war in East Africa is likely to change the dynamics of conflict, and to generate new waves of refugees. Because of the religious character of the war, the new wave of refugees will largely consist of groups adhering to the Islamic faith from Somalia, Sudan, and other pockets of East Africa.

The expansion of the refugee population has gone hand in hand with the increased presence of militias and militarization of refugee camps and the consequent decline of protection of refugee rights and freedoms. For instance, militias fighting in southern Sudan and Somalia have used Kakuma and Dadaab camps in northern Kenya, respectively, to organize, recruit, recuperate, and to exercise control and authority over refugee populations.[24] The presence of militias and criminal elements in camps has posed the classical problem of separating them distinguishing between them and refugees. This problem is also manifest in urban areas where, for example, it has been difficult to differentiate between Rwandese *génocidaires* or Somali fighters in Nairobi and bona fide refugees. Again, the war against terrorism complicates this problem because it is difficult to separate fighters from refugees.

Increasingly, arriving refugees or "recyclers"[25] are accompanied by armed militias and sometimes carry guns, which have a direct impact on the security of both refugees and their host communities. Illegal gunrunning in camps is directly responsible for increased incidences of armed violence. In the Kakuma camp at least two incidences of gun-related violence leading to deaths have occurred annually in the last five years. For instance, in April 2000 a fight between Sudanese groups in the camp, lasting for five days, claimed seven lives and left 160 refugees seriously wounded. By the same token, refugees, especially in Nairobi's Somali-dominated Eastleigh suburb, are blamed for trading in illegal arms, which are allegedly used in the proliferating armed intimidation, robbery, and other forms of criminality across Kenya.

There is also among refugees in East Africa an emerging and enlarging class of refugee entrepreneurs. This class, which has well-entrenched commercial operations within the camps, with local communities, and across borders, is neither under the control of the host states nor of UNHCR. It has been averred that this class, which is "adept at political machinations has the means to destabilize camp life and post-repatriation settlement initiatives."[26] While most of these entrepreneurs are involved in trading legal goods such as electronics, textiles, and leather, a section of them are involved in cross border trade in illegal arms, narcotics, minerals, precious stones, and money changing operations. An expanding network of monetary and financial assets associated with this commercial class can potentially aid terrorist networks and endanger the camps and suburbs where refugees live. This fear is real. East Africa has become a key transit point for illicit drugs owing to its geographic proximity to South Asia, its porous borders, long and largely unmonitored coastlines, and its communication networks including frequent international flights to Europe, the Indian subcontinent, and the Middle East. Drug traffickers based in Afghanistan and Pakistan have also reportedly established hubs in the predominately Muslim coastal city of Mombasa, and in nearby Zanzibar, Tanzania.[27] Additionally, al-Itihaad and other militant groups could exploit and benefit immensely from the weakness of Kenya's banking and financial institutions. Also, the trust-based *hawilad* or *hundi* banking system, which leaves no paper trail, is deeply entrenched in Somalia and in Somali enclaves, especially refugee camps and Somali-inhabited suburbs in Nairobi, Mombasa, Dar es Salaam, and Zanzibar.[28]

The search for intelligence along the Kenyan coast, in Somalia, and among Somali refugees and communities within Kenya by the global coalition has increased. This is likely to intensify human rights abuses, arrests, harassment, and ethnic profiling of Somali and Muslim refugees and communities. Preliminary activities on this front have begun to generate a backlash among refugees and Islamic groups across the region. So far, there is among Somali refugees increasing hostility and ill-feelings towards the notion of anti-terrorism, associated with developments that impact negatively on their lives. For instance, the closing down of the Yemen-based Al Barakat Bank, the main channel of remittances from the Somali Diaspora, significant to the survival of Somali refugees in East Africa, is perceived as punitive.[29] To counter what some Somali refugees see as machinations of America to punish Somalis for their acts against the American-led UN campaign against Farah Aideed in 1993, Somali refugees have begun to conduct religious training that is akin to Pakistan-styled *madrasa* classes in refugee camps, allegedly in preparation for defending Islam and Somali nationhood.[30] By the same token, al-Qaeda and al-Itihaad cells could exploit the laxity in security, unprotected borders, and the group determination criteria used for Somali asylum seekers to take refuge in camps and urban areas. Already, there are indications that terrorist cells may be present in Uganda while interviews with Kenyan Somalis reveal the possible presence of *Al-Itihaad* fighters in Dadaab camp.[31]

These developments pose critical dilemmas for UNHCR: the agency has neither the mandate nor capacity to control underground movements. Although it has played a critical role in boosting the security capacity of governments in areas around camps, UNHCR cannot deal with armed terror groups. Secondly, the war against terrorism will inevitably generate large influxes of refugees. Any such influx will not only overwhelm the capacity of UNHCR but also complicate its role of protecting refugees. Thirdly, there is a trend by the international community to sacrifice human rights and democracy at the altar of security. This trend is likely to erode refugee rights.

The Future of Protection in the Age of Terror

As Gil Loescher observes regarding the future of refugee protection in view of changing global politics, it is crystal clear that the war against terrorism paints a gloomy picture for refugee protection in East Africa in the years ahead.[32] Refugee protection is increasingly subsumed under the imperatives of security and strategic priorities of hosting states, perhaps more than during the Cold War era. In East Africa, refugees are not only viewed as a people in need of protection and assistance but also as a potential threat to national and regional security. Therefore, securing refugee protection in the era of anti-terrorism requires striking a delicate balance between the imperatives of humanitarianism underpinning refugee protection and, often, legitimate state fears of insecurity posed by refugees, among other groups. Related to this is the emerging trend by states and global actors, sometimes out of sheer political opportunism, to privilege anti-terrorism over issues of human rights, and democracy. This will increase the vulnerability of refugees to violation of rights by hosting states. In the same vein, regimes, eager to ensure the relaxation of conditions regarding democratization and human rights and to secure financial aid, are likely to amplify the security dimensions of the refugee phenomenon.

Besides, persuading refugee-receiving states not to conceive refugees as part of their security strategy, in situations where refugees are generated within the context of anti-terrorist war, is a difficult task. There is a need, therefore, to establish criteria of determining refugee eligibility and mechanisms for separating them from criminal elements, militias or terrorists, without compromising international norms regulating refugee protection. To that end, it is imperative to revitalize and build the capacity of government structures, particularly status determination committees, to foster effective and efficient processing of asylum claims. Besides, states should hasten the process of establishing policy and legal frameworks to regulate humanitarian activities, to guarantee refugees' access to justice and protect refugees from being unduly criminalized and persecuted. Such frameworks would go a long way in reducing the possibility of militias and criminal elements holding refugees hostage in camps as happened in Ngara (Tanzania) and Goma (DR-Congo). Existing laws and proposed refugee bills in East Africa should be reviewed in light of the complex realities posed by the war against terrorism.

Further, it is no longer feasible to marginalize the state in the management of refugee affairs and expect a guarantee of protection of refugee rights. There is a need to rethink the role of the state and its bureaucratic structures in the emerging humanitarian regime and to encourage it to take a more central role in the management and protection of refugees. States in East Africa should get more involved in the governance of refugee camps to minimize conflict and secure refugees from the grip of militias and criminal groups.

All three states are lacking in the capacity to secure their long porous borders, coastlines and airports and, by extension, to control not only the flow of refugees but also of militias, arms, drugs, and other contraband. Radicalized citizens with long-standing grievances arising from political and economic marginalization against the state are likely to support or shelter terrorists. It is already clear that Kenya's Muslim population in the North Eastern and Coast provinces—variously estimated from 15 to 30 percent of the population—is split on the issue of terrorism. East African governments should, therefore undertake to build bridges with these populations and render their support in hosting refugees and by the same breath exposing the presence of militant elements amongst them.

Dealing with refugees' involvement in cross border trade, especially contraband, requires a regional approach. The framework provided by regional structures such as the East African Cooperation (EAC) and the Inter-Governmental Agency on Development (IGAD), which are key players in addressing regional emergencies, can collaborate with the UNHCR to address this problem. Although it is not targeted to refugees, the draft Protocol on the Proliferation of Small Arms and Light Weapons[33] in the Greater Horn of Africa can be a reference point for stemming the flow of arms into camps and refugee-occupied areas. Simultaneously, UNHCR and its local and international partners should step up support to legitimate refugee business and protect refugee entrepreneurs from harassment and extortion by security personnel. They should also assist in enhancing the state's law enforcement and judicial institutional capacity around the camps. This will make justice accessible to refugees, check money laundering, narcotics trafficking, illegal arms flows, stem banditry, and counter possible terrorist activities that make refugee protection difficult.

In the age of anti-terrorism, advocacy on refugee rights has become a great point of contestation, which the UNHCR alone cannot sufficiently address. There is an urgent need for local and regional civil society organizations to strengthen their refugee rights programs to reinforce UNHCR's refugee protection work. In the past, there has been mutual suspicion between UNHCR and such civil society organizations as Refugee Consortium of Kenya, the Kenya Human Rights Commission and local chapters of the Commission of International Jurists, which run programs on the protection of refugee rights. This has changed drastically and UNHCR is collaborating with these organizations to defend refugee rights and to influence policy. In recent years the UNHCR has engaged such organizations as the International Federation of Women Lawyers (FIDA–Kenya) to give legal services in the protection of women victims of rape in Dadaab camp. Such experience offers valuable lessons for enhancing refugee protection in the future.

Conclusion

Refugee protection in East Africa is, first and foremost, complicated by the absence of viable legal and policy frameworks to determine asylum claims, assist, protect, and search for durable solutions. Where such frameworks exist, as in Uganda and Tanzania, they have become increasingly restrictive, hostile to refugees, and undermining of refugee rights. As a region, East Africa is yet to develop a comprehensive framework for protecting refugees, depriving partner states of a higher point of reference for the treatment of refugees. The absence of robust legal and policy frameworks at the national and regional levels has made it difficult to separate bona fide refugees from criminal elements, militant groups, and terrorists. Subsequently, the tendency has been to collectively criminalize refugees and view them within the security prism. This trend is likely to be exacerbated by the war against terrorism.

Refugee protection has also been a victim of the declining capacity of both the state and humanitarian agencies, particularly UNHCR. Marginalization of the state has deprived other humanitarian actors of the benefits of its structures. The absence of the state in the refugee sector has manifested itself in escalating insecurity in refugee hosting areas, undermining the protection of refugees. At another level, the abdication of the state has overburdened and strained the resources available to UNHCR, accentuating the protection crisis in camps and urban areas.

The size, character, and changing dynamics of refugee population in East Africa have also tended to compromise protection. Refugee population in the 1990s has overwhelmed the humanitarian capacity in East Africa, complicating the task of protection and assistance. Arriving from war-torn countries, refugees are accompanied by militia and criminal elements that take refuge in camps and use them for recuperation, and to recruit and mobilize for ongoing conflicts in their countries of origin. Such activities aggravate insecurity in camps and their environs, and undermine protection work. Besides, some refugees are increasingly getting involved in legal as well as illegal cross-border trade in narcotics, small arms and lights weapons, contraband, minerals, and precious stones. Criminal or terrorist networks can potentially exploit these legal and illegal conduits. These dynamics have heightened state insensitivity, suspicion, and mistrust of refugees and serve as a subterfuge to privilege security over human rights protection. The war against terrorism is likely to exploit these prejudices and, therefore, accentuate the problem of refugee protection.

In the light of the above developments, post–September 11, 2001 refugee protection in East Africa requires a number of policy adjustments. First, there is a need to bring back the state and to fully involve it in refugee protection and assistance. Second, apart from enhancing the capacity of both state and humanitarian actors, there should be a shift of emphasis from relief to human rights protection. Finally, refugee protection requires the establishment of mechanisms for separating refugees from criminal elements and groups without compromising the human rights of refugees. The East African region has rudimentary frameworks, experience, and regional focus to deal with refugee protection. These need to be revitalized to deal with the complex protection environment precipitated by the ongoing war on terror.

13
Refugee Protection in Europe and the U.S. after 9/11

JOANNE VAN SELM

By September 13, 2001, as the numbness instilled by the previous days' events started to lessen, NGO activists and other refugee advocates in the U.S. awoke to the fear that some of the hijackers involved in the attacks on New York and Washington D.C./Virginia would transpire to have been in the U.S. or Canada claiming to seek asylum, and were concerned about the impact that could have. That had been the case in the bombing of the World Trade Center in 1993, and the fact that terrorists had then abused the asylum system to gain access to the U.S. had inspired legal changes causing detention of certain asylum seekers to become mandatory. In fact, those fears were misplaced. Thirteen of the nineteen hijackers had entered the U.S. with valid documentation, it was reported some weeks later. The other six were not accounted for, but had not lodged asylum claims. However, the hijackings and use of passenger planes as weapons of terror still had an immediate and obvious impact on refugee protection in the U.S. as the resettlement program came to a halt. In Europe too, asylum and refugee protection came under immediate scrutiny in the weeks after 9/11.

At the heart of this chapter is the question of whether there will be a lasting impact from fears aroused by 9/11 on refugee protection in Europe and the U.S. Are there grounds for new state fears and state restrictions on the granting of protection? Are the existing tools of refugee protection sufficient to deal with any new perceptions or genuine changes? In what ways are refugee protection and the security of democratic, developed states inextricably linked? And what policy consequences does new attention to the links bring?

In investigating the answers to these questions, I will first reflect on the reasons for which the new atmosphere of security awareness is inextricably linked with matters of refugee protection. Among the issues to be referred to in this context are matters relating to the means of entry of asylum seekers in the West and the exclusion clauses. We will then turn to look at any immediate changes that have taken place, first at the EU level, including thoughts on the need to change any of the proposals for directives that the European Commission had already tabled with the Council of Ministers. We will also reflect on the immediate reactions linking security and asylum in two member states.

Second, we will turn to the other side of the Atlantic and the U.S. Finally, taking these thoughts on immediate changes to a more international level, we will look at the discussions between the EU and U.S. on security and related migration issues, pertaining to refugees. Throughout, reference will be made to both the impact of 9/11 on the general approach taken towards refugee protection, and the specific details of reactions to displacements in and from Afghanistan following the start of the U.S.-led military operations in that country. The chapter will conclude by drawing out some of the possible answers to the questions of the previous paragraph.

Why Are Security Awareness and Refugee Protection Inextricably Linked?

The issues of security and refugee protection have always been inextricably linked, if only implicitly—or selectively. There are many types of security: it is an essentially contested concept in and of itself—but can also be applied to many different contexts. There is also no single form of refugee protection. Ways in which the two have been linked include the fact that protection itself implies the offering of security to people fleeing an insecure situation. Furthermore, the security of those assisting refugees, or protecting them in an assistance and physical security type of way in camp situations have been issues which have seen another form of linkage, especially as so many aid workers have been killed during crises in the Great Lakes Region of Africa, in Somalia, and in East Timor, for example. A third form of linkage was also made in the context of a changing security environment, as some thinkers in the immediate post–Cold War Europe located migration as a potential threat to cultures and identities.[1] Those linkages were viewed by many, including this author, as somewhat spurious attempts to locate new threats, and above all as dangerous ways of lending credence to xenophobic tendencies.[2] Xenophobia has certainly not disappeared from the European (or any western) landscape. However, if 9/11 had any immediate effect in the field of immigration integration thinking in the U.S., it was to show that regardless of origins, all Americans are Americans. Symbolic gestures by politicians such as President Bush, in visiting the Washington D.C. Islamic Center, were very important in countering hate-crimes (even as profiling increased—see below). It might be hoped that one impact of the attacks on democracy, freedom, and peace in the West will be for the Western states to embrace the victims of those who oppose them (as indeed refugee law allowed them to do during the Cold War) and to exclude those who genuinely need to be excluded from the provisions of refugee protection.

While the linkage of the issues of security and refugee protection is not new, the form of the linkage is perhaps novel. It must be borne in mind that any arrival in a country, an immigrant of any sort (on a tourist, student or business visa, or an asylum seeker) could be a potential terrorist, nevertheless it is a needle in a haystack search. Twenty of the border crossings into the U.S.

in 2000–2001 are known to have been made by terrorists. There are estimated to be 500 million border crossings each year. Twenty out of 500 million: the odds of finding these people through the immigration system seem relatively small. And none of them were refugees or asylum seekers.

Two specific areas of concern will be highlighted in this background section: the means of arrival, including trafficking and smuggling, and the exclusion clauses.

Means of Arrival

If any aspect of migration could grab the world's attention, by the end of the 1990s, it was smuggling. When fifty-eight Chinese migrants were found dead in a tomato truck at the port of Dover, England, having spent their journey from the Netherlands without air, the developed world suddenly sat up and paid genuine attention to a phenomenon that had been on the rise for years. This was not the largest single incident in terms of deaths caused, many boats had sunk on their way to Italy, Greece, and Australia, for example, or traveling between developing countries, carrying migrants—including asylum seekers. However it was a dramatic and graphic incident that grabbed the imagination of people who may never previously have devoted any attention to how asylum seekers and unauthorized immigrants were arriving in their countries. The night-vision filmed scenes of over a hundred people storming the Channel Tunnel compound, or individuals trying to creep under the canvas of trucks preparing to board tunnel trains or conceal themselves under the carriages of the Eurostar trains from France to the UK have had a similar effect. These images have drawn the attention not only of policy makers, NGO activists, and transport workers, but of all citizens, concerned in one way or another about people risking their lives in this way to reach some place where they feel they'll be better off: safer, richer, happier? All of these images have brought questions of security to the fore: primarily matters of border control—but for people concerned with human rights and dignity (as one might argue we all should be)[3] also the security and inherent vulnerability of individuals who somehow feel forced to use such unsafe means of travel and arrival.

Many of the measures under consideration post 9/11 also have these entry control issues in mind. It may be that some of them could in fact benefit some of those people seeking asylum and refuge by ensuring other, safer, means of arrival, including the expansion of resettlement (see UK below).

Exclusion and Screening

The 1951 Convention Related to the Status of Refugees includes the following article:

> 1.F. The provisions of this Convention shall not apply to any person with respect to whom there are serious reasons for considering that:

(a) he has committed a crime against peace, a war crime or a crime against humanity, as defined in the international instruments drawn up to make provision in respect of such crimes;

(b) he has committed a serious non-political crime outside the country of refuge prior to his admission to that country as a refugee;

(c) he has been guilty of acts contrary to the purposes and principles of the United Nations.

Clearly, those drafting the convention in 1950–1951 were aware that some people should not be included within its protective remit. They were also clearly aware in this case as in many others within the document, that while needing to be precise, if the convention was to last, they needed a certain breadth too. Following 9/11, the terrorist attacks on the U.S. were described by many figures in positions of authority within the UN as well as in state governments as "crimes against humanity"—and any of the perpetrators or accomplices who might have sought asylum anywhere would surely have been excluded. As will be described below however, several people have noted that asylum is the least likely route for terrorists to take to enter any Western state.

Furthermore, they would only have been excluded from refugee status if governments had taken the time to use the clauses in question. For decades administrations dealing with asylum and refugee protection have not rigorously applied these exclusion clauses. A telling article in the London-based *Economist* reported that such laws had not been used appropriately:[4]

> Time was when North African diplomats called Britain "Europe's terrorist heaven", and its capital was known as Londonistan. Hundreds of veterans of *jihad* struggles in Afghanistan and North Africa settled in Britain. Where else, they ask, could terrorists receive housing, unemployment benefit and legal protection just by applying for asylum?

The strict application of the exclusion clauses may, at times, have been seen to be controversial, inappropriate (had he applied for asylum in London before being arrested in South Africa, Nelson Mandela might have been excluded, for example), and at times as conflicting with a regime of welfare state provision for all "from the cradle to the grave." However, since 9/11, documents released by European Union institutions, the UN and states have all indicated that the moment is politically ripe for more serious, consequential and rigorous use of these exclusion clauses—as well as for appropriate and rigorous use of those clauses relating to inclusion.

The Immediate Response and Changes

In the immediate aftermath of 9/11 there was a rush to create documents within international and regional forums, as well as at the national level, which expressed the horror at what had happened and sought to reassure citizens that governments were in control and could try to avoid a recurrence of such attacks. The keys in the first instance were to seek out terrorists, and those regimes that harbor them, and to cut off their financial support. A second level of the approach sought to demonstrate the way in which immigration laws generally could prevent terrorists from entering countries to commit such acts. The general tone in both Europe and the U.S. could be summed up as being one that showed that the tools for keeping terrorists out were all there on paper, but the implementation needed strengthening. Of concern to advocates of refugee protection was the fact that regard for the right to seek asylum, and for *non-refoulement* seemed sometimes to be potential sacrifices on the combating terrorism pyre.

In this section we will assess how both the EU and the U.S. responded in terms of documents issued outlining the approach to refugee protection issues as impacted by 9/11.

EU Level

Often accused of being a slow-working bureaucracy, the European Commission was seemingly remarkably quick to react to the events of September 11, as new proposals on combating terrorism, irregular migration, and the return of irregular migrants came virtually tumbling out of the door. In fact, the various branches of the Commission's Directorate on Justice and Home Affairs had been working on these issues for some months, and there was what might be called a tragic, if useful, coincidence of timing. In this section, after briefly assessing the specific history of integration on Justice and Home Affairs issues between the EU's member states, and the impact of this as background to any post 9/11 changes in policy, we will turn to the policies on refugee protection being developed within the context of the immigration and asylum branch of the so-called "Area of Freedom, Security and Justice," created by the 1997 Amsterdam Treaty. This is focused on "internal" EU jurisdiction and affairs, that is matters within and between the fifteen member states. We will then turn to look at the EU as a collective foreign policy actor, including specifically the realm of humanitarian and development assistance as this relates to refugee protection and assistance. Finally we will look at snapshots of two EU member states in order to have examples of domestic debates.

History

In discussing the EU level responses to the terrorist hijackings, and particularly with regard to the linkage with asylum, refugee protection and migration more widely, a few points of European Union history must be borne in mind. Firstly, the initial stages of cooperation on Justice and Home Affairs, in the form of inter-governmental working groups in the 1980s, saw two groups emerging, which asylum and refugee protection advocates always feared were linked in nonbenign ways. These were the TREVI group, which considered a range of trans-border criminal issues, including terrorism, and the Ad Hoc Working Group on Asylum and Immigration, which involved many of the same ministers and civil servants. These two groups within the pre-Maastricht Treaty framework of the European Communities reflected the workings of the smaller Schengen group of states, in a less formal setting. These activities of the 1980s, either ad hoc or consisting of only a subset of member states were, in retrospect, somewhat "amateurish" attempts at coordination, compared with the post-Amsterdam, post-Tampere steps on the road to development of a real community level system. The key point is that in the eyes of the world, and to an extent in fact, the EU member states had, collectively, regularly exchanged thoughts on both migration and terrorism, and the linkage had at least not been alien to them. Second, in the search for practical means of cooperation on immigration and asylum policy, almost as an easy way out of the great difficulties of discussing substantive policy issues and differences, information systems had been developing between the European states. The thirteen Schengen states had already established the Schengen Information System, with which non-Schengen states, such as the UK had over the years also sought links. Furthermore, as the Dublin Convention that would determine that member state was responsible for an individual asylum claim in cases where there was doubt floundered due to lack of proof and information, states had decided to establish the EURODAC system of collecting fingerprints from asylum applicants, so they could be sent back to the state in which their claim had been initially lodged, if that was the outcome of the application of the Dublin rules. EURODAC had not got off the ground due to a range of technical difficulties, and many commentators suggested it never really would work effectively, as inputing someone's fingerprints would mean that a state agrees to take them back, which none apparently want to do. However, the idea of sharing information, and means of protecting data and privacy, had been discussed. Additionally, an organization providing for cooperation between member state police forces was established: EUROPOL. EUROPOL was also developing a system for the centralisation of certain types of information. There were thus three developing systems for information gathering and sharing. One major problem, from a security perspective, is that none of these systems were designed to speak with the others.

The Area of Freedom, Security, and Justice

The Amsterdam Treaty created a so-called Area of Freedom, Security, and Justice (ASFJ) in the EU. Not exactly a hip slogan, this designation has lead several people to ask for whom each of those qualities might be set aside, with many concluding that none are apparently aimed at newly arriving immigrants or asylum seekers.[5] The areas of European integration falling under this heading include those relating to asylum and immigration, cross border criminal issues such as issues of concern to all such as drugs and terrorism and judicial and police cooperation. As explained above, these issues have consistently been linked during the integration process, as matters of Justice and Home Affairs. The events of 9/11 and their aftermath, involving combating terrorism, and asylum and immigration questions, have brought the AFSJ to the forefront of EU politics.

Combating Terrorism

With the above history in mind, it is interesting initially to note that the European Commission's proposal for a Council Framework decision on combating terrorism released on September 19, 2001 makes no mention of refugees, asylum, or the exclusion of any persons seeking refugee status.[6] In its observations on this proposal UNHCR notes that "while there is no obvious linkage between the subject matter of the draft Framework Decision and the 1951 Convention relating to the Status of Refugees, internationally agreed criteria for characterizing certain acts as "terrorist offences" may be relevant to the interpretation and application of the so-called "exclusion clauses" of the refugee definition of the 1951 Convention." According to UNHCR, the wording of the Exclusion Clauses makes it clear that if properly applied they should "make it impossible for terrorists to benefit from the protection of the 1951 Convention." However, UNHCR is, on the basis of this document, clearly wary of the over-enthusiastic connection between exclusion and terrorism in the absence of carefully crafted definitions of terrorist acts, leaving a wide margin for state interpretation. While terrorists clearly should not be included in the remit of Convention status

> UNHCR notes that, in the context of article 1 F (b) of the 1951 Convention, the serious and grave nature of the offence must clearly be established. Any listing of terrorist acts in legislative instruments must maintain the connotation of particular gravity. In addition, UNHCR wishes to point out that it is also important that the particular circumstances of the individual case be fully examined and, hence, that any unwarranted automaticity between the draft Framework Decision and the application of the exclusion clauses be avoided in asylum cases generally. The international standards developed in respect of the exclusion clauses require either personal participation or personal knowledge and responsibility in the sense of contributing to the impugned acts, or failing to stop them. Strict observance of these standards is particularly important when assessing whether certain acts carried out by an applicant for asylum may constitute terrorist acts, as the person's intent and motivation are an integral part of the definition of such offences. Whereas in some cases the personal knowledge and responsibility of the individual may be established on the basis of the person's position and his or her level of participation in the acts in question, there may be cases where such a conclusion would be unwarranted, and the person should be

given the opportunity to show that he or she had no personal knowledge or was not directly involved in those acts.[7]

State interpretation of terrorist acts on a relatively rash basis might exclude people from Convention status who in fact should have been included (the reference above to the question of how someone such as Nelson Mandela might have been treated at different points in history is relevant here). Whereas the European Commission, as will be seen below, set out a position from which the evidentiary requirement for exclusion from refugee status was markedly lower than that for a criminal case, UNHCR was sounding a note of caution, which should be expected of it.

The Council's common position of December 27, 2001 on the application of specific measures to combat terrorism[8] defines terrorism at length (Article 1.3) including seizure of means of public transport, and includes a list of names of individuals suspected of terrorist activities, and their identity card numbers. The former point is interesting not only for its connection to the means of committing terrorist acts used on September 11, but also for the potential link to smuggling arrivals and rescue at sea, in incidents such as that of the MV Tampa off the coast of Australia in August 2001. The list of names and ID card numbers consists mostly of Basque separatists, whose names were provided by the Spanish government. This is interesting in the context of this chapter for the connection to the EU's protocol on the seeking of asylum by European Union citizens in member states other than their own. That protocol, attached to the Amsterdam Treaty, effectively prohibits citizens of EU member states from seeking asylum in other EU states, and was provoked largely by Spain's dissatisfaction when a number of Basque separatists had sought asylum in Belgium.

The ETA and Real/Continuation IRA terror groups, 'native' to the EU, were among those whose existence had a major impact on the formulation of anti-terror measures post-9/11. To an extent it seemed that some EU governments were seizing the moment to get agreement at EU level on measures related to these existing 'problems', which had been of concern to them for a long time. In July 2001 already, a European Parliament report on terrorism, by Graham Watson, had contained nothing on refugees or migration, and had been focused on acts in Europe and largely by Europeans and the need for coherent legal systems and policies in all member states. One result of that process, somewhat accelerated in the post 9/11 atmosphere, was the creation of a uniform arrest warrant, replacing the need for extradition procedures between the member states.

Asylum and Immigration Measures

At its first emergency meeting following September 11, the Justice and Home Affairs Council decided to "harness all the measures already adopted at European Union level to combat these heinous acts" and also to "speed up the process of creating an area of freedom, security and justice and to step up cooperation with its partners, especially the United States."[9] Measures dealing with judicial and police cooperation took very much the front seat above immigration and asylum. Individual ministers and top level administrators within the EU's institutions frequently wear all the hats relating to justice matters, and have both criminal matters and immigration matters in their portfolios. Both within Europe and in dialogue with the U.S., these officials seemingly gave priority to justice matters in the earliest days; however, immigration matters linked to terrorism cannot have been far from their minds.

The conclusions of the September 20 meeting related chiefly to judicial/police cooperation.[10] Migration enters the picture in the following ways:

- The need to examine whether to extend, in the context of counter-terrorism, SIS access to other public services (i.e. immigration data).
- The recommendation that the Member States exercise the utmost vigilance when issuing identity documents and residence permits (particularly in the case of duplicates). [25]
- The request that the Member States apply procedures for the issue of visas with maximum rigour and to this end step up local consular cooperation.
- The invitation to Commission to submit proposals for establishing a network for information exchanges concerning the visas issued. [26]
- The invitation to the Commission to urgently examine the relationship between safeguarding internal security and complying with international protection obligations and instruments. [29]
- The request that the Commission examine whether the EU needs to provisionally apply the Council Directive on temporary protection—in case special arrangements are required in the EU due to the situation in relation to countries and regions where there is a risk of large-scale population movements as a result of heightened tensions. [30]

On following up on the penultimate request and considering the need to make changes to the embryonic asylum system in the EU, the European Commission wrote that "rather than through major changes to the refugee protection regime, a scrupulous application of the exceptions to refugee protection available under current law is the appropriate approach."[11] One of the ways of scrupulously applying current law regarding refugees, in a way which had not always been done in the past, would be the correct application of the exclusion clauses as outlined above. In fact, however, while terrorists might use asylum channel (in EU only student or family unity would be likely other legal options for immigration) the European Commission expressed its sense that "in practice terrorists are not likely to use the asylum channel much, as other, illegal, channels are more discreet and more suitable for their criminal practices."[12] Thus, measures aimed at preventing irregular, unauthorized immigration would be more necessary than a tightening of the asylum channel. In fact, if those many commentators who blame the restrictions on asylum in Western Europe for the rise in use of unauthorized immigration routes are even partially correct, it would be most politically advisable for European states to investigate more closely means of permitting the entry of genuine refugees more easily, and in a more controlled, well managed way (e.g., through resettlement—see below on the UK).

On December 5, 2001, the Commission of the European Communities issued a Working Document entitled *The Relationship between Safeguarding Internal Security and Complying with International Protection Obligations*.[13] This document forms the first official commentary from the European Commission on the links between terrorism and refugee protection. It was written in response to Conclusion 29 of the Extraordinary Justice and Home Affairs Council meeting of September 20, 2001. At that meeting, the Council invited the Commission to "examine urgently the relationship between safeguarding internal security and complying with international protection obligations and instruments."

The Commission working document is built on two main premises:

1. That bona fide refugees and asylum seekers should not become victims of the recent events; and
2. That there should be no avenue for those supporting or committing terrorist acts to secure access to the territory of the Member States of the European Union.

On the basis that some potential terrorists might make use of the asylum channel, however unlikely the scenario could be, the Commission addresses both the general question of how refugee protection can be upheld without compromising security, and the specific details of how many of the proposals on the European Council's table, intended to form the first building blocks of a Common European Asylum System, might be impacted by a new focus on terrorism.

Addressing the general question, the European Commission supports UNHCR's claim that the existing basis to refugee protection in international law provides sufficiently for the exclusion of terrorists with global reach.[14] What is needed is a more rigorous application of that existing legal principle, not a reformulation of the principle itself.

Among the specific different approaches the Commission outlines are:

A. Exclusion[15] and Cancellation of Status

- The choice is between freezing the examination of an asylum claim where an extradition request is made on the applicant (i.e. where suspicions have already been raised about the claimant) and making the claim inadmissible. Freezing the examination would mean that access to asylum procedures would be granted, and the procedures then suspended where person indicted by international criminal tribunal or where there is a pending extradition request from a country other than the country of origin of the asylum seeker, relating to serious crimes.

- That Article 1(f), the exclusion clause, should be used within the asylum procedures, in order that *refoulement* be avoided in all cases where the claimant, even if he or she should be excluded from refugee status, cannot be returned to a potentially life-threatening situation.
- That the exclusion clauses need not be applied to every asylum application—but only in those cases in which an initial admissibility procedure has shown that exclusion might be relevant to that particular case.
- That if it is already known that there are sufficient grounds to consider exclusion then the individual should be the subject of an accelerated procedure, starting with exclusion clauses rather than inclusion grounds.
- That full criminal proceedings are not necessary in order to exclude an individual from refugee status—rather "It is sufficient to establish that there are serious reasons for considering that the person has committed those acts. The basis for such a conclusion must be clearly established." In addition, the person must be able to appeal exclusion finding.
- That all member states should consider following the lead of those which have special units to deal with exclusion, and all security risk cases and cases of suspected involvement in serious violent acts or violations of human rights.
- That the creation of EU level guidelines on the use of exclusion clauses should be considered.
- That there should be an exchange of information on people excluded from Refugee Convention status.
- In the Proposal on Minimum Standards for Asylum Procedures there is provision for the cancellation of status on the grounds of information coming to light after the processing of claims. However, this may need to be re-worded to provide also for the suspension of the procedure, or inadmissibility of the claim.

The Commission also notes that, in line with Article 7 of the European Convention on the Suppression of Terrorism (agreed under the wider Council of Europe), a person excluded from refugee status must either be prosecuted or extradited to face justice for the crimes on which their exclusion is based.[16] This requirement means that in fact, as matters of jurisdiction and of the admissibility of evidence are different in criminal and extradition proceedings that in consideration of the applicability of the exclusion clauses, the suggestion of a lower level of proof for exclusion might be challenged.[17]

B. Reception Conditions and Detention

A proposal from the Commission on Reception Conditions was tabled in 2000. In this paper on post 9/11 thoughts, the Commission suggests that reception provisions would be withdrawn for terrorists (or suspected terrorists) although no reference is made to what should happen to those removed from reception facilities. Elsewhere, the Commission notes that:

> where there is evidence to show that an individual asylum-seeker has criminal affiliations likely to pose a risk to public order or national security, detention would be an appropriate tool. It must however be acknowledged that in most systems there are limits to the detention of asylum applicants; also the legality and necessity of detention is subject to judicial review. [1.6]

Indeed, detention is rarely used in asylum cases in EU member states: the UK provides a limited exception to that general rule (see below). However, a pragmatic approach following 9/11 would imply that those people who might credibly pose a risk to security, for example, through known links to terrorism, should be detained in line with any judicial proceedings concerning their actions.

C. Equal Treatment

Given that 'toeing the line' has been a problem between the member states of the European Union, particularly obvious in areas in which the need to toe the line represents a need to present a unified face to the world, it is perhaps not surprising that the Commission pointed out that: "If a terrorist is not granted an international protection status in one Member State or if the status is withdrawn or cancelled, he/she should expect the same treatment of his/her case in all other Member States." [3]

D. Temporary Protection

Temporary Protection is one of the very few areas in which a commission proposal for a directive has resulted in the adoption of EU law since the entry into force of the Amsterdam Treaty. Article 28 (1)(b) of that directive, the Commission points out, provides for exclusion. However, the Commission does not point out that in practice this would mean that individuals would need to be assessed for exclusion within a group determination process which is intended to save on administrative time during the arrival of a significant group of refugees. The Commission also suggests that EURODAC will help with providing an informational basis for temporary protection. Again, however, in practice, this could only be true if states do indeed fingerprint people seeking asylum (and there is some doubt that they will, when fingerprinting someone will mean accepting responsibility for processing their claim should they re-apply in another state).

E. Non-refoulement

Article 33(2) of the 1951 Convention clearly sets out that *non-refoulement* is not a right of those who pose a danger to the security of the receiving state. It says that the:

> benefit of [*non-refoulement*] may not, however, be claimed by a refugee whom there are reasonable grounds for regarding as a danger to the security of the country in which he is, or who, having been convicted by a final judgement of a particularly serious crime, constitutes a danger to the community of that country.

The Commission suggests that we should expect there to be a need for future rulings of ECHR on whether Article 3 of the European Convention on Human Rights, which also deals with non-return, is really nonderogable, as past rulings have implied, protecting all people, including people who are a potential security risk themselves, from return to a situation in which their own life might be at risk. The whole discussion surrounding *non-refoulement* and terrorism in connection with the seeking of asylum is indeed likely to be long-drawn out, and very complex. On the surface it conjures up immediately images of "terrorists in orbit" in place of the "refugees in orbit" who have so long been of concern (in various ways) in Europe. "Terrorists in orbit" sound somewhat more dangerous for everyone.

In any discussion of a Commission document it must be recalled that the system is such that the Commission drafts texts, but does not have any implementing role. Ultimately, what goes down on paper is only a guide for states, and it is what the states do, and will do, which really counts.

The EU as an International Actor

While the ASFJ is for the most part a matter of how the European Union's member states coordinate internal affairs, the EU has also been developing as an international actor, as much in the areas of humanitarian assistance, development aid, and foreign policy, in recent years, as in the more traditional area of trade. How the member states have acted as the EU in assigning humanitarian assistance, and in supporting the anti-terror measures and action of UN and U.S. are therefore important matters to take into account in assessing the impact of 9/11 on the EU's approach to refugee protection broadly speaking.

Humanitarian and Development Assistance

Besides concern for the domestic impact of 9/11, specifically on the issue of refugee protection, the European Commission, as part of the assessment of the economic impact of events, was looking at its role in financing assistance to Afghanistan and for regional refugee protection. The Commission noted that humanitarian assistance to Afghanistan after September 11, and before the end of October, 2001 totaled €310m from the EU as a whole, with over €100m from the European Commission.[18] Of that €100 million in Commission aid, €5.5 million had been decided upon and/or allocated after September 11 in response to the worsening situation.[19] The €100 million also included €22.5 million in the 'Aid to Uprooted People' budget, to programs for IDPs and refugees in Afghanistan, Pakistan, and Iran. Poul Nielson, European Commissioner for Development Cooperation and Humanitarian Aid noted that from the "Aid to Uprooted People" budget, €19 million had been given to Afghanistan, €3 million to Pakistan and €2 million to Iran.[20]

The Commission's October 17 report specifically linked development and poverty reduction with terrorism.[21] It also noted that need for international judicial and police cooperation as: "[r]ecent events have added a new 'security' dimension to the European Union's international perspective. The Union should take the lead."

The link between development and poverty reduction, as well as between security and refugee issues had already been made within the sphere of foreign policy thinking on consular, and thus immigration and asylum affairs. The Commission made no reference to this in its paper on the economic impact of 9/11. Indeed, the arena within which the linkages had been made had been relatively silent for some time. The High Level Working Group on Asylum and Migration (HLWG) had been formed in late 1998, as the result of a Dutch initiative. A cross pillar group, encompassing foreign policy (second pillar), development policy (first pillar) and asylum and migration policies (transitioning from third to first pillar) the HLWG had published a report and action plan on Afghanistan and neighboring states in 1999.[22] The action plan could not really be put into effect, as part of the purpose was to stimulate relations with the governments of sending and transit states, and there were no or only limited relations with the Taliban (no relations) and the regimes in Islamabad and Teheran. However, the EU had been supporting projects of UNHCR and other organizations on the ground in the region. Were security policy to be more closely integrated in the workings of that group, it could both breath new life into the initiative and broaden its cross-pillar perspective, as third pillar issues of judicial and police cooperation would be a clear matter for concern.

Supporting the UN and U.S. in Combating Terrorism

The Council's Common Position of December 27, 2001 on combating terrorism[23] mirrors the language of UN Security Council Resolution 1373 of September 28, 2001. The texts states that "Safe haven shall be denied to those who finance, plan, support or commit terrorist acts, or provide safe havens,"[24] and that action should be taken to "prevent the movement of terrorists or terrorist groups by effective border controls and controls on issuance of identity papers and travel documents, and through measure for preventing counterfeiting, forgery or fraudulent use of identity papers and travel documents"[25] The EU

Ministers added to this latter statement that "the Council noted the Commission's intention to put forward proposals in this area, where appropriate."

Of relevance to this chapter, both documents noted that:

> Appropriate measures shall be taken in accordance with the relevant provisions of national and international law, including international standards of human rights, before granting refugee status, for the purpose of ensuring that the asylum-seeker has not planned, facilitated or participated in the commission of terrorist acts. The Council noted the Commission's intention to put forward proposals in this area, where appropriate.[26]

And that:

> Steps shall be taken in accordance with international law to ensure that refugee status is not abused by the perpetrators, organisers or facilitators of terrorist acts and that claims of political motivation are not recognised as grounds for refusing requests for the extradition of alleged terrorists. The Council notes the Commission's intention to put forward proposals in this area, where appropriate.[27]

The new emphasis on the need to strictly adhere to the existing provisions for the exclusion of people whose previous acts have been contrary to the principles of the UN and included crimes against humanity and war crimes, has thus been noted at both UN and EU level. The Commission's proposals, and the member states fair implementation of the existing rules remain to be seen at the time of writing.

Individual Member States

While the EU is increasingly acting as a unit, as noted above, it is in fact still what the states do, often individually, that really counts, not what they collectively write on paper, or what the European Commission drafts on their behalf. In looking at the member states, it would be impossible to take in all fifteen of them. The focus here will therefore be on the UK and the Netherlands as they give us examples of a large and a small state. Both have been facing increased asylum seeker numbers in recent years and making policy changes independent of EU level discussions to deal with those. They offer different approaches, what is more, as one, the Netherlands, is a central player in the discussions on asylum and immigration, while the other, the UK, has an 'opt in' to integration in this area, meaning it can select those common policies of which it wishes to be part. As of March 2002, the UK had opted in to every discussion in the asylum field.

UK

European states became aware soon after September Eleventh that several of the hijackers had been in European states: none of them had sought asylum in any of the fifteen states, but several had been students, or had visas for other

purposes. In the stories that have surfaced either out of government willingness to assess and talk, or of news investigations by early 2002, the only country known to have refused a visa to any of the hijackers was Finland. The BBC
reported that Home Secretary David Blunkett had admitted that none of the
eleven men who had been in the UK were under surveillance during that
time.[28] Without knowledge of future terror plans, people who had committed
no crimes could not be prevented from entering the UK, they were effectively
"clean" terrorists (i.e. prior to terrorist acts being committed or exposed as in
the planning). "Individuals who have no previous involvement in terror present one of the most difficult challenges to the security service personnel deciding who is to be put under surveillance in the UK."[29] This position would
naturally also apply to asylum seekers and any thoughts that authorities might
have of applying exclusions.

On October 3, 2001, in his speech to the Labour Party conference, Blunkett
made two points that would have a direct impact on asylum seekers, and on
the nature of refugee protection in the UK, and another that could impact
those excluded from refugee status on Convention grounds:[30]

- Giving law enforcement agencies full access to passenger and freight
  information which air and sea carriers will be required to retain;
- Amending the Immigration and Asylum Act 1999 to ensure those
  suspected or convicted of terrorist involvement cannot be considered
  for asylum
- Also; complete overhaul of UK's extradition system, making a four-
  tier system with streamlined procedures

The first of Mr. Blunkett's points is linked to the issue of the means of arrival of
asylum seekers discussed in the introduction to this chapter. As such, it is not
only a measure to deal with the security issues at hand in the post-9/11 atmosphere of concern about terrorism, but is also a means of extending control on
an area of conflict with current immigration and asylum policies. If passenger
manifests are to be maintained with close attention to documentation and so
on this forms an additional means to attempt to prevent smuggling and trafficking and to allow for the control of undocumented or unauthorized arrivals
using fraudulent documentation. Like other measures, such as carrier sanctions, it could form another barrier to legitimate refugees exercising their right
to seek and enjoy asylum in countries other than their own.

The second point was reinforced when, on October 16, 2001, the Home
Secretary announced plans to suspend elements of the human rights laws to
enable the internment of suspected foreign terrorists in Britain. This meant
that the UK would derogate from Article 5 of the European Convention on
Human Rights (which had been incorporated into UK law with the Human
Rights Act in 1998) and make use of the provision of Article 15 (also ECHR),

allowing such derogation when national security required it. The new power would be used in cases where a suspect could not be deported either because there was no extradition agreement with the country of origin or transit or because he or she would face torture or death if returned to that country. The decision under this new provision, to certify someone as a threat to national security, is to be based on an assessment by British intelligence services and not simply on the basis of a request made by another country. This new power would, explained one newspaper, "enable asylum claims from those suspected of terrorist associations to be rejected by the home secretary issuing a certificate declaring them to be a threat to national security." In explaining the provision, Mr. Blunkett rightly called on the 1951 Convention for support.[31] However, the workings of the provision would require close monitoring by NGO groups, and undoubtedly a number of interesting and controversial court cases could result from its application and the appeals process.

In the midst of concerns over immigration and terrorism, an appeal case was heard with direct relevance in terms of issues and concepts, if not in terms of facts. Four Iraqi Kurds had been fighting the lawfulness of their detention. On October 19, 2001, the Court of Appeal ruled that they could be lawfully detained, rejecting their case. The wisdom of judgement was questioned by Louise Pirrouet, a representative of Oakington Concern (a group established to monitor detainee conditions): "Anyone looking at this in the wake of what happened in New York would, I suggest, have had those events in their minds and I cannot help but think this judgement has been warped by those feelings. Oakington is not a prison and should not be used as one."[32]

An increasing number of asylum seekers have been detained in the UK in recent years, often due to concerns about document fraud (and that in spite of Article 31 of the 1951 Convention which specifies that penalties will not be imposed on the basis of illegal entry). Detention on immigration charges became a prevalent issue in the U.S. in the wake of 9/11 as will be seen below. Interestingly, in reflecting on David Blunkett's desire to derogate from Article 5 of the European Convention on Human Rights, commentator Hugo Young retold a story from May 1940, when a man called Robert Liversidge, aka Perlzweig, was sent to Brixton prison as a threat to public safety. The home secretary, Sir John Anderson gave no reason, and under recent emergency legislation, he only needed "reasonable cause" to believe a suspect was a person "of hostile associations," Many people, 1,426 to be exact, were in the same predicament—and no judges were willing to hear the cases. The case went to House of Lords, where only one judge rejected the view that the politician could subjectively be the judge of what was required for national security. That judge was then derided, but has been held up as a hero by many ever since; he is regarded as a symbol of how the judicial process must be distinct from the executive branch of government.[33] Young tells this story as warning about Blunkett's actions—but it also reflects the 2001–2002 situation in the U.S.

Finally, in February 2002, the Labour government issued a White Paper *Secure Borders, Safe Haven, Integration with Diversity in Modern Britain.* This White Paper included the proposed development of a resettlement program, turning to a means of managing refugee immigration to the UK and away from the practice of resettling only the ten plus extremely vulnerable cases referred by UNHCR each year. This proposal, it is suggested in the paper, is intended to deter people from using smuggling to arrive in the UK. It might certainly be a step in the direction of permitting more people to arrive in an organized and legitimate way in the UK, avoiding the need for lengthy and stigmatized processing there, as they would arrive as refugees. However, any resettlement program, however large, cannot totally deter people from seeking asylum spontaneously—or better said, from exercising their human right to seek and enjoy asylum from persecution in another country. While the proposal of a resettlement program was to be expected in the light of speeches made by Mr. Blunkett's predecessor, Jack Straw,[34] and to be welcomed for all the positive benefits it could bring to some refugees, it has been greeted with notes of caution by advocates who see that it is contained in the same White Paper as several paragraphs on stricter border controls.[35] As the British Refugee Council points out, to have any impact a UK resettlement program would have to deal with thousands of people, not only hundreds. And in the wake of 9/11, as will be seen below, the only country whose resettlement program deals with thousands of arrivals each year, has cut back its program enormously in the months immediately following 9/11.

The Netherlands

In the immediate wake of September 11, the Netherlands returned to a long drawn out debate about multiculturalism, which had last been prominent in the media in late 2000, but has been a subject of discussion and tension for more two decades.[36] A poll of Muslims in the Netherlands suggested that 56 percent of them approved of the attacks in the U.S.[37] In reaction to this, another poll of Dutch citizens indicated that 63 percent of them felt radical Muslims, who expressed such approval, should be removed from the country. Meanwhile, two-thirds of the Dutch population was reported to fear that the integration of Muslims into their society would be hindered by the reactions to the attacks.[38]

A comfortable majority wanted border controls between Schengen states to be reinstated. At least two major parties (VVD and CDA) also supported this view.[39] In fact, on October 5, it was announced there would be an expansion in the number of officers performing tasks of oversight and control close to the borders (ANP).

In considering the situation of Afghans, the cabinet discussed revoking its position that Pakistan was a safe third country in which Afghans could achieve protection.[40] Ruud Lubbers, the UN High Commissioner for Refugees requested the country of which he had been Prime Minister for twelve years, via a TV appeal, to establish a quota of some thousands to ten thousand refugees from Afghanistan. As the bombing campaign by the U.S. seemed to achieve its goals of ridding Afghanistan of both the Taliban and al-Qaeda, the Dutch Immigration Service in fact exacted a 'stay of decision' on all new Afghan cases, and while the Netherlands gave almost $30 million to UNHCR for the reception of refugees in the South Asia region, Secretary of State for Justice, Ella Kalsbeek said it would be problematic to bring in more Afghans, beyond the 26,000 already in the Netherlands. The Dutch embassy in Pakistan closed after the attacks in the U.S., so family reunification for Afghans was effectively stopped as their visas could not be processed. While permission had already been given for family reunification visas for at least sixteen families, they were thereby stranded in Pakistan.[41]

While the actual acts of sitting politicians were directly impacting the lives of the 26,000 Afghans already in the Netherlands, other political developments were giving them ever-greater cause for concern about their futures. Sensing dismay with the ruling "Purple Coalition," a maverick figure, Pim Fortuyn, had caught a wave of public discontent with day to day life in the Netherlands (concerned with economic and social policies) and linked that to the ever populist tendencies of xenophobia to create two new parties, which in the run up to the May 15, 2002 general election looked likely to completely transform the landscape of Dutch politics.[42] In response to this new element, the existing political parties were forced to turn to the asylum and migration issues: Ella Kalsbeek, on the eve of municipal elections in March 2002, stated bluntly in an interview that involuntary returns to Afghanistan may become necessary in the longer-term. Although she added that before such a policy would be developed, one had to be sure of the safe future for the returnees in their country, the damage was done in terms of making the existing Afghan population feel less secure than ever in the Netherlands.[43]

United States

The events of 9/11 could certainly be expected to have their greatest impact in the country directly hit. American confidence in its relative geographic isolation and untouchability was rocked to the core. While the populations of New York and Washington walked numbly through city centers, eerily silent as all overhead flights were banned, others were feeling the impact in a different, but perhaps even more significant way. Thousands of refugees, awaiting resettlement from countries of first asylum around the world, having been through months of extensive screening, found themselves vulnerable and hit again, as their flights to the U.S. were cancelled, and their travel postponed. As the U.S. authorities put all non-terrorism related business aside, a new act passed though Congress: "Uniting and Strengthening America by Providing Appropriate Tools Required to Intercept and Obstruct Terrorism (USA PATRIOT

ACT) Act of 2001." Two elements of that act are of particular relevance to this chapter: those relating to the northern border and to profiling.

Resettlement Program Slow Down

The U.S. is one of the few traditional resettlement countries with a substantial annual quota for people preselected and arriving, in an organized way, as refugees on its territory. Only ten countries have practiced resettlement on a consistent basis since the 1980s: six of these are European states with quotas numbered in the hundreds on an annual basis, and arrival, through UNHCR referral, which sometimes number in the dozens.[44] Australia, Canada, and New Zealand have, like the U.S., had resettlement quotas running in the thousands. The U.S. has significantly reduced its annual ceiling on refugee resettlement admissions during the course of the 1990s and into the first decade of the twenty-first century. Importantly, the number decided upon annually by the president, on the basis of a tri-department proposal that must first advance through Congress, is a ceiling.[45] Actual arrivals have fallen significantly short of the ceiling consistently for the last decade.

The passage of the proposal through Congress in September 2001 was delayed due to the inevitable focus on post-9/11 needs and concerns. The administrative delays continued through to November 2001, at which point the President signed in a ceiling of 70,000 for the fiscal year 2002 (running from September 2001). Some delay in the signing in of the annual details is not unusual. However, this delay was very long, and in the meantime, due to a variety of security concerns and administrative hold ups, even refugees who had been cleared for arrival were not traveling to the U.S. In the first quarter of FY2002, only a few hundred people arrived instead of almost 20,000. In February 2002, Senator Edward Kennedy pointed out during a Senate sub-committee hearing that only 2,000 refugees had arrived by that point in the program year, whereas in February 2001 more than 14,000 had arrived.[46] Kennedy further suggested that the decline could not be attributed to the war on terrorism alone: the previous decade had seen refugee admissions falling. Many NGOs attributed this decline to mismanagement and an absence of desire to fulfil the aims of the program by those tasked to do so within the State Department.[47]

Anecdotal evidence of the impact of this resettlement slow down comes from media stories. For example, the New York Times on October 29, 2001 ran a story describing families due to leave Islamabad on September 13, 2001, who were still stuck there; forty Afghans scheduled to arrive at Kennedy International Airport from Pakistan on September 29, 2001, who had sold everything, and were now facing eviction and an uncertain future, still in Pakistan. Those prevented from carrying out the resettlement for which they had already been approved were not only Afghans (for whom the security concerns had of course the added impact of the war on terror within Afghanistan.) There were also people from elsewhere affected by this total stop: Armenian Christians from Iran, on their way to the U.S. from Austria, whose movement was cancelled; a Jewish family from Ukraine scheduled to fly out of Moscow. With the actual arrivals well below the quota level, Lavinia Limon (former Clinton State Department official, now executive director of Immigration and Refugee Services of America) was cited as saying: "If you wanted to come to this country as a terrorist, coming as a refugee has to be the stupidest way to come."[48]

The Northern Border

The PATRIOT Act contains provisions related to Protecting the northern border (ensuring personnel numbers; access to information; fingerprint identification), Enhanced Immigration Provisions (definition relating to terrorism; visa integrity and security; machine readable passports etc.) and the Preservation of Immigration Benefits for Victims of Terrorism (relating to those directly affected by 9/11). The issue which might in fact become the most important for refugee rights advocates is in fact not contained in the PATRIOT Act, but part of the quid pro quo arrangements with the Canadian authorities to engage their commitment to strengthening the security of the common border. This is the resurgence of interest in the drafting of a Memorandum of Understanding between the two countries, declaring each other as safe third countries. An attempt at such drafting took place in the late 1990s, without success.[49] In 2002, it is difficult to see how such an MOU could have the results the Canadians seem to require (fewer applicants there, more in the U.S.) and survive scrutiny by courts, advocacy groups and so on, as there is no attempt being made to harmonize the systems, as is the case within the EU where the Dublin Convention provides a similar, mutual partners type arrangement, or between the EU member states and their eastern neighbors, where the EU is in effect exporting levels of immigration policy control strictness in exchange for the promise of membership of the Union at some point.[50]

Profiling

From September 11 onwards, stories surfaced of hundreds of immigrants, predominantly men of Arab appearance, being detained, frequently on the basis of immigration violations, with no criminal charges being filed. Six months after 9/11, media stories were still circulating of people in jails with no idea what the reason for their incarceration might be. Most often there was no private access to lawyers, causing significant concern among immigrant advocacy and civil rights groups. In total more than 1,200 people were detained—and their plight seemed to provoke little general sense of sympathy in a population preoccupied with anti-terror security measures. While there is widespread lip service paid in the U.S. to the need not to target people of specific ethnic origins, there is much concern with the ways and means of finding that needle in the haystack—the single terrorist among the millions of people. There are widespread claims that profiling on the basis of behavior, for example, rather than ethnicity, is the way to go—though the stories of the nineteen hijackers indicate that they were either masters of disguise with regard to drawing attention to themselves, or that they were in fact by all regular behavioral measures fairly normal, except for their intent to kill on a massive scale, an intent hidden until the moment of action. Airlines took immediately to using random searches, with a variety of different means of selecting their "random" targets (seat numbers; an 's' prior to the boarding card number, etc). The concern has to be, however, that profiling of a less random sort may develop in such programs as the resettlement program, in which foreign policy and national interest have always played a major role.

Humanitarian Assistance

As their bombing campaign above Afghanistan began, the United States announced that as well as bombs, it was dropping food packages to try to alleviate the hunger of thousands of Afghans who, it had been feared even without the added intense bombings, would suffer starvation as a drought had persisted in the war-torn country for several years. The food packages came to symbolize for many the tension which had been increasing in recent humanitarian emergencies between civil and military ends of operations all nominally designed to help people. International organizations had pulled all international personnel out of Afghanistan prior to the military action. Only Afghan personnel were still on the ground, with no new supplies reaching them, and some existing supplies becoming the erroneous targets of smart bombs gone astray. The food packages, contained in yellow bags, with instructions on the outside, contained such non-Afghan goodies as jam and peanut butter. Many in the aid community decried these minimal efforts to feed millions of starving people. Others pointed out that although few got to eat, it was better than no one eating. The critics noted that the food packs could easily lead people into minefields, as their targeting could not be precise, and the country was littered with mines and new, unexploded warheads. They were "a Band-Aid measure to humanize [the] bombing campaign . . . [but] potentially lethal" some aid workers said.[51]

The symbolic food drops were followed by other actions to add a humanitarian strand to the U.S. attacks on those harboring terrorists and the delivery of the Afghan people from the Taliban regime. In a news conference on October 11, 2001, President George W. Bush announced the establishment of America's Fund for Afghan Children. It was presented as a fund to which American children would contribute in order to improve the lives of their Afghan counterparts. By March 19, 2002, the Fund had received and processed 390,614 letters containing donations of $4,289,455.11, and when online and other donations were added the total came to: $4,648,516.63.[52] Administered by the Red Cross of America, the Fund called for letters to be sent to the White

House address—an announcement derided at the time when letters containing anthrax had been delivered in the Capitol area.

Already in March 2002, the total U.S. provision of aid to Afghanistan for the fiscal year 2002 stood at $237,305,125. The President had announced a $320 million aid package in October 2001, and nearly $180 million had been provided during 2001. In making a statement on a new tranche of this budget (of $19 million, to be divided between UN agencies and the ICRC) the State Department noted that:[53]

> The United States believes that humanitarian assistance for refugees, displaced persons, conflict victims and other persons at risk and the pursuit of solutions for humanitarian crises are a shared international responsibility. We call on other donors to be generous in their response to the humanitarian emergency in Afghanistan

The comparison with the EU figures given above, if all figures are accurate and all aid is truly reaching its target, is reasonable, although some $600 million would not cover all the agencies involved for their operating costs as well as covering the massive amounts of assistance of all sorts really necessary in the country. In his State of the Union Address, George W. Bush noted that the U.S. had been spending $30 million per day on waging war on terror in Afghanistan. Ten days of war was equivalent thus to assistance, including for rebuilding war damage, for months.[54]

Links between U.S. and EU

In the days immediately following 9/11, representatives of the European Union were among the first to make the journey to the U.S. when its air space reopened. Meetings were held in Washington between the U.S. and three top EU figures: Belgian Foreign Minister Louis Michel (representing the presidency, which was with Belgium at that time), Chris Patten (Commissioner for External Affairs), and Javier Solana (EU High Representative for the Common Foreign and Security Policy). Although the Commissioner for Justice and Home Affairs, Vitorino, was not present, top civil servants dealing with those issues within the European Commission were, in their capacity as terrorism and criminality experts rather than for their knowledge of immigration and asylum policies—although that latter expertise may not have come amiss. The two sides agreed to 'vigorously pursue' cooperation in the following areas:[55]

- Aviation and other transport security
- Police and judicial cooperation, including extradition
- Denial of financing of terrorism, including financial sanctions
- Denial of other means of support to terrorists
- Export control and nonproliferation

- Border controls, including visa and document security issues
- Law enforcement access to information and exchange of electronic data.

There was, indeed, a widespread desire for better coordination in watch lists, within regions (even just within the U.S.) and between regions. The U.S. undertook to extend a more detailed list of areas of interest for cooperation to the EU. However, the window of opportunity for discussion in these areas appeared short-lived, as that list seemingly was interpreted as a wish list, and little response apparently came from the EU states or its Belgian presidency. In the area of justice and home affairs issues, even as they pertain to foreign policy matters, it seems Henry Kissinger's well known lament of there being noone to call in Europe may be applicable.

Conclusions

This chapter started out with a series of questions, none of which can be fully answered here, although we can seek the beginnings of answers perhaps. The questions were:

- Whether there will be a lasting impact from fears aroused by 9/11 on refugee protection in Europe and the U.S.?
- Are there grounds for new state fears and state restrictions on the granting of protection?
- Are the existing tools of refugee protection sufficient to deal with any new perceptions or genuine changes?
- In what ways are refugee protection and the security of democratic, developed states inextricably linked?
- And what policy consequences does new attention to the links bring?

Whether there will be a lasting impact of the fears aroused by 9/11 on refugee protection in Europe and the U.S. depends to a large extent on the answers to the other questions. In principle, it should not be impossible for developed states, seeking to strengthen their fundamental principles of democracy, freedom, justice, and humanitarianism in the face of terrorist attacks return to some basics. One way of doing that would be to return to those documents which emerged from humanity's enormous attacks on itself in the early and mid-twentieth century and to again see human rights and refugee protection not so much as state privileges but as essentials to the crafting of a humane world.

Surely, states will fear that their humanitarian approach to a measure such as refugee protection could allow the isolated terrorist to gain access across borders that might otherwise be closed to him or her. However, the economic activities of the twenty-first century, of the globalized world, have not stopped as a result of 9/11—and neither has the crossing of borders by human beings, almost by definition. Refugees are among the most scrutinized migrants in the world—because they are not arriving offering a service for which there is a market demand, as many economic migrants do, but are arriving, or seeking to flee, because they have nothing. As such, there are grounds for being more careful about the implementation of border controls, about sharing information, and about applying rules that exclude some people from refugee protection fairly and broadly. The existing tools for determining refugee status are sufficient for this task: the political will to be harsh as well as kind—and harsh where that is needed in order to guarantee security for all, citizens and real refugees—is needed.

Protecting refugees is arguably one of the trademarks of a secure state: only a state that can offer safety can truly protect. During the 1990s, developed states turned increasingly to poorer states, neighboring conflict zones, to take up the burden of refugee protection. With only 5 percent of the world's refugees reaching the developed states, it must be time to rethink this approach, within the context of thinking on poverty, development, and security post-9/11.

What policy consequences might the reactions to 9/11 bring for refugee protection? Of course, the answer to that could be increasing restrictions, more burden of protection on developing states—perhaps with greater financial assistance from developed states. In order to truly make the world secure, however, this cannot be the answer: it cannot be forgotten that many of the Taliban and al-Qaeda members who turned to radicalism and terror campaigns learned their trade, and developed their hatreds within the confines of refugee camps in the developing world. By no means do all people in refugee camps fall under such influences: but in this as in other areas, some lessons need to be learned, and education campaigns funded by post-9/11 appeals are a start to that.

Data systems need to talk; exclusion must take place where necessary and appropriate. In all of these areas, the right safeguards need to be in place to ensure that no victims fall through the gaps, and are made vulnerable a second or third time. The inefficiencies not of the 1951 Convention but of how states have used the convention need to be dealt with, and the inefficiencies of a refugee protection regime that puts the largest burden on those states which can least carry it need to be dealt with. One way in which that might be done is in an area on which there have been conflicting signals since 9/11: resettlement. While the UK has proposed a new resettlement program (albeit with the false hope that this might reduce its asylum seeker numbers and avoid smuggling), the U.S. has limited its longstanding program. Yet here is an area in which work could be done to deal with some of the existing inefficiencies referred to above.

Ultimately, the real question is: do states want to sacrifice the right to seek and enjoy asylum and the principle of *non-refoulement* on the "combating terrorism pyre"? If they are serious about fighting terrorism and maintaining democratic, just, and humanitarian principles, I would suggest that this is a sacrifice they should not make.

Notes

Chapter 1
UNHCR at Fifty

1. UNHCR, 2000, *The State of the World's Refugees: Fifty Years of Humanitarian Action*, Oxford: Oxford University Press: 309–310.
2. Ibid.
3. This chapter draws heavily upon Gil Loescher, 2001, *The UNHCR and World Politics: A Perilous Path*, Oxford: Oxford University Press.
4. See Mark Walkup, March 1997, "Policy Dysfunction in Humanitarian Organizations: The Role of Coping Strategies, Institutions, and Organizational Culture," *Journal of Refugee Studies*, Vol. 10, no. 1: 37–60.
5. There is a growing literature on the impact of ideas and norms in international politics and international organizations. See: Martha Finnemore, Spring 1996, "Norms, Culture and World Politics: Insights from Sociology's Institutionalism," *World Politics*: 325–48; Thomas Risse, Stephen Ropp, and Kathryn Sikkink, eds., 1999, *The Power of Human Rights: International Norms and Domestic Change*, Cambridge: Cambridge University Press; and Margaret Keck and Kathryn Sikkink, 1998, *Activists Beyond Borders: Advocacy Networks in International Politics*, Ithaca, NY: Cornell University Press.
6. UNHCR, 2000, *UNHCR Global Report 1999*, Geneva, UNHCR: 32.
7. Ibid. 33.
8. For background see: Gil Loescher and John Scanlan, 1986, *Calculated Kindness: Refugees and America's Half-Open Door: 1945 to Present*, New York: The Free Press.
9. Benjamin Schiff, 1995, *Refugees unto the Third Generation: Aid to Palestinians*, Syracuse: Syracuse University Press.
10. Gene Lyons, 1961, *Military Policy and Economic Aid: The Korean Case*, Columbus, Ohio: Ohio University Press.
11. For background see: Cecilia Ruthstrom-Ruin, 1993, *Beyond Europe: The Globalization of Refugee Aid*, Lund: Lund University Press.
12. UNHCR interview with Auguste Lindt, Bern, Switzerland, February 4, 1998.
13. Ibid.
14. For background see: Gervase Coles, 1985, *Voluntary Repatriation: A Background Study*, Geneva: UNHCR.
15. B.S. Chimni, 1993, "The Meaning of Words and the Role of UNHCR in Voluntary Repatriation," *International Journal of Refugee Law*, Vol. 5: 442–459.
16. Michael Barnett, Spring 2001, "Humanitarianism with a Sovereign Face: UNHCR in the Global Undertow," *International Migration Review*; and B.S.

Chimni, (forthcoming), "Post-Conflict Peace Building: Return and Repatriation," *Refugees and Human Displacement in Contemporary International Relations: Reconciling State and Individual Sovereignty*, Ted Newman and Joanne van
Selm, eds.

17. See the chapter in this volume by Beth Whitaker, "Changing Priorities in Refugee
Protection: The Rwandan Repatriation from Tanzania."

18. Arthur Helton, 1994, "UNHCR and Protection in the 90s," *International Journal
of Refugee Law*, Vol. 6, No. 1: 1–2.

19. Arthur Helton, September 1990, "What is Refugee Protection?" *International
Journal of Refugee Law*, (Special Issue): 119.

20. Philip Alston, 1995, "The Downside of Post-Cold War Complexity: Comments
on Hathaway," *Journal of Refugee Studies*, Vol. 8, No. 3: 303–304.

21. See: Alex Cunliffe and Michael Pugh, 1997, "The Politicization of the UNHCR in
the Former Yugoslavia", *Journal of Refugee Studies*, Vol. 10, No. 2: 134–153; and
1999, "UNHCR as Leader in Humanitarian Assistance: A Triumph of Politics
over Law?," *Refuge Rights and Realities: Evolving International Concepts and
Regimes*, Frances Nicholson and Patrick Twomey, eds., Cambridge: Cambridge
University Press: 200–219.

22. For an account of these organizational changes see: Gil Loescher, 2001, *The
UNHCR and World Politics: A Perilous Path*, Oxford: Oxford University Press.

23. Critiques of UNHCR's new approach to refugee problems can be found in
Guy Goodwin-Gill, 1999, "Refugee Identity and Protection's Fading Prospect,"
Refugee Rights and Realities: Evolving International Concepts and Regimes, Francis
Nicholson and Patrick Twomey, eds., Cambridge: Cambridge University Press:
220–252; and "UNHCR and Internal Displacement: Stepping into the Legal and
Political Minefield," *World Refuge Survey 2000* (Washington, D.C.: U.S. Commit-
tee for Refugees, 2000): 26–31.

24. This point is also made by William Maley, (forthcoming), "A New Tower of
Babel? Reappraising the Architecture of Refugee Protection," in Ted Newman
and Joanne van Selm, eds., *Refuges and Human Displacement in Contemporary
International Relations: Reconciling State and Individual Sovereignty*.

25. Voluntary contributions from governments raised another $44 million during
2000. But as Mary Robinson, the UN High Commissioner for Human Rights
stated: "if human rights are so important, they must be funded out of the core
budget." *The Financial Times*, March 20, 2001.

26. See the chapter in this volume by Elizabeth G. Ferris, "The Role of Non-Governmental Organizations in the International Refugee Regime."

27. See the chapter in this volume by Brian Gorlick, "Refugee Protection in Troubled
Times: Reflections on Institutional and Legal Developments at the Crossroads."

Chapter 2
What Is Refugee Protection?

1. Arthur Helton, 1990, "What is Refugee Protection?" *International Journal of
Refugee Law*, (Special Issue): 119–129.

2. Arthur Helton, 1994, "UNHCR and Protection in the 90s," *International Journal of Refugee Law*, Vol. 6, No. 1:

3. Arthur Helton, 1990, "What is Refugee Protection?" *International Journal of Refugee Law*, (Special Issue): 119–129.

4. United Nations Convention Relating to the Status of Refugees, adopted by the Conference of Plenipotentiaries on the Status of Refugee and Stateless Persons, convened under UNGA Res. 429 (V), 14 Dec. 1950. Adopted 28 July 1951; entered into force 22 April 1954: 189 UNTS 137 (No. 2545); text in UNHCR, *Collection of International Instruments Concerning Refugees* (1979): 10.

5. United Nations Protocol Relating to the Status of Refugees, adopted by ECOSOC Res. 1186 (XLI). 18 Nov. 1966; see also UNGA res. 2198 (xxi), 16 Dec, 1966; entered into force 4 Oct, 1967: 606 UNTS 267 (No. 8791): text in UNHCR, *Collection* (above, note 1): 40. At 31 May 1990, l06 States were parties to either the Convention or Protocol or both. As of 2001, 140 states were parties.

6. Art. 1 A(2), 1951 Convention relating to the Status of Refugees (above, note 1).

7. Statute of the Office of the United Nations High Commissioner for Refugees, adopted by UNGA res. 428(V), 14 Dec. 1950. See Lawyers Committee for international Human Rights and Americas Watch, 1984, *El Salvador's Other Victims: the War on the Displaced*: 252–55, discussing instances in the Sudan, Guinea-Bissau, Mozambique, Angola, Laos, and Chad, where UNHCR provided assistance to displaced persons between 1972 and 1981. See also UNGA resolutions 37/175, 38/91, 39/105, 40/133, concerning assistance to displaced persons in Ethiopia, and UNGA resolutions 39/106, 40/136, concerning assistance to displaced persons in Chad, for more recent examples of mandate extensions in 1982, 1983, 1984, and 1985.

8. UNBRO was created in 1982 to coordinate services provided to Cambodians detained in camps along the border of Thailand.

9. Article I(2), OAU Convention Governing the Specific Aspects of Refugee Problems in Africa, adopted by the Assembly of Heads of State and Government at its Sixth Ordinary Session on 10 Sept. 1969; entered into force 20 June 1974: 1001 UNTS 45 (No. 14691); text in UNHCR, *Collection* (above, note 1): 193.

10. The Cartagena Declaration an Refugees (published as a pamphlet by UNFICR, also contained in *La protección internacional de los refugiados en America, México Central y Pánama: problemas juridícos y humanitarios*, Universidad Nacional de Colombia: 332); part III (containing the conclusions) also reproduced in Annual Report of Inter-American Commission on Human Rights, 1984–1985, OEA/Ser.L/V/II.66, Doc. 10, rev. 1: 190–193. See also Gros Espiell, H. Picado, S., Valladares Lanza, L., 1990, "Principles and Criteria for the Protection of and Assistance to Central American Refugees, Returnees and Displaced Persons in Latin America," 2 *IJLR* 83 (background document prepared for the International Conference on Central American Refugees [CIREFCA] in April 1989).

11. See author 1981, *Report of the Working Group on Current Problems in the International Protection of Refugees and Displaced Persons in Asia*, San Remo, International Institute of Humanitarian Law.

12. H. P. Gasser, Jan.–Feb 1988, "A measure of humanity in internal disturbances and tensions: proposal for a Code of Conduct," 262 *International Review of the Red*

Cross: 38. See also Meron, T., "Draft Model Declaration in Internal Strife," ibid.: 59. For another perspective, see Cohen, R., 7. Feb. 1990, "UN Human Rights Bodies Should Deal With the Internally Displaced," mimeo, Refugee Policy Group.

13. See Article 35, 1951 Convention, above, note 1; Article 2, 1967 Protocol, above, note 2.

14. UNHCR, l979, *Handbook on Procedures and Criteria for Determining Refugee Status* (hereinafter, *Handbook*), para. 51. A re-edited *Handbook* was issued by UNHCR in 1992, which did not affect the substance of the provisions cited in this essay.

15. Cf. A. Grahl-Madsen, 1966, *The Status of Refugees in International Law*, vol. I: 195, 214.

16. See *Handbook*, above note 11, paras 54, 55.

17. See *Handbook*, above note 11, para, 65.

18. Ibid.

19. Art. I A (2), 1951 Convention.

20. See *Handbook*, above, note 11, paras. 66–79; also Helton, 1983, "Persecution on Account of Membership in a Social Group as Basis for Refugee Status," 15 *Columbia Human Rights Law Review*: 39.

21. See *Handbook*, above, note 11, paras. 80–86. *See also Maldonado-Cruz v. INS*, 883 F.2d 788 (9th Cir. 1989); case no. *IJRL/0040*, 2 *IJRL* 289 (1990).

22. 1966 International Covenant on Civil and Political Rights, adopted by UNGA Res. 2200 (XXI), 16 Dec. 1966, entered into force 23 Mar. 1976; 21 UN GAOR Supp. (No. 16), at 52, UN doc. A/6316 (1966); text in UNHCR, *Collection*, above, note 1: 104.

23. 1966 International Covenant on Economic, Social and Cultural Rights, adopted by UNGA Res. 2200 (XXI), 16 Dec. 1966, entered into force 3 Jan. 1976: 21 UN GAOR Supp. (No. 16), at 49, UN doc. A/6316 (1966); text in UNHCR, *Collection*, above, note 1: 128.

24. *Non-refoulement* provisions are included in several United Nation documents, including the 1951 Convention/1967 Protocol; see Art. 33. A similar provision is also Article 3 of the Declaration on Territorial Asylum, adopted by UNGA res. 2312 (XXII), 14 Dec. 1967. United States domestic law reflects this policy; see 8 U.S.C. § 1253 (h). Even States not parties to the United Nations instruments are bound to respect *non-refoulement* as a fundamental principle of customary international law; see G.S. Goodwin-Gill, 1983, *The Refugee in International Law*: 97; *Conclusion No. 6* (XXVIII), in UNHCR, *Conclusions on the International Protection of Refugees adopted by the Executive Committee of the High Commissioner's Programme* (1980): 14; Report of the twenty-eighth Session of the UNHCR Executive Committee, (1977): UN doc. A/AC. 96/549, para. 53.

25. See Lawyers Committee for Human Rights, 1990, *Refugee Refoulement: The Forced Return of Haitians Under the U.S.–Haitian Interdiction Agreement*; Lawyers Committee Human Rights, 1989, *Refuge Denied: Problems in the Protection of Vietnamese and Cambodians in Thailand and the Admission of Indochinese Refugees into the United States*: 65 (hereafter *Refuge Denied*); A. C. Helton, 1989, "Asylum and Refugee Protection in Thailand," 1 *International Journal of Refugee*

Law (IJRL): 21, 27; U.S. Committee for Refugees, 1987, *The Plight of Vietnamese Boat People.*

26. The term "first asylum" is not a term of art in international law. It is used to describe the limited character of a host country's recognition of an obligation toward refugees. See Report of the Secretary-General: UN doc. A/34/627, para. 35.

27. European Consultation on Refugees and Exiles, 1989, *Refugees Policy in a Unifying Europe* London, European Council on Refugees and Exile; H. Meijers, 1990, "Refugees in Western Europe: 'Schengen' affects the entire Refugee Law," 2 *International Journal of Refugee Law* (IJRL) no. 3. Much, of course, has happened since 1990 in this harmonization process. See, e.g., E. Guild, 1999, "The impetus to harmonize: asylum policy in the European Union," in *Refugee Rights and Realities*, Cambridge: 313–335. eds Frances Nicholson and Patrick Twomey, Cambridge University Press.

28. See A. C. Helton, 1986, "The Legality of Detaining Refugees in the United States," 14 *NYU Review of Law and Social Change*: 353, 366–7.

29. Office of the United Nations High Commissioner for Refugees: International Conference on Indo-Chinese Refugees, *Report* by the Secretary-General: UN doc. A/44/523 (1989). For text of the CPA, see 1 *IJRL* (1989): 474.

30. See Lawyers Committee for Human Rights, 1989, *Inhumane Deterrence: The Treatment of Vietnamese Boat People in Hong Kong.*

31. See generally, Lawyers Committee for Human Rights, 1990, *The Implementation of the Refugee Act of 1980: A Decade of Experience.*

32. For example, the Thai government maintains that it has no duty to police inside the camps along its border with Cambodia. The United Nations has recognized a de jure Cambodian government-in-exile, which the Thai government maintains is responsible. However, the de jure government, while on Thai soil, has no actual authority to protect Cambodians through the exercise of legal control. Thus, the Thai government has passed off the duty of protection to a "government" which is unable to govern or to enforce law. Cf. Chim Chan Sastra, "The Human Rights Situation in Site II," below: 130–2; Sang Ha Pry, "Justice in Site II Refugee Camp," below: 133–6; and see Helton, "Asylum and Refugee Protection in Thailand," above, note 22: 37–9.

33. Art. 7, 1951 Convention; see also Helton, "Asylum and Refugee Protection in Thailand," above, note 23: 36f.

34. See I. Brownlie., 1973, *Principles of Public International Law*, 3rd. ed.: 504.

35. See Helton, "Asylum and Refugee Protection in Thailand," above, note 23: 41; C. Amerasinghe, 1967, *State Responsibility for Injuries to Aliens*: 44. See also *Barcelona Traction and Light Co.*, I.C.J. Rep. (1970): 32 (State bound to protect foreign nationals admitted on to its territory).

36. Helton, "Asylum and Refugee Protection in Thailand," above, note 23: 42.

37. Helton, "Asylum and Refugee Protection in Thailand," above, note 22: 39; see also above, note 21, and accompanying text.

38. At times countries have instituted policies towards asylum seekers specifically designed to discourage those who would seek refuge within its borders. See, Helton, "Asylum and Refugee Protection in Thailand," above, note 22: 41; C. Petersen,

Feb. 1990, "Stepped Up Voluntary Return of Boat People Widely Praised," BC *Cycle*: 22.

39. Conclusion No. 19 (XXXI) on Temporary Refuge, adopted by the UNHCR Executive Committee in 1980, states: "The Executive Committee (a) *Reaffirmed* the essential need for the humanitarian legal principle of *non-refoulement* to be scrupulously observed in all situations of large-scale influx; . . . (c) *Took note* of the extensive practice of granting temporary refuge in situations involving a large-scale influx of refugees; . . . (e) *Stressed* the exceptional character of temporary refuge and the essential need for persons to whom temporary refuge has been granted to enjoy basic humanitarian standards of treatment . . ." UNHCR, *conclusions*, above, note, 21: 41.

40. See UN Charter, arts. 1, 2, 55, 56.

41. UNGA res, 217A(III), 10 Dec. 1948: UN doc, A/810 (1984).

42. Helton, "Asylum and Refugee Protection in Thailand," above, note 23: 43 (quoting R. Lillich, 1984, *Human Rights of Aliens in Contemporary International Law*: 42).

43. "Other treaties include the 1966 Covenant on Civil and Political Rights, UNGA res. 2200 (XXI): UN doc. A/6316 (1966), which protects the right to life, to be free from cruel, inhuman, or degrading treatment, punishment or torture, the right to be treated with humanity, and freedom of movement; the 1969 American Convention on Human Rights: 1969 I.L.M, (1970) 673, which declares the right to humane treatment and that "every person has the right to have his physical, mental, and moral integrity respected" Sec also American Declaration of Rights and Duties of Man, 2 May 1948, O.A.S. Off. Rec. OEA/Ser.L/V/II. 23, doc. 21, rev. 6 (English 1979).

44. UNGA res. 40/144, 13 Dec. 1985.

45. Articles 5 and 6, respectively.

46. See UNHCR Executive Committee Conclusion No. 39 (XXXVI) on Refugee Women and International Protection (1985): UNHCR, *Conclusions*, above, note 21: 84; Conclusion No. 54 (XXXIX) (1988); texts in 1 *IJRL* 253 (1989). See also Conclusion No. 60 (1989): text in 2 *IJRL*: 152 (1990); A. B. Johnsson, 1989, "The International Protection of Women Refugees," 1 *IJRL*: 221; N. Kelley, 1989, "Report on the International Consultation on Refugee Women, held in Geneva, 15–19 November 1988," 1 *IJRL*: 233. On children, see UNHCR Executive Committee Conclusion No.47 (XXXVIII) (1987); text in 1 *IJRL*: 257 (1989); Conclusion No, 59 (XL) (1989); text in 2 *IJRL*: 150 (1990).

47. Conclusion No, 39, above, note 46, at para. (h).

48. Declaration on the Protection of Women and Children in Emergency and Armed Conflict: UNGA res. 3318(XXIX), 14 Dec 1974.

49. See, for example, *Refuge Denied*, above, note 22: 60.

50. Declaration of the Rights of the Child: UNGA Res. 1386 (XIV), 20 Nov. 1959.

51. UNGA Res. 45/24, 20 Nov. 1989.

52. Art. 9.

53. Art. 9(1).

54. Standard Minimum Rules for Treatment of Prisoners, adopted at the first United Nations Congress on the Prevention of Crime and Treatment of Offenders: ap-

proved by ECOSOC resolutions 663 C(XXIV), 31 Jul. 1957 and 2076 (LXII), 13 May 1977. See also Declaration on the Human Rights of Individuals Who are not Nationals of the Country in Which They Live, above, note 47.

55. *United States Diplomatic and Consular Staff in Tehran*, I.C.J. Rep. (1980): 42.

56. Arthur Helton, 1994, "UNHCR and Protection in the 90s," *International Journal of Refugee Law*, Vol. 6, No. 1: 1–2.

57. See generally *The State of the World's Refugees: Fifty Years of Humanitarian Action*, 2000 (Oxford Univ. Press): passim.

58. See UNHCR *Briefing Notes*, 29 March 2001.

Chapter 3
The Legal and Ethical Obligations of UNHCR

1. See generally, UNHCR's background papers for informal meetings with government experts on temporary protection, entitled Background Notes to the Informal Meeting on Temporary Protection [hereinafter Background Notes] (Jan. 18, 1993, 23 March 1993, 23 March 1994, 20 April 1995) and UNHCR, Note on International Protection UN, U.N. doc. A/AC. 96/830 (1994) [hereinafter Note on International Protection]. The gist of UNHCR's thinking on TP is contained in this latter document and we shall mainly refer to it in our discussion on TP below.

2. The General Assembly (GA) established UNHCR through G.A.. Res. 319 A (IV), 3 Dec. 1949. The Statute of UNHCR was adopted in 1950 as an Annex to G.A.. Res 428 (V), 14 Dec. 1950. Both resolutions were passed pursuant to U.N. Charter Art. 22. The mandate of UNHCR was initially limited to three years. However, the GA has continuously renewed UNHCR's mandate on a five year basis. Most recently, the GA decided to continue the Office until 31 Dec. 2003 through G.A. Res. 52/104, 9 Feb. 1998.

3. Convention Relating to the Status of Refugees 28 Jul. 1951 [hereinafter 1951 Convention]. The 1951 Convention was adopted by the United Nations Conference of Plenipotentiaries on the Status of Refugees and Stateless Persons convened under G.A. Res. 429 (V), 14 Dec. 1950. It entered into force 22 April 1954.

4. The Protocol Relating to the Status of Refugees entered into force 4 Oct. 1967. Its purpose is to extend the personal scope of the 1951 Convention. As of 2002 a total of 143 states have acceded to one or both of these instruments (10 Mar. 2002) <http://www.unhchr.ch/html/intlinst.htm> [Hereinafter when we refer to the 1951 Convention we mean the 1951 Convention and its 1967 Protocol].

5. See also, Preamble to the 1951 Convention ("Noting that the United Nations High Commissioner for Refugees is charged with the task of supervising international conventions providing for the protection of refugees, and recognizing that the effective co-ordination of measures taken to deal with this problem will depend upon the co-operation of States with the High Commissioner. . . .").

6. See 1951 Convention Art. 1 (A).

7. The whole idea of human rights is that they pertain to everyone by virtue of their nature as human beings. This is ingrained in the very notion of "universal

human rights" and follows unmistakably from the language used in all key human rights instruments. See, e.g., the Preamble to the U.N. Charter ("We the Peoples of the United Nations Determined to . . . reaffirm faith in fundamental human rights, in the dignity and worth of the human person. . . ."); Preamble to the Universal Declaration of Human Rights, G.A. Res. 217A(III), 10 Dec. 1948. [hereinafter UDHR] ("Whereas recognition of the inherent dignity and of the equal and inalienable rights of all members of the human family is the foundation of freedom, justice and peace in the world . . ."); UDHR art. 1 ("All human beings are born free and equal in dignity and rights. They are endowed with reason and conscience and should act towards one another in a spirit of brotherhood."); Preamble to the International Covenant on Civil and Political Rights, Dec. 16, 1966 (hereinafter ICCPR) ("Considering that, in accordance with the principles proclaimed in the Charter of the United Nations, recognition of the inherent dignity and of the equal and inalienable rights of all members of the human family is the foundation of freedom, justice and peace in the world. . . ."); ICCPR art. 2 (1) ("Each State Party to the present Covenant undertakes to respect and to ensure to all individuals within its territory and subject to its jurisdiction the rights recognized in the present Covenant, without distinction of any kind, such as race, colour, sex, language, religion, political or other opinion, national or social origin, property, birth or other status."). Cf. Preamble to the 1951 Convention ("Considering that the Charter of the United Nations and the Universal Declaration of Human Rights approved on 10 December 1948 by the General Assembly have affirmed the principle that human beings shall enjoy fundamental rights and freedoms without discrimination . . . Considering that it is desirable to revise and consolidate previous international agreements relating to the status of refugees and to extend [emphasis added] the scope of and the protection [emphasis added] accorded by such instruments by means of a new agreement . . .")

8. Cf, e.g., Guy S. Goodwin-Gill, 1999, "Refugee identity and protection's fading prospect," in *Refugee Rights and Realities Evolving International Concepts and Regimes* 243 in Frances Nicholson and Patrick Twomey eds., Cambridge: Cambridge University Press, (Stressing the conflict of interest that may arise if UNHCR assumes the responsibility of monitoring the human rights situations in countries of origin.); *id:* 246 (noting that "UNHCR has no authority to protect persons within their own country. . . .") and James C. Hathaway and R. Alexander Neve, 1997, "Making International Refugee Law Relevant Again: A Proposal for Collectivized and Solution Oriented Protection," *Harvard Human Rights Journal* 10:115–211, 133–137 [hereinafter Hathaway and Neve] (criticizing UNHCR for introducing the dubious notion "the right to remain"). But, cf., Volker Türk, "The role of UNHCR in the development of international refugee law," in Nicholson and Twomey, supra at 160 (Arguing that "[U]NHCR's standard-setting function in the area of international law apply equally to asylum seekers, stateless persons, returnees and, to a limited extent, to the internally displaced, as well as persons threatened with displacement or otherwise at risk, to

the extent that the General Assembly has charged UNHCR with specific protection functions").

9. Including the ideals and values of a democratic society cf. UDHR art. 21 (3) ("The will of the people shall be the basis of the authority of government. . . .").

10. Cf. Goodwin-Gill, *supra* note 8, at 223 ("The pursuit of protection objectives necessarily results in a tension between the state and individual, and between states and the international agency charged with that responsibility. UNHCR cannot expect always to please all sides, but the art is to stay close to principles, not to throw them overboard in an excess of 'realistic' cohabitation").

11. Of course, UNHCR's legal opinions must always rest on a sound international legal methodology. Further, it is not argued here that UNHCR can or should assume a very liberal teleological methodology, akin to that of the European Court of Human Rights (see, e.g., Golder v UK, 18 Eur. Ct. H.R. (ser. A) (1975)) It is argued, however, that UNHCR should be closer to that approach than to the other extreme. That is, UNHCR should put appropriate emphasis on the humanitarian object and purpose of the 1951 Convention, and in cases of doubt, all other things being equal, should operate with a presumption in favor of individual rights, rather than restrictions.

12. EXCOM was established by G.A. Res. 1166 (XII), 26 Nov. 1957, and E.S.C. Res. 672 (XXV), 30 Apr. 1958. See also UNHCR's Statute par. 4.

13. Cf. U.N. Doc. A/37/18 (1976), paras. 288–315 (on the conflict between the GA and the Committee on the Elimination of Racial Discrimination). Admittedly, the relationship between the GA and UNHCR is less clear cut than the relationship between the GA and treaty monitoring bodies exclusively set up by treaties, such as the Committee on the Elimination of Racial Discrimination and the Human Rights Committee. Nonetheless, if one concludes that UNHCR has a supervisory function under the 1951 Convention, which appears to be a correct conclusion, it seems reasonable to conclude that UNHCR acts with autonomy when exercising this function. The reasons for this are apparent. First, the GA (and at times ECOSOC) is comprised of member states that have not ratified the 1951 Convention or the 1967 Protocol. Second, decisions by these bodies are adopted by either two-thirds or simple majority. Third, and most importantly, neither the GA nor ECOSOC are, and were never intended to be, legislative bodies in an ordinary sense of the term. It is true that Article 22 of the U.N. Charter gives the GA the authority to "establish such subsidiary organs, as it deems necessary for the performance of its functions," and that the GA exercise full authority over such an organ (within the scope of the GA's powers under the U.N. Charter.) It is also true that the GA and ECOSOC oversee the drafting of treaties aimed at furthering the goals of the UN. But, importantly, neither the GA or the ECOSOC can impose treaty obligations on states, nor can they with binding effect modify them once in force. In theory, the GA could discontinue UNHCR, which would force the contracting states to the 1951 Convention to consider whether to replace the Office with another treaty monitoring body. But as long as UNHCR has a function under the 1951 Convention, neither the GA nor the ECOSOC should

indirectly force it to neglect it. Finally, whereas the role of GA and ECOSOC under the 1951 Convention is somewhat of a gray area, what is crystal clear is that EXCOM does not exercise any formal function under the 1951 Convention. Hence, EXCOM cannot authorize UNHCR to adopt practices that conflict with the Office's function under the 1951 Convention or, for that matter, under UNHCR's Statute. Nor can EXCOM ex posto facto validate such practices with any legal effect.

14. See, e.g., Alex Cunliffe and Michael Pugh, "UNHCR as leader in humanitarian assistance: a triumph of politics over law," in Nicholson and Twomey *supra* note 8 (arguing that UNHCR was partly responsible for its unfortunate role as the "lead agency" in the war in the former Yugoslavia).

15. Cf. Terje Einarsen, 2001, Refugee Protection Beyond Kosovo: Quo Vadis? *Journal of Refugee Studies* 14:119–127, 120 ("Refugee policies should—in accordance with democratic theory, and a rule of law-based regime of thoughts—be implemented within the existing framework of international law such as the 1951 Convention, as long as the law itself is not revised according to given procedures.").

16. The main exceptions to this general rule are issues directly relating to national security or, at the other extreme, issues of minor importance. In these areas the executive branch of government may enjoy discretion to assume or change the state's international obligations. Also, in some jurisdictions the executive branch has the power to renounce treaties (albeit not a general right to adopt or modify them).

17. It may be objected here that we erroneously downplay the importance of the GA, ECOSOC, and EXCOM for the development of international refugee law. According to a modern view of international law, statements and votes cast by government representatives in international forum may constitute evidence of state practice. This, in turn, may constitute a source of interpretation for the purpose of determining the content of treaties. Yet, to avoid undermining the democratic legitimacy of international law, it is important not to exaggerate the weight of this type of evidence. Furthermore, the value of state practice with respect to treaty interpretation must be considered. The basic rule of treaty interpretation, as embodied in Article 31(1) of the Vienna Convention on the Law of Treaties 1969 (VCLT), is that "[a] treaty shall be interpreted in good faith in accordance with the ordinary meaning to be given to the terms of the treaty in their context and in the light of its object and purpose." Article 31 (3) (b) states: "There shall be taken into account, together with the context . . . any subsequent practice in the application of the treaty, which establishes the agreement of the parties regarding its interpretation."

Note that to fall within the meaning of Article 31 (3) (b), the subsequent practice must be coherent and shared by all parties to the treaty. Thus, with respect to the interpretation of the 1951 Convention, only a GA resolution accepted by all contracting states may fall within the scope of this provision. Still, while GA resolutions may constitute evidence of state practice, they are hardly conclusive evidence. Further, the relative weight of state practice per se depends on its clarity on the interpretative problem at issue. GA resolutions are often phrased in very general and ambiguous terms. Hence, even if accepted as evidence of state practice within the ambit of subparagraph b, such resolutions, rarely provide meaningful guidance as to how a particular treaty text should be interpreted. In this respect it is noteworthy that Article 31 attributes relatively more weight to the text of the treaty (the "ordinary meaning of the terms") than to the other basic means of interpretation. Finally, it should be mentioned that "state practice" which is not shared by all state parties to a particular treaty might constitute a supplementary means of interpretation in accordance with VCLT Art. 32. Thus, GA resolutions (not unanimously adopted), ECOSOC resolutions, and EXCOM conclusions may be used as supplementary means of interpretation. But again, caution is called for when inferring state practice from statements in these forums. In any case, supplementary means of interpretation are not conclusive. Their basic value is to confirm an interpretive result, already arrived at through the basic means of interpretation.

18. The basic thought of this tradition, which has its roots in the political and moral philosophy of Thomas Hobbes, is that the interaction of human nature and the absence of international government leads to the overriding role of power in international politics. As a result, the sole objective of foreign policy is to pursue "state interests," narrowly defined, in terms of security and economic power. In practice, this translates into mere power, or the balance of power, politics. Apart from "state interests," there are no external or internal ethical standards that govern, or should govern, states' actions in the international realm. To succeed in the delicate art of power or balancing of power politics, foreign policy needs to be left in the hands of "experts" as opposed to the public. This explains why the realist holds a deep admiration for "classic diplomacy" and invariably objects to any moralizing tendencies as this relates to international affairs writ large. What the public (through a democratic and constitutional process) has actually defined as "state interests"—by, for example, ratifying a treaty—is irrelevant.

Besides resting on doubtful empirical grounds and incorporating many inconsistencies, this doctrine is anathema to the values underlying modern democratic institutions as well as human rights. Yet, there is no question that this thinking continues to influence the way international business is conducted and the culture of the international community. More specifically, it appears to instill representatives of democratic states acting abroad with a sense of discretionary power that goes beyond constitutional limitations. No doubt, there is a need to reform how international business is conducted and the impetus for this change must come from domestic sources. However, U.N. agencies such as UNHCR have a responsibility in this regard as well. See generally, Ernst-Ulrich Petersmann, 1998, "How to Constitutionalize International Law and Foreign Policy for the Benefit of Civil Society," *Michigan Journal of International Law* 20:1–30 on the need for improved democratic accountability of foreign policy. See e.g., Jack Donnelly, 2000, *Realism and International Relations*, New York: Cambridge University Press, for a critical analysis on political realism in international relations theory.

19. Unfortunately, there is a decided tendency among many commentators in the "realist/utilitarian" camp to emphasize the need for pragmatic solutions—but without actually clarifying in what way a legal or principled approach conflicts with, or would impede, the "end." While these authors are often influenced by utilitarian thinking, the central element of such an approach, namely, an analysis of the possible consequences of the different causes of actions, is far too often missing or does not include all relevant variables (including the utility of the rule of law and respect for human dignity).

20. This "catch phrase" was recently used, without much explanation as to its content, in the summary conclusion of an "expert group" conveyed by UNHCR to discuss UNHCR's supervisory function. See Summary conclusions—Supervisory responsibility, Global consultations on international protection, Cambridge Expert Roundtable, 9–10 July 2001, (11 Mar. 2002) <http://www.unhcr.ch/cgi-bin/texis/vtx/home?page=protect>.

21. We use the terms public scrutiny in a broad sense, signifying an informed public participation at all relevant levels and areas in society, including both the political and judicial sphere.

22. Of course we do not rule out that the actions of UNHCR's staff in the field may occasionally and in certain circumstances have a very tangible impact on the protection of refugees. It needs to be clarified that what we are primarily concerned with here is the broader picture—not the micro level. Nor do we deny that UNHCR might face great dilemmas when dealing with oppressive and undemocratic regimes. But, as noted in the introduction, we are primarily concerned with UNHCR's interaction with democratic states, not warlords or rogue regimes.

23. However, it appears like UNHCR needs to become much more self-reflective (i.e., self-critical). See generally, Goodwin-Gill, *supra* note 8. Compare these observations with a statement by Robert Denhardt, March/April 1992, "Morality as an Organizational Problem," *Public Administration Review*, vol. 52, 105 ("[public organizations] and their members must not be moral only when it is efficient to do so, they must be efficient only where it is moral to do so'"). See also, Einarsen, *supra* note 15, at 119 (commenting on Suhrke et al., *The Kosovo Refugee Crisis: An independent Evaluation of UNHCR's Emergency Preparedness and Response*, Geneva, UNHCR).

24. See, e.g., U.N. Charter Art. 1; and Preamble to the UDHR (cited *supra* note 7).

25. Cf. *Human Rights Watch World Report 2000*; Amnesty International, *Annual Report, 2000*; Cf. also, Speech by Mary Robinson United Nations High Commissioner for Human Rights, Forum on intolerance in Stockholm 29 January 2001, (10 Mar. 2002) http://www.unhchr.ch [hereinafter Mary Robison]. She stresses the need to recognize the scale of racism and xenophobia in Europe, in particular:

    • The overall increase in intolerance towards foreigners, asylum seekers, and minorities.
    • Discrimination against minority groups by law enforcement, immigration, and other officials.

- Discrimination in the workplace and the service sector.
- The rise in support for far-right parties.
- The emergence of racist attitudes in places where it had not been so evident before and in wealthy societies where there is no threat to livelihoods.

26. Cf. Klaus Günther, 1999, "The Legacies of Injustice and Fear: A European Approach to Human Rights and their Effects on Political Culture," in Philip Alston, ed., *The EU and Human Rights,* Oxford: Oxford University Press: 118 ("The violation of human rights does not begin with their explicit negation or rejection, but with their implicit neutralization—at first with perceiving a human being as somebody who does not in all respects belong to the community of human beings, and secondly with the right to treat them as something which does not deserve the protection of human rights.").

27. Cf. Sergio Vieira de Mello, August 25, 1999, "Resist the Apartheid Temptation in the Balkans," *International Herald Tribune,* (emphasizing the need to continue spending resources in the Balkans to create a multicultural and tolerant environment).

28. Statement by Mr. Michael Banton (former Member of the Committee on the Elimination of Racial Discrimination) at a seminar organized by the High Commissioner for Human Rights/Centre for Human Rights on immigration, racism, and racial discrimination, held in Geneva from 5 to 9 May 1997, U.N. Doc. E/CN.4/1998/77/Add.1, para 68.

29. From a historical perspective, skepticism about Western Europe's commitment to human rights is understandable. Throughout history, European States have maintained notions of universal human rights—based on the notion of equality—but have consistently applied and interpreted these norms in an exclusionary fashion to serve their own interests. See generally, Antony Anghie, 1993, "The Heart of My Home: Colonialism, Environmental Damage and the Nauru Case," *Harvard International Law Journal* 34:445–506.

30. Philip Alston and J. H. H. Weiler, "An 'Ever Closer Union' in Need of a Human Rights Policy," in Alston, *supra* note 26. Alston and Weiler write:

> The promotion and protection of human rights is not a one-time undertaking and neither governments nor bureaucracies can be counted upon to remain consistently, let alone insistently, vigilant. There will always be occasions and issues in relation to which it will seem preferable to sweep human rights under the carpet ('temporarily', of course, and only in the interest of a more profound objective which is itself assumed to be human rights friendly).

Id. at 5.

31. See generally, Secretariat of the Inter-Governmental Consultations on Asylum, Refugee and Migration Policies in Europe, North America and Australia, Report on Temporary Protection in States in Europe, North American and Australia (1995) [hereinafter Inter-Governmental Consultation] Morten Kjaerum, 1994, "Temporary Protection in Europe in the 1990s," *International Journal of Refugee Law* 6:444–56; Hathaway and Neve, *supra* note 8.

32. More specifically, UNHCR referred to "standards such as those outlined in Conclusion 22 (XXXII) of the Executive Committee." Note on International Protection, *supra* note 1, par. 48.

33. *Id.*

34. See, e.g., Background Notes to the Informal Meeting on Temporary Protection (18 January 1993, 23 March 1993, 23 March 1994).

35. On TP in the case of Kosovo see, e.g., Joan Fitzpatrick, 2000, "Temporary Protection of Refugees: Elements of a Formalized Regime," *American Journal of International Law* 94:279–306.

36. Consolidated Version of the Treaty on European Union and Consolidated Version of the Treaty Establishing the European Community, Feb. 7, 1992, Mar. 25, 1957, Oct. 2, 1997, Art. 63(2)(a) (ex-Art.73k), 37 ILM 56, 90 (1998).

37. Council Directive 2001/55/EC of 20 July 2001. The directive authorizes the council to establish TP regimes valid on all member states (MS) "in the event of a mass influx or imminent mass influx of displaced persons." (Arts. 2 and 5). The directive defines mass influx as "the arrival to the community of a large number of displaced persons, who come from a particular country or geographical area, whether their arrival to the community was spontaneous or aided, for example, through an evacuation program." (Art. 2). The meaning of a "large number of persons" is not quantified. It is notable, in this respect, that an overburdening of MS's asylum procedures is not a prerequisite for the application of the Directive. It is also noteworthy that MS have, bilaterally and collectively, deployed the term "mass influx" in situations that clearly could not be characterized as such. There is a danger that TP is used in situations where it is more appropriate to use individual determination procedures. This risk is lessened by Article 3 of the directive which states that "[t]emporary protection shall not prejudge recognition of refugee status under the Convention." Moreover, Article 17 of the Directive states that "a person enjoying TP must be able to lodge an application for asylum at any time." At the same time, however, a MS can, according to Article 19 of the Directive, withdraw TP from a person who applies for asylum. This may act as a deterrent to apply for refugee status. The Directive greatly improved the standard of treatment to TP beneficiaries compared to earlier national TP regimes in MS. The benefits extended to TP beneficiaries include: residence permit and appropriate documentation; right to work (albeit this right may be restricted by giving precedence to EU nationals other legally resident third-country nationals at the discretion of MS); suitable accommodation; necessary assistance in terms of social welfare, means of subsistence and emergency medical care and essential treatment of illness; education for minors on roughly the same terms as for nationals; and family reunification (see Art. 8–16). While there are some positive aspects of the directive, it is important to see it the context of other EU measures aimed at keeping refugees away from the community. In this respect, it should be underscored that the directive does not impose a duty on the council to extend TP to nationals from countries experiencing large refugee outflows. And, as noted by ECRE, even when a TP regime has been established "[t]he Directive does not seem to do anything to ease ad-

mission to the territory for persons arriving outside evacuation programmes. . . ." (ECRE Information Note on the Council Directive 2001/55/EC
of 20 July 2001). Finally the directive does not clearly stipulate that the council
applies its authority under the directive in a non-discriminatory manner (a
principle that is ingrained in the 1951 Convention). This is unfortunate because
in view of increasing demands for cultural homogeneity in Europe, there is arguably a risk that a refugee group's cultural or ethnic composition will influence
future decisions on TP.

38. Note on International Protection, *supra* note 1, par. 28.

39. *Id.*, par. 29. Note that the legal basis that UNHCR in part relied upon for TP had,
in the Office's own words, "not generally been explored" but, according to the Office, "would appear to be consistent with TP." This rather hesitant language is
startling since it was articulated some time after UNHCR had embarked on this
policy.

40. See Background Notes, *supra* note 1.

41. Note on International Protection, *supra* note 1, par. 28.

42. *Id*, section IV (B).

43. See, e.g., UNHCR Information Note 'Temporary Protection' 20 Apr. 1995, par. 11.

44. Note on International Protection, *supra* note 1, section IV (C).

45. The only provision in the Convention that implies a right to derogate from the
obligations under the Convention is Article 9. It states: "Nothing in this convention shall prevent a Contracting State, in time of war or other grave and exceptional circumstances, from taking provisionally measures which it considers to
be essential to the national security in case of a particular person, pending a determination by the Contracting State that that person is in fact a refugee and that
the continuance of such measures is necessary in his case in the interest of national security." The purpose of Article 9 was to allow states some time, in a crisis
situation, to determine whether an individual asylum seeker might pose a threat
to national security. Article 33 unequivocally dictates that a State must adopt
such provisional measures on an individual and non-discriminatory basis. The
text of Article 9 and the *traveaux preparatoires* suggest that a real threat to the nation must exist. Finally, the measures taken must be proportional and can only be
made on an interim basis. In other words, Article 9 does not grant states a right to
suspend rights for groups of refugees to avoid strains on their asylum determination procedures or to facilitate their eventual return. On Article 9, see generally
James C. Hathaway and Anne K. Cusick, 2000, "Refugee Rights are Not Nego-
tiable," *Georgetown Immigration Law Journal* 14:481–539.

46. See *Handbook on Procedures and Criteria for Determining Refugee Status under
the 1951 Convention and the 1967 Protocol relating to the Status of Refugees* (1992)
par. 28 ("A person is a refugee within the meaning of the 1951 Convention as
soon as he fulfils the criteria contained in the definition. This would necessarily
occur prior to the time at which his refugee status is formally determined. Recognition of his refugee status does not make him a refugee but declares him to be
one. He does not become a refugee because of recognition, but is recognized because he is a refugee.").

47.   As Hathaway and Neve have argued:

> In elaborating what temporary protection is, and what rights it entails, the UNHCR has consistently emphasized only the duty of admission, respect for the principle of non-refoulement, for basic human rights as defined in Conclusion 22 of the UNHCR Executive Committee, and repatriation to the country of origin when conditions permit. In taking this position, UNHCR may be seen to suggest that states are not required to respect all obligations under the Refugee Convention in the context of providing temporary protection to refugees . . . [U]NHCR's failure to link standards of treatment expressly to the Refugee Convention and international human rights law sends an unfortunate and unwarranted signal that these legal standards are negotiable. . . . By grounding its protection efforts in a non-binding resolution of its Executive Committee rather than working from clear statements of relevant international law, UNHCR has, perhaps unwittingly, given solace to those who prefer to treat refugee protection as a matter of discretion, rather than of binding obligation. . . . There is often no recognition by UNHCR of the fact that refugees, whether protected temporarily or permanently, whether they arrive individually or as part of a mass influx, are prima facie entitled to the protections set by the Refugee Convention and international human rights law.

Hathaway and Neve, *supra* note 8, at 167–68.

48.   This principle has been affirmed on numerous occasions by different international treaty monitoring bodies, see e.g., the opinions of the Human Rights Committee in *Van Duzen v. Canada* U.N. Doc. A/37/40, p.150, pr.10.2; and the opinion of the European Court of Human Rights in *Engel and others v. Netherlands,* 22 Eur.Ct. H.R. (ser. A) (1976).

49.   See Hathaway and Cusick, *supra* note 45, at 205 (noting that the drafters specifically emphasized that it was the refugee's de facto circumstances which determined whether or not a person was to be considered as "lawfully in" or "lawfully staying in" a State Party).

50.   For a complete account on Western European states's TP practices during the war in the former Yugoslavia see Inter-Governmental Consultations, *supra* note 31.

51.   Cf. Article 34 of the 1951 Convention: "The Contracting States shall as far as possible facilitate the assimilation and naturalization of refugees. They shall in particular make every effort to expedite naturalization proceedings and to reduce as far as possible the charges and costs of such proceedings."

52.   Article 3 of the 1951 Convention states: "The Contracting States shall apply the provisions of this Convention to refugees without discrimination as to race, religion or country of origin." Article 3 contains an accessory standard of non-discrimination. This means that Article 3 is not directed against discrimination in general, but only against discrimination in relation to the provisions set out in the Convention. Thus, where a particular right falls outside of the ambit of the

Convention, Contracting States do not have an obligation to avoid discrimination between different categories of refugees. However, Article 3 should not be understood as applicable only to cases in which there is an accompanying violation of a material provision. Such a restrictive reading of Article 3 would be incompatible with the plain meaning of the terms used and would basically render it nonsensical. According to the principle of effectiveness, it must be presumed that Article 3 adds something to the Convention and that it has significance independent from the rights ensured by the Convention. (See, e.g., the Belgian Linguistics Case (Merits) 6 Eur. Ct. H. R. (ser. A) (1968), where the European Court of Human Rights confronted a similar problem with respect to article 14 of the European Convention on Human Rights). Rather, Article 3 must be understood to apply to discrimination that affects the enjoyment of rights guaranteed by the Convention and those provisions that establish obligations of a progressive nature. If a contracting state grants the right to family reunification for one group of refugees it has a prima facie duty to grant it to all refugees. Similarly, if a state allows one group of refugees the right to permanent settlement it should not deny the same opportunity to other groups of refugees on discriminatory grounds.

53. In contrast to Article 3 of the 1951 Convention, Article 26 of the ICCPR contains an "autonomous right" to freedom from discrimination. In other words, the application of Article 26 is not limited to the ambit of those or other rights that are provided for in the Covenant, but protects individuals from invidious distinctions in any field regulated and protected by the State. See Human Rights Committee, General Comment 18 on Non-discrimination (Thirty-seventh session, 1989), U.N. Doc. HRI\GEN\1\Rev.1 (1994). See also, Terje Einarsen, 1995, "Discrimination and Consequences for the Position of Aliens," *Nordic Journal of International Law*, 64:429–52.

54. See, e.g., Human Rights Committee, General Comment 18, Non-discrimination (Thirty-seventh session, 1989), U.N. Doc. HRI\GEN\1\Rev.1 (1994).

55. Note on International Protection, *supra* note 1, par. 49.

56. Note the exceptionally low standard (reasonable expectation) that, according to UNHCR, can justify "substantial differences in the standards of treatment of different groups of refugees." Indeed, it appears that "the mere hope" that a conflict will end is sufficient to trigger TP according to UNHCR. "One of the principle reasons for applying the "temporary" to protection given to persons fleeing conflicts or acute crises in their country of origin is the expectation—or at least the *hope*—that international efforts to resolve the crisis will, within a fairly short period produce results that will enable the refugee to exercise their right to return home in safety." See Note of International Protection, *supra* note 1, par. 50 (emphasis supplied).

57. Certainly in the case of Bosnia, UNHCR had no reasons to believe that western powers would commit themselves to solve the conflict and quite frankly no mandate to suggest that they would. The case of Kosovo was arguably different. In the latter case, NATO showed an unprecedented and unambiguous commitment to a military solution of the conflict. However, this level of commitment is rare. Fur-

ther, it is one thing to bring a military confrontation to an end. It is quite another thing to restore an environment that is presumptively safe for all individual refugees to go back.

58. Cf. Statement by Mrs. Sadako Ogata, United Nations High Commissioner of Refugees, on "A Comprehensive Refugee Policy" on the occasion of the Intergovernmental Consultations on Asylum, Refugee and Migration Policies in Europe, North America and Australia, London, 9 December 1993 (11 Mar. 2002) <http://www.unhcr.ch> ("I realize that the concept of temporary protection raises a number of issues which require further thought. This is why my Office has engaged in an *informal* dialogue with Governments about its implementation.") (emphasis supplied). See also, Volker Türk, *supra* note 8, at 170 (noting that TP was developed "through an *informal* and regular dialogue with states on the implementation of temporary protection, with the objective of elaborating on the nature of the protection required and standards applicable.") (emphasis supplied).

59. See Article 44 of the 1951 Convention and Article 9 of the 1967 Protocol.

60. Declaration of States Parties to the 1951 Convention and its 1967 Protocol Relating to the Status of Refugees. HCR/MMSP/2001/09.

61. Cf., Einarsen, *supra* note 15, at 120 (noting that the debate on international refugee protection within the international community often "bear[s] a certain resemblance to 'The Emperor's New Clothes'. . . . It is even questionable whether much improvement has been made with regard to the framework of international refugee protection since the 1951 Convention was adopted. . . . International refugee law is today de facto threatened with relegation to the sphere of policy discretion, as was formally the case before the United Nations and the contemporary refuges regime came into being. A key issue in this regard is the particular status accorded to groups of refugees from the Balkans, presented in the new clothes of 'temporary protection' almost as if refugee status is not 'temporary' by nature and asylum from persecution is not 'protection.'").

62. Gil Loescher, 1993, *Beyond Charity: International Cooperation and the Global Refugee Crisis*, New York: Oxford University Press, 137–38.

63. Goodwin-Gill, *supra* note 8, at 231.

Chapter 4
Defining Persecution and Protection

1. Bill Frelick, 1998, "Refugee Rights: The New Frontier in Refugee Protection," *Buffalo Human Rights Law Review*, 4: 262.

2. Alison D. Renteln, 1985, "The Unanswered Challenge of Relativism and the Consequences for Human Rights," *Human Rights Quarterly*, 7: 4; James W. Nickel, 1980, "Cultural Diversity and Human Rights," *International Human Rights: Contemporary Issues*, eds. Nelson and Green, New Brunswick, NJ: Human Rights Publishing Company.; Abdullahi Ahmed An-Na'im, 1992, "Towards a Cross-cultural Approach to Defining International Standards of Human Rights. The Meaning of Cruel, Inhuman or Degrading Treatment of Punishment," *Human*

Rights in Cross-Cultural Perspectives. A Quest for Consensus, ed. Abdullahi A. An-Anima, Philadelphia: University of Penn Press; Lone Lindholt, 1997, *Questioning the Universality of Human Rights: The African Charter on Human and People's Rights in Botswana, Malawi and Mozambique*, Aldershot, Brookfield, Dartmouth; John Klenig, 1981, "Cultural Relativism and Human Rights," *Teaching Human Rights*, ed. Alice Erh-Soon, Canberra: Australian Government Publishing Service.

3. Issa Shivji 1989,*The Concept of Human Rights in Africa*, London: Codesria: 16.

4. The reference to "Western" notions or traditions here and elsewhere in this work is merely for the purpose of clarity and to keep our discourse within a specific scope. It is recognized that to talk of a "western tradition of human rights" is to indulge in a degree of ideological generalization. Human rights traditions in the West vary not only from one geographical location and/or historical period to another, but also from one social class/group to another. Our reference to "Western traditions" may therefore actually mean no more than the standpoints of the dominant classes in particular sections of the West.

5. S. Prakash Sinha, 1981, "Human Rights: A Non-Western View Point," *Archiv für Rechts- und Sozialphilosophie*, 67: 77.

6. Nickel: 44.

7. Jack Donnelly, 1984 "Cultural Relativism and Universal Human Rights," *Human Rights Quarterly*, 6, 4: 400–19.

8. Jack Donnelly, 1989, *Universal Human Rights in Theory and Practice*, Ithaca: Cornell University Press.

9. Lars Adam Rohef and Tyge Trier, 1990, *Mennes keret Jurist-og Økonomforbundts Forlag*, Københvn: 52.

10. American Anthropological Association, 1947, "Statement on Human Rights by the Executive Board," *American Anthropologist*: 539–43.

11. Antonio Cassese, 1990, *Human Rights in a Changing World*, Philadelphia: Temple University Press.

12. William Theodore De Bary, 1998, *Asian Values and Human Rights: A Confucian Communitarian Perspective*, Cambridge: Harvard University Press MA.; Xiaorong Li, 1996, "Asian Values and the Universality of Human Rights," *Report from the Institute for Philosophy and Public Policy*, 16, 2.; Daniel A. Bell, 1996, "The East Asian Challenge to Human Rights: Reflections on an East West Dialogue," *Human Rights Quarterly*: 18; Joanne R. Bauer and Daniel A. Bell, eds., 1999, *The East Asian Challenge for Human Rights*, Cambridge, NY: Cambridge University Press.

13. Kofi Quashigah, 1991, "The Philosophical Basis of Human Rights and its Relation to Africa," *Journal of Human Rights Law and Practice*: 1, 2.

14. Yougindra Khashalani, 1983, "Human Rights in Asia and Africa," *Human Rights Law Journal*, 14, 4. Dunstan M. Wai, 1979, "Human Rights in Sub-Saharan Africa," *Human Rights: Cultural and Ideological Perspectives*, Ed. A. Pollis and P. Schwab, New York: Praeger.; L. Marasinghe, 1984, "Traditional Conceptions of Human Rights in Africa," *Human Rights and Development in Africa*, C. E. Welch and Ronald Meltzer eds. Albany: State University of New York Press.; Makau Wa Mutua, 1995, "The Banjul Charter and the African Cultural Fingerprint: An Eval-

uation of the Language of Rights and Duties," *Virginia Journal of International Law*: 35, 2.

15. Makau Wa Mutua, 1999, "Limitations on Religious Rights: Problematizing Religious Freedom in the African Context," *Buffalo Human Rights Law Review*: 5.

16. Xiaorong Li, 1996, "'Asian Values' and the Universality of Human Rights," 20.

17. Ibid.

18. Rhoda Howard, 1986, *Human Rights in Commonwealth Africa*, Rowman and Littlefield: Totowa, NJ: 25.

19. James C. Hathaway, 1991, *The Law of Refugee Status*, Toronto: Butterworth Legal Publishers: 108–11.

20. This statement has been credited to Colonel Acheampong of Ghana. Quoted in Rhoda Howard, 1983, "The Full Belly Thesis: Should Economic Rights take Priority over Civil and Political Rights? Evidence from Sub Saharan Africa", *Human Rights Quarterly*, 5, (4): 467.

21. Li.: 21.

22. CRDD (The Convention Refugee Determination Division)—Decisions de la Section du statut de refugie [DSSR], Case No. M91–04822 (1991).

23. Canada's Immigration and Refugee Board (IRB), 1993, "Guidelines on Women Refugee Claimants Fearing Gender Related Persecution," 7. Hereinafter, "Guidelines."

24. Guidelines, 1993: 4.

25. Chantal Bernier, 1997, "IRB Guidelines on Women Refugee Claimants," *International Journal of Refugee Law*; Kristine M. Fox, 1994, "Gender Persecution: Canadian Guidelines Offer a Model for Refugee Determination in the United States," *Arizona Journal of International and Comparative Law*: 11.; Valerie L. Oosterveld, 1996, "The Canadian Guidelines on Gender-Related Persecution: An Evaluation," *International Journal of Refugee Law*: 8.

26. Statement credited to Bernard Valcourt, Canadian Minister of Employment and Immigration, quoted in Audrey Macklin, "Refugee Women and the Imperative of Categories" *Human Rights Quarterly*, 17: 252.

27. Audrey Macklin, 1995, "Refugee Women and the Imperative of Categories,": 252.

28. Ibid: 254.

29. This tradition may not be as "innocuous" in all Islamic societies as some writers have suggested. An Iranian law makes a woman's failure to wear a chandor a criminal offense punishable by seventy-five lashes.

30. IRB (Immigration and Refugee Board—Refugee Division, Toronto, Ontario), Case of Khadra Hassan Farah, Mahad Dahir Buraleh and Hodan Dahir Buraleh (Ref: 13 Jul 1994, IRB Refugee Div. (Toronto) T93–12198, T93–12199, T93–12197) (1994).

31. Alberta Fabbicotti, 1998, "The Concept of Inhuman or Degrading Treatment in International Law and its Application in Asylum Cases," *International Journal of Refugee Law*, 10, 4: 637.

32. Article 5 UDHR and Article 7 ICCPR.

33. The fifth and sixth sessions of the Commission on Human Rights, 1949 and 1950, 151, cited in An'Naim, "Towards a cross-cultural Approach to Defining International Standards of Human Rights": 30.

34. An'Naim, 1992: 31.
35. Ibid: 37.
36. Ibid.
37. Fabbicotti: 661.
38. UNHCR (United Nations High Commissioner for Refugees), 1979, *Handbook on Procedures and Criteria for Determining Refugee Status*, Geneva: UNHCR: 51.
39. Macklin, "Refugee Women and the Imperative of Categories." Citing the Supreme Court of Canada's decision in *Ward* [1993 SCR 689. p 222].
40. See for example, the decision of the Immigration and Refugee Board, Convention Refugee Determination Division (Toronto, Canada.) of 1994, cited in 6 *International Journal of Refugee Law*, 662 1994. By this decision, Canada became one of the first countries to make FGM grounds for granting refugee status.
41. "Female Genital Mutilation" is described as such in most Western and Human rights discourse generally. However, there exists an active group of scholars, mostly from developing countries, opposed to this description. They argue that the term "Female Genital Mutilation" implies a value judgment and biases the discussion in favor of those opposed to the practice of traditional forms of "genital surgery." They argue that the term "female circumcision" is more appropriate because the intention of its practitioners is often not to mutilate but to circumcise. "Parents do not set out to mutilate their daughters; they simply want to circumcise them." See for example, Apena, "Female Circumcision in Africa and the Problem of cross-cultural Perspectives." In deference to these arguments I employ both terms interchangeably in this paper.
42. Ifeyinwa Iweriebor, Sping 1996, "Brief Reflections on Clitorodectomy," *Africa Update*.; Adeline Apena, Spring 1996, "Female Circumcision in Africa and the Problem of Cross-Cultural Perspectives," *Africa Update*.; Aisha Samad Matias, Spring 1996, "Female Circumcision in Africa," *Africa Update*. African Studies Program, Central Connecticut State University, New Britain, CT.
43. Iweriebor.
44. Connie M. Ericson, 1998, "In Re Kasinga: An Expansion of the Grounds for Asylum for Women," *Houston Journal of International Law*, 20: 3; Gregory A. Kelson, 1998, "Female Circumcision in the Modern Age: Should Female Circumcision Now be Considered Grounds for Asylum in the United States?," *Buffalo Human Rights Law Review*, 4: 185–208.
45. Fabbricotti, 1998: 660. Fabbricotti argues that "[f]rom a human rights point of view, the practice of FGM must be considered one of the most cruel and inhuman treatments and must be eradicated. This has nevertheless *nothing* to do with asylum and refugee status. . . . Permitting women at risk to reside abroad will not likely reduce this abhorrent phenomenon. Instead it will create new grounds of abuse of asylum procedures or at least, additional reasons for dispute" (Fabbricotti, 1998: 660). My emphasis.
46. In his groundbreaking study of Western discourses of non-Western societies, Edward Said describes Orientalism as a way of coming to terms with the Orient that is based on the Orient's special place in European Western Experience. The Orient is not only adjacent to Europe; it is also the place of Europe's greatest and

richest and oldest colonies, the source of its civilizations and languages, its cultural contestant, and one of its deepest and most recurring images of the Other. In addition, the Orient has helped to define Europe (or the West) as its contrasting image, idea, personality, experience. Edward Said, 1978 *Orientalism*. London: Routledge. Passim.

47. This binary structure is truer in the North rather than the South where states are both refugee producers and acceptors.

48. UNDP, 1993, United Nations Development Program, Human Development Report: 16.

49. Macklin: 26.

50. Ifi Amadiume, 1987, *Male Daughters, Female Husbands: Gender and Sex in African Society*, London: Zed Books: 5.

51. Valentine Mohandam, 1994, *Identity Politics and Women: Cultural Reassertions and Feminism in International Perspectives*, Boulder: Westview Press: 22.

52. Amadiume, 1987; Mohandam, 1994; Chandra Mohanty, 1991, "Under Western Eyes: Feminist Scholarship and Colonial Discourses," *Third World Women and the Politics of Feminism*, Ed. Chandra Mohanty et al, Bloomington: Indiana University Press.

53. Macklin, 1995: 273.

54. Bonny Ibhawoh, 2000, "Between Culture and Constitution: Evaluating the Cultural Legitimacy of Human Rights in the African State," *Human Rights Quarterly*, 22, 2; Abdullahi Ahmed An'Naim, ed., 1992, *Human Rights in Cross-Cultural Perspectives. A Quest for Consensus*, Philadelphia: University of Penn Press.

55. Elvin Hatch, 1983, *Culture and Morality: The Relativity of Values in Anthropology*, New York: Columbia University Press: 12.

56. An'Naim, 1992: 26.

Chapter 5
Refugee Protection in Troubled Times

1. Hathaway draws a telling comparison of refugee burden sharing in Northern and Southern states where he notes that: "Of the 26 states hosting at least one refugee per 100 citizens, 21 were among the world's poorest (i.e. they had a per capita income of less than $1000 per year) . . . The Refugee Convention speaks about the importance of sharing, but incorporates no mechanism to make it happen. Northern states each year spend at least $12 billion to process the refugee claims of about 15% of the world's refugee population, yet contribute only $1–2 billion to meet the needs of 85% of the world's refugees who are present in comparatively poor states. . . ." Keynote Address of Professor James Hathaway at New Delhi Workshop on International Refugee Law, *Indian Journal of International Law*, Vol 39, No 1, January–March 1999: 11.

2. Speech by the UK Home Secretary, Jack Straw, to the Institute for Public Policy Research, London, 6 February 2001 (on file with the author).

3. Adam Roberts, December 1998, "More Refugees, less Asylum: A Regime in Transformation" *Journal of Refugee Studies (JRS)*, Vol 11, No 4: 379.

4. Gil Loescher, "The UNHCR and World Politics: State Interests vs. Institutional Autonomy," Paper prepared for an international conference on "Commemorating UNHCR at 50: Past, Present and Future of Refugee Assistance," Columbia University, New York, 15–18 May 2000, forthcoming in *International Migration Review*.

5. "Between 1991 and 1997 the Security Council made specific reference to UNHCR assuming a leading humanitarian role more than 30 times, in contrast to merely four times prior to 1991 . . . In Kosovo, UNHCR worked in partnership with an overt party to a conflict even without the cover of a UN resolution, so that "its claim to be a neutral actor looked increasingly threadbare," as noted in B. S. Chimni, September 2000, "Globalization, Humanitarianism and Refugee Protection," *JRS*, Vol 13, No 3: 256.

6. See for example, S Alex Cunliffe and Michael Pugh, "The Politicization of UNHCR in the Former Yugoslavia," *JRS*, Vol 10, No 2 (1997); Michael Barutciski, 1996, "The Reinforcement of Non-Admission Policies and the Subversion of UNHCR: Displacement and Internal Assistance in Bosnia-Herzegovina (1992–1994)," *International Journal of Refugee Law (IJRL)*, Vol 8, No 1/2; Bill Frelick, "Preventing Refugee Flows: Protection of Peril?," *World Refugee Survey 1993*, U.S. Committee for Refugees, Washington, D.C. In a news article in *Le Monde* of 29 May 1997, a representative of Medicins sans Frontiere targeted UNHCR for criticism as head of the UN's repatriation operation for Rwandese refugees from the former Zaire thus: "Instead of standing up for the right of asylum and security guarantees for refugees in Rwanda itself, [UNHCR] is undertaking this repatriation under international pressure." The MSF representative went on to criticize the international community's "understanding" of the Rwandan government whose representatives "are killing refugees by the thousands," and then posed the question: "should UNHCR bring refugees back to the country of their oppressors in the name of humanitarianism?" Also see Edward N. Luttwak, July/August, 1999 "Give War a Chance," *Foreign Affairs*: 36–44. For a counterview see Nicholas Morris, 1997, "Protection Dilemmas and UNHCR's Response: A Personal View from within UNHCR," *IJRL*, Vol 9, No 3.

7. A press release from the Swedish Ministry of Foreign Affairs dated 29 March 2001 on support for the UN Trust Fund for Security of UN Staff members notes: "The lack of security for UN personnel has been highlighted on several occasions. Two serious incidents have occurred during the past week, one in the Democratic Republic of Congo where an employee of UNHCR was killed, and one in Mogadishu in Somalia where a number of international relief workers for Doctors without Borders and the UN were abducted and locally-employed Somalis killed. Since 1992, some 200 civilian UN staff members have lost their lives in the execution of their duty, and since 1994 some 240 have been held hostage or kidnapped. In addition, UN personnel have been victims of threats and assaults on many occasions, and humanitarian transport has been attacked."

8. It is perplexing to see certain refugee groups, Afghans in South Asia for example, being largely without direct financial or social assistance from UNHCR as a re-

sult of budgetary retrenchment measures. Prior to cuts in financial assistance to urban-based Afghan refugees in India, subsistence allowances were provided at the rate of approx. US$1 per refugee a day. Yet in another part of the world donors have provided funds for the establishment of legal aid resource centers for returnees to Bosnia and Herzegovina who wish to get their homes back. The resource allocation is often beyond UNHCR's control as a result of earmarking of funds by donor countries. This nevertheless leads to unequal treatment in providing international protection and assistance to certain groups of refugees. The Office has at times been the subject of strong criticism as a result of these operational imbalances.

9. The Statute of the Office of the UNHCR provides that: "The work of the High Commissioner shall be of an *entirely non-political character; it shall be humanitarian and social* and shall relate, as a rule, to groups and categories of refugees," General Assembly Resolution 428(V) of 14 December 1950, Chapter 1 'General provisions,' para 2. The Preamble of the 1951 Refugee Convention also expresses a similar sentiment: Expressing the wish that all states, *recognizing the social and humanitarian nature of the problem of refugees,* will do everything within their power to prevent this problem from becoming a cause of tension between states," 189 United Nations Treaty Series 137, as updated by the 1967 Protocol Relating to the Status of Refugees, 31 January 1967, 606 UNTS 267 (emphasis added).

    Mark Cutts, 1998, has suggested that: ". . . rather than attempting to universalize the ICRC approach to humanitarian action, perhaps what is needed is for a clear distinction to be drawn between the different types of humanitarian organizations. On the one hand there are independent organizations which espouse neutrality, which seek to avoid politics, which focus on palliatives rather than solutions and mitigation rather than prevention, and which operate only on the basis of consent. On the other hand there are those organizations, including the UN organizations such as UNHCR, which do not necessarily conform to any of these standards or philosophies. The UN is, after all, a political organization, and one which has enforcement powers of its own (sic)." "Politics and Humanitarianism," *Refugee Survey Quarterly,* Vol 17, No 1: 15; Also see David Forsythe, March, 2001 "UNHCR's mandate: the politics of being non-political," *New Issues in Refugee Research,* UNHCR Working Paper No 33, available online at: www. unhcr.ch/refworld/pubs/pubon.htm

10. Chimni, op cit, pp 252–53.

11. The perception that "vastly increased" numbers of asylum seekers and immigrants are invading Western Europe is deserving of further study. However, it is worth considering the following: Goodwin-Gill, 1999, has suggested that: "Numbers in and of themselves are not a problem. In the immediate aftermath of the First World War, Europe faced a refugee population of some 800,000 Russian refugees. They were soon joined by Assyrians, Armenians, Assyro-Chaldeans, Germans, Spaniards, and others. At the end of the Spanish Civil War, France received some 400,000 refugees within a period of ten days. After the Second World War, Europe was a refuge, often temporary, to over 1.6 million refugees and displaced persons. Other regions in other times have coped with as many or

more. . . .", "Editorial: Refugees and Security," *IJRL*, Vol 11, No 1: 2; In January 2001 the UNHCR Registration and Statistical Unit reported that provisional data provided by governments to UNHCR indicate that some 452,000 asylum applications were submitted in 25 European countries in 2000, 4% less than in 1999. In the 15 EU countries, the number of applications rose slightly from 387,000 in 1999 to almost 390,000 in 2000, with the UK receiving the largest number of asylum applications (approx. 97,900), followed by Germany (78,800), and the Netherlands (43,900). Slovenia received the largest number of asylum seekers in Europe during 2000 with 4.7 applications per 1,000 inhabitants, followed by Belgium (4.2), and Ireland (2.9). The three main nationalities of asylum seekers in Europe remained unchanged compared to 1999: citizens from the Federal Republic of Yugoslavia (FRY) submitted the largest number of applications (42,300), followed by nationals from Iraq (34,700), and from Afghanistan (28,800). The number of Iranian applications more than doubled from 12,100 in 1999 to 27,100 in 2000. Significant decreases were reported in the number of applications submitted by citizens from the FRY (−64%) and Somalia (−26%); *The Economist*, citing a United Nations' Population Fund report of 2000, noted that: "In order to keep its working-age population stable between now and 2050, at current birth and death rates, Germany would need to import 487,000 migrants a year . . . France would need 109,000, and the European Union as a whole 1.6 million. To keep the ratio of workers to pensioners steady, the flow would need to swell to 3.6 million a year in Germany, 1.8 million a year in France and a staggering 13.5 million a year in the EU as a whole." (*The Economist Mobile Edition*, 5 October 2000); Finally, for an excellent article which debunks a number of common myths about global migration see Demetrios Papademetriou, Winter 1997–1998, "Migration: Think Again," *Foreign Policy*.

12. Roberts, op cit, 382.

13. Reg Whitaker, 1998, "Refugees: The Security Dimension," *Citizenship Studies*, Vol. 2, No 3: 429–430.

14. A former UNHCR Director of International Protection has described some of these practices by states as: "the narrowing of formal recognition [of refugee status] to minimal levels; attempts to streamline procedures to the exclusion of fair appeals before deportation; efforts to constrict entitlement to basic rights for various categories of victims of civil conflict. Temporary protection has generally been a positive response by states to the problem [of refugees from the former Yugoslavia], but in some cases it, too, has kept refugees for years in temporary, albeit safe, limbo, sometimes unable to get work or to reunite with their immediate families. These tendencies are, of course, of particular concern to UNHCR when they involve the nations that founded our system of human rights and refugee protection, those whose jurisprudence continues to be closely followed by the rest of the world." Statement of Dennis McNamara to the Sub-Committee of the Whole on International Protection, Executive Committee of the High Commissioner's Program, 13 October 1995.

15. The interdiction, refugee-screening and "safe-haven" protection exercised by the U.S. government in July 1994 for Haitian asylum seekers and August 1994 for

Cubans, as well as the 'Tampa' boat incident off the coast of Australia in August 2001 which resulted in several hundred Afghan and Iraqi asylum seekers being processed for refugee status on the island of Nauru, are examples of extraordinary efforts by states to avoid receiving refugees on their territory. The writer participated in the UNHCR Haiti Operation in Jamaica aboard the US Naval Ship *Comfort* in 1994. This operation of offshore refugee screening was described by UNHCR at the time as ill-advised and something which should not be repeated. The proposal by the former UK Home Secretary to develop refugee determination and resettlement programs in regions of origin, an idea which has received initial endorsement from a number of Western European states, is another extra-territorial measure which would require careful consideration as to whether it complies with international principles of refugee protection.

16. For a discussion of "safe zones" in international law and practice see Karin Landgren, 1995, "Safety Zones and International Protection: A Dark Grey Area," *IJRL*, vol 7, no 3. A more critical analysis is offered by B. S. Chimni, 1995, "The Incarceration of Victims: Deconstructing Safety Zones," in *International Legal Issues Arising under the United Nations Decade of International Law*, N. Al-Naumi and R. Meese, eds., Kluwer Law International.

17. The use of detention of asylum seekers by states in Europe has been extensively documented by UNHCR. See "Detention of Asylum-Seekers in Europe," *UNHCR European Series*, Vol 1, No 2 (1995).

18. See "Working Paper on Readmission Agreements" prepared by the Secretariat of the Inter-Government Consultations on Asylum, Refugee and Migration Policies in Europe, North American and Australia, Geneva, August 1994.

19. See "An Overview of Protection Issues in Western Europe: Legislative Trends and Positions Taken by UNHCR," UNHCR European Series, vol 1, no 3 (1995): 12–14.

20. Ibid, 14–21.

21. See Erika Feller, 1989, "Carrier Sanctions and International Law," *IJRL*, vol 1, no 1; and R. I. R. Abeyratne, 1998, "Air Carrier Liability and State Responsibility for the Carriage of Inadmissible Persons and Refugees," *IJRL*, vol 10, no 4.

22. In addition to preinspection practices which have become routine with major airline companies and are specifically targeted to international airports where irregular travel is considered a problem, there is the phenomenon of police and immigration officials checking the travel documents of passengers upon arrival. The writer has experienced this on numerous occasions flying to European destinations aboard international flights originating in developing countries. Not only are such practices legally questionable, but more generally it begs the question of whether persons who wish to seek asylum are provided an opportunity to do so if they are subject to checks at the gate, or even at the door of the aircraft pursuant to authorities' efforts to control disembarkation or entry of persons without proper travel documents. See Saad Al Attar, 1996, "Preinspection of Travelers in Foreign Airports: An Obstacle to Asylum Seekers," *Journal of International Relations*, Vol 3, No 2, Dhaka, Bangladesh.

23. Concerning airport procedures in Europe refer to *Working Paper on Airport Procedures in Europe*, European Consultation on Refugees and Exiles (ECRE) (1993), and Maryellen Fullerton, 1998, "Restricting the Flow of Asylum-Seekers in Belgium, Denmark, The Federal Republic of Germany, and The Netherlands: New Challenges to the Geneva Convention Relating to the Status of Refugees and the European Convention on Human Rights," *Virginia Journal of International Law*, vol 29, no 1.

24. Aiken has described the case of a "sophisticated interdiction action involving a boat of 192 Tamil asylum seekers bound for Europe" in which none of the passengers were properly interviewed to determine whether they would be at any risk if returned to Sri Lanka. The entire group was deemed to be "economic migrants" and they were encouraged to consent to "voluntarily" repatriate under the "watchful eyes of Canadian officials." Reports and interviews with the detainees confirmed that all of the Tamils were arrested upon return to Sri Lanka and held in detention over several weeks. One of the individuals was rearrested a month later and tortured. The U.S. State Department Report for 2000 describes a long list of torture methods which are still in use in Sri Lanka. Sharryn Aiken, 2000, "Manufacturing 'Terrorists': Refugees, National Security and Canadian Law—Part II," *Refuge*, Vol 19, No 4.

25. In 1993, the former High Commissioner for Refugees expressed her concern on the measures taken by some European states to control illegal immigration, which may result in the creation of "unreasonable barriers and impossible burdens for people in need of protection." Much has been written on the European experience of common immigration control mechanisms and their negative impact on refugee protection. See, for example, Gregor Noll, 2000, *Negotiating Asylum: The EU Acquis, Extraterritorial Protection and the Common Market of Deflection*, Martinus Nijhoff Publishers; Jens Vedsted-Hansen, May 1999, *Europe's response to the arrival of asylum seekers: refugee protection and immigration control*, New Issues in Refugee Research, Working Paper No 6, UNHCR Geneva; Karin Landgren, June 1999, *Deflecting international protection by treaty: bilateral and multilateral accords on extradition, readmission and the inadmissibility of asylum requests*, New Issues in Refugee Research, Working paper no. 10, UNHCR. Also see *The trafficking and smuggling of refugees: the end game in European asylum policy?*, UNHCR-commissioned study prepared by John Morrison, Geneva, July 1999.

26. Others have argued that due to the current irrelevance of international refugee law to states there is a need to develop a new paradigm of refugee protection based on standards and mechanisms to implement common but differentiated responsibility towards refugees. Refer to James Hathaway and Alexander Neve, 1997, "Making International Refugee Law Relevant Again: A Proposal for Collectivized and Solution-Oriented Protection," *Harvard Human Rights Journal*, vol 10.

27. Background papers, conclusions, and participant lists from the UNHCR Global Consultations process, as well as the *Declaration of States Parties to the 1951 Convention and or its 1967 Protocol Relating to the Status of Refugees*, which was

adopted in December 2001 after the first meeting of States Parties to the international refugee instruments, are available on UNHCR's website: www.unhcr.ch.

28. Although several of the examples of obstacles to refugee protection have found their genesis in developed countries, serious protection problems also occur in less-developed countries. For a study of refugee protection problems in Africa see Lawyers Committee for Human Rights, 1995, *African Exodus: Refugee Crises, Human Rights & the 1969 OAU Convention,* New York. In the Latin American context a UNHCR report noted that: "Numerous countries [in the region] have indeed acceded to the 1951 Convention and/or 1967 Protocol, but few have a fully operational national legislation and, [for those that do] fewer do apply them systematically if UNHCR is not there to remind concerned authorities of their duties. While it is true that we are rarely confronted with very serious protection problems, there are still numerous situations in our countries which justify our presence and monitoring role. This is more so when we note that [UNHCR's] main challenge for this end of century is to ensure that effective protection of refugees and asylum-seekers goes hand-in-hand with activities geared to ensure effective institution building and training programs (on behalf of both governmental and non-governmental counterparts) and the enactment or revision and effective application of refugee law." (UNHCR Regional Office Costa Rica Report of 28 February 1996).

29. See for example Guy S. Goodwin-Gill, 1996, *The Refugee in International Law,* 2nd edition, Clarendon Press, Oxford: 20–25.

30. For a perspective which argues that the origins of the 1951 Refugee Convention are premised on its universal application to all refugee situations see Ivor C. Jackson, 1991, "The 1951 Convention relating to the Status of Refugees: A Universal Basis for Protection," *IJRL,* vol 3, no 3; also by the same author see, 1999, *The Refugee Concept in Group Situations,* Martinus Nijhoff Publishers, The Hague.

31. For example, Article 3 of the 1951 Convention provides that states parties shall apply the provisions of the Convention without discrimination as to race, religion, or country of origin of the beneficiary; Article 4 governs freedom to practice religion and religious education; Article 16 provides that a refugee shall have free access to the courts of law on the territory of all contracting states; Articles 17, 18, and 19 govern the granting of access to employment opportunities to refugees; and Article 21 provides that as regards housing, refugees shall be accorded treatment as favorable as possible and in any event not less favorable than that accorded to aliens generally in the same circumstances. Other rights granted to refugees include freedom of movement in the territory of the contracting state (Articles 26 and 31), and facilitating assimilation and naturalization (Article 34). Other provisions include freedom of association with non-political and non-profit-making associations and trade unions (Article 15), and provision of administrative assistance by the contracting state authority to allow a refugee to exercise a right under the Convention (Article 25).

32. Article 5 of the Refugee Convention would thereby require that any broader rights granted under international human rights treaties, for example, the UN Convention against Torture or the European Convention on Human Rights and

to which states are a party, be applicable to refugees and asylum seekers. For a comparative study of state practice in granting rights to refugees see James Hathaway and John Dent, 1995, *Refugee Rights: Report on a Comparative Survey*, York Lanes Press, Toronto.

33. Much has been written on reforming the UN treaty body system in recent years. Several practical proposals for reforming and reactivating this particular aspect of the UN human rights system are contained in the "Conclusions and Recommendation" from the proceedings of a Conference *Enforcing International Human Rights Law: The Treaty System in the Twenty-First Century* held at York University, Toronto, on 22–24 June 1997. Also see: *Future of UN Human Rights Treaty Monitoring*, Philip Alston, James Crawford, ed., Cambridge University Press (2000); Anne Bayefsky, 1995, "Making the Human Rights Treaties Work," in *Human Rights: An Agenda for the Next Century*, Louis Henkin and John Lawrence Hargrove eds., Studies in Transnational Legal Policy, No. 26, The American Society of International Law, Washington, D.C.; Interim report by Philip Alston entitled "Effective Implementation of International Instruments on Human Rights, Including Reporting Obligations under International Instruments on Human Rights," UN report ref: A/CONF.157/PC/62/Add.11/Rev.1 of 22 April 1993; Philip Alston (ed), *The United Nations and Human Rights: A Critical Appraisal*, Clarendon Press, Oxford, 1992.

34. One UNHCR colleague has described the situation as follows: "In many places . . . UNHCR offers very little protection and our assistance falls far below acceptable international standards. I don't mean to confuse you by deflecting attention from the moral and legal responsibilities of states which are failing to protect and respect the rights of refugees and asylum seekers enshrined in international and regional refugee and human rights instruments . . . but UNHCR also has a particular mandate and must be more vocal about the failure of international protection in the absence of political will. In many places we do not even have access to the people we are mandated to protect and when we do have access we may have one protection officer assigned to protect a population of 30,000 or more desperate refugees. . . ."

35. See chapter 2 of *The State of the World's Refugees*, "Defending refugee rights," UNHCR Geneva (1997); and William Clarence, 1997, "Field Strategy for the Protection of Human Rights," *International Journal of Refugee Law*, Vol 9, No 2.

36. The "UNHCR and Human Rights" policy paper inter alia notes that "UNHCR must strengthen its involvement in [refugee and human rights] standard-setting exercises, in particular with the UN, as well as in the development of case law by human rights Commissions and Courts. It must do so in order to ensure proper reflection of the Office's interests and concerns and to safeguard a liberal interpretation of these standards as they apply to refugees and others persons of concern." The paper is reproduced in the UNHCR RefWorld CD-ROM.

   UNHCR has also developed policy papers for its protection staff on the Office's strategy to use the European Convention on Human Rights and the UN Convention against Torture. Other human rights-related guidelines include the UNHCR Training Module "Human Rights and Refugee Protection" (Geneva

1995) and "A Practical Guide to Capacity Building as a feature of UNHCR's Humanitarian Programs" (Geneva 1999). Since 1993 UNHCR has maintained two professional officer posts in the Department of International Protection whose main tasks are training, liaison, and advocacy in relation to human rights and refugee issues.

37. The 1998 Note on International Protection submitted to the UNHCR Executive Committee began with the following observation: "There is a natural complementarity between the protection work of UNHCR and the international system for the protection of human rights. The protection of refugees operates within a structure of individual rights and duties and state responsibilities. Human rights law is a prime source of existing refugee protection principles and structures; at the same time, it works to complement them . . . UNHCR has . . . intensified its cooperative involvement with system-wide human rights promotion activities and protection mechanisms, where this was judged to be of tangible benefit to refugee protection, or to addressing the root causes of refugee flows. This cooperation has included support for national human rights institutions to strengthen local capacity to protect human rights; assistance in training the judiciary and government officials in refugee and related human rights concepts; and working along with non-governmental organizations to spread awareness of human rights instruments, principles and practices directly impacting on refugee situations. UNHCR has also intensified its cooperation with the human rights treaty implementation machinery, while at the operational level, a positive interaction is developing between the human rights field missions and UNHCR operations on the ground. At Headquarters, the cooperation between UNHCR and the Office of the UN High Commissioner for Human Rights has been very positive and is expanding . . . In all these activities, UNHCR has been guided by its clear awareness of the complementarity but difference between the refugee specific mandate of UNHCR and the broader human rights mandates of other concerned organs and institutions, including of the Office of the High Commissioner for Human Rights. The need to maintain the supportive but separate character of respective mandates is particularly clear in the area of monitoring. While human rights monitoring missions must investigate and encourage prosecution of human rights violations, action in support of refugees and returns is essentially humanitarian, involving confidence-building and creation of conditions conducive to peace and reconciliation. This being said, because the activities of human rights field operations are very relevant to UNHCR's work, UNHCR has been repeatedly supporting the need for a more operational human rights machinery as a necessary complement to its own protection efforts." UN Doc ref: A/AC/96/98 of 3 July 1998.

38. This point was made in the 1981 Commission on Human Rights "Study on Human Rights and Massive Exoduses" that was prepared by former UN High Commissioner for Refugees, Sadruddin Aga Khan, wherein he noted that: "Since the individual is the ultimate beneficiary in any system of international law and practice, the need to respect human rights is all the more important. These rights, as embodied in the 1948 *Universal Declaration of Human Rights*

constitute a set of guidelines, a code of conduct, of how, in an ideal society, the nation-state should deal with an individual. The former should not abuse the latter. The rule of law should reign supreme and impartial courts must enforce this even against governments. . . ." UN Doc ref: E/CN.4/1503 of 31 December 1981, 8–9.

39. *Charter of the United Nations*, Articles 55 and 56. The International Court of Justice has had the opportunity to consider the legal effect of these particular provisions and has stated, albeit as *obiter*, that they "bind member states [of the UN] to observe and respect human rights" (Advisory Opinion on *The Legal Consequences of the Continued Presence of South Africa in Namibia*, ICJ Reports 1971, 16). Or as Brownlie, 1990, stated: ". . . while it may be doubtful whether states can be called to account for every alleged infringement of the rather general [UN] Charter provisions, there can be little doubt that responsibility exists under the Charter for any substantial infringement of the provisions, especially when a class of persons, or a pattern of activity, are involved, *Principles of Public International Law* (4th ed.), Clarendon Press, Oxford: 570.

UN General Assembly Resolution 428 (V) of 14 December 1950, which established the Office of the UNHCR also calls upon governments to cooperate with the Office in the performance of its functions. The necessity for states to cooperate with UNHCR has since been acknowledged in successive General Assembly resolutions and in a variety of international instruments including the preamble to the 1951 Refugee Convention, the 1967 UN Declaration on Territorial Asylum, the Final Act of the 1968 Teheran International Conference on Human Rights, and the preamble to the 1969 OAU Convention Governing the Specific Aspects of Refugee Problems in Africa et al.

40. The *continuing nature* of international human rights treaty obligations was addressed by the UN Human Rights Committee in its General Comment No. 26 on "Issues relating to the continuity of obligations to the ICCPR" of 8 December 1997. In its comment, the Committee noted that the Covenant, along with the ICESCR, codifies in treaty form the universal human rights enshrined in the Universal Declaration of Human Rights. Accordingly, the Covenant does not have a temporary character typical of treaties where a right of denunciation is deemed to be admitted. The Committee noted that ". . . *once the people are accorded the protection of the rights under the Covenant, such protection devolves with territory and continues to belong to them, notwithstanding change in government of the state party,* including dismemberment in more than one state or state succession or any subsequent action of the state party designed to divest them of the rights guaranteed by the Covenant." (emphasis added)

In addition to the two International Covenants, only the CEDAW does not permit denunciation by a state party. The other human rights treaties including the CRC, CAT, and CERD allow for denunciation. However, denunciation of a human rights treaty obligation by a state is an extremely rare occurrence. It may be politically more expedient for a state to suffer periodic criticism of a treaty body and the international community for human rights violations, rather than be permanently marked as a state which has denounced a major human rights instrument.

41. As a general rule of international law, in the event of disparity between two or more human rights standards then the more generous provision would be applicable. In comparison with refugee law, some may argue that if the provisions in the international refugee instruments are more specific than those found in universal human rights instruments then the more specific legal provision should apply. This view can only be considered correct where the more generous provision is ambiguous or unclear as to whether it benefits refugees. Furthermore, as has been repeatedly emphasized by the human rights treaty bodies, states should not interpret the scope and content of their treaty obligations in an overly restrictive fashion.

42. The general comments as well as other documents and reports of the UN human rights treaty bodies are reproduced on the UNHCR RefWorld CD-ROM and on the website of the UN High Commissioner for Human Rights at: www.unhchr.ch.

    Of particular relevance in the refugee context is the Human Rights Committee General Comment No. 20 (Article 7) which provides: "It is the duty of the state party to afford everyone through legislative and other measures as may be necessary against the acts prohibited by article 7, whether inflicted by people acting in their official capacity, outside their official capacity or in a private capacity . . . The text of article 7 allows no limitation (and) no derogation . . . States parties must not expose individuals to the danger of torture or cruel, inhuman or degrading treatment or punishment upon return to another country by way of their extradition, expulsion or *refoulement*." (paras 2, 3, 9).

43. For example, the extra-territorial application of the rights under the ICCPR was addressed by the Human Rights Committee during consideration of the report of the United States of America under Article 40, in which the Committee expressed its "concern" that excludable aliens are dealt with by lower standards of due process that other aliens. The Committee also expressed concern regarding "the situation of a number of asylum seekers and refugees." The Committee added, in what was clearly a reference to the practice adopted in 1994 of not permitting Haitian asylum seekers to enter the United States, that it "does not share the view expressed by the government that the Covenant lacks extraterritorial reach under all circumstances." The Committee took the position that such an opinion as expressed by the United States government "is contrary to the consistent interpretation of the Committee on this subject, that, in special circumstances, persons may fall under the subject matter jurisdiction of a state party even when outside that state territory," Comments of the Human Rights Committee, Fifty-third session, at its 1413th meeting held on 6 April 1995.

44. *The UN and Refugees' Human Rights: A manual on how UN human rights mechanisms can protect the rights of refugees*, Amnesty International and the International Service for Human Rights, (1997) UK. This manual is an excellent compilation and sourcebook on the workings of the principal UN human rights bodies and includes suggestions and practical information on how NGOs, advocates or other actors may access these bodies to raise refugee protection issues. The manual also includes a chapter on how refugee advocates can lobby UNHCR

to act on particular issues. It is available from the International Service for Human Rights office, 1 rue de Varembe, P.O. Box 16, 1211 Geneva.

45. In 1970, ECOSOC adopted resolution 1503 which established a procedure for the consideration of communications alleging that governments have committed a "consistent pattern of gross and reliably attested violations of human rights and fundamental freedoms." Although the Commission makes the decision as to whether action will be taken on a communication submitted under the 1503-procedure, it is the Sub-Commission on Human Rights which initially assesses a communication with regard to its admissibility. In practice, a five-member Working group meets for two weeks just before the Sub-Commission's annual session to consider all the communications and governments' replies it has received (which between 1972 to 1991 numbered over 800,000 communications and several thousand government replies). It is estimated that the working group currently deals with 20,000 to 25,000 communications annually. The 1503-procedure is confidential, so it is not possible to assess whether the procedure functions fairly and effectively. There is nothing preventing refugee protection issues from forming the basis of a communication under this procedure, although the volume of communications received and the delay which is inevitably associated with this process make it impractical for redress in urgent cases.

46. Sub-Commission Resolution 1996/7. Clearly the language of this resolution was adopted as a result of some Iranian refugee leaders being murdered in Germany. These murders later resulted in criminal charges being brought by the German authorities against the perpetrators who were deemed to be agents of the Iranian state. Iran vehemently denied these allegations.

47. The authority for Committee against Torture to get engaged in such matters is found in article 20 of the CAT which provides that: "If the Committee receives reliable information which appears to it to contain well-founded indications that torture is being systematically practiced in the territory of a state party . . . a confidential enquiry [can be made and] in agreement with that state party such inquiry may include a visit to its territory." The Torture Committee has only exercised Article 20 authority twice in relation to Turkey and Egypt. The Committee on the Rights of the Child has also been involved in field visits jointly organized by UNICEF and the Office of the High Commissioner for Human Rights in order to assist the Committee to gain firsthand experience concerning the problems in safeguarding the human rights of children.

On 24 July 2002 the UN Economic and Social Council (ECOSOC) adopted an Optional Protocol to the Convention against Torture. The Optional Protocol provides authority to the Committee against Torture to establish a system of regular visits to places of detention by an international body of experts, complemented by national visiting bodies, in order to monitor and improve the treatment of people in detention as well as conditions of detention, and to ensure that they are not subjected to torture or cruel and degrading treatment or punishment. This would be an unprecedented mechanism in the UN system, in that previously visits by the Committee only took place where there were indications that systematic torture had been committed. While the majority of ECOSOC members from all regions of the world voted in support of the Optional Protocol in July, countries which did not support it include the U.S., China, Cuba, Egypt, Iran, Libya, Saudi Arabia, and the Sudan.

48. Lists of states parties to the international human rights treaties as well as those states which have made declarations to permit individual and/or inter-state complaints are maintained on the website of the Office of the UN High Commissioner for Human Rights at: www.unhchr.ch.

49. For a full review of the law and procedures governing the work of the UN Committee against Torture, the Committee on the Rights of the Child and the Human Rights Committee, including the 'conclusions' and 'jurisprudence' of these bodies which is of direct benefit to refugee protection, see Brian Gorlick, October 2000, "Human Rights and Refugees: Enhancing Protection through International Human Rights Law," New Issues in Refugee Research, UNHCR Working Paper No 30: 29–51, available online at: www.unhcr.ch/refworld/pubs/pubon.htm.

   The work of the Committee against Torture is particularly important. The protection provided for refugees under the concept of *non-refoulement* under the 1951 Refugee Convention is paralleled in Article 3 of the CAT, which prohibits the return (*refouler*) of any individual who would face "torture or cruel, inhuman or degrading punishment or treatment." Unlike international refugee law, the CAT is devoid of any exclusion provisions (see *Tapia Paez v Sweden*, Communication No 39/1996). However, what the CAT does provide is the universal jurisdiction of states parties to criminally prosecute a person who has committed acts of torture.

   Of the UN treaty bodies, the Committee against Torture has also been the most active in terms of developing jurisprudence in cases involving individual complaints, most of whom are *rejected* asylum seekers. A detrimental sign of the committee's relative success in this area is that some states parties have begun to express concerns about how the committee handles these cases, including how it assesses an applicant's credibility. Not surprisingly, the very states which have been subject of several decisions by the committee are now voicing such concerns.

50. The relevance and interest of the work of the international human rights mechanisms has not been lost on UNHCR. Indeed, the Office's interest in these bodies can be summed up as follows: "As a rule, UNHCR's interaction with the human rights mechanisms generally, and the torture provisions (in the Convention against Torture) in particular, should be linked to its mandate to protect from *re-foulement*, all bona fide refugees and other individuals "of concern" to the Office. Where the treaty mechanisms and the torture provisions can be used to prevent the *refoulement* of bona fide refugees or other cases of concern, then UNHCR will have a legitimate interest in those alternative and parallel systems." (UNHCR Memorandum Nos 57/98 & 61/98 of 28 August 1998, at para 1.9, on file with the author).

51. An example is the refusal by Egypt in 1996 to permit the Committee against Torture to conduct a field investigation pursuant to its authority under Article 20 of the CAT.

52. In 1997, Canada carried out a deportation in contravention of a request by the Committee against Torture, *Tejinder Pal Singh v Canada*, Communication No 99/1997. Mr. Singh was expelled from Canada on the basis that he posed a security risk. Mr. Singh acknowledged that he was an active member of the Dal Khalsa movement, a Sikh militant group. In finding a violation of Article 3 CAT against Canada, committee member Guibril Camara issued an additional individual opinion which noted the time to assess whether there are substantial grounds for believing that the concerned individual would be in danger of being subjected to torture is at the moment of expulsion, return, or extradition. The committee member further noted, in what may be considered a positive pronouncement for asylum seekers, that:

> The facts clearly show that, at the time of his expulsion to India, there were substantial grounds for believing that the author would be subjected to torture . . . the fact that in this case the author was not subsequently subjected to torture has no bearing on whether the state party violated the CAT in expelling him. *The question of whether the risk—in this case, of acts of torture—actually materializes is of relevance only to any reparation or damages sought by the victim or by other persons entitled to claim. The competence of the Committee against Torture should also be exercised in the interests of prevention.* In cases relating to article 3, it would surely be unreasonable to wait for a violation to occur before taking note of it. (at paras 16.3 & 16.4, emphasis added)

53. Statute of the International Tribunal for Yugoslavia, 32 *International Legal Materials (ILM)* 1163 (1993).

54. Statute of the International Criminal Tribunal for Rwanda, 33 *ILM* 1604 (1994).

55. Rome Statute of the International Criminal Court, Adopted by the UN Diplomatic Conference of Plenipotentiaries on the Establishment of an International Criminal Court on 17 July 1998, UN Doc ref: A/CONF. 183/9, 37 *ILM* 999 (1998).

56. *Pinochet Ugarte, Re,* (1999) All ER 97; Also see G. S. Goodwin-Gill, 1999, "Crime in International Law: Obligations Ergo Omnes and the Duty to Prosecute," in Goodwin-Gill and S. Talmon, ed., *The Reality of International Law: Essays in Honour of Ian Brownlie,* Clarendon Press, Oxford: 199–223; The Pinochet Precedent: How Victims can Pursue Human Rights Criminals Abroad, Human Rights Watch, New York (March 2000); *Universal Jurisdiction and absence of Immunity for Crimes against Humanity,* Amnesty International Secretariat, UK, Report EUR 45/001/1999 of (January 1999); *Hard Cases: Bringing Human Rights Violators to Justice Abroad: A Guide to Universal Jurisdiction,* International Council on Human Rights Policy, Geneva (1999).

57. Developments such as the Constitutional Council of Cambodia giving its approval to legislation creating a court to try surviving Khmer Rouge leaders for crimes against humanity; attempted criminal prosecution against Pinochet in his home country; the convictions of three ex-Serbian soldiers for rape as a war crime by the ICTY; the decision of the Federal Republic of Yugoslavia to crimi-

nally prosecute Slobodan Milosevic; the indictment in Senegal of the Former Chad Head of State Hissene Habre; and the request for extradition of Miguel Cavallo from Mexico to Spain for alleged torture in Argentina, which all have occurred over the last year, are very positive for the development of international criminal and human rights law. Similar to the Pinochet case, Habre and Cavallo are accused of the crime of torture under the CAT. Articles 4–9 of the CAT recognize the criminal jurisdiction of any state whose citizens were the victims of acts of torture. The CAT also recognizes the jurisdiction of any state to criminally prosecute an individual who is in its territory even though the alleged acts of torture took place elsewhere. Also see "Pinochet is Freed, But no Ex-Dictator Should Feel Safe," *The Wall Street Journal*, 3–4 March 2000.

58. Crimes against humanity include systematic or widespread acts of murder, extermination, enslavement, torture, deportation or forcible populations transfers, arbitrary imprisonment, enforced disappearance of persons, persecution on political, religious, racial, or gender grounds, and rape, sexual slavery, and other serious forms of sexual violence. Practices like apartheid and genocide are also crimes against humanity.

59. War crimes are largely defined in the Four Geneva Conventions and their Protocols. The most serious war crimes include killing of prisoners or civilians, unlawful deportation or transfer, the taking of hostages, attacks on the civilian population, killing of prisoners or civilians, torture, and conducting unfair trials.

60. *UNHCR and the Establishment of an International Criminal Court: Some Comments on the Draft Statute*, Department of International Protection, UNHCR Geneva, June 1998 (on file with the author).

61. Statement by the former Assistant High Commissioner for Refugees, Soren Jessen-Petersen, at the UN Diplomatic Conference of Plenipotentiaries on the Establishment of an International Criminal Tribunal, Rome, 16 June 1998.

62. For an extensive treatment of the law of "exclusion" in international refugee law, including its relationship to international criminal law and regional experiences of its application in Africa, Europe and North America, see the Special Supplementary Issue of the *IJRL* on "Exclusion from Protection," Vol. 12 (2000).

63. Chaloka Beyani, 1995, "State Responsibility for the Prevention and Resolution of Forced Population Displacements in International Law," *IJRL*, (Special Issue): 130.

64. Nina Jorgensen, 2000, *The Responsibility of States for International Crimes*, Oxford Monographs in International Law, Oxford University Press: 217.

65. A strong argument and review of developments in international law which favor the transnational responsibility of states for human rights violations committed through state policies or their agents is provided by Mark Gibney, Katarina Tomasevski and Jens Vedsted-Hansen in 'Transnational State Responsibility for Violations of Human Rights', *Harvard Human Rights Journal*, Vol 12 (Spring 1999).

66. See Dinah Shelton, *Remedies in International Human Rights Law*, Oxford University Press (1999), at chapter 4 on 'Reparations in the Law of State Responsibility for Injury to Aliens'; Steven Ratner, Jason Abrams, *Accountability for Human*

Rights Atrocities in International Law, 2nd ed, Oxford University Press (2001); Jorgensen, *op cit*, at pp 192–207; John Murphy, 'Civil Liability for the Commission of International Crimes as an Alternative to Criminal Prosecution', at pp 28–56, *Harvard Human Rights Journal*, Vol 12 (1999); Christian Tomuschat, 'State Responsibility and the Country of Origin', in Vera Gowland-Debbas, editor, *The Problem of Refugees in Light of Contemporary International Law Issues*, Martinus Nijhoff Publishers (1995); David Matas, *No More: The Battle against Human Rights Violations*, Dundurn Press Limited, Toronto (1994), chapter 12 on 'Compensation'; Luke Lee, 'The Right to Compensation: Refugees and Countries of Asylum', *American Journal of International Law*, Vol 80 (1986); Payam Akhavan and Morten Bergsmo, 'The Application of the Doctrine of State Responsibility to Refugee Creating Situations', *Nordic Journal of International Law*, Vol 58, Nos 3–4 (1989), at pp 253–254; and 'Austria Begins Payment to Jews', *International Herald Tribune*, 3 April 2001, at p 5.

67. Luke Lee, 1997, "Questions of Responsibilities and Reparation," *Refugee Survey Quarterly*, Vol. 16, No. 3: 157.

68. "The right to restitution, compensation and rehabilitation for victims of gross violations of human rights and fundamental freedoms," Final report of the Special Rapporteur, Mr. M Cherif Bassiouni, submitted in accordance with Commission resolution 1999/93. Commission on Human Rights Doc ref: E/CN.4/2000/62 of 18 January 2000. Section VII (Victims' Right to a Remedy), paragraph 11 of the *Basic Principles and Guidelines on the Right to a Remedy and Reparation for Victims of Violations of International Human Rights and Humanitarian Law*, which are annexed to the above-noted report, notes that:

> Remedies for violations of international human rights and humanitarian law include the victim's right to: (a) Access justice; (b) Reparation for harm suffered; and (c) Access the factual information concerning the violations.' Section XII (Non-Discrimination among Victims), paragraph 27 of the Principles also provides that: 'The application and interpretation of these principles and guidelines must be consistent with internationally recognised human rights law and be without any adverse distinction founded on grounds such as race, color, gender, sexual orientation, age, language, religion, political or religious belief, national, ethnic or social origin, wealth, birth, family or *other status*, or disability. (emphasis added)

69. See, for example, The Cairo Declaration of Principles of International Law on Compensation to Refugees, *American Journal of International Law*, Vol 87, No 1 (1993), at pp 157–59. Principle 4 of the Cairo Declaration provides that: "A state is obligated to compensate its own nationals forced to leave their homes to the same extent as it is obligated by international law to compensate an alien." Principle 7 further states that: "The United Nations may, in the discharge of its role as guardian of the interests of refugees, claim and administer compensation funds for refugees."

Article VIII of the Asian-African Legal Consultative Committee's (AALCC) 1966 'Bangkok Principles' on the Status and Treatment of Refugees, as revised by the open-ended working group meeting held in New Delhi on 26–27 February 2001, inter alia provides that: "1. A refugee shall have the right to receive compensation from the state or the country which he left or to which he was unable to return. 2. The compensation . . . shall be for such loss as bodily injury, deprivation of personal liberty in denial of human rights, death of a refugee or of the person whose dependant the refugee was, and the destruction of or damage to property and assets, causes by the authority of the state or country, public officials or mob violence. 3. Where such person does not desire to return, he shall be entitled to prompt and full compensation by the government or the authorities in control of such place of habitual residence as determined, in the absence of an agreement by the parties concerned, by an international body designated or constituted for the purposes by the Secretary-General of the UN at the request of either party. . . ." (On file with the author.)

70. For example, the Report of the 'Working Group on Solutions and Protection' submitted to the forty-second Session of the UNHCR Executive Committee makes no mention of compensation, restitution or reparation being made available to refugees. Although in its recommendations, the Working Group inter alia asserted that "the international community should vigorously pursue the enhanced promotion and implementation of international humanitarian and human rights law and further develop the concept of state responsibility as it relates to redressing the root causes which lead to mass flows of persons." (Section B, para (s)). UN Doc ref: EC/SCP/64 of 12 August 1991, available on the UNHCR RefWorld CD-ROM.

71. This point was reflected in February 2001 meeting in New Delhi on the revision of AALCC 1966 "Bangkok Principles" that was attended by delegates from thirty-one Asian and African states. In discussions on article VIII *supra*, the governments of Sudan, Pakistan, Turkey, Jordan, and Tanzania expressed reservations to paragraph 1 in view of the financial and economic implications.

72. Chimni, op cit, September 2000: 257–58.

Chapter 6
A Rare Opening in the Wall

1. UNHCR, 1979, *Collection of International Instruments*, Geneva: UNHCR.

2. Bret Thiele, 2000, "Persecution on Account of Gender: A Need for Refugee Law Reform," *Hastings Women's Law Journal*, Vol. 11, No. 2: 227.

3. Emily Copeland, 2000, "Gender Politics within the Refugee Regime," Paper presented at the IRAP conference, Johanesburg South Africa.

4. A summary of interpretations and practices of other states can be found on the CRS web site: http://www.web.net/~ccr/gendpers.html.

5. Thiele, 2000; Isabelle R. Gunning, 1999, "Global Feminism at the Local Level: Criminal and Asylum Laws Regarding Female Genital Surgeries," *Journal of Gender, Race and Justice*, No. 3: 45–62; Caryn L. Weisblat, 1999, "Gender-Based Persecution: Does United States Law Provide Women Refugees with a Fair Chance?,"

Tulane Journal of International and Comparative Law, Vol 7: 407–430; Gregory Kelson, 1998, "Female Circumcision in the Modern Age," Buffalo: *Buffalo Human Rights Law Review*, Vol. 4; Deborah Anker, 1995, "Women Refugees: Forgotten No Longer," *San Diego Law Review*, 32: 771; Kristin Kandt, 1995, "United States Asylum Law: Recognizing Persecution Based on Gender Using Canada as a Comparison," *Georgetown Immigration Law Journal*, 9: 137; Todd Stewart Schenk, 1994, "A Proposal to Improve the Treatment of Women in Asylum Law: 'Gender' Category to the International Definition of 'Refugee'" *Indiana Journal of Global Legal Studes*, 2: 301 (Fall).

6. See Emily Copeland, 2000.

7. Cited in Christiane Berthiaume, 1998, "Do We Really Care?," http:www.unhcr.ch/issues/women/rm1002.htm (10/16/98).

8. Elizabeth Ferris, 1993, *Beyond Borders: Refugees, Migrants, and Human Rights in the Post-cold War World*, Geneva: WCC Publications: 115.

9. Elisabeth Prugl and Mary Meyer, 1999, *Gender Politics in Global Governance*, Lanham: Rowman and Littlefield.

10. Gene Dewey, Former Deputy UN High Comissioner for Refugees, interview with the author, 1998.

11. Dewey, 1998.

12. Michael Malloy, Former Canadian representative to the UNHCR Executive Committee, correspondence with the author, 1999.

13. Thiele, 2000: 222.

14. Musala, 1998: 361–370.

15. Stephen Knight, Hastings Center correspondence with the author, 2001.

16. Gregory Kelson, 2001, "Giving Formal Recognition to Gender-Based Persecution: Proposing a Protocol to the Convention on the Status of Refugees." Paper presented at the International Studies Association Conference (February). Cited with permission of author.

17. Thiele, 2000.

18. Kelson, 2001.

19. There have been two other regional attempts to modify the definition, but the first—the 1969 OAU Convention Governing the Specific Aspects of Refugee Problems in Africa—applies only to Africa and the second—the 1984 Cartagena Declaration—is nonbinding.

20. Art: 26.

21. Transcribed interview with Mr. Laurence Dawson, 1969, Interviewed by Louise Holborn, March 5. Holborn archives (uncateloged). Schlesinger Library, Harvard University.

22. Dawson, 1969.

23. See Atle Grahl-Madsen, 1980, *Territorial Asylum*, Stockholm: Almqvist and Wiksell International.

24. Paul Weis, 1969, "The United Nations Declaration on Territorial Asylum," *Canadian Yearbook of International Law*, No. 7: 94.

25. Ibid: 95.

26. Paul Weis, 1979, "The Draft United Nations Convention on Territorial Asylum," *British Yearbook of International Law*: 151.

27. Emily Copeland, 1996, *The Creation and Evolution of the Refugee and Economic Migration Regimes: Testing Alternative Frameworks*, Ph. Dissertation, The Fletcher School of Law and Diplomacy: ftn 57.

28. Weis, 1979: 152.

29. Goodwin-Gill, 1983.

30. Report on the Nansen Symposium on Territorial Asylum, reprinted in Grahl-Madsen, 1980.

31. F. Leduc, 1977, "L'asile territorial et la Conference des Nations Unies de Geneve Janvier 1977," *Annuaire francais du droit international*, 23: 221–267.

32. Grahl-Madsen, 1980: 64.

Chapter 7
The Role of Non-Governmental Organizations in the International Refugee Regime

1. The inadequacy of the term "non-governmental organization" has long been recognized by NGOs and academics (see for example, Smillie, 1995; Clark, 1991; Korten, 1990; and Hancock 1989 for a particularly critical assessment.) Within the NGO community, some prefer a term with a more positive connotation, such as voluntary agency, rather than a term that defines an organization by what it is not. Critics have questioned whether agencies receiving substantial amounts of government funding can be considered *non*-governmental. A range of alternative terms have been proposed, from volag to community-based development organization. While recognizing the inadequacies of the terminology, this paper nevertheless uses the term "NGO" to refer to organizations which have been established by individuals and groups to promote the public welfare and which are not formally a part of government.

2. J. Bruce Nichols, 1988, *The Uneasy Alliance: Religion, Refugee Work and US Foreign Policy*, New York: Oxford University Press: 32–34.; Michael R. Marrus, 1985, *The Unwanted: European Refugees in the Twentieth Century*, Oxford: Oxford University Press: 83–84.; Maggie Black, 1992, *A Cause for Our Times: Oxfam, the first Fifty Years*, Oxford: Oxfam.; Randolph C. Kent, 1987, *Anatomy of Disaster Relief: The International Network in Action*, London: Pinter Publishers: 21–41.

3. Nichols, 1988: 32–33.

4. Marrus, 1985: 83.

5. Gilbert Jaeger, "Participation of Non-Governmental Organizations in the Activities of the United Nations High Commissioner for Refugees," *Pressure Groups in the Global System*, ed. Peter Willets, London: Francees Pinter Publishers: 171.

6. See Mann and Estorick (1939: 142–154) for a description of NGO efforts around the ill-fated Evian conference.

7. Louise Holborn, 1975, *Refugees: A Problem of Our Time. The Work of the United Nations High Commissioner for Refugees, 1951–1972*, Metuchen, NJ: Scarecrow Press: 26.

8. Ibid: 125.

9. Peter Willets, 1982, "Pressure Groups as Transnational Actors," *Pressure Groups in the Global System,* ed. Peter Willets, London: Frances Pinter: 10.; See also Lowell W. Livezy, 1989, "PVOs, Human Rights and the Humanitarian Task," *The Moral Nation: Humanitarianism and US Foreign Policy Today,* ed. Bruce Nichols and Gil Loeshcer. Notre Dame: 192–209.; C.M. Nchama, 1991, "The Role of Non-Governmental Organizations in the Promotion and Protection of Human Rights," *Bulletin of Human Rights,* 90/1, 50: 93.; and Henry J. Stein, 1991, *Diverse Partners: Non-Governmental Organizations in the Human Rights Movement,* Cambridge: Harvard University for descriptions of the role of NGOs in the development of human rights standards.

10. Holborn, 1975: 125.

11. Ibid: 40.

12. Cited by Nichols: 68.

13. "The Non-Governmental Order," *The Economist,* 11 December (1999).

14. Ibid.

15. United Nations High Commissioner for Refugees, 2000a, *The State of the World's Refugees,* Oxford: Oxford University Press: 194.

16. Vanessa Houlder "Fighting to Be Heard," *Financial Times,* Sept. 20, 2000.

17. Ibid: 194.

18. The Red Cross and Red Crescent Movement have long insisted that they are not non-governmental organizations.

19. Cited by Doug Hellinger, 1987, "NGOs and the Large Aid Donors: Changing the Terms of Engagement," *World Development,* Oxford: Pergamon Press (Autumn): 137.

20. Joseph Hanlon, 1991, *Mozambique: Who Calls the Shots?,* Bloomington: Indiana University Press.

21. Roger Winter, 2000, "The Year in Review," *World Refugee Survey,* Washington: U.S. Committee for Refugees: 24.

22. Tim Brodhead and Brent Herbert-Copley with Anne-Marie Lambert, *Bridges of Hope: Canadian Volunteer Agencies and the Third World,* Ottawa: North-South Institute (1988).

23. Open Society, "Eurasia's Dispossessed: NGOs and Human Security," (www. reliefweb.int/library/documents/eurasia.html) (1999).

24. Brian Smith, 1987, "An Agenda of Future Tasks for International and Indigenous NGOs: Views from the North," *World Development,* Oxford: Pergamon Press: 87.

25. For examples of codes of conduct drawn up by groups of NGOs, see Minear 1988; SCHR 1994; Relief and Rehabilitation Network 1997; InterAction 1996; and Sphere 1998.

26. Sphere Project, 1998, *Humanitarian Charter and Minimum Standards in Disaster Response,* Geneva: Steering Committee for Humanitarian Response and InterAction.

27. UNHCR 2000a: 194.

28. Ibid.

29. Christine Bloch, Jesuit Refugee Service, Interview, Geneva, December 2000.

30. UNHCR "Humanitarian Impact of Funding Shortfall." Mimeo, Geneva November 2002.

31. Cf. Rachel Reilly, 2000, "UNHCR at 50: What Future for Refugee Protection?," *Human Rights Watch Background Paper*, New York: Human Rights Watch.; United Nations High Commissioner for Refugees, 2000b "Note on International Refugee Protection," A/AC.96/930, Geneva: UNHCR, Winter.

32. Reilly: 21.

33. UN Security Council Resolution 1261 (1999).

34. Jean-Christophe Rufin, 2000, "The Economics of War: a New Theory for Armed Conflict," in *ICRC Forum: War, Money, and Survival*: 22–27.

35. Ibid: 23.

36. Mary B. Anderson, 1999, *Do No Harm: How Aid can Support Peace—or War*, Boulder: Lynne Rienner Publishers.; Hugo Slim, "The Continuing Metamorphosis of the Humanitarian Professional: Some New Colours for an Endangered Chamelon," Paper presented at the 1994 Development Studies Association Conference "Challenging the Orthodoxies," Lancaster, UK (September).; Larry Minear and Thomas G. Weiss, 1995, *Mercy Under Fire: War and the Global Humanitarian Community*, Boulder: Westview Press.

37. Cf Thomas G. Weiss, 1996, "NGOs and Internal Conflict," *The International Implications of Internal Conflicts*, Ed. Michael E. Brown, Cambridge: MIT Press: 435–39.

38. Reilly: 4–6.

39. See for example, the annual NGO statements at the UNHCR Executive Committee (ICVA 2000).

40. Larry Minear, 1999, "Partnerships in the Protection of Refugees and Other People at Risk: Emerging Issues and Work in Progress," *UNHCR Working Paper no. 13*, Geneva: UNHCR.

41. World Council of Churches, 2001, "Recommendations of the Amman Process Meeting in Beirut, 12–14 January 2001," Geneva: WCC.

42. Slim 1994: 11.

43. Hugo Slim, September 1997, "Doing the Right Thing: Relief Agencies, Moral Dilemmas and Moral Responsibility in Political Emergencies and War," *Disasters* 21, 3: 4.

44. United Nations High Commissioner for Refugees, 1999b, "Report on the Consultations on Strengthening Collaboration between UNHCR and Humanitarian and Human Rights NGOs in Support of the International Refugee Protection System," Geneva: UNHCR.

Chapter 8
Changing Priorities in Refugee Protection

1. The repatriation exercise was actually announced several days earlier by senior government officials and UNHCR representatives in Karagwe District, which was host to more than 100,000 Rwandan refugees.

2. The country's name was changed to the Democratic Republic of Congo in 1997, after Laurent Kabila overthrew longtime dictator Mobutu Sese Seko.

3. This paper is based on data collected by the author in western Tanzania from October 1996 to August 1998. Funding for the field research was provided by a Fulbright-Hays Doctoral Dissertation Abroad Fellowship, a P.E.O. Scholar Award, and an Institute for the Study of World Politics Doctoral Dissertation Research Fellowship. The support of these institutions is gratefully acknowledged.

4. In October and November 1996, a series of attacks on refugee camps in eastern Zaire forced roughly 600,000 Rwandans to return to their home country.

5. The fact that December 6 was a Friday is important, because most NGOs did not send staff to the camps on Saturdays. Thus, the mass exodus from the camps was not discovered by aid workers until Sunday morning, when Tanzanian police began to make frantic announcements over the communications radio.

6. *The Daily Mail*, November 13, 1998.

7. United Nations High Commissioner for Refugees, 1997, *The State of the World's Refugees: A Humanitarian Agenda*. New York: Oxford University Press.

8. Sadako Ogata, 1997. Remarks at the U.N. Security Council, New York (April 28), available at http://www.unhcr.ch/refworld/unhcr/hcspeech/28ap1997.htm.

9. UNHCR 1997: 80.

10. Marjoleine Zieck, 1997, *UNHCR and Voluntary Repatriation of Refugees: A Legal Analysis*. Boston: Martinus Nijhoff Publishers.

11. UNHCR, 1997: 81.

12. Myron Weiner, 1998, "The Clash of Norms: Dilemmas in Refugee Policies." Paper presented at the Conference on the Growth of Forced Migration: New Directions in Research, Policy and Practice, Refugee Studies Programme, University of Oxford (March 25–27).

13. Agnès Callamard, 1994, "Malawian refugee policy, international politics, and the one-party regime." *Journal of International Affairs* 47, 2: 525–556.

14. Jeff Crisp, 1984, "The Politics of Reptariation: Ethiopian Refugees in Djibouti, 1977–1983." *Review of African Political Economy* 30: 73–82.

15. Andrew Bruce Kendle, 1998, "Protecting whom? The UNHCR in Sri Lanka, 1987–1997." *Round Table* (October).

16. For an examination of UNHCR's involvement in this operation and the extent to which it was voluntary, see Kendle (1998).

17. B. S. Chimni, 1999, "From resettlement to involuntary repatriation: towards a critical history of durable solutions to refugee problems." New Issues in Refugee Research Working Paper #2. Centre for Documentation and Research, United Nations High Commissioner for Refugees.

18. It should be noted, as Chimni (1999) argues, that UNHCR and host governments, rather than refugees themselves, generally determine when conditions in the home country are "safe" for return.

19. Sadako Ogata, 1998, "The future of refugee work (Excerpt of a speech given by the United Nations High Commissioner for Refugees on May 22, 1998)," *Migration World Magazine* 26, 5 (September-October).

20. Chimni, 1999.

21. *Reuters*, September 29, 1996.

22. Aristide R. Zolberg, Astri Suhrke, and Sergio Aguayo, 1989, *Escape from Violence: Conflict and the Refugee Crisis in the Developing World*. New York: Oxford University Press.

23. *The New York Times*, December 21, 1996.

24. Beth Elise Whitaker, 1999, *Disjunctured Boundaries: Refugees, Hosts, and Politics in Western Tanzania*. Doctoral dissertation at the University of North Carolina at Chapel Hill.

25. Mel McNulty, 1999, "The collapse of Zaire: implosion, revolution or external sabotage?" *Journal of Modern African Studies* 37, 1: 53–82.

26. Human Rights Watch. 1997. Democratic Republic of the Congo: What Kabila is Hiding: Civilian Killings and Impunity in Congo. New York: Human Rights Watch.; René Lemarchand, 1998. "Genocide in the Great Lakes: Which Genocide? Whose Genocide?" *African Studies Review* 41, 1 (April): 3–16.

27. If history is any lesson, Tanzania had ample reason to be concerned. In 1972, the Burundi army bombed villages in western Tanzania in retaliation for attacks on its territory by rebel groups operating there.

28. International refugee law actually allows for this eventuality with the "cessation clause." Under this mechanism, refugee status can be withdrawn when fundamental changes have taken place in the refugees' country of origin. The standards for applying this principle are relatively high, however, and were only met in fifteen cases between 1975 and 1996 (UNHCR 1997).

29. See Raimo Väyrynen, 2001, "Funding Dilemmas in Refugee Assistance: Political Interests and Institutional Reforms in UNHCR." *International Migration Review* 35, 1 (Spring): 143–167 for an interesting analysis of the effect of UNHCR funding dilemmas on refugee relief operations. Although alluding to the possibility, the author does not explore the impact of these dilemmas on refugee protection decisions.

30. Tony Waters (*Bureaucratizing the Good Samaritan: The Limitations of Humanitarian Relief Operations*. Boulder: Westview Press, 2001) argues that the international refugee relief regime in Tanzania was unable to adapt its programs to changing funding realities. The bureaucratic dogma of the situation dictated that the Rwandan refugees be fully-supported in densely populated camps; when funding declined, officials were not able or willing to change this approach and promote refugee self-sufficiency.

31. This trend continued in 1999, when the refugee situation in the Balkans caused increasing concern within humanitarian organizations that the plight of refugees in Africa would fade even further from international attention (*The New York Times*, May 9, 1999). By October 1999, donor countries had given UNHCR 90 percent of the money it needed for the Kosovo refugee operation, but only 60 percent of its budget for more than 6 million refugees in Africa (*The Washington Post*, October 8, 1999).

32. Discussion with author, February 16, 1999.

33. Many observers accused the French intervention in Rwanda in July 1994 (*Opération Turquoise*) of allowing perpetrators of genocide to slip out of the country unpunished rather than protecting humanitarian interests. For more on this perspective, see Prunier, Gérard. 1995. *The Rwanda Crisis: History of a Genocide.* New York: Columbia University Press.

34. Arthur C. Helton, 2001, "Book Review: United Nations High Commissioner for Refugees, *The State of the World's Refugees: Fifty Years of Humanitarian Action.*" *International Journal of Refugee Law* 13, 1/2: 269–274.

35. Amnesty International. 1997. *Great Lakes Region Still in Need of Protection: Repatriation, Refoulement and the Safety of Refugees and the Internally Displaced.* London: International Secretariat (January 24).

36. Press release, December 17, 1996.

37. According to one UNHCR official, "The international community . . . never told Tanzania to change its get-tough policy [toward refugees]. In fact, they were told they did the right thing with the Rwandans. So there was no incentive to stop being tough."

38. Augustine Mahiga, 1995, "The United Nations Higher Commissioner for Refugees' Humanitarian Response to the Rwandan Emergency." Paper presented at the International Workshop on the Refugee Crisis in the Great Lakes Region, Arusha, Tanzania (August 16–19).

39. Ben Barber, 1997, "Feeding refugees, or war? The dilemma of humanitarian aid." *Foreign Affairs* 76, 4: 8–14.

40. Eventually, though, the perception of the Rwandan refugees as guilty affected UNHCR's ability to raise funds to support the relief operation (Waters 2001).

41. The International Criminal Tribunal for Rwanda was established in Arusha, Tanzania, by the UN Security Council in November 1994.

42. Discussion with author, February 16, 1999.

43. Burundi in particular has threatened to open up an "eastern front."

44. Sadako Ogata, 1997. Remarks at a conference of the Carnegie Commission on the Prevention of Deadly Conflict, Geneva (February 17), transcript p. 4.

45. James Fennell, 1997, "Hope Suspended: Morality, Politics and War in Central Africa." *Relief and Rehabilitation Network Newsletter* 9 (November).

46. Ibid.

47. Zolberg et al, 1989.

48. In Kenya, UNHCR has provided funding for a local NGO partner to focus on protection issues and ensure that they are not overlooked.

Chapter 9
The Marginalization of Palestinian Refugees

1. I would like to thank a number of people for their suggestions and comments, particularly Gail Boling and Terrence Rempel from Badil and Mark Gibney. I am also grateful for initial comments provided by Gil Loescher, Lex Takkengburg, and Niklaus Steiner. Last but not least, I would like to thank Mr. Matar Saqer, for-

mer Public Information Officer at UNRWA's Headquarters in Amman, Jordan for his invaluable insight into UNRWA's political, social, cultural, and economic history. Conversations and interviews with him over the past few years have provided me with a deeper understanding of the agency.

2. Ernie Ross, MP, Chair of the Joint Parliamentary Middle East Councils Commissions of Enquiry—Palestinian Refugees, Dundee, Scotland, March 9, 2001.

3. *The State of the World's Refugees,* The United Nations High Commissioner for Refugees (UNHCR) 2000: 279. In a report submitted by BADIL Resource Center for Palestinian Residency and Refugee Rights to the Human Rights Inquiry Commission (hereafter, Inquiry Commission), established by the UN Commission on Human Rights (CHR) in 2001, the number of Palestinian refugees is estimated at 5.5 million refugees. The report also posits that: "eighty percent of [refugees] live within 100 km of their villages of origin. Globally, approximately one-in-three refugees are Palestinians." The report concludes that when the internally displaced Palestinians within Israel, the West Bank, and the Gaza Strip and those displaced by the 1967 war are included, the total number of Palestinians displaced or uprooted comprises three-quarters of the Palestinian people.

4. G. Goodwin-Gill, 2000, "Return and Compensation," in *The Final Status Negotiations on the Refugee Issue: Positions and Strategies. Ramallah and Jerusalem:* Department of Refugee Affairs: Palestine Liberation Organization: 43.

5. Edward Said, 1994, *The Politics of Dispossession. The Struggle for Palestinian Self-Determination 1969–1994.* New York: Pantheon Books, 63–64.

6. S. Gazit, 1995, *The Palestinian Refugee Problem,* Jaffee Center for Strategic Studies: Tel Aviv University: 8–10.

7. R. Lapidoth, 2001, "Do Palestinian Refugees Have a Right to Return to Israel?" http://www.mfa.gov.il/mfa/go.asp?MFAH0j8r0.

8. Since its establishment, Israel has attempted to maintain a Jewish majority and Jewish control over the land confiscated from Palestinian Arabs. Thus, the term Israel in this article does not include the viewpoint of Palestinian Arabs who became Israeli citizens. For further information on the Israeli policies of maintaining a demographic Jewish majority, see for example: The Koenig Report (1976) on Handling the Arabs of Israel, Israel, Koenig, Ministry of Interior; Section 1: The Demographic Problem; published in *Swasia* vol. 3 No. 41 (15 October 1976).

9. The New Israeli historians include scholars such as Simha Flapan, Tom Segev, Benny Morris, Avi Shlaim, and Ilan Pappe. Although they differ ideologically and politically, they have contested the official state history propagated in the public arena. Benny Morris was the first to utilize Israeli military archives, which clearly demonstrated the Israeli responsibility for the flight of the Palestinians from their homes and that armed violence was used in the process of eviction. For more information on this subject see Rogan and Shlaim, eds., 2001, *The War for Palestine: Rewriting the History of 1948;* Benny Morris, 1987, *The Birth of the Palestinian Refugee Problem, 1947–1949;* and Ilan Pappe, 1999, *The Israel/Palestine Question Rewriting Histories.* London: Routledge.

10. Established under UNGA 194 (III) on 11 December 1948.

11. The Inquiry Commission (19 October 2000) was established under the terms of the UN Commission on Human Rights Resolution E/CN.4/S-5/1, endorsed by the Economic and Social Council (22 November 2000). The Commission's terms of reference were ". . . to gather and compile information on violations of human rights and acts which constitute grave breaches of international humanitarian law by the Israeli occupying Power in the occupied Palestinian territories and to provide the Commission with its conclusions and recommendations, with the aim of preventing the repetition of the recent human rights violations . . ." The members of the Committee were: Professor Richard Falk, American expert in international law, Princeton University; Dr. Kamal Hossein, former Minister of Bangladesh; and Professor John Dugard, South African international expert on human rights law, Leiden University. The United States also established the Mitchell Fact-Finding Committee following the Sharm al-Shaikh Summit between Israel and the Palestine Liberation Organization (PLO) in October 2000.

12. Since 1972, the U.S. has cast thirty-five vetoes (Security Council) regarding the Arab-Israeli conflict and of these twenty-two relate to the Palestine issue, particularly the situation in the occupied Palestinian territories, including Jerusalem. These vetoes adopted the Israeli position, which had negative repercussions on Palestinian attempts to seek redress from the Security Council following Israeli violations. ("Security Council Resolutions on Palestine Vetoed by the U.S." http://www.pna.org/minfo/cause/un/veto-pal.htm).

13. A. Hourani, 1991, *A History of the Arab Peoples*, Cambridge: Harvard University Press: 316.

14. The Agreement was manuevered by Sir Mark Sykes, under secretary to the British War Cabinet and George Picot of the French Foreign Office. The "agreement was concluded soon after the conclusion of the McMahon/Hussein treaty which stipulated the independence of those Arab territories." Tannous, who served on several international conferences at the time, including UN sessions, noted that "Sir Mark Sykes and George Picot attached a map to the agreement which they marked blue, red and brown. France in the Blue Area (Lebanon and Syria) and Great Britain in the Red Area (Transjordan and Iraq), shall be at liberty to establish such direct administration or control as they may desire . . ." (ibid: 62).

15. Izzat Tannous, 1988, *The Palestinians. A Detailed Documented Eyewitness History of Palestine under British Mandate*, London: I.G.T. Company, 62–63.

16. Balfour quoted in Tannous, 1988: 65.

17. Koestler quoted in "Facts and Figures about Palestinians." The Centre for Policy Analysis on Palestine. Information Paper #1, Washington, DC 1992: 10.

18. T. W. Mallison, 1982, "The United Nations and the National Rights of the People of Palestine," in I. Abu-Lughod ed., *Palestinian Rights Affirmation and Denial*, Wilmette, Ill: Medina Press: 23.

19. Tannous, 1988:107.

20. Mallison, 1992:23.

21. Rashid Khalidi, 2001, "The Palestinians and 1948," in *The War for Palestine*, edited by Eugene Rogan and Avi Shlaim: NY: Cambridge University Press: 19.

Khalidi shows that in stark distinction to the other 'Class A' mandates, which were governed under their British and French commissioners by a Prime Minister in Syria and Lebanon and *amir* (prince) in Transjordan, the Palestinians were not given any significant authority in the British mandatory government. Ibrahim Abu-Lughod ed., *Palestinian Rights: Affirmation and Denial,* Wilmette, IL: Medina Press: 1982.

22. The pro-Zionist policy of the British Mandate was slightly modified following the 1936–39 Palestinian Arab Rebellion. For several reasons, such as Palestinian resistance, British interests and regional politics, Britain (for example, in the 1939 White Paper), attempted to control land transfer to Jews and immigration according to Palestine's absorptive capacity. As a result, Zionist leaders began to turn to the United States, the new emerging power for support. Moreover, the British became targets of Jewish para-military organizations. On November 6, 1944, for example, the Stern Gang, led by Yitzhak Shamir (former Israeli Prime Minister), assassinated the British Minister of State in Cairo, Lord Moyne. Another attack by the Irgun Zvai Leumi, led by Menachim Begin (also was a Prime Minister), blew up the King David Hotel in Jerusalem on July 22, 1946, killing more than a hundred people (Tannous 1988: 336–353).

23. Hadawi, 1979: 44.

24. S. Hadawi, 1976, *Palestine: Loss of Heritage,* San Antonio: The Naylor Company Book Publishers of the Southwest, 24–25.

25. The Haganah was a highly organized underground paramilitary organization of the "Yishuv" or the Jewish immigrants in Palestine. A great deal of its arms were acquired through a "massive, covert arms acquisition" campaign in the West by Ben-Gurion. The Haganah, as the largest Jewish para-military organization, and the predecessor of the Israeli Defence Forces (IDF) after June 1948, was able to purchase "thousands more weapons," or stole these from withdrawing British forces during the first months of the war in 1948. In addition, between October 1947 and July 1948, it had factories producing millions of bullets, as well as sub-machine guns and mortars. See B. Morris, *The Birth of the Palestinian Refugee Problem 1947–1949.* Cambridge: Cambridge University Press 1987.

26. S. Farsoun and C. Zacharia, *Palestine and the Palestinians,* Boulder: Westview Press 1997.

27. E. Rogan and A. Shlaim, eds., *The War for Palestine: Rewriting the History of 1948.* Cambridge: Cambridge University Press 2001.

28. S. Abu-Sitte, 1998, *The Palestinian Nakba 1948.* London: The Palestine Return Center, 1–4.

29. W. Khalidi, ed., 1992, *All That Remains: The Palestinian Villages Occupied and Depopulated by Israel in 1948,* Washington, D.C.: Institute for Palestine Studies: xxxi–xxxii.

30. Admission of Israel to Membership in the United Nations. A/Res/273 (III), May 11, 1949.

31. G.A. Res. 194, U.N. GAOR, 3rd Sess., U.N. Doc. A/810/ (1948).

32. A day after the UN Mediator submitted this report in September, he was assassinated by members of the Jewish Stern Gang, led by Yitzhak Shamir.

33. Progress Report of the UN Mediator on Palestine, U.N. GAOR, Third Sess., supp. No. 11 at 5, U.N. Doc. A/648 (1948).

34. G.A. Res. 194, UN GAOR, Third Sess., U.N. Doc. A/810/ (1948).

35. G. Boling, 2001, *Palestinian Refugees and the Right of Return: An International Law Analysis,* BADIL Brief No.'s 1 and 8, Bethlehem: BADIL Resource Center for Palestinian Residency and Refugee Rights.

36. For a detailed study of the UNCCP, see Terry Rempel 2000, "The United Nations Conciliation Commission for Palestine, Protection, and a Durable Solution for Palestinian Refugees," Issue no. 5, Bethlehem: BADIL Resource Center.

37. E. Zureik, 1996, "Palestinian Refugees in the Arab World: Refugees and the New World Order," in H. Hopfinger and H. Kopp, eds., *Wirkungen von Migrationen auf aufnehmende Gesellschaften,* Neustadt an der Aisch: Verlag Degener & Co., 66–67. The plan consisted of six main elements: (1) To destroy the largest possible number of Arab villages; (2) Prevent Arabs from ever working their deserted land, including sowing and harvesting the fields; (3) Preventing the creation of a "vacuum" by settling Jews in a number of Arab towns and villages; (4) Passing laws to prevent the return of the refugees; (5) Mounting a campaign of propaganda to prevent the return of the refugees; and (6) To help Arab countries absorb the refugees. Ben-Gurion approved all the elements, except for the last one, which was not an Israeli priority at the time.

38. N. Masalha, 1992, *Expulsion of the Palestinians,* Washington, D.C: Institute for Palestine Studies.

39. L.Takkenberg, 1998, *The Status of Palestinian Refugees in International Law.,* Oxford: Clarendon Press: 60.

40. GAOR, fifth sess., third comm. 328 mtg. Para. 52, quoted in Takkenberg, 1998: 62.

41. T. M. Rempel, 2000, *The United Nations Conciliation Commission for Palestine: Protection, and a Durable Solution for Palestinian Refugees.* Brief No. 5. Bethlehem: BADIL Resource Center: 13.

42. Letter and Memorandum dated 22 November 1949 concerning Compensation, received by the Chairman of the Conciliation Commission from Mr. Gordon R. Clapp, United Nations Economic Survey Mission for the Middle East, UN Doc. W/32, 19 January 1950.

43. The areas of operation of UNRWA were Jordan, which included the West Bank until 1967, Gaza, Syria, Lebanon and until 1952 the Agency provided services to refugees within Israel, which included a small number of Jews and for a short time operated in Iraq. Today, the Agency's areas of operation are: Gaza, the West Bank, Jordan, Lebanon and Syria.

44. B. Schiff, 1995, *Refugees Unto the Third Generation: UN Aid to Palestinians.,* New York: Syracuse University Press: 29.

45. Ibid.

46. This is based on a study conducted by the author between 1995–1999 in Palestinian refugee camps in the region, see Ph.D. Thesis submitted to the University of Toronto, 1999 Anthropology Department, titled "Popular Memory and Reconstructions of Palestinian Identity."

47. Takkenberg, 1998: 288.

48. See the 1999–2000 Annual Report by the Commissioner-General, Peter Hansen to the UNGA.
49. See BADIL published reports: www.badil.org.
50. UNRWA HQ, Amman.
51. Takkenberg, 1998: 83. According to Rempel, it is important to question as to what happened to the UNCCP draft definition of a Palestine refugee, which preceded UNRWA, although it was a very broad and non-discriminatory definition (Terry Rempel, personal communications, July 22, 2001).
52. Public Information Office, UNRWA HQ, Amman.
53. "Refugees" are generally identified as those who originate in the territories occupied during the 1948 war and the 'displaced persons' are those who were uprooted during the 1967 war and are the habitual residents of the West Bank and Gaza. In reality, the classifications which are utilized when referring to Palestinian refugees, have in fact added to the confusion surrounding refugees. According to Boling, it is best to refer to the 1967 refugees to distinguish them from those displaced during the 1948 war (personal communication).
54. Takkenberg, 1998: 93.
55. Takkenberg, 1998: 90.
56. BADIL 2001: 6.
57. Susan M. Akram and Guy Goodwin-Gill, 2002, *Brief Amicus Curiae*, United States Department of Justice Executive Office For Immigration Review, Board of Immigration Appeals, Falls Church, Virginia, p. 3.
58. A. Grahl-Madsen, *The Status of Refugees in International Law*, vol. 1, Refugee Character, Leyden, Sijthoff 1966: 247, quoted in Akram and Goodwin-Gill 2002: 40.
59. Akram and Goodwin-Gill 2002: 3.
60. There are exceptions, such as UNHCR 2000, *The State of the World's Refugees*, NY: Oxford University Press, where two pages are dedicated to Palestinian refugees and in which their "exceptionalism" is highlighted.
61. Syria, Lebanon, and Egypt issued refugee documents for Palestinians. In the case cited here, the refugee held a document issued by the Egyptian government. Egypt had administered (not annexed as is the case with Jordan) the Gaza Strip following the 1948 war until it was occupied by Israel during the 1967 war. Since then, Israel has prohibited Palestinians who had been living outside Gaza during the war (such as students and labourers, etc.) from returning. UNRWA refers to refugees from Gaza as the "ex-Gaza refugees."
62. This information is based on interviews with Palestinian asylum seekers in the UK conducted by the author in March and April 2001.
63. Takkenberg, 1998:104–107.
64. Takkenberg, 1998: 101.
65. For more information on this questionnaire, contact info@badil.org.
66. In the Introduction of the Report by the Commissioner General of UNRWA to the General Assembly, A/49/13, 21 September 1994, he states: "The historic developments that took place during the year under review—1 July 1993 to 30 June 1994—had a profound impact on the work and responsibilities of the United Na-

tions Relief and Works Agency for Palestine Refugees in the Near East (UNRWA). With the establishment of the Palestinian Authority in the Gaza Strip and the Jericho area and the anticipated extension of self-rule to the rest of the West Bank, UNRWA entered a new era in its relationship with the Palestinian people. *Thenceforth, in addition to maintaining the services that it had provided for over 40 years, the Agency would soon begin a process of preparing for the eventual hand-over of its installations, services and programmes to the Palestinians in the West Bank and Gaza Strip"* (emphasis added).

67. The Peace Implementation Programme was launched in October, 1993. General Assembly Official Records, Fifty-fifth session, Supplement No. 13 (A/55/13).

68. In the past few months and since the writing of this article, Israel has included UNRWA vehicles and ambulances in its military attacks in Palestinian territories in addition to UNRWA administered camps, schools, clinics, and community centers, obstructing the provision of basic health and relief services, including medicine and food rations to refugees.

69. For more information on the internally displaced Palestinians in Israel, see www.adalah.org.

70. Matthew Lee "Israel Demands Changes to UN Agency for Palestinian Refugees," Agence Franie Presse, 6/26/02.

71. Schiff, 1995: 251.

72. Matthew Lee "Israel Demands Changes to UN Agency for Palestinian Refugees," Agence Franie Presse, 6/26/02.

73. Comment, 'Keeping the UN in Line'. *The Nation,* July 15, 2002. Articles criticizing UNRWA include: Dov B. Fischer, 'The Overseers of Jenin, What exactly is the UN doing in its refugee camps? (with our money)? *The Weekly Standard,* 05/13/2002; Mortimer B. Zuckerman, editor-in-chief, 'A tragic miscalculation', *U.S. News and World Report,* May 20, 2002; AIPAC For the Press, AIPAC Facts: UNRWA Camps Used as Terrorist Strongholds,' May 20, 2002; and, Congressman Eric Cantor, Chairman, 'Task Force on Terrorism and Unconventional Warfare', U.S. House of Representatives, Washington, D.C. May 22, 2002.

74. Takkenberg, 1998: 65–66.

75. This issue was raised by Terry Tempel while communicating with the author.

76. S. Akram, 2001, "Temporary Protected Status and Its Applicability to the Palestinian Case", BADIL Resource Center: www.badil.org.

77. R. Falk, 2001, *Right of Return, Joint Parliamentary Middle East Councils Commissions of Enquiry Palestinian Refugees,* London: Labour Middle East Council, Conservative Middle East Council, Liberal Democrat Middle East Council, 6. Richard Falk authored the introduction only.

Chapter 10
Arguing about Asylum

1. This figure of 15 million refugees does not include "Other People of Concern to UNHCR:" internally displaced people, returnees, war-affected populations, and others groups benefiting from UNHCR's protection and assistance activities. To-

gether, "refugees" and "other people of concern to UNHCR" totaled 27.4 million in 1995. See United Nations High Commissioner for Refugees *The State of the World's Refugees: In Search of Solutions* (Oxford: Oxford University Press, 1995) and United Nations High Commissioner for Refugees, *The State of the World's Refugees: A Humanitarian Agenda* (Oxford: Oxford University Press, 1997).

2. Myron Weiner, 1993, "Introduction: Security, Stability and International Migration," in *International Migration and Security*, ed. Myron Weiner, Boulder, CO: Westview Press: 1. He notes that asylum and migration is overlooked by such standard international relations works such as: Robert Gilpin, 1987, *The Political Economy of International Relations*, Princeton: Princeton University Press; Robert O. Keohane and Joseph Nye, 1977, *Power and Interdependence: World Politics in Transition*, Boston: Little, Brown; Robert O. Keohane, 1984, *After Hegemony: Cooperation and Discord in the World Political Economy*, Princeton: Princeton University Press; Stephen D. Krasner, 1978, *Defending the National Interest: Raw Materials Investment and U.S. Foreign Policy*, Princeton: Princeton University Press; Kenneth Waltz, 1979, *Theory of International Politics*, Reading, MA: Addison-Wesley.

3. For more on this critique of neoliberalism and neorealism, see a new set of literature known variously as "constructivist," "reflectivist," "post-modernist," "interpretivist," "structurationalist," "post-structuralist," and "sociological institutionalist." This literature shares the basic belief that interests are not exogenous to the political process and that norms are not merely intervening variables between interests and behavior. Instead, interests, norms, and behavior are all part of a dynamic environment in which each component affects the others, and each is constantly being interpreted and reinterpreted by actors who are themselves, part of this environment. These claims, which are a significant departure from those of neoliberalism and neorealism, have been fueled by the failures of these conventional theories to explain the dramatic transformation of the international system brought by the end of the Cold War. See, for example, Alexander Wendt, Spring 1992, "Anarchy Is What States Make of It: The Social Construction of Power Politics," *International Organization* 46, 2: 391–426; Peter Katzenstein, ed., 1996, *The Culture of National Security: Norms and Identity in World Politics*, New York: Columbia University Press; Audie Klotz, 1995, *Norms in International Relations: The Struggle against Apartheid*, (Ithaca: Cornell University Press; Cecelia Lynch, 1997, *Beyond Appeasement: Interpreting Inter-War Peace Movements in World Politics*, Ithaca, NY: Cornell University Press; Rey Koslowski and Friedrich Kratochwil, Spring 1994, "Understanding Change in International Politics: The Soviet Empire's Demise and the International System," *International Organization* 48, 2: 215–48; Martha Finnemore, 1996, *National Interests in International Society*, Ithaca: Cornell University Press; Friedrich Kratochwil and John Gerard Ruggie, Autumn 1986, "International Organization: A State of the Art on an Art of the State," *International Organization* 40, 4: 753–76; Friedrich Kratochwil, 1989, *Rules, Norms, and Decisions: On the Conditions of Practical and Legal Reasoning in International Relations and Domestic Affairs*, Cambridge: Cambridge University Press.

4. Andrew E. Shacknove, 1988, "American Duties to Refugees: Their Scope and Limits," in *Open Borders? Closed Societies?*, ed. Mark Gibney, New York: Greenwood Press.

5. Samuel P. Huntington, 1968, *Political Order in Changing Societies*, New Haven: Yale University Press; John C. Harles, 1993, *Politics in the Lifeboat: Immigrants and the American Democratic Order*, Boulder, CO: Westview Press.

6. Alan Dowty, 1989, *Closed Borders: The Contemporary Assault on Freedom of Movement*, New Haven: Yale University Press.

7. For more on asylum in the Cold War see, for example, Gil Loescher and John A. Scanlan, 1986, *Calculated Kindness: Refugees and America's Half-Open Door, 1945 to the Present*, New York: Free Press; Kim Salomon, 1991, *Refugees in the Cold War*, Lund: Lund University Press.

8. Daniéle Joly, 1996, *Haven or Hell?: Asylum Policies and Refugees in Europe*, New York: St. Martin's Press; Zig Layton-Henry, 1992, *The Politics of Immigration: Immigration, 'Race' and 'Race' Relations in Post-War Britain*, Oxford: Blackwell; Marilyn B. Hoskin, 1991, *New Immigrants and Democratic Society: Minority Integration in Western Democracies*, New York: Praeger.

9. Gil Loescher, 1989, "Introduction," in Gil Loescher and Laila Monahan, eds., *Refugees and International Relations*, Oxford: Oxford University Press; Sarah Collinson, 1993, *Beyond Borders: West European Migration Policy Towards the 21st Century*, London: Royal Institute of International Affairs; Andrew Shacknove, 1993, "From Asylum to Containment," *International Journal of Refugee Law* 5, 4: 516–33; Daniéle Joly and Robin Cohen, eds., 1989, *Reluctant Hosts: Europe And Its Refugees*, Aldershot, England: Avebury; Daniéle Joly, 1996, *Haven Or Hell?: Asylum Policies And Refugees In Europe*, New York: St. Martin's Press.

10. While relatively little has been written on refugees in Europe, much good work has dealt with immigrants and guest workers in Europe. See, for example, James Hollifield, 1992, *Immigrants, Markets, and States: The Political Economy of Postwar Europe*, Cambridge, MA: Harvard University Press; Mark Miller, 1981, *Foreign Workers in Western Europe: An Emerging Political Force*, New York: Praeger; Tomas Hammar, ed., 1985, *European Immigration Policy: A Comparative Study*, Cambridge: Cambridge University Press; Zig Layton-Henry, 1990, *The Political Rights of Migrant Workers in Western Europe*, London: Sage Publications; Rosemarie Rogers, ed., 1985, *Guests Come to Stay*, Boulder, CO: Westview Press; Rogers Brubaker, ed., 1989, *Immigration and the Politics of Citizenship in Europe and North America*, Lanham, MD: University Press for America; Hans-Joachim Hoffmann-Nowotny, 1973, *Soziologie des Fremdarbeiterproblems: Eine Theoretische und Empirische Analyse am Beispiel der Schweiz*, Stuttgart: Ferdinand Enke Verlag; Daniel Kubat, ed., 1993, *The Politics of Migration Policies*, 2nd ed., New York: Center for Migration Studies; Stephen Castles and Godula Kosack, 1985, *Immigrant Workers and Class Structure in Western Europe*, 2nd ed., Oxford: Oxford University Press. On making the distinction between refugees and immigrants, see Gil Loescher, ed., 1992, *Refugees and the Asylum Dilemma in the West*, University Park, PA: Pennsylvania State University Press; Elizabeth, G. Ferris, 1993, *Beyond Borders: Refugees, Migrants and Human Rights in the Post-Cold War*

Era Geneva: WCC Publications; Mary M. Kritz, Lin Lean Lim, and Hania Zlotnik, eds., 1992, *International Migration Systems: A Global Approach*, Oxford: Clarendon Press; Sarah Collinson, 1993, *Beyond Borders: West European Migration Policy towards the 21st Century*, London: Royal Institute of International Affairs.

11. Alasdair Mackensie represents this anti-government position when he argues in *New Statesman and Society* (12/8/1995), "Refugee advisers agree that the overwhelming majority of asylum-seekers is sincere. If anyone is abusing the system, it is not refugees, but the government."

12. Article 33 of the 1951 Refugee Convention states: "No Contracting State shall expel or return ('*refouler*') a refugee in any manner whatsoever to the frontiers of territories where his life or freedom would be threatened on account of his race, religion, nationality, membership of a particular social group or political opinion."

13. For more on these international asylum norms, see, for example, Guy S. Goodwin-Gill, 1983, *The Refugee In International Law*, Oxford: Clarendon Press; Atle Grahl-Madsen, 1985, *The Emergent International Law Relating To Refugees: Past, Present, Future*, Bergen: University of Bergen Law Faculty; Richard Plender, 1990, *The Right Of Asylum*, Dordrecht, NL: Martinus Nijhoff; Jack Donnelly, 1993, *International Human Rights*, Boulder, CO: Westview Press; Erika Feller, 1989, "Carrier Sanctions And International Law," *International Journal of Refugee Law* 1, 1: 48–66; Kay Hailbronner, 1988, "Nonrefoulement And 'Humanitarian' Refugees: Customary International Law Or Wishful Legal Thinking?," in *The New Asylum Seekers*, ed. David A. Martin, Dordrecht, NL: Martinus Nijhoff Publishers; Kay Hailbronner, 1990, "The Right To Asylum And The Future Of Asylum Procedures In The European Community," *International Journal of Refugee Law* 2, 3: 341–60; James C. Hathaway, 1988, "International Refugee Law: Humanitarian Standard Or Protectionist Ploy," in *Human Rights And The Protection Of Refugees Under International Law*, ed. Alan E. Nash, Halifax, Nova Scotia: Institute for Research on Public Policy; James C. Hathaway, 1991, *The Law Of Refugee Status*, Toronto: Butterworths; Claudena M. Skran, 1995, *Refugees in Inter-War Europe: The Emergence of a Regime*, New York: Oxford University Press.

14. For more on this conception of morality, see Hans-Balz Peter, 1995 "Die Internationale Sozialpolitik und der Weltsozialgipfel 1995—Sozialethische Perspektive," Referat im Rahmen der Tagung *Weltsozialgipfel 1995: Gute Nachrichten für die Armen?* gemeinsam veranstaltet von der Kammer für Kirchlichen Entwicklungsdienst der Evangelischen Kirche in Deutschland und der Wissenschaflichen Arbeitsgruppe für weltkirchliche Aufgaben der Deutschen Bischofskonferenz, Bonn, Januar 1995.

15. For more on morality and asylum, see for example Elizabeth Ferris, 1993, *Beyond Borders: Refugees, Migrants and Human Rights in the Post-Cold War Era*, Geneva: WCC Publications; Robert F. Gorman, 1993, *Mitigating Misery: An Inquiry Into The Political And Humanitarian Aspects Of U.S. And Global Refugee Policy*, Lanham, MD: University Press of America; John H. Elliott, 1985, "The Bible From The Perspective Of The Refugee," in *Sanctuary*, ed. Gary MacEoin (San Francisco: Harper & Row; Joseph H. Carens, 1992, "Migration And Morality: A Lib-

eral Egalitarian Perspective," in *Free Movement,* ed. Brian Barry, and Robert E. Goodin, University Park, PA: Pennsylvania State University Press; Francis X. Sutton, 1987, "Refugees And Mass Exoduses: The Search For A Humane, Effective Policy," in *Population In An Interacting World,* ed. William Alonso, Cambridge: Harvard University Press; Peter Singer and Renata Singer, 1988, "The Ethics Of Refugee Policy," in *Open Borders? Closed Societies?,* ed. Mark Gibney, New York: Greenwood Press.

16. For more on the difference between explaining and understanding, see Martin Hollis and Steve Smith, 1990, *Explaining and Understanding International Relations,* Oxford: Clarendon Press.

17. In the German case, I read the debates surrounding the 1978 *Gesetz zur Beschleunigung des Asylverfahrens,* the 1980 *Zweites Gesetzes zur Beschleunigung des Asylverfahrens,* the 1986 *Gesetz zur Aenderung asylverfahrensrechtlicher, arbeitserlaubnisrechtlicher und ausländerrechtlicher Vorschriften,* and the 1993 *Gesetz zur Aenderung des Grundgesetzes (Artikle 16 und 18)* as transcribed in *Verhandlungen des Deutschen Bundestages, Stenographische Berichte* (Bonn: Bonner Universitaets-Buchdruckerei, various years) and *Verhandlungen des Deutschen Bundesrates, Stenographische Berichte* (Bonn: Bonner Universitaets-Buchdruckerei, various years). In the Swiss case, I read the debates over the 1979 *Asylgesetz,* the 1986 *Asylgesetz Revision,* and the 1994 *Zwangsmassnahmen im Ausländerrecht,* as transcribed in *Amtliches Bulletin der Bundesversammlung, Nationalrat,* (Bern: Sekretariat der Bundesversammlung, various years) and *Amtliches Bulletin der Bundesversammlung, Ständerat,* (Bern: Sekretariat der Bundesversammlung, various years). In the British case, there were no significant asylum debates until the mid-1980s, so I read the debates surrounding the 1987 *Immigration (Carriers' Liability) Act* and the 1993 *Asylum and Immigration Appeal Act,* as transcribed in *Parliamentary Debates (Hansard), House of Commons Official Report,* (London: H. M. Stationary Office, various years). Each of these parliamentary debates resulted in tighter asylum legislation, except for the 1979 Swiss debate, which loosened asylum.

18. *House of Commons,* v111: 740.
19. *Bundestag,* 1993: 13506.
20. *Bundestag,* 1993: 13512.
21. *Bundestag,* 1993: 13509.
22. *Bundestag,* 1993: 13534.
23. *Bundestag,* 1993: 13519; 11603.
24. *House of Commons,* v112: 729.
25. *House of Commons,* v112: 723.
26. *Nationalrat,* 1994: 89.
27. *Nationalrat,* 1994: 87.
28. *Nationalrat,* 1986: 724.
29. *House of Commons,* v112: 730.
30. *Ständerat,* 1994: 112.
31. *House of Commons,* v213: 106.
32. *Bundestag,* 1993: 13516.
33. *Nationalrat,* 1994: 150.

34. *Nationalrat*, 1994: 81.

35. On Britain's poor wartime refugee policy, see for example Bernard Wasserstein, 1979, *Britain And The Jews Of Europe 1939–1945*, Oxford: Clarendon Press; Michael R. Marrus, 1985, *The Unwanted: European Refugees In the Twentieth Century*, Oxford: Oxford University Press; Colin Holmes, 1991, *A Tolerant Country? Immigrants, Refugees And Minorities In Britain*, London: Faber and Faber; Tony Kushner, 1989, *The Persistence Of Prejudice: Anti-Semitism In British Society During The Second World War*, Manchester: Manchester University Press.

36. *Bundestag*, 1978: 7371.

37. *Bundestag*, 1985: 12213.

38. *Bundestag*, 1985: 12220–1.

39. *Bundestag*, 1993: 13600.

40. *Ständerat*, 1994: 123.

41. *House of Commons*, v213: 45.

42. *Nationalrat*, 1986: 266.

43. For a good overview of this debate, see Christian Joppke, ed., 1998, *Challenge to the Nation-State: Immigration in Western Europe and the United States*, Oxford: Oxford University Press.

44. See, for example, David Jacobson, 1996, *Rights across Borders*, Baltimore, MD: Johns Hopkins University Press; Saskia Sassen, 1996, *Losing Control? Sovereignty in an Age of Globalization*, New York: Columbia University Press; Yasemin Soysal, 1994, *Limits to Citizenship: Migrants and Postnational Membership in Europe*, Chicago: Chicago University Press; Wayne Cornelius, Philip Martin, and James Hollifield, eds., 1994, *Controlling Immigration: A Global Perspective*, Stanford: Stanford University Press.

45. Gary Freeman, 1998, "The Decline of Sovereignty? Politics and Immigration Restrictions in Liberal States," in *Challenge to the Nation-State: Immigration in Western Europe and the United States*, ed. Christian Joppke, Oxford: Oxford University Press.

46. For more on domestic constraints see, for example, Christian Joppke, June 1997, "Asylum and State Sovereignty," *Comparative Political Studies* 30, 3; Christian Joppke, January 1998, "Why Liberal States Accept Unwanted Immigration," *World Politics* 50; Gary Freeman, Winter 1995, "Modes of Immigration Politics in Liberal States," *International Migration Review* 29, 4; Gary Freeman, July 1994, "Can Liberal States Control Unwanted Migration," *Annals of the American Academy of Political and Social Science* 534.

47. Gary Freeman, 1998, "The Decline of Sovereignty? Politics and Immigration Restrictions in Liberal States," in *Challenge to the Nation-State: Immigration in Western Europe and the United States*, ed. Christian Joppke, Oxford: Oxford University Press.

48. Christian Joppke, January 1998, "Why Liberal States Accept Unwanted Immigration," *World Politics* 50.

49. Gary Freeman, Winter 1995, "Modes of Immigration Politics in Liberal States," *International Migration Review* 29, 4; Christian Joppke, January 1998, "Why Liberal States Accept Unwanted Immigration," *World Politics* 50.

50. Christian Joppke, "Why Liberal States Accept Unwanted Immigration," *World Politics* 50 (January 1998).
51. Bundestag, 1978: 7373; House of Commons v 112 p. 738.
52. *House of Commons*, v112: 769; v113: 628.
53. Bundestag, 1993: 13512; House of Commons

Chapter 11
Post-Conflict Reintegration and Reconstruction

1. The annual UNDP *Human Development Reports* elaborate and measure these factors.
2. Peter Uvin, 1999, *The Influence of Aid in Situations of Violent Conflict,* Synthesis Paper on lessons learned from Case Studies on Limits and Scope for the use of Development Assistance Incentives and Disincentives for Influencing Conflict Situations: OECD, Development Assistance Committee.
3. UNDP, Evaluation Office, January 2000, *Sharing New Ground in Post-Conflict Situations: The Role of UNDP in Support of Reintegration Programmes,* New York: 5.
4. UNHCR, September 1999, *A Practical Guide to Capacity Building as a Feature of UNHCR's Humanitarian Programmes,* Geneva: 10.
5. These are micro projects undertaken by communities heavily populated by repatriates, and involving collective decision making and involvement. They are short-term and very modestly funded, with no built-in follow-up mechanisms.
6. UNHCR, June 1996, "Mozambique: An Account from a Lessons Learned Seminar on Reintegration," Geneva: 3.
7. UNHCR, 1999: 7.
8. Ibid: 10.
9. The name, (translated) Conference on Refugees of Central America, derived from the conference where the plan was determined, in 1989.
10. Development Program for Refugees, Displaced Persons and Repatriates.
11. Farabundo Marti National Liberation Front.
12. The fact that both the UN appointed Special Representative who headed ONUSAL and the Head of UNDP were in different ways the leaders of the United Nations programs in El Salvador created difficulties. Further, the beneficiary population of UNHCR and PRODERE programs tended to overlap.
13. The IFIs did not at first share the vision. The structural adjustment programs on which they insisted essentially obliged the government to choose between meeting the demands for restrained public spending or violating these demands in order to fund the promised peace programs. The government was more than willing to choose the former, bestowing on the international community the responsibility for funding the peace programs. (Alvaro de Soto and Graciana del Castillo, Spring 1995, "Obstacles to Peacebuilding," *Foreign Policy,* no. 94.) The criticism of this approach in El Salvador and elsewhere, however, had a salutary effect in raising the debate within the World Bank and leading that institution not only to modify its approach but to take stronger leadership roles subse-

quently in post conflict reconstruction programs. A special Post-Conflict Unit was later created for these purposes.

14. Cambodia signed a peace agreement in October 1992 that gave the UN mission, UNTAC, far greater authority in governing the country, but it left the country precipitously after the May 1993 elections.

15. William Stanley and Charles T. Call, 1997, "Building a New Civilian Police Force in El Salvador," *Rebuilding Societies after Civil War,* Krishna Kumar, ed, Boulder, Colo.: Lynne Reinner Publishers.

16. Margaret Popkin, 2000, *Peace Without Justice: Obstacles to Building the Rule of Law in El Salvador,* Pennsylvania State University Press: chapter 6.

17. What was hoped to be a definitive peace accord between the then Hutu government of Rwanda and the Rwandan Patriotic Front (RPF) opposition was signed in Arusha, Tanzania in August 1993. The accords led to the deployment of a UN mission, UNAMIR, to the return of large numbers of exiled Tutsis and, most important, to an increased level of activities by militant extremists among the Hutus.

18. USAID, July 1996, *Rebuilding Postwar Rwanda, The Role of the International Community,* Evaluation Special Study Report No. 76, Washington, DC: 7.

19. These were Tutsis who began leaving the country in 1959. In 1990 they had mounted an armed offensive to return that was foiled by the Hutu dominated army, but led to the Arusha negotiations and peace accord. Some 700,000 in this group finally did return with the RPF victory.

20. Sue Lautze, Bruce Jones and Mark Duffield, 1998, "Stategic Humanitarian co-ordination in the GreatLakes Region 1997–1997," An Independent Assessment for the UN Department of Humanitarian Affairs, New York: 1998.

21. UNDP mounted a pledging roundtable conference in January, 1995.

22. Danish Ministry of Foreign Affairs, March 2001, *Donor Response in Conflict-Affected Countries: Implementation Partnerships in Rwanda,* Issues Paper; OECD, Development Assistance Committee, Task Force on Conflict Peace and Development Cooperation, June 1999, Anton Baare, David Shearer, Peter Uvin with Christian Scherrer, *The Limits and Scope for the Use of Development Assistance Incentives and Disincentives for Influencing Conflict Situations, Case Study: Rwanda*: 14.

23. There have been local level elections, however.

24. UN General Assembly, 17 September 1999 A/54/359, *Situation of Human Rights in Rwanda,* Report prepared by the Special Representative of the Commission on Human Rights, 54th Session.; OECD/DAC, 1999.

25. Amnesty International expressed strong reservations and urged the international community to monitor the trials assiduously. Press Release June 19 2002. Reference AFR 47/003/2002.

26. OECD/DAC, 1999; Iain Guest, 1998, "Protection Information in the Great Lakes." Report prepared for the UNHCR and furnished by the author. The UNDP has coordinated a number of governance projects, but these areas did not receive major donor funding.

27. UNHCR, 2000.

28. Building some 177,000 houses at a cost of nearly US$184 million (Danish Ministry of Foreign Affairs, March 2001: 10.)

29. UNOCHA, December 1, 2000. UNOCHA estimated 1.5 million people in Rwanda live in a refugee-like situation.

30. UN General Assembly, 1999.; OECD/DAC, 1999.; Guest, 1998.; Danish Ministry of Foreign Affairs, March 2001. Human Rights Watch has been particularly critical of the manner in which relocations are carried out.

31. OECD/DAC, 1999: 27.

32. OECD/DAC, 1999; Guest, 1998; Philip Gourevitch, 1997, *We Wish to Inform You that Tomorrow We Will Be Killed With Our Families,* New York: Farrar, Straus and Giroux.

33. That year the results of a multi donor evaluation of international responses criticized the latter: It blamed the limited effectiveness of assistance on "lack of in-depth knowledge of the historical, political, social and economic context of the crisis;" and for its failure "to provide adequate support for the government." And, reminiscent of El Salvador, the evaluation criticized World Bank policies on grounds that: "conditionality on economic restructuring exacerbated social tensions and undermined efforts to improve human rights through political conditionality." (World Bank, 1998, *Post-Conflict Reconstruction: The Role of the World Bank,* Washington, DC: 22.)

34. OECD/DAC, 1999: 29,

35. A 1999 UNHCR-UNDP-World Bank initiative to better coordinate donors in moving from relief to development. UNHCR was especially concerned that smoother transitions would follow its departure.

36. The participants, as of March 2001 included: UNDP, UNHCR, Denmark, Germany, UK, Japan, Sweden, and USAID.

37. Danish Ministry of Foreign Affairs, March 2001: 9.

38. Ibid: 9.

39. UN General Assembly, 1999.

40. UNHCR estimated 2,000 returnees from the DRC as of April 2002. "Rwanda: Interview with UNHCR representative Kalunga Lutato, 24 May 2002, (*reliefWeb: UN/OCHA*).

41. UNHCR, November 1998, *Evaluation and Policy Analysis: Review of the UNHCR Housing Programme in Bosnia and Herzegovina,* by Walter Irvine.

42. OECD, DAC, Task Force on Conflict, Peace and Development Cooperation, June 1999(b), Nicola Dahrendorf and Hrair Balian, *The Limits and Scope for the Use of Development Assistance and Disincentives for Influencing Conflict Situations: Case Study: Bosnia,* Paris: 13.

43. Ibid: 14.

44. Article 1 (2).

45. Ian Smillie, 1998, *Relief and Development: The Struggle for Synergy,* Occasional Paper #33, Thomas J. Watson Jr. Institte for International Studies, Providence, RI: 12–16.; U.S. Institute of Peace, December 21, 1999, "Balkan Returns: An

Overview of Refugee Returns and Minority Repatriation," Special Report, Washington, DC: 7–8.

46. Total refugee returns from all countries during 1977 were 60,257 and during 1998 90,503, according to IOM figures: www.iom.int. Those from Germany represented by far the largest group.

47. Sandra Coliver, 2000, "The Contribution of the International Criminal Tribunal for the Former Yugoslavia to Reconciliation in Bosnia and Herzegovina: Lessons for the International Criminal Court," *International Crimes, Peace and Human Rights: The Role of the International Criminal Court*, Dinah Shelton, ed, Transnational Publishers, Inc.

48. For example by requiring that owners reclaim the property within a few days of the end of the war.

49. UNHCR figures derived from local reporting of property claims and repossessions, as of 7/02.

50. UNHCR figures as of August 2002 reported a total of some 880,000 repatriations from the end of the war. Associated Press, August 6, 2002.

51. Quoted in a Reuters report of December 4, 2000.

52. Ibid.

53. U.S. Department of State, PRM, Fact Sheet, September 4, 2002.

54. A Swiss project will devote funds to closing the collective centers, with priority for Serbia.

55. FRELIMO (the present government) and RENAMO (now a political opposition party) in Mozambique; the Guatemalan government and the URNG (former guerrilla forces) in Guatemala.

56. UNHCR, 1996: 6.

57. UNHCR, 1996.

58. Interviews in November, 1999 with UNHCR officials who formerly served in Mozambique.

59. Interview with person who wished to remain anonymous, 2000.

60. UNHCR, 1996.

61. Sam Barnes, 2000, "International Assistance and Incentives for Peace: The Case of Mozambique," presented to the Bergen Seminar on Development 2000, March 27–29, 2000, Bergen, Norway.

62. Ibid.

63. A 1994 Swiss Cooperation water project in Gaza Department is one of the few that survived. It was turned over to the national Railroad Association for implementation, with Swiss financial support. The fact that a government entity took responsibility for it from the outset, according to the donors, assured its durability Interview Mr. Gregor Binkert, formerly Swiss representative in Mozambique, February 2001.

64. OECD/DAC, 1997, *Conflict, Peace and Development Cooperation of the Threshold of the 21at Century*, binding. In the Balkan region the "Stability Pact" has proved to be a fairly effective inter-government entity to set priorities, guide donor actions, and mobilize funding.

Chapter 12
Securing Refuge from Terror

1. In February of 2002, the U.S. sought Kenyan basis to support the launching of attacks on alleged al-Qaeda cells in Somalia. The request was granted by presidential consent.

2. Since 1995, Sudan has been blacklisted as a terrorist-sponsoring state following its refusal to extradite Islamic fundamentalist agents, accused of attempting to assassinate the Egyptian President, Hosni Mubarak. Reacting to this, the United Nations Security Council passed Res. 1044, Res. 1054 and Res. 1070 (all in 1996), censuring Sudan for sponsoring Islamic "fundamentalist" groups from the Middle East.

3. In August 1998, terrorists bombed U.S. embassies in Kenya and Tanzania, killing more than 200 people and maiming over 4,000 others.

4. After the terrorist attack on the U.S. in 2001, Kenya's President Moi personally led a historic demonstration against terrorism and has since offered unequivocal support, including the use of Kenya's territory and military facilities, to the coalition against terrorism. These military facilities are offered under an existing agreement on base rights, which permits the United States to land large transport aircraft at twenty-four hours notice, and use Mombasa as a port stop for U.S. Navy personnel. Under this agreement, signed in 1970, the U.S. has maintained military access agreements with the Kenyan government that permit use of Kenyan sea and air bases. These facilities were used extensively in administering humanitarian assistance to Somalia in the early 1990s, to post-1994 Rwanda, and to Sudan. Mombasa was also used as a port of call for U.S. carriers during the Gulf War. See Joel Barkan and Jennifer G. Cooke, 2001, "US Policy Toward Kenya in the Wake of September 11: Can New Antiterrorist Imperatives Be Reconciled with Enduring US Foreign Policy Goals?" Centre for Strategic and International Studies, Washington D.C.

5. See Amnesty International, 1997, *In Search of Safety: The Forcibly Displaced and Human Rights in Africa*. London: Amnesty International.

6. See Jeff Crisp, 2000, "A State of Insecurity: The Political Economy of Violence in Kenya's Refugee Camps" *African Affairs* vol. 99: 601–632.

7. Monica K. Juma, 2000, "The Politics of Humanitarian Assistance: The State, Non-State Actors and Displacement in Kenya and Uganda,1989–1998," D. Phil Thesis, Oxford: 175–181.

8. See Gulgielmo Verdirame, 1999, "Human Rights and Refugees: The Case of Kenya," *Journal of Refugee Studies*. vol. 12, No. 1. 54–77.

9. See Marc-Antoine Perouse de Montclos, 2001, "Elections Among the Kenya Somali: A Conservative But Marginalized Vote" in *Out for the Count: The 1997 General Elections and Prospects for Democracy in Kenya* (eds.) M. Rutten, A. Mazrui, and F. Grignon. Kampala: Fountain Press: 296–314.

10. Refugee assistance and protection has been highly targeted and concentrated in camps located among deprived communities such as the Turkana, Somalis and

Acholi, making them islands in oceans of poverty. This has increased competition and envy between refugees and host communities.

11. Somalis are divided into six major clan-families: Hawiye, the Issaq, the Dir, the Digil, the Darod, and the Rahawayn occupying parts of Ethiopia, Djibouti, and Kenya and predominantly in Somalia.

12. At independence, Kenya's Somalis voted to secede and join the "Greater Somalia." This culminated in the *Shifta* (bandit) war (1964–67). After losing this war, Kenyan Somalis were exposed to years of institutional discrimination, marginalization, and a general pattern of communal punishment under the emergency law, which lasted until 1991 when it was lifted. See Kathurima M'Inoti, 1992, "Beyond Emergency in North Eastern Province: An Analysis of the Use of Emergency Powers," *Nairobi Law Monthly* no. 41.

13. See footnote no. 61 in Monica K. Juma, Ibid: 154.

14. One of such tragic incidences involved an attack on the Acholi Pii refugee settlement in 1996, which left eighty-six refugees dead and property worth millions of shillings razed to the ground. See Monica K. Juma, Ibid: 306.

15. Binaifir Nowrojee, 2000, *In the Name of Security: Erosion of Refugee Rights in East Africa*. U.S. Committee for Refugees. October 2000: 1.

16. See Bonaventure Rutinwa (forthcoming), "Addressing Humanitarian Problems Through Regional Organisations: The Potential Role of the East African Community" in Monica Kathina Juma and Astri Suhrke, (eds.) *Eroding Local Capacity: The Nature and Consequences of Humanitarian Assistance*. Uppsala: African Nordic Institute; "EAC Refugees: A Responsibility for All Member States" *Refugee Insights*, vol 1 April, 2001: 6.

17. Monica K. Juma, op. cit.: 177.

18. Gil Loescher, 2001, "UNHCR and the Erosion of Refuee Protection," *Forced Migration Review*, no. 10: 29.

19. Of the three East African countries, Kenya has the largest resettlement quota of approximately 4,000 refugees annually. Uganda and Tanzania have no quota and benefit from resettlement only when specially deserving cases are identified.

20. So far, the investigation has exposed the existence of a cartel involving refugees, UNHCR current and former staff and resettled refugees in the diaspora.

21. In Kenya, mobile courts operate in the Dadaab camp complex and Kakuma, and since they were established in the mid-1990s, poor staffing and irregular scheduling have hindered effective operation.

22. Gulgielmo Verdirame, 1999, Ibid. p. 62–63.

23. Peter Kagwanja, "Subjects of the Good Samaritan: 'Traditional' Culture and Refugee Protection in the Kenyan Camps" in *Politique Africaine*, 2002; G. Verdirame, op. cit.

24. "Dadaab: The Nightmare Won't End" *Refugee Insights*, No. 1, 2001: 3; Refugee Consortium of Kenya, "Kakuma Camp-Refugee camp or Recruitment Ground?" in *Refugee Insights*, no. 1, April 2001: 13.

25. Proscribed by UNHCR in the mid-1990s, the term is used by humanitarian agencies to describe refugees that move back and forth between camps, their coun-

tries of origin, and other countries. The introduction of fingerprinting and photographs in the documentation of refugee arrivals within the region in the late 1990s was aimed at stemming this "irregular" movement of refugees and asylum seekers.

26. Jelvas Musau, 2001, "Protecting Refugees in Dadaab: Processes, Problems and Prospects," *Forced Migration Review*, no. 11: 36.
27. See Joel Barkan and Jennifer G. Cooke, ibid.: 1–2.
28. M. P. de Montclos, and P. M. Kagwanja, 2000, "Refugee Camps or Cities: The Socio-economic Dynamics of the Dadaab and Kakuma Camps in Northern Kenya" *Journal of Refugee Studies*, vol. 13, no. 2: 205–222; Joel Barkan and Jennifer Cooke.
29. Marc-Antoine Perous de Montclos, 2002, "A Refugee Diaspora: When the Somali Go West," in Khalid Koser, ed. *New African Diasporas*, London: Routledge.
30. Interview with a Dadaab based Somali Councilor in Garissa, February 28, 2002 (anonymity requested).
31. UNHCR BO in Nairobi vehemently denies the view that terrorist elements might be in the camps in Kenya. Yet, it is consulting with its partners and preparing to receive a possible influx of refugees from Somalia. Interview with a UNHCR Official in Nairobi, March 29, 2002.
32. Gil Loescher, "UNHCR at Fifty: Refugee Protection and World Politics," chapter one of this volume.
33. The first of its kind, the draft protocol was sponsored by EAC and IGAD in June 2001.

Chapter 13
Refugee Protection in Europe and the U.S. after 9/11

1. See e.g., O. Waever, B. Buzan, M. Kelstrup, and P. Lemaitre, 1993, *Identity, Migration and the New Security Agenda in Europe*, London: Pinter.
2. J. van Selm, 2000, "Introduction" *Kosovo's Refugees in the European Union*, London: Continuum.
3. See M. Frost in Newman, E. and J. van Selm, *Refugees and Forced Displacement: International Security, Human Vulnerability and the State*. Tokyo: UN University Press 2003.
4. 'Farewell, Londonistan?' January 31, 2002 *The Economist* (print edition)
5. Joanne van Selm, 1998, "Asylum in the Amsterdam Treaty: a harmonious future?," *Journal of Ethnic and Migration Studies*, vol. 24, no. 4; and Pieter Boeles, 2001, "Introduction: Freedom, Security and Justice for All," in E. Guild and C. Harlow, eds. *Implementing Amsterdam: Immigration and Asylum rights un EC Law*, Oxford: Hart.
6. Proposal for a Council Framework decision on combating terrorism (19.9.2001) COM(2001) 521 final 2001/0217 (CNS). Similarly, the reports issued by the European Parliament on terrorism, both in July 2001, so prior to 9/11, and after 9/11 do not dwell on either immigration of refugee issues. Report on the role of

the European Union in combating terrorism (2001/2016(INI)) Committee on Citizens' Freedoms and Rights, Justice and Home Affairs, Rapporteur: Graham R. Watson European Parliament final A5–0273/2001 12 July 2001.

7. Common Position of 27 December 2001 on the application of specific measures to combat terrorism (2001/931/CFSP) OJ L 344/93 28.12.2001.

8. Conclusions adopted by the Council (Justice and Home Affairs) Brussels, 20 September 2001 SN 3926/6/01.

9. Conclusions adopted by the Council (Justice and Home Affairs) Brussels, 20 September 2001 SN 3926/6/01.

10. Commission of the European Communities, Commission Working Document: The relationship between safeguarding internal security and complying with international protection obligations and instruments, COM(2001) 743 final, Brussels, 05.12.2001: 1.

11. Ibid.: 1.

12. Ibid.

13. See Article 1F of the 1951 Convention Relating to the Status of Refugees, set out above.

14. Ibid.: 1.4 and 1.5.

15. Ibid.: 2.1 and 2.2.

16. See also on UNHCR above.

17. Commission of the European Communities, "Report from the Commission: Overview of EU action in response to the events of 11 September and assessment of their likely economic impact," Brussels, 17.10.2001 COM(2001) 611.

18. Humanitarian response to the Afghan Crisis, Memo/01/2001 18 October 2001.

19. Statement on humanitarian situation in Afghanistan and the region European Parliament Plenary Session Strasbourg, 2 October 2001, SPEECH/01/431. The figures cited total to 24 million which does not match the 22.5 million indicated in the Commission paper.

20. Commission of the European Communities, "Report: economic impact," op. cit.

21. See broadly J. van Selm, 2002, "Immigration and Asylum or Foreign Policy: The EU's Approach to Migrants and Their Countries of Origin" in S. Lavenex and E. Uçarer, eds., *Migration and the Externalities of European Integration*, Lexington Books. Lanham, Maryland.

22. Common Position of 27 December 2001 on combating terrorism (2001/930/CFSP)—Act adopted pursuant to Title V of the Treaty on European Union.

23. Article 6 (EU Common Position) and 2(c) Security Council Resolution.

24. Article 10 (EU) 2(g) SC.

25. Article 16 (EU) and 3(f) SC.

26. Article 17 (EU) and 3(g) SC.

27. "UK's surveillance dilemma" BBC News 27 September 2001 www.news. bbc. co.uk.

28. Ibid.

29. See Labour Party website www.labour.org.uk.

30. Alan Travis, "UK to intern terrorist suspects," *The Guardian*, 16 October, 2001.

31. "Court rules refugees can be detained," *Guardian Online*, 18 October 2001.

32. Young, Hugo, "Hijacking Justice in the name of national security," *Guardian Online,* 23 October 2000.

33. Rt. Hon. Jack Straw MP, 2001, "An Effective Protection Regime for the Twenty-first Century," speech at the Institute for Public Policy Research, London, 6 February 2001.

34. British Refugee Council, Response to "Secure Borders, Safe Havens, Integration with Diversity in Modern Britain," February 2002, http://www.refugeecouncil.org.uk/infocentre/asylumprops/white_paper.htm.

35. See van Selm, Joanne, July 2002, "The Netherlands: tolerance under pressure," *The Migration Information Source,* www.migrationinformation.org.

36. FORUM Persbericht, Utrecht, 18 September 2001, "Extra kabinetsinspanning nodig tegen dreigende tweedeling in multiculturele samenleving." Forum Press Release, ("Additional Cabinet attention necessary to avert a threatened split in the multicultural community"—author's translation), FORUM is an association representing immigrants in the Netherlands, with a strong focus on Muslim—primarily Moroccan immigrants.

37. "Radicale moslims moeten land uit," *De Volkskrant,* 26 September 2001, ("Deport Radical Muslims"—author's translation.)

38. Ibid.

39. "Kabinet wil soepler asiel voor Afghanen" *De Volkskrant,* 3 October 2001. ("The Cabinet wants easier asylum for Afghans"—Author's translation.)

40. Vluchtelingen Werk NL, "Behandeling gezinshereniging Afghaanse vluchtelingen gestopt" (Handling of Family Reunification cases for Afghan Refugees stopped—author's translation), 9 October 2001.

41. Pim Fortuyn was assasinated on 6 May 2002, just nine days before the elections. His eponymous party, the "Lijst Pim Fortuyn" went on to win 27 seats in the 150 seat parliament, and to become one of three coalition governing partners (with the Christian Democrats [CDA] and the Liberals [VVD]).

42. "Het Gevaar is nog altijd niet geweken," (The danger is still there—author's translation), *Vrij Nederland* 16 February 2002 and A. Faquiri, 2002 (forthcoming), "September 11: Has Anything Changed?," *Forced Migration Review,* No.13.

43. The countries are Denmark, Finland, the Netherlands, Norway, Sweden, and Switzerland.

44. The Departments of State, Justice and Health and Human Services submit the proposal in July—and a decision is reached in September—under section 207(e) (1)–(7) of the Immigration and Nationality Act.

45. "Statement of Senator Edward M. Kennedy at the Immigration Subcommittee hearing on the US Refugee Program," 12 February 2002.

46. NGO testimony at the same hearing.

47. Somini Sengupta, "Refugees at America's door find it closed after attacks," *New York Times,* 29 October 2001.

48. See J. van Selm, "Access to Procedures: Safe third countries, safe countries of origin and time limits." Paper for the UNHCR Global Consultations, June 2001 to be found under www.unhcr.ch.

49. See Lavenex, S. and E. Ucarer, op. cit.

50. Kremmer, Christopher, "US food aid drops under fire," *The Age*, 9 October 2001, theage.com.au.

51. http://kidsfund.redcross.org/about.html.

52. "Afghanistan: US contributes additional $19,125,000," http://www.state.gov/r/pa/prs/ps/2002/7356.htm.

53. State of the Union Address, 20 January 2002. http://www.whitehouse.gov/news/releases/2002/01/20020129–11.html.

54. Joint EU—U.S. Ministerial Statement on combating Terrorism, 20 September 2001, http://ue.eu.int/newsroom/loadDoc.asp?max=1&bid=109&did=67801 &grp=3772 &lang=1.

Biographies

Emily Copeland received her Ph.D. from the Fletcher School of Law and Diplomacy in 1996. When this chapter was written, she was an assistant professor in the International Relations Department at Florida International University in Miami. She was also the lead project director for an eight university consortium program on "Transnationalism, International Migration, Race, Ethnocentrism and the State." Current projects include: an examination of gender politics in the refugee regime and an edited volume exploring the nexus between security and migration issues. She is co-author of *Forced Migration: Policy Issues in the Post-Cold War World* (1993) and several articles. She has also worked with UNHCR in the Sudan, Save the Children in Pakistan, and the Refugee Policy Group in Washington, D.C.

Patricia Weiss Fagen is currently a senior associate at the Institute for the Study of International Migration ISIM, Georgetown University. Until recently she was an official of UNHCR. While associated with ISIM, Dr. Fagen has been a consultant to projects related to post-conflict reconstruction and refugee/returnee integration for UNHCR, IDRC (Canada), the Christian Michelsen Institute (Norway), the International Center for Research on Women, and the U.S. Peace Corps. Dr. Fagen received her Ph.D. in History from Stanford University. She served on the Executive Committee of the Latin American Studies Association for three years. She was a member of the Executive Committee and Board of Directors of Amnesty International, USA for six years and, in 1985, was Vice Chair of the Board of the U.S. Section. Her most recent publication is "El Salvador and Guatemala: Refugee Camp and Repatriation Experiences," with S. Yudelman, a chapter in Krishna Kumar, ed., *Women in Civil War: Impact, Organization, and Action* (2001). She is the author of several articles, book chapters, and monographs in the fields of Latin American studies, human rights, and worldwide refugee problems.

Randa Farah is an assistant professor in anthropology at the University of Western Ontario and an associate researcher at the Refugee Studies Center (RSC) at the University of Oxford, where she co-teaches a course titled *Palestinian Refugees and the Universal Declaration of Human Rights.* Farah acquired her Ph.D. at the University of Toronto where she examines the relationship of Palestinian popular memory and identity following the political shifts in the nineties and in the context of prolonged displacement.

Farah was also a research associate with CERMOC, a French research institution in Jordan, where she was involved in their research initiative on the United Nations Relief and Works Agency (UNRWA). In the past few years, she has been conducting research in projects supervised by the RSC and funded by the Mellon Foundation. These projects include a completed regional and long-term study on Palestinian refugee children and currently she leads the research team in a similar and on-going project on refugee children of Western Sahara living in camps in the Algerian desert. Her writings and lectures reflect her interest in the areas of displacement and refugees, memory/history and identity, nations and nationalism, humanitarian aid, and children and youth.

Elizabeth G. Ferris presently serves as executive secretary for International Relations at the World Council of Churches in Geneva, Switzerland. In this capacity she is responsible for coordinating advocacy on refugee, migrant and IDP issues, administering support for refugee projects in seventy countries, and analyzing global trends in humanitarian assistance. After receiving M.A. and Ph.D. degrees from the University of Florida in Latin American Studies and International Relations respectively, she spent ten years teaching at various U.S. universities and spent a year at the Universidad Nacional Autónoma de México as a Fulbright Professor. From 1985–91, she served as Study and Interpretation Secretary in WCC's Refugee Service. From 1991–93 she was Research Director at the Life & Peace Institute in Uppsala, Sweden, where she supervised the work of some seventy researchers in all regions on various research projects. In 1993 she was appointed Director of the Church World Service Immigration and Refugee Program of the National Council of Churches in New York. In that capacity she managed programs on resettlement, asylum, advocacy and international concerns, and supervised 100 staff in New York, Washington, Miami, and Nairobi. In January 1999, she returned to Geneva to take up her current position. She has written or edited six books and written numerous articles and research papers on a range of topics.

Mark Gibney is the Belk Distinguished Professor in the Humanities at UNC-Asheville. His main field of interest is human rights, especially the intersection between ethics, law, and politics. His publications include the edited volumes *Open Borders? Closed Societies: The Ethical and Political Issues* (1988), *World Justice? U.S. Courts and International Human Rights* (1991), and *Judicial Protection of Human Rights: Myth or Reality?* (2000). Recent writings on refugee issues include "In Search of a U.S. Refugee Policy," in David Forsythe (ed.) *The United States and Human Rights: Looking Inward and Outward,* and "Ethics and Refugees," in Jean-Marc Coicaud and Daniel Warner (ed.) *Ethics and International Affairs: Extent and Limits* (2001).

Brian Gorlick joined the Office of UNHCR in 1991, prior to which he worked as legal counsel in the areas of refugee and immigration law in Toronto. He has worked as legal officer at the UNHCR Branch Office in Turkey, the Department of International Protection in Geneva, the Office of the Chief of Mission in India, and presently the Regional Office for the Baltic and Nordic Countries in Sweden. He is a graduate of the University of Winnipeg (B.A.), York University, Toronto (M.A.), the Osgoode Hall Law School (LL.B.) and the London School of Economics and Political Science (LL.M., with distinction). Mr. Gorlick has published a number of articles on international refugee and human rights law.

Arthur C. Helton is Director of Peace and Conflict Studies, and Senior Fellow for Refugee Studies and Preventive Action at the Council on Foreign Relations. At the Council, he prepared a book on U.S. and international responses to refugee emergencies since the end of the Cold War, *The Price of Indifference: Refugees and Humanitarian Action in the New Century* (2002). His article in the March/April 2002, issue of *Foreign Affairs* "Rescuing the Refugees," applies the ideas in his new book to recovery policy in Afghanistan. Mr. Helton also co-authored *Forced Displacement and Human Security in the Former Soviet Union: Law and Policy* (2000), and has written over ninety scholarly articles on refugee and migration subjects. He is a member of more than thirty organizational boards in the field. In 2002, Mr. Helton received the Award for Distinction in International Law and Affairs of the New York State Bar Association. He received the Immigration and Refugee Policy Award of the Center for Migration Studies in 2001, the Ninoy Aquino Refugee Recognition Award conferred by the President of the Republic of the Philippines in 1991, and the Public Interest Award conferred by the NYU Law Alumni Association in 1987. Mr. Helton is a Lecturer in Law at the Columbia Law School. He graduated from Columbia College in New York City in 1971, and the NYU Law School in 1976.

Bonny Ibhawoh is an assistant professor in African studies and international politics at the University of North Carolina at Asheville. He is also a visiting lecturer in history and development studies at Edo State University, Nigeria. He was formerly a research fellow and consultant to the Carnegie Council on Ethics and International Affairs, New York; the Danish Center for Human Rights, Copenhagen and an Associate Member of the Center for African Studies, School of Oriental and African Studies (SOAS), University of London. His research interests include culture, human rights and international development. His latest works include *Human Rights and NGO Activism in Nigeria* (2001); "Cultural Tradition and National Human Rights Standards in Conflict" in Kristin Hastrup ed.

Legal Cultures and Human Rights: The Challenge of Diversity, (2001). His articles on African studies and human rights have appeared in *Human Rights Quarterly, Netherlands Quarterly of Human Rights* and *Comparative Studies in South Asia, Africa and the Middle East.*

Monica Kathina Juma is a senior analyst at Safer Africa, Pretoria (South Africa). A political scientist who researches and lectures in issues of humanitarian assistance, conflict management, and refugee studies/forced migration, she holds a Ph.D. from the University of Oxford. In 2000, Dr. Juma served as a member of the International Academic Advisory Group to UNHCR in the production of *The State of The World's Refugees* (2000) and serves as a Board Member to the Refugee Consortium of Kenya and the Eastern African Network for the Study of Forced Migration. She has been a research associate at the International Peace Academy's Africa program in 2001, where she directed a project assessing the capacity of African institutions to respond to crises and conflicts in eighteen countries in Sub-Saharan Africa. Dr. Juma is a lead researcher and coordinator of the East African component of the Project on Humanitarian Assistance and Conflict in Africa, undertaken by African and Nordic research institutions. She is also a team leader in a project assessing disaster readiness for countries under the United States Central Command and the European Command in Eastern Africa. Dr. Juma has written on displacement, human rights, and regional security issues, and is currently co-editing a book entitled *Eroding Local Capacity: The Nature and Consequences of Humanitarian Assistance in Africa.*

Peter Mwangi Kagwanja has contributed a number of articles, chapters, and commissioned reports on human rights, forced migration, governance, and conflict. He has served as a lecturer in history and political science, as a research associate in the Centre for Refugee Studies at Moi University, Kenya, and as a research associate at the Kenya Human Rights Commission. Kagwanja is currently a Fulbright Fellow at the University of Illinois, Urbana-Champaign, where he is completing his doctoral work on refugees and human rights in Eastern Africa.

Gil Loescher is a senior fellow for migration, forced displacement, and international security at the International Institute for Strategic Studies in London and the author of the first independent history of UNHCR entitled: *The UNHCR and World Politics: A Perilous Path* (2001). He received his doctorate from the London School of Economics and Political Science, and he was a professor of international relations at the University of Notre Dame for twenty-six years. In recent years, he served as a senior adviser to the policy research unit of the Office of UNHCR in Geneva. He is also a member of the External Research Advisory Board for UNHCR's publication *State of the World's Refugees* and has been its past chair. He has held visiting research appointments at The International Institute for Strategic Studies (IISS) in London, at Princeton, Oxford, and the London School of Economics, and has been a visiting scholar at the U.S. State Department's Bureau of Humanitarian Affairs. Loescher has received grants for his research from the Open Society Institute, the U.S. Institute of Peace, the Ford Foundation, the Twentieth Century Fund, the Rockefeller Foundation, the John D. and Catherine T. MacArthur Foundation, the Institute for the Study of World Politics, and the Fulbright Commission, among others. He is the author of the Twentieth Century Fund book *Beyond Charity: International Cooperation and the Global Refugee Problem* (1993) and an IISS Adelphi Paper *Refugee Movements and International Security* (1992). He is also co-author of *Calculated Kindness: Refugees and America's Half-Open Door, 1945 to Present* (1986) and co-editor of *Refugees and International Relations* (1989) among numerous other works.

Erik Roxström is a Research Fellow at the University in Bergen Law School in Norway. He gained his Masters in Law from Uppsala University Law School in 1994. He has previously worked as a practicing lawyer in Sweden and in that capacity represented asylum claimants. From 1995– 1997 he was a legal consultant at the Secretariat of the inter-governmental consultation on asylum, refugee, and migration policies in Europe, North America, and Australia. He is presently pursuing a doctorate in human rights law.

Joanne van Selm is Senior Policy Analyst at the Migration Policy Institute, a Washington D.C. based think tank devoted to the study of international migration. Dr. van Selm is also senior researcher at the University of Amsterdam's Institute for Migration and Ethnic Studies. She holds a Ph.D. in International Relations from the University of Kent at Canterbury. Dr. van Selm is co-editor of Oxford University Press' *Journal of Refugee Studies*, and is on the Executive Committee of the International Association for the Study of Forced Migration, for which she ran the Program of its January 2001 conference on *The Refugee Convention at 50* hosted at the University of the Witwatersrand, South Africa. Dr. van Selm's publications include *Kosovo's Refugees in the European Union* (2000) and *Refugee Protection in Europe: Lessons of the Yugoslav Crisis* (1998). She has also published some twenty articles and book chapters on global migration, European integration in asylum and migration affairs, Dutch politics, and international refugee policies. In 2001 she wrote the background paper "Access to

Procedures: 'safe third countries', 'safe countries of origin' and time limits" for UNHCR's Global Consultations on Refugee Protection.

Niklaus Steiner is associate director of the University Center for International Studies and adjunct professor in the Curriculum of International Studies at the University of North Carolina-Chapel Hill. A native of Switzerland who moved to the U.S. in his youth, Steiner has had the good fortune of being able to move back and forth between two cultures all his life. This life experience has shaped his academic focus. Steiner earned a B.A. in international studies at UNC-Chapel Hill and a Ph.D. in political science/international relations at Northwestern University. His research interests include refugees, nationalism, and national identity, and he has published a number of articles on these topics. Steiner has recently published *Arguing about Asylum: The Complexity of Refugee Debates in Europe*.

Beth Elise Whitaker is assistant professor of political science at the University of North Carolina at Charlotte. Her research focuses on refugee and security issues in Central Africa. She conducted field research in Tanzania from 1996 to 1998 for her dissertation, which examined the impact on host communities of the presence of more than one million refugees from Rwanda, Burundi, and Congo. She completed her Ph.D. at the University of North Carolina at Chapel Hill in 1999. Prior to her current position, Dr. Whitaker taught African politics and international relations at George Washington University and worked for a USAID-funded project of the American Council on Education. Dr. Whitaker has also done research projects for the Social Science Research Council, the Brookings Institution, the UN Foundation, Save the Children Fund, CARE, and the U.S. Institute of Peace.

Index

AALCC. *See* Asian-African Legal Consultative Committee (AALCC)
Abu-Lughod, Ibrahim, 159
accountability, 4, 44, 81, 94, 125. *See also* Humanitarian Accountability Project
Acholi, 324*n*10, 324*n*14
Afghanistan
  9/11 and, 238, 249–250, 258–259
  asylum applications in, 287*n*11
  drugs and, 232
  jihad in, 240
  military in, 146
  nation building in, 30
  NGOs/war in, 127
  refugees from, 19, 250
  UNHCR in, 143, 202
  war-to-peace transitions in, 220–221
Afghans, 166, 254–255, 285*n*8, 288*n*15
Africa, 5. *See also* Asian-African Legal Consultative Committee (AALCC); Organization of African Unity (OAU); *specific cities; specific countries*
  banking systems in, 232–233
  conflicts in, 13
  criminal tribunals and, 95
  displaced persons in, 21, 30, 31–32
  on gender persecution, 104
  human rights in Asia and, 62–66, 231
  humanitarian aid in, 19
  jihad in, 240
  NGOs in, 120, 127
  polygamy in Islamic societies and, 71
  protection in, 235–236, 290*n*28
  refugee camps in, 323*n*10
  "Refugee Sundays" in, 132
  on Territorial Asylum Conference, 112
  terrorism and, 225–226, 231
  UNHCR in, 83, 235–236
African Charter of Human and Peoples' Rights, 65
African Union, 32
Aga Khan, Sadruddin (High Commissioner), 292*n*38
agriculture, 146–147, 231
aid, 85. *See also* assistance ; humanitarian aid; *specific countries*
  to displaced persons, 26–28, 250
  governments on conflicts and, 128
  human rights records and, 44
Aideed, Farah, 233
airport regulations, 86, 258, 259, 288*n*22
Akram, Susan, 165
Al Barakat Bank, 233
al-Itihaad, 225, 233
al-Nakbah (the Catastrophe), 159–160
al-Qaeda, 225, 233, 255, 261, 323*n*1
Albanians, 30
Algerian refugees, 108
Algerian War of Independence, 8–9

aliens, refugees *v.*, 23–24
American Anthropological Association, 64
American Jewish Committee, 118
Amnesty International, 150, 320*n*25
Amsterdam Treaty, 241, 242, 244. *See also* Area of Freedom, Security and Justice (ASFJ)
Angola, 127, 143, 153, 220
animals, 231
An'Naim, Abdullahi Ahmed, 71, 75
Annan, Kofi, 169
anti-populist norms, 193
Anti-Racism Convention, 186
Arab-Israeli conflict, 156–157, 163, 169–170, 309*n*12
Arab states, 112, 158–159, 171. *See also specific states*
Area of Freedom, Security and Justice (ASFJ), 241–243
Argentina, 298*n*57
Armenia, 117
Armenian Committee for Relief in the Near East. *See* Near East Relief
Armenian refugees, 286*n*11
arms trade, 127, 133, 232, 234–236
Arusha negotiations, 320*n*19
Asia, 5
  Afghans in, 285*n*8
  conflicts in, 13
  drugs and, 232
  human rights in Africa and, 62–66, 231
  NGOs in, 120
  refugee definition in, 21
  on Territorial Asylum Conference, 112
Asian-African Legal Consultative Committee (AALCC), 299*n*69, 300*n*71
assets, seizure of, 160, 169, 172, 189
assimilation, and naturalization, 290*n*31
assistance, 13, 128, 131, 136. *See also* material assistance; social assistance
  conflicts' prolonging of, 31, 83, 128, 134, 153
Assyrian refugees, 286*n*11
Assyro-Chaldean refugees, 286*n*11
asylum, 22, 26, 80, 84, 286*n*11. *See also* "first asylum"; Territorial Asylum, 1977 Conference on
  appeals for, 173
  applications for, 80, 179, 230, 284*n*1
  claim processing for, 234, 235, 246–247
  communism and, 7
  detention and, 86, 248
  deterrents for seekers of, 86
  exclusion clause and, 237
  FGM and, 72–73
  foreign policy and, 179–180, 183, 185
  gender and, 101, 104, 107–108, 113–114
  human rights and, 182
  identity and, 193–194
  immigration and, 191, 244–249